Global Youth Unemployment

Global Youth Unemployment

History, Governance and Policy

Ross Fergusson

Senior Lecturer in Social Policy, The Open University, UK

Nicola Yeates

Professor of Social Policy, The Open University, UK

EE **Edward Elgar**
PUBLISHING

Cheltenham, UK • Northampton, MA, USA

Published by
Edward Elgar Publishing Limited
The Lypiatts
15 Lansdown Road
Cheltenham
Glos GL50 2JA
UK

Edward Elgar Publishing, Inc.
William Pratt House
9 Dewey Court
Northampton
Massachusetts 01060
USA

A catalogue record for this book
is available from the British Library

Library of Congress Control Number: 2021932267

This book is available electronically in the **Elgar**online
Sociology, Social Policy and Education subject collection
http://dx.doi.org/10.4337/9781789900422

ISBN 978 1 78990 041 5 (cased)
ISBN 978 1 78990 042 2 (eBook)

Printed and bound by CPI Group (UK) Ltd, Croydon, CR0 4YY

Contents

Figures

Tables

Appendices

Acknowledgements

This book is the product of many years' work gravitating around different aspects of youth unemployment, social policy, social justice, and globalisations that we have pursued separately and together. Various aspects of it have been formally shared and discussed with colleagues at academic gatherings of the UK Social Policy Association at Durham, Lincoln and York Universities (UK), the International Sociological Association's RC19 meetings in the Universities of Vienna (Austria) and Toronto (Canada), and at global social policy discussions at the University of Bremen (Germany) and Lingnan University (Hong Kong). We do not underestimate the great value of the planned and fortuitous informal collegial discussions that are such an intrinsic part of academic research and ideas development. We have greatly benefited from exposure to and participation in discussions about what it means to think about the social relations of work, joblessness, inequality, marginalisation and social policy in international and global contexts, and about the politics and policy of mass and endemic youth unemployment as persistent and entrenched global phenomena.

Many colleagues have read and commented on nascent ideas, papers and draft chapters. Our ideas – expressed in draft form with all the clumsiness that that entails – met with intellectual engagement, collegial warmth, critical insights, and boundless enthusiasm. In particular, we thank (in alphabetical order): Armando Barrientos, Vickie Cooper, Alvaro Faria, Malcolm Fergusson, John Foster, Heidi Gottfried, Al Green, Chris Grover, Tony Hirst, Chris Holden, Kirsten Martens, Stephen McBride, Stuart Parris, Jo Phoenix, Jane Pillinger, Raia Prokhovnik, Robin Simmons and Rebecca Surender. They variously received, read, listened, commented, questioned, encouraged and challenged, pushing us to realise more of the expansive potential of this long-evolving project. Sarah Tipping, our statistics consultant for Chapter 6, has been a meticulous analyst, an indispensable source of highly valued advice, and an excellent, patient and educative co-author and colleague. The usual disclaimer applies: no one but ourselves bear any responsibility for any of the book's content and arguments, nor for any errors or omissions.

We also thank all at Edward Elgar who responded promptly, cheerfully and patiently to all our requests and queries, including in relation to deadlines, and for providing outstanding editorial and production support – in particular, Commissioning Editors Catherine Elgar, Harry Fabian and Saffron Watts, Graphic Designer Karen Jones, Catherine Cumming, Senior Desk Editor and Digital Specialist, Isobel McLean, freelance indexer, and to freelance copy editor Brian North.

At The Open University, we extend our sincere thanks and utmost gratitude to Mrs Virginia Alitta for her timely work on the References list, and to Kirsty Ternent and Sarah Batt for their support with research finance and administration aspects of this project. Financial support from the Innovation, Knowledge and Development research centre, the Harm and Evidence Research Collaborative, the School of Social Sciences and Global Studies, and the Faculty of Arts and Social Sciences substantially helped with the completion of the book.

We had completed most of the text before the full global significance of the Covid-19 Coronavirus pandemic became evident. We have been able to acknowledge its prospectively transformative importance only in a brief closing section in Chapter 9 that looks back to the recent history of global youth unemployment for some guidance as to what may lay ahead, while avoiding the precarious clairvoyance of anticipating a future that has probably never been more unstable and uncertain in modern history. In this, and much else, we are thankful for our intellectual partnership, which is a source of ongoing mutual encouragement, support and inspiration. It is our best hope that its realisation through this text might make a tangible contribution to thinking, debate and policy in a field of social policy, globally and nationally, that was never so much in need of advancement and development.

Note: The author attribution for Chapter 6 is Ross Fergusson, Sarah Tipping and Nicola Yeates. The author attribution for all other Chapters is Ross Fergusson and Nicola Yeates.

Abbreviations and acronyms

ALMP	active labour market policy/programme
ASEAN	Association of South-East Asian Nations
AU	African Union
BIS	Bank for International Settlements
BoE	Bank of England
BPO	business process outsourcing
CIG	country income group
DJY	Decent Jobs for Youth
ECOSOC	Economic and Social Council of the United Nations
ECOWAS	Economic Community of West African States
EPZ	export processing zone
EU	European Union
EYU	endemic youth unemployment
EzC	Eurozone crisis
GATT	General Agreement on Tariffs and Trade
GCP	global Coronavirus pandemic
GCfYE	Global Compact for Youth Employment
GDP	gross domestic product
GenU	Generation Unlimited
GFC	global financial crisis
GIDJY	Global Initiative on Decent Jobs for Youth
GNI	gross national income
GPYE	Global Partnership for Youth Employment
GRAoYL	global reserve army of youth labour
GSC	global supply chain
HDI	Human Development Index
HIC	high-income country
IBE	International Bureau of Education
IBRD	International Bank for Reconstruction and Development
ICESCR	International Covenant on Economic, Social and Cultural Rights

ICPE	International Conference on Public Education
ICT	information and communications technology
IGO	international governmental organisation
ILC	International Labour Conference
ILO	International Labour Organization
IMF	International Monetary Fund
INGO	international non-governmental organisation
IO	international organisation
IT	information technology
ITES	information technology-enabled services
IYF	International Youth Federation
LIC	low-income country
LMIC	lower middle-income country
LNHO	League of Nations Health Organization
LoN	League of Nations
MDGs	Millennium Development Goals
MIC	middle-income country
MS	member state
NEET	not in education, employment or training
NGO	non-governmental organisations
NIDL	new international division of labour
NIDYL	new international division of youth labour
OBR	Office for Budget Responsibility
OECD	Organisation for Economic Co-operation and Development
RAoL	reserve army of labour
RoSLA	Raising of the School Leaving Age
S4YE	Solutions for Youth Employment
SDGs	Sustainable Development Goals
SSA	sub-Saharan Africa
TVE	technical and vocational education
TVET	technical and vocational education and training
UDHR	Universal Declaration of Human Rights
UK	United Kingdom of Great Britain and Northern Ireland
UMIC	upper middle-income country
UN	United Nations
UNDESA	United Nations Department for Economic and Social Affairs

UNGA	United Nations General Assembly
UNICEF	United Nations International Children's Emergency Fund
UNDP	United Nations Development Programme
UNESCO	United Nations Educational, Scientific and Cultural Organization
UNIDO	United Nations Industrial Development Organization
UNSG	United Nations Secretary-General
USA	United States of America
WB	World Bank
WDR	*World Development Report*
WEP	World Employment Programme
WHO	World Health Organization
WTO	World Trade Organization
YEN	Youth Employment Network
YEP	Youth Employment Programme
YLM	youth labour market
Youth-SWAP	System-wide Action Plan on Youth
YU	youth unemployment

1. Introduction: globalising endemic youth unemployment

1.1 THE ENTRENCHMENT OF YOUTH UNEMPLOYMENT

Unemployment is widely recognised as a major feature of the extreme social and economic inequalities that are characteristic features of the contemporary world order. A great deal of research and thought has been expended in charting how the social organisation of the economy, education, work and welfare have contributed to its production, maintenance and mitigation, and while there is no consensus on this, one thing is clear: involuntary unemployment is devastating and life-changing at any age, but its impacts are particularly adverse for young people. As myriad studies have shown, unemployment indelibly 'scars' the lives of young people and those around them way beyond their immediate lack of income. It adversely affects their health, their transition to social and financial independence, and their prospects of accessing and keeping hold of the quality jobs that are fundamental to socio-economic security and human capability throughout the life-course. At a wider level, youth unemployment (YU) undermines the personal and collective resources invested in education and skills development. At a societal level, sustained rates of high YU challenge liberal notions of inclusive citizenship as a foundation of modern societies and of the social and political order itself – as both liberal and authoritarian democracies have discovered to their cost in recent years.

These are all good reasons to be alarmed about how YU has remained a large-scale, enduring and entrenched feature of the world economy. According to the most authoritative data provided by the International Labour Organization (ILO), over the last twenty years the global rate of YU has remained consistently in the 12–14 per cent range. Absolute annual totals of young unemployed people aged 15–24 have fluctuated between 70 and 80 million (ILO, 2017a). A decade on from the global financial crisis (GFC), which produced a dramatic and immediate spike of 76 million young unemployed people in 2009 followed by a decline to 67 million by 2018, the YU rate was already slowly, steadily increasing again and projected to do so further, even before the onset of the Covid-19 Coronavirus pandemic in 2020. These figures do not include forms of non-participation in the formal labour market which are not counted among the official unemployment figures. These statistics take no account of the more than 700 million young people worldwide who are classified as being 'not in the labour force', irrespective of whether this is by choice and preference or imposed by a range of prevailing adverse socio-economic conditions or hostile circumstances.

The Executive Summary of ILO's most recent annual *Global Employment Trends for Youth* report (ILO, 2020a: 13) offers a single headline comment that is of direct relevance to the persistent levels of YU in the wake of the GFC: '[y]oung workers continue to face high rates of poverty and are increasingly exposed to non-standard, informal and less secure forms of employment'. Unemployment is of course referred to elsewhere in the report but at no point are its extremes mentioned in the Summary. There is no headline that highlights, for example, that the *mean* YU rate has been above 30 per cent for one year in every two since 1991 (including the last five years) in Northern Africa; or that the *average* YU rate amongst the world's second poorest group of countries (more than one country in every five) has shown an almost continuous five percentage point rise over three decades (16 per cent in 2019), with no hint of recovery from the GFC. In our view, the ILO currently understates the seriousness of the depth and extent of global YU – even allowing that official ILO data do not take into account hidden and 'invisible' forms of unemployment referred to above.

Five years into the 15-year period of the United Nations' Sustainable Development Goals (SDGs), realising the youth (15–24 age group) employment aspects of Goal 8.5 – 'achieve full and productive employment and decent work for all women and men, *including for young people* and persons with disabilities, and equal pay for work of equal value' (our emphasis) – by 2030 looks a remote prospect, even before the Covid-19 pandemic took hold. In 2019, the UN reported ambivalent progress on unemployment, in that:

> The global unemployment rate has finally recovered from the global economic crisis. In 2018, the global unemployment rate stood at 5.0 per cent – matching pre-crisis levels. Youth were three times more likely to be unemployed than adults.[1]

Goal 8.6 pledges that by 2020 the world will have 'substantially reduce[d] the proportion of youth not in employment, education or training'. Yet, realising this goal for this sub-group of young people still has a long way to go:

> In 2018, one fifth of the world's youth were not in education, employment or training, meaning that they were neither gaining professional experience nor acquiring or developing skills …. There is a stark gender difference. Young women were more than twice as likely as young men to be unemployed or outside the labour force and not in education or training.[2]

In all, data of this kind for the period 2000–19 underpin two unprecedented claims that lie at the core of this book. The first is that YU had *already* become a prevalent social phenomenon by the time of the GFC. At the onset of the GFC in 2008, young people comprised 16 per cent of the world's population and 25 per cent of its working-age population but accounted for 43.7 per cent of the unemployed, meaning that 'almost every other jobless person in the world is between the ages of 15 and 24' (UNDESA, 2007: 238). *Prior* to the GFC, the rate of young people's participation in the labour market in many countries around the world, not just in the OECD and European Union (EU), had been in a marked and steady decline for many years.

---

[1]   Progress of Goal 8 in 2019, https://sustainabledevelopment.un.org/sdg8 (accessed 2 August 2019). See also on the same site: 'The global unemployment rate in 2017 was 5.6 per cent, down from 6.4 per cent in 2000. The decline has slowed since 2009, when it hit 5.9 per cent. Youth are three times more likely to be unemployed than adults, with the global youth unemployment rate at 13 per cent in 2017' (Progress of Goal 8 in 2018). And: 'The global unemployment rate stood at 5.7 per cent in 2016, with women more likely to be unemployed than men across all age groups. Youth were almost three times as likely as adults to be unemployed, with unemployment rates of 12.8 per cent and 4.4 per cent, respectively, in 2016' (Progress of Goal 8 in 2017).

[2]   Progress of Goal 8 in 2019, https://sustainabledevelopment.un.org/sdg8 (accessed 2 August 2019).

The second claim is that since the onset of the GFC there is substantial evidence that YU has made a quantum shift to become *endemic*. We use the adjective 'endemic' deliberately, and we mean it in three senses. One in that, more than ten years on from the GFC, YU is largely sustained at totals at, or close to, the peaks of the early 2010s. Two, it has continued at broadly similar levels long after the end of the 'formal' recessionary conditions after 2008 that characterised the economies of much of the Global North. Three, it has effectively normalised significantly-raised expectations of YU levels across most parts of the world. We return in detail to these observations, but in effect, as this book will argue, there seems to be a degree of medium-term acceptance of levels of YU that greatly exceed those of most of the period since the end of the Second World War.

This book encapsulates these claims in the term endemic youth unemployment (EYU). The new evidence we bring to bear here shows that EYU is a persistent and prevalent feature of contemporary global social organisation. It is a feature of all continents, most regions, and a great many countries, state-types and political-economic and welfare system types. In much of Africa and parts of Asia, Europe and beyond, unemployment has been consistently sustained between 30 per cent and 50 per cent of the youth labour force. EYU is not the prerogative of poorer countries. Fourteen European countries had YU rates above 30 per cent for several years following the GFC, including in some OECD countries where rates exceeded 50 per cent – for up to nine consecutive years in two cases. Modelled rates of YU for most current and recent major conflict and post-conflict zones of the world considerably exceed most of the rates cited above.[3] Unemployment rates of young women are predominantly higher than those of young men.

The data cited above begin to illustrate our core argument that EYU is a major *global* issue. They suggest that EYU can be expected to prevail for decades ahead unless major and significant interventions are made in social organisation and political-economic environments, and at levels above those that can be achieved by local interventions and domestic actors alone. Realising the global policy ambition to 'leave no one behind, anywhere' requires a different order of analysis and action than that which has dominated to date. Most academic scholarship on work and welfare landscapes for young people has failed to grasp how *transnational* structures, processes and sites of capital accumulation, political engagement and types of consciousness bear on the production, maintenance, distribution and mitigation of YU. Indeed, the integration of transnational analytics into social, economic and public policy analysis has not yet reached the study of how young people are positioned and re-positioned in labour and welfare systems, or of how this positioning plays out across a range of development contexts worldwide. The precepts of methodological nationalism and advanced country biases to which studies of young people and social policy have remained unusually susceptible are, we argue, wholly insufficient for recognising and interpreting the emergent normalised levels of YU. The dominance of such precepts invisibilise the links, ties and activities that stretch beyond

---

[3]   No YU data have been available since 2005 or earlier for other current or recent major conflict zones (Afghanistan, Iraq, Myanmar, Niger, Rwanda, Senegal, Sierra Leone or South Sudan, Syria): ILO WESODATA (https://www.ilo.org/wesodata, accessed 3 August 2020) provides modelled data where national returns of data are not available. Much unemployment is not captured in official rates which take no account of multiple forms of unrecorded unemployment or of casual, informal and insecure employment.

the domestic sphere, and how these refract back into it to restructure economic and social organisation.

There is a pressing need for a transnationalist social policy analytics capable of comprehending how the causes of YU are rooted in international and not just national social, economic and political structures or in dysfunctional local labour markets, ineffective welfare systems or in unemployed individuals' lack of motivation and skills. This book is born from that imperative. Eschewing facile globalisation narratives that over-simplify the complexities of major social and economic transformations of our time (Yeates, 2001), we elucidate major features of the worldwide, border-spanning 'systemic tendencies' that tangibly condition work and welfare landscapes and the early labour market experiences of young people. Specifically, we elaborate a transnational social policy analytics of YU that is rooted in world economy dynamism and the re-making of welfare systems that together structure global social organisation. We address 'upstream' conditions that give rise to EYU worldwide and the role of institutions of global governance in those processes. Sensitivity to the maximum variety of political-economic and development contexts opens up differences and similarities, divergence and convergence, and, with this, the prospect of deeper, more nuanced insights into the structural causes of YU than most studies of YU to date have offered. Finally, our *social policy* focus routes attention to labour organisation and economies not as an end in themselves but as means of social participation, inclusion and equality. By invoking a multi-dimensional concept of YU and the necessity of multi-sectoral analysis and action, we propose an alternative to the economic reductionism which accounts for the major share of globalist analyses of YU and labour markets to date.

We make no claim to the novelty of these maximally internationally-extensive global policy 'optics', but it remains rare for them to be combined at once, even in Global Social Policy studies. This book is the first extended study of young people that deploys such optics. Our focus on young people brings specificity and contextualisation into these global analytics, at the same time as these analytics bring a fresh look at the restructuring of youth education, work and welfare landscapes that have been a feature of welfare restructuring internationally. In this, the book charts an incipient and exciting new research terrain. It defines a new global social (policy) field and subjects it to historically grounded, policy-relevant, internationally-oriented critical social analysis that brings transnational structures, processes, institutions and actors to the foreground as major protagonists in the (re)making of YU. The work of demonstrating the centrality of the study of social policy to that of YU, nationally, regionally and globally (and vice-versa), begins in Chapter 2 and continues throughout the book.

The next part of the chapter elaborates on these opening statements and arguments. It discusses our choice of unemployment as a central conceptual framework (Section 1.2), elaborates the concept of EYU (Section 1.3), and explains the analytical value of the prefix 'global' (Section 1.4). It then elaborates the aims, scope and debates structuring the book (Section 1.5), our methods and data (Section 1.6), and our key terms (Section 1.7).

1.2   UNEMPLOYMENT AS A CENTRAL ORGANISING CONCEPT

Our choice of unemployment as a central organising category for this global study may be considered peculiar by readers who are well-versed in social policy. Although unemployment is the most frequently measured labour market indicator and one of the best available measures of labour under-utilisation, it is also a highly restrictive category that struggles to capture the complexity of relationships to work, employment and joblessness. For example, some official unemployment rates are based on those people who fulfil all the eligibility criteria attached to the receipt of an income support benefit expressly designated as intending to 'compensate' for periods of joblessness as provided for under the terms of the scheme. The strictures of needing to be available for, and actively seeking, work limit receipt of unemployment payments in practice and reduce the number of people officially counted as unemployed. Other measures of unemployment (including some official ones) are based on surveys of whether people have looked for work during a particular period, even if they are not immediately available. This is a more permissive definition, but it does not include people not actively seeking a job but who want one and are available to start, still less hidden unemployment (ILO, n.d.).

The nature of the problem is compounded when we consider that unemployment is not a social risk covered by the social security system in most countries of the world. Dixon (1995) showed that 60 per cent of countries did not cover unemployment at all, and the rich countries of Europe and Asia (including the former Soviet countries) and America (USA and Canada plus 12 Latin American countries) formed the preponderant share of the 40 per cent of countries that did cover it. The picture has hardly changed since then. Only just over a fifth (21.8 per cent) of unemployed workers actually receive unemployment benefits. This leaves 152 million unemployed workers without social protection, most of whom live in poorer countries in Asia-Pacific, the Americas and Africa (ILO, 2017a). This global divide means that although unemployment no longer leads *inevitably* to unacceptable levels of hardship and poverty in a small number of countries, the majority of the world's working-age population in general and its unemployed people in particular are outside such provision as is made by their country's social security system – and thus also for all practical purposes from official unemployment itself (Van Ginneken, 1999).

This brief foray into some issues in delineating unemployment starts to illuminate the considerable divergence in what unemployment means as well as where and how it is manifested. The relationship to work, employment, joblessness, and thus also of poverty, needs to be understood as an entirely different dynamic for the majority of the world's unemployed than for the minority in the world that commands the overwhelming share of research attention. This is a social division that, broadly speaking, falls on a Global North–South axis. In many ways, the economic structures of the latter are so structurally different from those of the former as to render defunct the idea that there is a single universally applicable meaning of unemployment. Worldwide, waged jobs in the formal economy are the exception rather than the rule. Most countries have a very large informal economy that absorbs the vast number of people for whom there is no formal waged work and who are pursuing their own livelihood strategies, mostly as self-employed in the service sector or, for those in rural areas, in agriculture. In the absence of social safety-nets, people have to work one way or another. As Fox et al. (2016: i3) cogently state in relation to low- and middle-income countries of sub-Saharan Africa (SSA), 'unemployment is not high as it is considered a "luxury"'. They elaborate this statement thus:

> [M]ost working age people in SSA cannot afford to be unemployed. Many families cannot fully support a recent graduate while he or she looks for a job, and many youth did not graduate from secondary school so would not qualify for a formal job anyway … They will have to make their own livelihood, either by getting some land and farming, or starting a non-farm business. (p. i7)

In essence, the informal sector absorbs most unemployment, which becomes hidden or disguised because unemployed people have to work to survive, even though they do not have a stable wage-paying job. The problem of unemployment thus reappears as marginal employment (often referred to as marginal attachment to the labour force), underemployment and, above all, in-work poverty where people cannot find enough sufficiently paid work to sustain them. Fox et al. (2016) illustrate this key point thus:

> In low-income African countries, less than 20% of employment is in a wage-paying job, and about half of that wage employment is casual or temporary … A more common situation in Africa is full-time employment but low earnings (often with high income variability), and widespread underemployment (not being able to work as many hours as desired, either in wage or self-employment) especially in rural areas. (p. i9)

The absorptive qualities of the informal sector together with the larger share of the economy that this sector occupies in lower-income countries means that unemployment headcounts cannot be taken as wholly reliable indicators of the 'health' of the labour market, household income, or of the wider economy more generally. It is also clear that although unemployment is inseparable from underemployment and informality, this inseparability is not unique to the informal sector. Thus, informal employment is also increasingly found in enterprises in the formal sector, in the form of 'atypical' employment such as 'clandestine employment, involuntary part-time work, work on short-term contract or no contracts, casual work', as well as 'labour on call' (ILO, 1993: 13–14, cited in Benanav, 2019: 124). The growth of such jobs reflects a process of casualisation and 'social dumping' whereby deregulatory measures create a pool of poorly paid and insecure urban workers that employers can use to replace many of the better paid, well-protected workers whom they employed (Benanav, 2019: 124). Casualisation goes hand in hand with falling numbers of official unemployment, further disguising the 'true' level of unemployment. This is because the terms of these jobs are such that unemployment is highly unlikely to be included as a coverable social security risk. (Indeed, the point of deregulation is to reduce employers' costs – or 'taxes' on jobs, as they might call them – and increase their power to set the working conditions of their labour force.) Equally, working in any capacity at any point in a reference period (primarily forms of underemployment such as short hours in multiple small jobs, or 'gigs'), disqualifies jobless people from being classed as unemployed.[4]

Young people are generally not eligible to be unemployed. Even in countries that in principle cover unemployment as a social risk, they mostly fail to pay the requisite number of contributions to insurance-based unemployment benefit schemes within the given amount of time. This does not prevent them from signing on, but there is little incentive to do so if they are not eligible for benefit payment. Also, many countries have instituted measures to divert young people from unemployment, either by assisting them into a job or removing them from the ranks of the economically active and thus also the potential to end up as openly unemployed. Examples include lengthening the period of compulsory schooling, expanding further and/or higher education and vocational training schemes, extending periods of skills development,

---

[4]   For this reason supplementary measures of labour under-utilisation, such as time-related underemployment and the potential labour force, and associated concepts of available and unavailable jobseekers, are sometimes used as indicators (ILO, n.d.).

and instituting employment and business start-up schemes for young jobless people. Because of these measures, young people of working age feature disproportionately in the working-age economically inactive population than their share of the population would suggest. This point holds for nearly all countries, irrespective of income-level, with the exception of poorest (low income) countries that lack comprehensive post-compulsory education or welfare provision.

Education and class are major factors affecting the social composition and rate of YU. Studies of YU rates in countries that provide very little or no unemployment protection for under-25-year-olds typically find that YU tends to be higher amongst better educated groups (especially young graduates) but low amongst those with little or no education. The availability of family (financial) support to young people unable to secure or maintain a job is a key factor here. Godfrey's (2003) extensive study shows that in some lower middle-income countries (LMICs) (for example Cambodia, Egypt, Indonesia, Pakistan and Sri Lanka), historically, graduates have relied on the support of their relatively affluent families to maintain them during periods of prolonged initial job search for professional employment, while young people without any schooling or qualifications became vulnerably employed workers within the family (or nominally 'own-account' or casual workers when opportunities arose). The financial pressure for a young person to engage in job search, actually take a job and keep it is offset in cases where family support through intra-familial (informal) cash transfers is forthcoming. This is confirmed by Fox et al. (2016: i7) in relation to low-income countries (LICs) and LMICs in SSA:

> Hidden in the low overall youth unemployment rate in low-income countries is a high unemployment rate among urban graduates. It is no coincidence that these graduates primarily come from the top end of the income distribution; only richer parents can afford to support youth in an extensive job search.

They cite the example of Mozambique, a LIC, half of whose population is classified as extremely poor. Here, although rural YU is 'almost non-existent' (at 1.7 per cent), in urban areas, as much as 20 per cent of young people are unemployed. Education is a predictor of this risk of unemployment: '[t]hose with secondary education and above are way over-represented in the unemployed group. Two-thirds of all urban unemployed reported that they had been in this status for over 1 year' (p. i7). This relationship between unemployment and education applies in higher-income SSA countries where broader social protection systems than those in LMICs or LICs exist. South Africa, an upper middle-income country (UMIC), for example, has a high official rate of YU, which (in 2014) stood at 42 per cent of 15–29-year-olds compared with 25 per cent of the working-age population (Bhorat et al., 2016; Fox et al., 2016: i7). In high-income countries, extensive schemes for unemployed workers that provide temporary financial support and help prevent unemployed workers from slipping into informality (ILO, 2017b: 40) do not obviate class-based social inequalities in the likelihood of entering unemployment – whether in its open or disguised forms. The availability of family support is a key explanatory factor in this.

These insights may well contribute to why the principal difference between the proportion of the 15–24-year-old population who are recorded as being unemployed across all country

income groups (CIGs) is that, against reasonable expectation, YU is lowest *by far* in LICs.[5]
But it cannot be assumed that this is universally applicable across LICs and LMICs.[6] Leaving
aside the well-educated respondents in Godfrey's (2003) study of LMICs who declare themselves to be formally unemployed, the opportunities for other young people in LICs to find
'vulnerable employment' (typically one-off, seasonal or 'gig economy' work) beyond or
within the household might be expected to be more limited. In practice, though, in LICs, 43
per cent are vulnerably employed, compared to 15 per cent in LMICs. This major difference
is clearly reflected in the relative proportions of young people who are economically inactive:
43 per cent in LICs versus 66 per cent in LMICs. One interpretation of these data is that young
people's opportunities to survive while being economically inactive in LMICs (and in many
UMICs and high-income countries (HICs)) are far greater than those of their counterparts in
LICs. However, reliable data on how the young people survive in these latter countries in the
absence of state-provided social protection are extremely sparse.

Such complexities are amplified for young people because they are at the outset of their
working life when education and family support combined with other measures to divert them
from registered unemployment feature strongly. Despite its limitations, unemployment is
a well-known concept that commands a great deal of attention internationally. It remains the
most commonly used indicator of the 'health' of labour markets and economies that, for all its
flaws, is widely respected. It is also capable of visibilising harms generated by labour systems
and mobilising wider action for economic and social justice in ways that no alternative concept
can. Used sensitively, with caution and specificity, informed by an appreciation of the quali-
fiers we have briefly outlined and how they shape the overall prevalence, social composition
and structure of unemployment, the concept remains a powerful one. We are, in sum, confident
that unemployment is a productive analytical category, *providing that* an expansive definition
of it is used – one that recognises, first, the inseparability of unemployment, underemployment
and informality as structural characteristics of labour systems internationally, and, second,
the intersecting familial, educational, welfare, and labour domains that produce the worlds of
work and welfare in which young people are embedded.

1.3   ENDEMIC UNEMPLOYMENT: DEFINING THE CATEGORY

We deploy the term 'endemic' in the concept of EYU as a defining generic category of
(youth) unemployment. This is to avoid the complexity of multiple versions of unemployment
used by labour economists and others, and to differentiate our approach in order to provide
greater clarity about some of the key characteristics of YU with which this book is concerned.
Economists differentiate primarily between frictional unemployment, structural unemployment (sometimes called technological unemployment), cyclical unemployment, systemic
unemployment and political unemployment. Structural, systemic and political unemployment
are of most relevance here. Structural/technological unemployment is typically defined in

---

[5]   The respective proportions of young people who are wage workers, vulnerably employed and economically inactive vary hugely between country income groups. But despite these differences and the
vast gulf between those countries, the proportions of young people recorded as unemployed actually vary
remarkably little: 5 per cent (LMICs) and 9 per cent (UMICs): see Chapters 3 and 5.

[6]   Godfrey et al. (2003) point out that YU is weaker in Latin American countries, and is inverted in
'transition' countries – typically Eastern Europe and Central Asia.

terms of unemployment that arises because of a decline in demand for the goods or services produced by firms or organisations; or because labour-saving technologies that are more economically productive, efficient and/or profitable enable firms and organisations to reduce the size of their workforces. Political unemployment is unemployment deemed to be the result of interjections in the predominant organisation of production and labour on the part of powerful interest groups, organisations and governments that seek to alter the structures or processes of employment for their own advantage or the advantage of those whom they represent or are governed by. The most widely recognised and used categories of political unemployment are protectionism (typically as exercised by trades unions) and labour flexibilism (typically on the part of managers, owners, investors or of capital itself). One of the purposes and effects of interventions by the former group is to prioritise securing members' job security, while those of the latter group are to maximise profits accruing to owners, etc. Systemic unemployment is 'allowed' to accumulate when convenient, such that a fraction of the total labour force is normally reliably without work and waiting to be employed – either available to start work if there is an increase in demand for goods and services, or accustomed to their status as unemployed when they are no longer needed if demand falls. 'Full employment' and minimal frictional unemployment are relatively rare, at least at national levels. On one interpretation, systemic unemployment provides a reliable, flexibly available 'reserve army of labour' (RAoL) – a concept we revisit in Chapter 3 in particular.

YU 'at scale' is typically primarily the product of one or more of these categories of unemployment at any time or place, assuming young people are ready and able to take up the jobs on offer. Historically, much large-scale YU has been explained using theories associated with the concept of cyclical unemployment. In free-market capitalist economies, the 'business cycles' of any country are liable to peaks and troughs related to the confidence consumers and service-users have in the state of the economy, to what they believe their money buys now and in the near future, and to consequent fluctuations in demand and in supply at prices that are acceptable to all parties directly or indirectly involved in financial transactions.

Our argument is that structural unemployment and cyclical unemployment alone no longer provide adequate explanations for the nature of YU or for trends in YU globally. The GFC – like the Great Depression of the early 1930s – was undoubtedly an example of (almost worldwide) instability in financial markets that resulted in an extreme form of cyclical unemployment, combined with the key characteristics of structural unemployment (Tooze, 2018). But, as Chapter 5 will show, the scale of YU had already been much greater than that of adult unemployment for several decades *before* the GFC (sometimes at extreme levels in some countries like the UK in the 1980s and 1990s, for example), and continued to be so, long *after* adult unemployment rates had recovered in all but the very worst-affected countries.

To capture this, we deploy the term EYU to convey a fundamentally different set of meanings about the nature and causes of YU worldwide from those that are normally used. Although the concept 'endemic' has its origins in epidemiology regarding the spread of disease following epidemic trajectories, our use of the adjective endemic is intended to encapsulate a social meaning of *prevalence*, *persistence* and *permanence*. As a social science concept, it conveys the sense of a harmful phenomenon that spreads across borders and barriers, does not 'naturally' die out, but is reproduced, sustained and endures over time, with no reliable or anticipated end-point. EYU is the product of failures whether on the part of governments, warring armies, criminals, fraudsters or – as we shall argue – institutions of global governance to intervene to prevent the privations, extremes of poverty and reduced life-expectancy asso-ciated with extended and unrelieved periods of unemployment.

Adopting the terminology of EYU circumnavigates alternative terminology that is inherently imprecise, unsatisfactory or unreliable as a way of conveying the seriousness of the nature of EYU. In many cases and at certain junctures, the scale and volume of YU might seem to warrant the term 'mass unemployment' – a term which was historically only widely deployed in public discourse and academic literature after the Great Depression of the 1930s. We have generally avoided using this term unless essential, in part because it is inherently ephemeral in terms of the conditions it captures, but especially because it overlooks *persistence over time* as a crucial characteristic of many instances of unemployment that are distinctively harmful without ever receiving attention of the kind that is reserved for 'global emergencies' like the Great Depression and the GFC. Put simply, EYU recognises that *duration* is at least as impor-tant as scale in many contexts.

1.4   INSCRIBING 'THE GLOBAL' INTO ENDEMIC YOUTH UNEMPLOYMENT

The long shadows cast by the GFC and its political management have been a source of renewed interest in ongoing processes of the globalisation of social and economic policy and transformations of the global social system. The last decade has seen a resurgence of critical scrutiny of how international banking and finance have been governed and regulated, not just by domestic institutions but by global ones, and of how international organisations (IOs) have responded to the social and economic fall-out of the GFC (Schoenbaum, 2012; Tooze, 2018). This particular financial crisis reinforced like no other the salience of global macro-analytics and of attending to the structural features of capital accumulation and the institutions of global governance. Comprehending this crisis, its origins, unfolding, and aftermaths, has required not just a country-scale analysis but a truly global one capable of understanding how the crisis spread rapidly across multiple countries, regions and continents of the world, drawing in ever-wider areas of public policy and numbers of people affected. Connecting this global dynamism with the micro-worlds of everyday lived experience was given new impetus, particularly when the impacts of ensuing programmes of economic austerity and welfare restructuring were taken into account. These analytical threads provided insight into the sources of social conflict that pre-existed the GFC but which were aggravated and intensified by it. Fuelling insurgencies of many kinds, and fragmenting the international order that had governed the world economy for more than half a century, by some accounts the GFC marked the beginning of a new dynamic of 'de-globalisation' (Livesey, 2018; see also van Bergeijk, 2017).

Remarkably few of the tenets of such powerful analyses of the global system as have (re) emerged during this time have been tested in the realm of YU. Global restructuring remains, it seems, merely a remote, abstract feature of the contemporary social, economic and political conditions shaping young people's labour market experiences, if we are to go by the preoccu-pations of youth studies in recent years, that is. Although analyses of country-specific YU data abound, YU is still seen as primarily *national* in its causes and effects; that is, the analytical focus lies with *domestic* institutions, *domestic* spheres of governance and *domestic* policy actors conditioning *intra-national* processes. Furthermore, since 2008 there has been a proliferation of (mainly economics-led) academic literature on YU, a much sparser sociological and political-economic literature, and a notable dearth of social policy literature (almost all in the form of papers in reputable social science peer-reviewed journals or from international governmental organisations (IGOs)). Dominating these debates, consequently, is a focus on formal labour markets and training, education and employment policy sectors. Analysis of YU as an expansive *social policy* issue has attracted remarkably little coherent attention.

One problem is that the analytical paradigms used in the study of YU globally remain firmly rooted in the methodologically 'thinnest' sense of 'global', equating it with 'worldwide'. And even this turns out to be much less than genuinely globe-spanning. For example, Peter Blossfeld et al.'s (2008) otherwise majestic comparative study of eleven 'modern societies' (their term), *Young Workers, Globalisation and the Labor Market* was restricted to some European countries plus the USA. Despite invoking globalisation, it was posited as contextual, in the background vaguely somewhere, but in no way taken up through investigation of how different sorts of globalising structures actively condition youth labour markets or the quality of youth employment. Undoubtedly, forensic studies of young people's encounters with employment pathways are important, but on the question of how globalisation processes tangibly impact on these, Blossfeld et al. obscure more than they reveal.

In similar vein, Alan France's (2016) study, entitled *Understanding Youth in the Global Economic Crisis*, had a great deal to commend it as a response from youth sociology to the GFC, but the depth and breadth of its analysis of mass YU offered is also peculiarly narrow. Its claim to international coverage in the context of a global financial crisis is limited. Its geographical coverage is highly selective, covering the UK, the British Commonwealth of the (affluent) 'Global North' (Canada, Australia, New Zealand), three European countries (Spain, Norway, Poland) and Japan. Like Blossfeld et al., France's invocation of 'global' obscures rather than reveals transnational modes of production and governance of youth (un)employment.

Most recently, *The Crisis of Global Youth Unemployment* by Tamar Mayer, Sujata Moorti and Jamie K. McCallum (2019), with especially its interesting opening chapter on global labourscapes (cf. Appadurai, 1990) intended to convey 'the variegated effects of youth unemployment, including the new cultural and political formations that [revolve around precarity] have come into being as a result' (p. 2), turns out to be a fairly conventional international study of YU, albeit one that extends its gaze to a commendably wider range of development contexts than those usually covered by such volumes. Unusually, it includes countries from the Global South – China, Pakistan, South Africa, and 15 countries comprising West Africa – as well as those from the Global North. Still, with the exception of the West African contribution (Bergson et al., 2019), the youth 'labourscapes' that the volume depicts are all too familiarly constructed around 'container' notions of the nation state. Only Bergson et al.'s chapter approaches a sense that *transnational* sites of political engagement and action, in the form of global and sub-global institutions such as the Economic Community of West African States (ECOWAS), EU, World Bank (WB) and International Monetary Fund (IMF), have any bearing on the (re)making of 'global youth labourscapes'. Beyond that, the ostensibly-central notion of 'global society' referenced in the introductory chapter is taken up by none of the later chapters.

These books and others from the social science canon from which they emanate pay scant serious attention to globalising dynamics of YU. Indeed, almost all of the ostensibly relevant sociological volumes since 2008 are indicative of an entrenched methodological nationalism combined with advanced country bias that result in insufficient attention to: the extensive international scale of YU, including outside high-income development contexts where the majority of the world's youth labour force and young unemployed people reside; the implications of greater international interconnectedness and interdependence for how institutions of work and welfare for young people are organised, and how these bear upon YU; and the ways in which YU has been taken up as a policy issue within cross-border spheres of governance together with the forms that global institutions' interventions take and their impacts on the course of national policy-making or on domestic economic and social structures.

The omission of globalist narratives in studies of YU is surprising. It is now well-established that a major characteristic of contemporary world history is the intensification and expansion of capitalism on a global scale, and that employment structures are shaped by global forces (Dicken, 2009, 2011; O'Brien, 2014). Just as global analytics of the world economy is understood as necessary to grasp the structure of employment, so too this point applies to unemployment. As Benanav (2014), a historian, argued, unemployment is a 'story' that actively requires 'the global' be fully integrated into any modern history of it. This is because the worldwide expansion of unemployment since 1950.

> … was in large part the result of processes that unfolded at the global level: first, a massive increase in the world's population, and in particular, its working population; second, a global 'Green Revolution,' which significantly reduced the price of food, but also resulted in a worldwide wave of agricultural exit; and third, a global wave of deindustrialization, which unfolded not only in the high-income countries, as is well known, but also, across the low-income world. The result was a huge increase in the global supply of labor, relative to a weak demand, and that in turn created a gigantic population of unemployed people …. (p. 6)

This does not deny the complexities and variations in where and how these processes have unfolded, including how they 'touch down' in historically and geographically context-specific ways. However, powerful social forces such as these are essential to understanding who gets which jobs and who is excluded from a job, why, how, under what conditions and with what effects, outcomes and impacts (ILO, 2016). How global restructuring distributes benefits, risks and costs is, we argue, conditioned by international institutions and policies and not just national ones. Indeed, international institutions have been active agents in the (re)making of unemployment. Benanav's study of half a century of ILO involvement in the making of such labour market realities shows this all too well (Benanav, 2019).

Young people and YU have been largely invisible from academic theoretical or empirical literatures on global economic restructuring. Social divisions and fractures of class and gender shaping the course, timing and outcomes of contemporary 'globalisations' and the (re)making of contemporary capitalisms are, relatively speaking, well-trodden paths compared with those of age. The voluminous literature on global labour, corporate restructuring and international institutions contains next to no dedicated attention to how they re-position young people's labour. As a result, we know less than we should by now about the 'youth' dimension of unfolding global economic processes and their impacts on structures of unemployment on a world scale. Yet there have long been clues that there is a distinct youth story to be told. For example, long before the GFC, youth labour markets worldwide had begun to change significantly, and in some sectors radically, as a result of North Atlantic neo-liberal globalisation and the restructuring of many labour markets that it brought about. In turn, much of the change in youth labour markets (YLMs) is a particular version of labour market transformation to which the contexts and conditions of YLMs were amenable. This is just one example to illustrate the general point. As will become increasingly evident throughout this book, the ostensibly fluid, adaptive, absorbent attributes of young people and the YLMs in which they are embedded represent a mix of qualities that are apparently well-suited to the very forms of the labour flex-ibilisation upon which labour markets transformed by neo-liberal globalisations both depend and also help to foster.

Our inscription of young people into these 'global labour shifts' (cf. Dicken, 2009) is cognisant of the structural differentiation of both capital and labour and how they remain embedded in socio-institutional contexts that vary across time and place (Silver, 2003; Hardy et al., 2016). Cognisance of this differentiation is vital when it comes to young people because, as we will show, they are distinctly placed within labour forces. Not only are they the most likely of all age groups to be jobless, but those with jobs are more likely to be in 'precarious' forms of employment in 'disorganised' workforces – whether because they have eschewed collective forms of action or because they are prohibited by law and policy from forming or joining labour unions. Irrespective of how we label this (for example, 'surplus labour', 'global youth reserve army', 'flexible labour force'), the underlying dynamics of social organisation that position young people in this way is not well enough understood.

1.5   AIMS, SCOPE AND DIALOGIC TERRAINS

As we hope will be clear by now, the premise of this book is that YU is best understood as a *global* phenomenon necessitating broad-based *social policy* analysis. The nature of *global* YU, we argue, is such that it can *only* be understood by reference to global(ising) processes unfolding over time across the interlinked spheres of economic organisation, labour systems and social policies. Our commitment to a transnational analytics is driven by a deep frustration with the lack of scrutiny of the relationship between YU and macro-level conditions of devel-opment in general, and with the shifting social foundations of capitalism more specifically. This frustration with the lack of such a perspective has grown during our ongoing collabora-tion over the last decade to monitor and analyse evolving global policy on YU (Fergusson and Yeates, 2012, 2013, 2014; Fergusson, 2016a, 2016b, 2017, 2021). That work highlighted to us the need now more than ever for an extended project capable of bringing to bear a new way of looking at the production and governance of EYU as a global phenomenon. That extended project is this book.

At the same time, we are of course cognisant that no single study can make good all these limitations or come close to doing full justice to the many complexities of YU as a social policy field – global or otherwise. Many important facets of the causes, nature and effects of global YU are beyond the scope of this study. Prioritising an analysis through the lens of social policy limits the scope to do justice to some sociological and most psychological paradigms, for example – a point on which we expand briefly below. We have not attempted to pay more than passing attention to many important adverse 'multiplier effects' of being young and unemployed (or unskilled and poor) – not only for individuals but for the lost societal and economic benefits of engagement in paid work and its associated socially integrative effects. Relatedly, questions of how young people's interests are represented inside the workplace, and especially when they are excluded from it, deserve consideration that we do not have space to pursue. The voluminous migration of young people across national and continental borders is now deeply inherent in regional (mal)distributions of (un)employment, and are deserving of a parallel comprehensive global study in their own right: disconnected glimpses into this domain are at serious risk of masking much more than they reveal in terms of understanding the global dynamics of YU. The final chapter of the book makes a challenging and radical suggestion as to how IOs might lead a set of major interventions that would address endemic YU at a genuinely global scale, but space and the need to maintain focus and coherence have otherwise prevented us from considering national or localised policy-driven solutions to YU.

Partly in recognition of these caveats, we limit the book to five principal aims. These are to:

1. Identify the salience of EYU as a major social policy issue of global significance;
2. Elaborate a transnational analytics of global EYU;
3. Scrutinise how global EYU is manifested across diverse development contexts;
4. Examine how global EYU is responded to by transnational social actors, institutions, and policies;
5. Consider the implications of our analytical findings for research and policy.

Breaking down these broad aims into specific objectives, these are to:

1. Highlight inequalities and social and economic injustices of age and gender amongst young people worldwide (expressed as the likely immanent failure to meet or substantially progress SDGs 8.5 and 8.6);
2. Advance understanding of the diverse manifestations and persistent underlying causes of EYU, at scale;
3. Extend analysis of the institutional architectures and functioning of transnational policy, as seen through how YU is taken up and responded to by international actors in spheres of cross-border governance.

Based on rigorous original analysis and research, and bringing new, robust evidence to light for the first time, we offer the first sustained major academic social policy research study into global YU as an endemic and universal feature of contemporary social organisation world-wide. We argue that YU is a *global* phenomenon that requires multi-disciplinary theoretical and empirical social policy research. We add our voices to those of many colleagues who are already convinced that it is not meaningful to research and analyse the contemporary organisation of labour and welfare solely in terms of domestic economies, institutions, governance and policy. And we hope to persuade others of the merits of a transnational analytics in relation to this issue and others. To both, we offer some ways of thinking about how our study can enhance efforts to understand the causes of YU and the array of responses to it, and how future research might take forward this study through further research.

As such, this book aims to contribute to ongoing assessments of the condition of labour and the state of welfare within the contemporary world order. From Chapter 2 onwards, it 'speaks' to debates about the sources and growth of social inequalities, the effectiveness of responses to their causes and consequences, and key social policy issues and priorities in the light of the SDGs. Within this, three principal dialogic terrains structure our discussion. These are outlined below.

1.5.1 Global Economic Restructuring and Endemic Youth Unemployment

The first terrain concerns how populations, welfare systems and economies are differentially embroiled in globalisation processes and their wider social and developmental impacts. Key debates revolve around the global economic dynamics of inclusion and exclusion, and the extent to which the terms of international integration have brought net gains to previously marginalised economies and labour forces or whether they have accentuated inequalities and undermined socially sustainable forms of economic growth and development. Are these transnationalising dynamics indelibly and universally bound to a trajectory of widening and deepening socio-economic insecurity? Or is a more complex narrative warranted – one that recognises multiplicity and complexity, and which entertains the possibility of parallel and contradictory forces at work simultaneously?

Principal questions centre on the implications for employment and jobs – who accesses them, where, and on what terms (Munck, 2002; ILO, 2016)? Unemployment as one form of labour market exclusion has featured as a barometer of the 'new' global dynamics of exclusion and inequality, but remarkably few studies evidence a dedicated and sustained focus on young adults. By examining these processes through the prism of YU, we aim to provide important new evidence about the global restructuring of labour markets and labour systems, together with the specific forms that inclusion/exclusion and inequality take. Some have suggested that young people's labour market position is actually improved as a result of economic globalisation (de Lange et al., 2014). However, the strength of accompanying evidence about how globalising economic dynamics restructure labour markets and the implications for the quality of jobs within the rich countries is unclear. There is even less clarity about this in relation to the poorer countries. In this context, we scrutinise whether such dynamics re-position young people in labour markets: do 'new' sorts of differentiation and inequality emerge in this process and are existing ones mitigated or dissolved? What are the 'new' social edifices being built that help interpret the production, distribution and composition of EYU, globally? These debates and questions are the focus of Chapters 3 and 4.

1.5.2 The Global Financial Crisis and Endemic Youth Unemployment

The second terrain concerns the impacts of the GFC on EYU. The GFC that began in 2008 and the consequential Eurozone crisis (EzC) that erupted in its wake combined to raise international awareness of the scale and impact of economic and financial failures on young people's lives and prospects. Triggering echoes of the global economic depressions of the early 1920s and 1930s and the poverty, suffering and unrest caused by mass unemployment, the GFC and EzC brought to public and political attention the effects of unemployment that were persistent and in many contexts endemic. Of particular concern was the extent to which the effects of these crises fell especially heavily on young people – initially school leavers, then progressively those up to and beyond the age of 25 years – and persisted in some world regions and countries long after the most immediate financial and economic effects of crisis had been ameliorated (Verick, 2009; Bell and Blanchflower, 2010, 2011; Scarpetta et al., 2010; Choudhry et al., 2012). The overarching sources of debate and contention concerned why young people were so badly affected over such an extended period as to become popularly labelled as 'generation jobless' in the Global North (Dorling, 2013; Vogel, 2015); why mass YU remained persistent

(Bruno et al., 2014; Caporale and Gil-Alana, 2014); and why the geographies of the scale and persistence of YU were so variable (O'Higgins, 2012; Mai, 2014).

Beneath these debates lie more fundamental questions and concerns that remain largely unanswered. Was the GFC unprecedented in its effects on the scale and persistence of YU, or was it so internationally notable because of its acute impact on high-income countries? Prior to the GFC and since the Second World War, has the partial recovery from the GFC in the Global North largely allayed the threat of EYU at scale, and if so how far has it done so by transforming the norms, policies and conditions of youth labour markets? Were the scale and profiles of mass YU that followed the GFC exceptional only in the context of the Global North, and are they entrenched characteristics of youth labour markets in many countries of the Global South? These debates and questions are the focus of Chapters 5 and 6.

1.5.3   Global Governance and Endemic Youth Unemployment

The third terrain concerns processes of global social governance and policy formation. Transnational actors, such as IOs, occupy a key place in these, not only because they are, for some, an expression of the apparent erosion of state sovereignty in a globalising world, but also because they are major participants in processes of 'changing norms about the legitimate role of the state in the economy and in the provision of security' (Biersteker, 1992: 104, 2013; Weiss and Wilkinson, 2014). It is by now well understood that *socio-economic* security and social policy are an essential dimension of this (re)configuration of norms and that IOs are meaningful social policy actors therein. IO programmes of global social regulation, redistribution and rights influence domestic policy content and outcomes, and individual and collective welfare worldwide (Biersteker, 1992; Deacon et al., 1997; Yeates, 1999, 2002, 2007, 2014; Lee et al., 2002; Orenstein, 2008; Jakobi, 2009; Kaasch and Martens, 2015; Martens et al., 2020; Yeates and Holden, forthcoming).

A great number of studies now abound of IOs and other transnational social actors in processes of global social problem construction and global policy formation. These variously address the processes by which social issues become defined as ones of immense importance to global society and as matters for global social policy, the forms that global social policies take, and the contexts, sources of legitimacy and mechanisms that enable IOs to become and remain meaningful and influential actors in shaping global social welfare outcomes (Yeates and Holden, forthcoming). Knowledge of global social policy formation in relation to different policy sectors and issues has developed significantly in recent years, but not in relation to young people or on matters of unemployment, with the exception of our own contributions.[7] How is YU viewed and addressed in this context? Is it an exclusively economic issue or one that is the sole prerogative of country-level action, or is understood as a social and political issue that has consequences beyond nation states and as a matter for collective action on an international scale and a subject of action led by institutions of global governance? What powers do IGOs have to address YU, and how have they exercised them? How have organisational values and cultures translated into priorities for action, and what kinds of action have they instituted? How have IGOs collaborated with one another, and with what results? How successful have they been in terms of influencing collective action? By charting *how* YU has

---

[7]   See Fergusson and Yeates, 2012, 2013, 2014; Fergusson, 2016a, 2016b, 2017, 2021.

come to be defined as an ongoing matter for global social governance and policy over the course of a century, and with what effects, our study helps locate EYU within a global institutional field of policy and action that is an integral part of the contemporary global social organisation of work and welfare. These debates and questions are the focus of Chapters 7 and 8.

1.6 VALUES, METHODS AND EVIDENCE

The normative standpoint of this research is that the extent, prevalence and apparent permanence of high levels of YU are a matter of social and economic *in*justice. Extended periods of YU reflect wider social inequalities and exacerbate them, inflicting long-term individual and societal harms. EYU contravenes international norms and goals, and tackling it is a priority of the first order in socio-political projects aiming for egalitarian, inclusive and cohesive social structures.

Epistemologically, we adopt a nomothetic approach to the nature of relevant knowledge in this field and to our methods of data collection and analysis. In practical terms, this means we focus on prevailing trends, general tendencies, and generalisable propositions perceived through broadly based surveys and analyses of material conditions, social and economic structures, political processes and their priorities and loci and distributions of power.[8] In the context of this study, we have limited interest in the personal experiences, psychological characteristics or behaviours of young people who are most harshly affected by YU – not because these considerations are unimportant, insubstantial or resistant to social science analysis, but because the scale and scope of our study places such considerations beyond what can be encompassed here. Our evidence base is comprised entirely of policy sources and statistical and qualitative data. Our research did not involve human participants. Our data and the four datasets we constructed are described below.

1.6.1 Quantitative Surveys of Worldwide Youth Unemployment Trends and Dynamics

We undertake quantitative analyses of worldwide YU based on three datasets constructed for this study. The datasets are derived from publicly available data and help analyse YU rates or trends at the level of countries and/or groups of countries.

The first dataset collates key aspects of youth labour data from the ILO's statistical database, ILOStat. It collates the total cumulative employment status of all 15–24-year-olds in all countries for which such data are available. This amounts to data on 757 million young people across 142 countries and territories. We use this descriptively in Chapter 3 to better understand how YU is distributed worldwide and its compositional basis. We group the data according to four categories: wage workers, vulnerably employed, unemployed and economically inactive. We further group it according to the standard WB country income groups: high income,

---

[8] This approach is perhaps most readily understood in contradistinction to idiographic methods and analyses that prioritise foci on specific cases, events or individuals, their personal understandings and expressed meanings, their 'lifeworlds' and their constitution as unique entities, and the specific instances and effects of their actions.

upper-middle income, lower-middle income and low income. Further information about the dataset, its scope and limitations, is provided in Section 3.3 of Chapter 3.

In order to understand better how EYU is socially structured on a worldwide basis we turn to international datasets of the ILO, WB and United Nations Development Programme (UNDP). ILO and WB data are useful for describing broad trends in YU over time and their manifestation across diverse development contexts (Chapter 5), but in order to understand better the relationships between long-run YU rates and wider economic and social factors (Chapter 6) we constructed two further datasets. The first of these collates long-run aggregated YU rates and GDP between 1980 and 2018 for 74 countries. It enables further exploration of the relationship between annual changes in whole-population YU rates and annual changes in economic growth, country by country, on a worldwide basis. It also facilitates comparison with a validated relationship of correspondence between degrees of change in terms of changes in total unemployment rates across all age ranges and changes in GDP, as postulated by Okun's Law. Our dataset and findings from it greatly extend preliminary assessments of the relationship between changes in GDP and YU by focusing exclusively on young unemployed people and for a far wider range of countries worldwide and over longer periods (Chapter 6). A second dataset cross-tabulates the mean national YU rates of 73 countries for the period 1991–2017 against the mean national UN Human Development Index (HDI) rating for the same period.[9] This representation of the standing of these countries facilitates a close reading of the relationship between the prevalence of long-term YU and human development factors that go beyond the state of the economy. The dataset enables us to differentiate this relationship by country income group. An important feature of both these datasets is that they enable us to test specific propositions regarding the impact of the GFC on YU on a worldwide basis.

All data used for these datasets have been extracted directly from ILO, UNDP and WB sources, using the most recent approved data available (mostly (up to) 2018/19). These data are publicly available open access data. Appendices 6.1, 6.2, 6.3 and 6.4 describe the data, present modelling methods and outputs, and provide data values. This enables readers to check and test our analyses. Some of the countries we wished to include in our analyses do not have complete data over the time periods of our analyses (and we note more generally that there are established and particular difficulties with sourcing accurate standardised data, for example in low-income countries and war and armed conflict zones: see Chapter 5 and Jerven, 2013). We made informed decisions as to the appropriate limits of using incomplete data of this kind, and recorded these decisions in footnotes at the relevant points in the text and in Appendices 6.1–6.4.

1.6.2   Qualitative Survey of Global Youth Unemployment Policy

A parallel study based on archival research and qualitative data relating to the history of global policy on EYU was carried out (Chapters 7 and 8, Appendices 7.1 and 8.1). We trace these responses from the beginning of the twentieth century when the ILO was established (1919) to 2020, by which time the organisational features of the policy field had developed

---

[9]   The HDI is a composite index for each country, calculated on the basis of the health and longevity of its population (life-expectancy index), its knowledgeability (education index), and its standard of living (gross national income (GNI)).

considerably, in terms of the participants and their interactions, and the scope and range of their interventions.

Policy can be tracked through a range of genres (policy reports, official reports, political speeches, interviews, press releases, briefings and media reports), and the historical contours of most public policy action can usually be traced through these. We focused on official documents to trace the 'evidential fingerprints' of IOs' contributions to shaping the policy field over time. These included reports (annual, thematic or special/ad hoc reports), quasi-technical documents (for example, monitoring and evaluation guides for practitioners), Minutes, Notes, Resolutions and formal statements. We considered working papers and evaluation reports prepared by external consultants if they were published by the organisation, though they were assigned lesser weight than official documents of the organisation. All of the documents examined are publicly accessible. Each document is an individual piece of evidence that, taken by itself, has fairly low probative value, but cumulatively can strengthen evidence of a wider pattern or tendency within a sequence of interventions.

Our primary sources were the UN's libraries system, notably the Dag Hammarskjöld Library, the ILO Library (including its online database, Labordoc), the Library of the UN Office of Geneva (UNOG) which hosts the League of Nations Archive resources, UNICEF's Office of Research-Innocenti virtual library, and UNESCO's resource documentation (UNESDOC). We also consulted the e-libraries of the OECD, WB and IMF. Other website-sourced documentation from the UN and elsewhere helped construct the involvement of other international policy actors from the corporate and third sector in the policy field.

Our analytical aims were to identify the major organisational characteristics of the global policy field, its ideational, discursive, institutional, agentic and programmatic structures and the axes of alignment and divergence, cooperation and contestation underpinning them. Guided by process tracing methodology, we used a descriptive inference method to generate 'mechanistic' evidence about all these organisational aspects of the field. Such evidence is essential to delineating and probing previously unchartered policy terrains, though in and of itself the observations it gives rise to and the empirical record into which it feeds do not warrant causal inferences that can logically or robustly be linked to specific outcomes within the chosen case or comparatively with other cases (Beach, 2017; Collier, 2019). That said, our method proved more than adequate for our aim of systematically charting the principal organisational features of global YU policy. We did not seek to test causal relationships about why these actors responded as they did. In this, our method may be termed process tracing 'lite' (Beach, 2017).

Our analysis initiated search terms beginning with 'youth', 'youngster(s)', 'young people', 'unemployment', 'employment', 'labour' and 'work' to identify key documents and sift them for dominant cognate concepts used in the field. We repeated the document searches for concepts – for example, 'employment', 'underemployment', 'informal', 'informality', 'insecurity', 'precarity' and 'youth development' – either on a standalone basis or in combination with one another. We constructed a descriptive timeline of relevant events, milestones, organisational actors and programmes, by sifting documents. We looked for an evidential trace of different kinds of interventions, regarding institutional development and processes of policy formation, as well as of substantive matters of policy content. Each year was covered to construct the long-term timeline. We coded qualitative aspects of observed activity using manual techniques. We wanted to understand not just the frequency of activity, but also its nature – for example, whether the discursive intervention(s) was ephemeral (for example, a passing reference) or more substantial (for example, fully fledged analysis); whether the corresponding action (if any) was a one-off intervention or indication of a sustained presence. The volume of documentation we sifted was substantial. For example, the UN General Assembly's (UNGA) Resolutions database is a vast resource comprising nearly 20,000 entries. The annual proceedings of the International Labour Conference routinely run to over 300 pages each. Similar volumes of documentation exist for other organisations.

Conflict of interest declaration: The research was not financially supported, directly or indirectly, by any entity or organisation that is the subject of this study. We declare no conflict of interests that may cast doubt on the integrity of our research or its reliability.

1.7   A NOTE ON TERMINOLOGY

Unless otherwise stated, the default age range of our study is 15–24 years old. This range corresponds with the UN definition of youth and therefore provides the most stable and universally-applicable definition of youth. We recognise, however, that youth is a constructed, contested and ever-changing social category, as well as the fact that the de facto starting working age for young people in parts of the world is less than 15 years old (an age that the rich world would class as falling within the ambit of childhood). We take due account of this as far as is reasonably possible for a study of this kind.

Unemployment has multiple meanings and casual use of this term can be a major source of confusion as well as analytical bluntness. We therefore distinguish between 'open' or official unemployment and 'hidden' or 'disguised' unemployment. We preface which sort of unemployment we mean by using one of these terms, wherever appropriate. For maximum clarity, we also identify which measure of unemployment we are using. We reserve use of the term 'endemic' adjectivally and specifically to mean (youth) unemployment that is prevalent, persistent and permanent (see Section 1.3, p. 9 and Chapter 5).

We use the term 'international organisation' (IO) as an umbrella term to encompass international governmental organisations (IGOs) (for example, ILO, WB, IMF) and international non-governmental organisations (INGOs) (for example, International Trade Union Confederation). However, we use IGO or INGO as appropriate where we are deliberately referring to one rather than the other. The GFC and its effects are recurrent concepts throughout the book. We refer to 'pre-GFC' and 'GFC' periods but avoid reference to any 'post-GFC' period: there is no universally applicable definition or marker of when the GFC and its downstream effects 'ended' (or will 'end') in any given country or group of countries. Where unavoidable, the need for any such reference refers to periods following the peak of the GFC and/or its apparent peak effects.

The variety of terms used to portray and categorise the countries of the world is immense. None stands out as wholly or universally satisfactory. In this book, we restrict ourselves to two categorisations. The first is geographical place, in the sense of a region (for example, Western Europe, South America, Northern Africa, East Asia) or a continent of the world (Europe, America, Africa, etc.). Where we refer to politically constructed regional groupings of countries, such as the European Union, the Association of South-East Asian Nations (ASEAN) and so on, we term these world-regions (though the African Union is, strictly speaking, a continental grouping). The second categorisation is the delineation of countries in terms of their 'development' status, the most commonly used of which is the World Bank's four-fold classification of countries by income/GDP/GNI, and the UN's HDI which, in addition to GDP, also incorporates measures of education and health. We use both the WB and UN's country classifications. We permit ourselves the occasional foray into the language of 'rich' and 'poor' countries, and other terminologies (such as core, semi-periphery and periphery). We use the term capitalist and capitalism in a general sense, unless we expressly state we are using it in a more specific (Marxist or Marxian) sense.

2. Endemic youth unemployment: a social policy issue

2.1 INTRODUCTION

This chapter builds on the foundational idea set out in Chapter 1 that endemic youth unemployment (EYU) is first and foremost a matter of social policy. We mean this in three senses. First, EYU is inseparable from the organisation, governance and operation of public institutions, and ultimately from issues of social order and civil stability, on which individual and collective welfare depend. Second, EYU is variously 'produced', maintained, managed and mitigated through a wide range of social sectors – from employment policy through social security and education policy to housing policy – all of which form major parts of the wider institutional environment shaping economies and labour forces. Third, current models of development founded on economic growth will not solve EYU, and transformative social policies are needed to comprehensively prevent and mitigate it. In all far too little attention has been afforded to the ways in which the social relations and organisation of welfare shape the trends and trajectories of youth unemployment (YU), even though they are critical foci for analysing the causes and harms of persistent YU.

By elaborating this argument, we mount a sustained critique of dominant approaches to YU. One is that YU is typically treated as a private trouble in public and political discourse – one whose incidence, costs and harms are essentially removed from social structures and institutions shaping everyday life, and which are individualised and invisibilised. As we show in this chapter through our coverage of the invidious, long-lasting effects of YU on individual and collective welfare, there can be few more striking examples of failure to exercise a 'sociological imagination' (Mills, 1959) that this be so. A second aspect of our critique is that research and debate about YU has long been dominated by labour economists, sociologists and psychologists. Economic analysis in particular has tended to dominate accounts of burgeoning YU, especially in advanced economies, but in explaining YU in terms of the economics of labour markets, or as the product of economic processes, business cycles, labour market fluctuations or financial crises, it invariably lapses into economic reductionism. Psychologically-inclined analyses tend to explain YU in terms of individual psychological factors rooted in the personalities of young people that render them unable to adapt sufficiently well to labour market exigencies. These are equally unconvincing claims at the best of times, but especially when it comes to the massification of YU and, indeed, EYU on a global scale.

This chapter is therefore devoted to expanding on our claim that endemic YU is, inherently, a social policy issue as well as a political and economic one, and that a political economy of welfare perspective is needed to comprehend the dynamics of EYU. This is not a particularly contentious claim. After all, governments regularly make (often tacit and un-transparent) political choices within defined legal and institutional constraints as to how far economic change should be allowed to shape the scale and trajectories of all forms of (un)employment, but especially that of YU.

In much of what follows in this chapter, of necessity, we confine our arguments to considering YU at multiple national levels of policy. Subsequent chapters reverse this emphasis, focusing, as we have already signalled (Chapter 1), on the 'upstream' conditions that give rise to EYU worldwide and the institutions of global governance that shape them. Focusing on the 'downstream' national effects of EYU is more informative and insightful than merely instantiating these effects 'on the ground', however: it lends the indispensable perspective of demonstrating that social policy is as much a lens through which to scrutinise the proliferation of EYU *and its under-representation and under-estimation* in 'official' unemployment records and welfare accounts (see Chapter 1) as it is a path towards mitigating EYU. By gaining an initial, if necessarily selective, view of YU across a wide range of countries worldwide, we aim to depict some of the downstream effects of EYU without capitulating to methodological individualism, methodological economism, or methodological nationalism.

This chapter is organised as follows. We begin by considering the so-called scarring effects of YU and their consequences for social policy, especially with regard to young people's incomes and their mental health and well-being (Section 2.2). Section 2.3 reviews some of these consequences through the lens of housing and the crisis of its supply for an ever-widening segment of the youth populations of many countries, especially those without work or reliable incomes. These and other difficulties have direct impacts on social protection for unemployed young people. Section 2.4 reviews the literature that focuses on the links between EYU and social welfare and protection worldwide. This leads us to consider manifestations of discontent and social unrest amongst young people, and then to review the critical issue of states' endeavours to manage and govern young populations experiencing rising levels of EYU (Section 2.5). The closing section summarises and draws conclusions across the chapter.

In the face of the current trends of burgeoning YU internationally, social policy (both as a configuration of state practices and policy-making, and as a field of academic study and research) has been slow to foresee and diagnose 'problems in the making' at scale for young people who are denied 'decent work'. Wherever YU has 'become' EYU, it has also become an intractable issue for social policy and for the maintenance of social stability and civil order in all its manifestations. Recognising this is essential if collective action is to respond to and avert increasingly troubling and potentially threatening harmful outcomes at individual and societal levels, nationally and globally.

2.2 THE SCARRING EFFECTS OF YOUTH UNEMPLOYMENT

The concept of scarring in relation to YU implies early harms that endure in tangible form and impair financial security over the life-course (Kinsella and Kinsella, 2011; Cuervo and Wyn, 2016; Hvinden et al., 2019a, 2019b; Kuchibhotla et al., 2019; Wright et al., 2019). A long-established concept, it has been widely demonstrated that significant damage occurs as a result of exclusion from and/or delayed entry to labour markets, insecure forms of employment, poor labour market entry credentials, and lack of demand for young people's labour in over-subscribed labour markets – as well as of the self-compounding effects of lack of work experience and poor employment records. The consequential experiences of intermittent incomes, low pay, stigmatisation and loss of confidence readily trigger increased anxiety, fears concerning job performance, poor mental and physical health, and higher rates of morbidity and mortality. It is therefore important to interpret the scarring effects of YU within a life-course perspective: its effects can be deeply damaging as well as life-long.

2.2.1 Income and Employment

Copious studies across many countries and regions over three decades have demonstrated the nature and impacts of scarring.[1] Historically at least, the literature has tended to attribute scarring to actual degradation or loss of skills resulting from lack of active labour market participation in the form of human capital decay (Schmelzer, 2011), or to assumed loss of motivation, or by the application of conscious or unconscious sexist, racist or other stigmatisation (Omori, 1997). Either way, the effects on the life chances of young people are profound. Cockx and Picchio (2013) analysed the trajectories of 15,000 Belgian 18–25-year-olds who remained unemployed nine months after leaving school, for the period 1998–2002. They found that 'prolonging unemployment drastically decreases the chances of finding employment but hardly affects the quality of subsequent employment' (p. 951). A year after the nine-month period, for those who remained unemployed, 'the probability of finding a job in the following two years decreases from 60% to 16% for men and from 47% to 13% for women' (p. 977). In the UK, Zuccotti and O'Reilly (2019) find that having been unoccupied in school, college or a job in 2001 reduced by more than 30 percentage points the probability of being employed in 2011 – for both men and women' (p. 576); and that 'all ethnic minority groups have lower employment probabilities than White British women' (p. 578). These findings highlight the early scarring signs of cumulative disadvantage that risk becoming life-long. Economic scarring in particular appears to endure beyond the immediate timeframe within which it occurs following periods of economic retrenchment and recession. There is considerable agreement that for some generations recovery is difficult for most of those affected by unemployment, and effectively impossible for some. Chauvel's study, for example, finds that, in France:

> This 'scarring effect' is even clearer concerning earnings: the cohorts of new entrants in the labor market in a time of downturn have to accept lower wages; conversely, for young workers, a strong economy allows them to negotiate better earnings. After this entry point, the earning gaps remain *because of the lack of a catch-up effect on earnings*: some generations are about 10 points above or below the long-term trend, because of the point at which they entered the workforce, and after age 30 the relative benefit or handicap remains stable ... Age-period-cohort analysis shows that cohorts who experienced a difficult (favorable) entry because of a context of recession (expansion), continue to suffer (benefit) from a relative delay (advancement) in upward mobility when they are compared to the average situation. ... Those who are 'lost in transition' do not make up for their early difficulties. (Chauvel, 2010: 80, 83, 84, emphasis added)

---

[1]   For studies relating to future employment and incomes, see Becker and Hills (1980), Ellwood (1982) and Lynch (1989) (USA); Ackum (1991) (Sweden); Gregg (2001) and Gregg and Tominey (2005) (UK); Nilsen and Reiso (2014) (Norway).

Other international research confirms these long-term effects. Researching 11 West European countries, Brandt and Hank (2014) found long-term scarring in a sample of more than 13,000 men and women.[2] Their study highlighted

> a large positive total effect of having experienced unemployment in the first three years of one's career on further unemployment risks before and after age fifty ... early and mid-life experiences of unemployment have independent and strong associations with the risk of losing one's job after the age of fifty. (p. 736)

The chances of recovery from YU are limited and for many its impacts are life-changing. There is little to suggest that the predominant modes of the social organisation of welfare in and beyond advanced economies address these self-compounding trends.

One of the most assiduous analyses of scarring addresses the full effects of the global financial crisis (GFC) on young people in the UK. It estimated that 7–9 per cent of young people were adversely affected by the GFC, and that young people who became unemployed at this time would be

> more likely to be unemployed and welfare-dependent later in life; with the average young unemployed person spending an extra two months per year out of work by their late twenties ... [and] ... likely to be paid less in later life; with the average young unemployed person earning £1,800–£3,300 less per year by their early thirties. (ACEVO, 2012: 12)

The net costs of post-GFC YU to the UK Treasury were calculated as being approximately £28 billion (ACEVO, 2012: 4). We return to these macro-level costs later in the chapter.

2.2.2 Mental Health and Well-being

Numerous studies draw direct connections between unemployment scarring and mental health and well-being as well as those mediated though experiences of poverty. Many of these experiences are prolonged; some become permanent and are matters of serious concern amongst epidemiologists. Bell and Blanchflower's (2011) definitive UK study incorporated the effects of the GFC, and found that

> Those currently unemployed are less happy; there are enduring effects from spells of unemployment while young, which continues to lower happiness more than two decades later ... The currently unemployed are less healthy than full-time employees. The longer the spell of unemployment while young the lower the happiness when they are older ... spells of unemployment are especially harmful to the individual—and to society—when young people become unemployed. A spell of unemployment when young continues to have a negative impact in later life. And the longer the initial spell of unemployment the larger the subsequent negative impact ... With [one] important proviso, our results add to the range of evidence on the negative personal and social impacts of youth unemployment associated with the Great Recession. (pp. 263–4)

---

[2]   Austria, Belgium, Denmark, France, (West) Germany, Greece, Italy, the Netherlands, Spain, Sweden and Switzerland. See also Mojsoska-Blazevski et al. (2017) and Petreski et al. (2017) for studies of Central and Eastern Europe.

The authors' conclusion is a disturbing depiction of many young people's long-term trajectories:

> ... youth unemployment has adverse effects that extend well beyond the present ... Of particular concern are the group of youngsters with the lowest levels of education and skills, especially when they belong to racial and ethnic minorities. These are the ones most impacted in a recession as jobs requiring relatively low levels of skills are taken by those with higher levels of skills. (p. 264)

This authoritative evidence underscores the life-course-related meaning of scarring (and the vulnerability of this birth-cohort to recessions in the 1980s and 1990s: see Chapter 5). Copious other studies in advanced economies demonstrate the nature and impacts of scarring concerning mental health and well-being.[3] All agree that the material and psychological scarring effects of YU are deep, long-lived and ostensibly internationally ubiquitous, at least in the Global North. There is less agreement on what the long-run damage from scarring to employment prospects, employability and personal and social viability over the life-course means for tangible social policy reforms, however.

2.3   HOUSING AND YOUTH UNEMPLOYMENT

Second only to scarring are the acute housing needs of young people without work. In many higher-income countries, young people who are employed even at the early stages of professional careers are often unable to meet the revenue or capital requirements to ensure housing security by rental or purchase. The possibilities of living independently for a significant proportion of employed young people have been greatly restricted by changes in earnings, entitlements and the availability of suitable housing stocks. In some countries of the Global North, in comparison with the 1960s–1990s, the scope for leaving the parental home for an independent household has been greatly limited by extended studentship, the reduced value of the earnings and the curtailment of rights to housing benefit. In turn, these issues have been significantly exacerbated by demographic trends away from cohabitation and joint and shared housing, in contexts of critical shortages for families with children, the accelerating gravitation of populations towards urban locations, uneven regional distributions of jobs and earnings, and, especially, consequent surges in house prices in many countries and regions. The increasing dependence of the sons and daughters of middle-class and affluent families on parental assistance to finance first-time renting and house-buying is emblematic of many of the above trends. Intergenerational transfers of capital on or before the death of a grandparent or parent that became common even in lower sections of the middle class – as a result of the high earnings, enlarged pensions and higher morbidity rates that proliferated during the 1960s–1980s – incrementally dwindled and, for many, vanished from the 1980s–1990s onwards, as older generations have lived longer and need more care.[4] The possibilities for young people who are

---

[3]   Morrell et al. (1994); Goldsmith et al. (1997); Clarke et al. (2001); Tyler (2013); Mars et al. (2014); Power et al. (2015); Strandh et al. (2015); Goldman-Mellor et al. (2016); Lee et al. (2019).

[4]   Failures of the so-called 'intergenerational contract' in monetary form in higher-income countries have other complex, extensive significances for young people from lower socio-economic classes. For critical reassessments of this concept, see Göransson (2013). For an informative review of key literatures, see France (2016). See also Bessant et al. (2017) and Hammer et al. (2018) for further critiques.

unemployed to enter any housing market without parental or other sources of financial support are negligible.

Pressing and immediate problems at this interface between YU and housing arise from urgent, under-financed, ill-planned, or premature departures from the parental home into the typically chaotic and often unsafe environments of overcrowded shared rental accommodation, 'sofa-surfing' and street homelessness. Where 'home' is a seat of conflict, unemployment and homelessness among young people as co-existing risk factors intensify for parents and young people alike (Hagan and McCarthy, 1998; Whitbeck et al., 1999; Van den Bree et al., 2009). This is the crux at which lack of employment and housing problems combine to generate acute vulnerability and specific needs for care and protection. Yet there is significant evidence in the UK that those young people who seem most vulnerable often fail to meet vulnerability tests that, if 'passed', would entitle them to safe housing (Carr and Hunter, 2008). In some other European countries, the increasing specialisation of responses to vulnerability in relation to homelessness has also had the perverse effect of intensifying competition for safe accommodation such that reasonable needs cannot be met (Levy-Vroelant, 2010).

The lived experiences of young adults facing such difficulties are well documented. Ford et al. (2002) found commonplace opportunistic and disorderly trajectories after leaving the parental home. MacDonald and Marsh (2005) reported how difficult lives produced unstable and troubled housing careers that were nonetheless grounded in relatively inclusive communities from which second-generation individuals and families were reluctant to depart. Here the provision of social housing was key to 'moves to independent living regardless of ... progress in the labour market' (p. 168). At the same time, some respondents in MacDonald and Marsh's study claimed that local councils clustered unemployed young people with groups associated with crime and drug dealing. 'Postcode discrimination' allegedly resulted – in the form of exclusion from job opportunities, indicating a spiral of self-reinforcing disadvantages (p. 168). For many young people, such routes to living alone without work have become progressively scarcer whatever their consequences, especially in cities and affluent regions.[5]

In the USA, high housing costs and economic uncertainty and decline have long-since delayed departure from the parental home (Haurin et al., 1997; Toro et al., 2011). Amongst homeless young Canadians, stable employment is a significant factor for finding accommodation (although young homeless people find employment at the same rate as others) (Hagan and McCarthy, 1998). Northern Europe is typified by early home-leaving, in contrast to Southern and Eastern Europe, where home-leaving is more commonly delayed (Billari, 2004; Guerrero, 2017). In lower-income countries, UNICEF estimated that 80 million children and young people live apart from a parent or responsible adult (Van der Ploeg and Scholte, 1997). For them, the relationship between employment, housing and the need for social care is different and may even be inverted: the need for any form of employment, however erratic, takes precedence over housing and care of an adult, as a tactic for survival.

This brief review of homelessness in relation to lack of employment or low or unreliable incomes demonstrates the complexities and challenges facing policymakers and, above all, young people, keen to realise their reasonable rights and aspirations. Interdependency between

---

[5]   See Simmons et al. (2014: 214–15), especially regarding the important distinction between living alone and the more frequently used term 'living independently'.

these two policy sectors interacts in vicious policy circuits of mutual ineligibility that render inaccessible fundamental necessities for young people's self-sustaining survival.

2.4   YOUTH UNEMPLOYMENT AND SOCIAL PROTECTION

Multi-sectoral interdependencies like those between YU and housing are compounded in other policy spheres. The most direct interface is between YU and social protection in the form of benefit entitlements and other non-monetary forms of social protection that accrue to being unemployed, for some. The bilateral interaction between these policy spheres typically intensifies wherever YU rates increase significantly and entitlements to social protection are triggered. Whenever the supply of youthful labour outstrips labour-market demand it typically poses multiple challenges to states and governments. Although not universally, higher-income countries conditionalise or reduce entitlement when YU rates surge, especially during recessions and financial or other crises. Elsewhere, such provision is minimal or entirely absent. We consider each in turn.

2.4.1   Europe

The responses of successive UK governments when faced with expanding youth cohorts during periods of substantial labour surplus have been more extreme than in most advanced economies. A copious academic literature on some of the more radical policy changes between the early 1980s and the mid-2000s charts waves of the erosion, gradual withdrawal and deletion of young people's entitlements to unemployment and related benefits.[6] Since 1983, at least 30 withdrawals of welfare-related entitlement, impositions of additional charges and altered thresholds of obligation and entitlement have negatively affected 16–24-year-olds (Muncie, 2015). These major changes amounted to what Coles (1995) termed 'precarious transitions without [the] benefit of a safety net' (p. 52) and a 'threat to young people's entitlements' (p. 54) (see also pp. 52–6 and pp. 118–24).[7]

EYU over several periods since 1983 was incrementally translated from being a problem of weak labour market demand to being an opportunity to reform social and education policy. The dramatic peaks in YU rates of 15–19-year-olds and 20–24-year-olds lent pragmatic legitimacy to the effective withdrawal of the state from provision for the youngest group of the unemployed, and its substantial diminution for young adults.[8] These escalations in

---

[6]   For the early years of responses to burgeoning YU, see Coffield et al. (1983); Fiddy (1983); Watson (1983); Bates et al. (1984); Roberts (1984). For the effects of benefits cuts by UK Conservative governments to 1997, see Coffield et al. (1986); Finn (1987); Wallace (1987); Harris (1989); MacDonald (1994); Coles (1995). For critiques of New Labour policies (1997–2011), see Fergusson et al. (2000); MacDonald and Marsh (2001); Fergusson (2002, 2004, 2016b); Finn (2003); Mizen (2003, 2004); Webster et al. (2004); Furlong and Cartmel (2006).

[7]   Coles (1995) viewed these changes as erosions of young people's citizenship – a theme central to the work of his predecessors and successors (Harris, 1989; Bynner et al., 1997; Dean, 2006; Furlong, 2013).

[8]   26 per cent and 17 per cent unemployment, respectively, for the two age groups totalling 1.2 million in 1983; 19 per cent and 17 per cent (0.9 million) in 1993; 31 per cent and 17 per cent (1.0 million) in 2011. Data from https://www.ilo.org/shinyapps/bulkexplorer49/?lang=en&segment=indicator&id=UNE _TUNE_SEX_AGE_NB_A (accessed 5 December 2019).

YU, unprecedented since the 1930s depression (see Chapter 3), gave credence to extensive deregulation of employment and wages. They were also an opportunity to extend compulsory schooling and massively expand capacity in further and higher education – in many cases without full or adequate funding for the new wave of students. Much of the financial costs of YU fell on parents or on third sector (charitable) organisations where familial support was unavailable or refused. In the UK, YU policies have been inseparable from social protection and welfare policies, primarily in the sense that the latter were deployed as means of downplaying, re-narrating and reconfiguring what was to count as YU.

The circumstances and policy shifts associated with EYU for much of the last four decades in the UK depict the opportunities it offered successive governments for redefining YU and breaking the historic post-Second World War link between unemployment and social protection. Compared with its European neighbours, the UK was atypical in its neo-liberal policy turns and in the way in which the youth labour force became the anvil upon which labour market deregulation and restructuring was forged across all age groups (Craig, 1988; Peck, 2001; Mizen, 2004; MacDonald and Marsh, 2005). Indeed, across the full youth and adult age range, UK policy was an outlier amongst unemployment protection regimes in Europe in the 1980s–1990s (Gallie and Paugam, 2000). In descending order of levels of protection provided to young unemployed people by the state, Gallie and Paugam's defining typology identified four regime types: universalistic, employment-centred, liberal/minimal and sub-protective regimes. It focused on the degree of coverage of unemployment benefits, the level and duration of entitlements to benefits and the use or otherwise of active employment policies. In the liberal/minimal regimes, coverage is identified as incomplete, and the levels and duration of cover as weak. In sub-protective regimes coverage is very incomplete and the level and duration of coverage are very weak. The typology covers 12 European countries (all but one EU member states at the time of the analysis). The UK and Ireland alone were identified as liberal/minimalist; Greece, Italy, Portugal and Spain were closest to sub-protective. The remaining six countries all provided higher levels of protection.

More recently, when the GFC began to shrink youth labour markets at dramatic rates, Scarpetta et al. (2010) showed that two of every three OECD countries provided no or highly conditional unemployment benefits for school leavers. Only Germany, Finland, Ireland and Sweden provided full benefits on a par with adults' entitlements.[9] In some countries, entitlement is mitigated in cases of demonstrable social distress, for those above the age of 18 or 25 years. In others, being made redundant from insecure or casualised modes of employment did not confer eligibility, although these strictures were moderated in some countries as the crisis took hold.

Most recently, Leschke and Finn (2019) differentiate provision between age groups and timeframes across all EU countries, offering a wider perspective on the effects of the GFC, and a substantially more detailed analysis. For 15–24-year-olds, in 2013, the mean benefit coverage across the EU27 was approximately 32 per cent of adult benefits. This average

---

[9]   It is a mark of the rapid reconfiguration of unemployment benefit entitlements for young people following the GFC that such data are at constant risk of dating. For example, countering Scarpetta et al.'s data, Lorentzen et al. (2014: 41) found that 'earnings-related unemployment benefits now cover only 10 per cent of unemployed Swedes and Finns and 45 per cent of unemployed Norwegians aged 24 years or younger'. See also Madsen (2015).

conflates a remarkably wide range of entitlements – from 122 per cent of adult entitlement in Romania, to zero entitlement in Luxembourg and Latvia, with most countries' entitlements ranging between 15 per cent and 50 per cent of adult entitlements.[10] The comparable entitlements for 25–29 year-olds are substantially higher in every country except Romania, Lithuania and Spain, and the differences between the EU27 countries are notably smaller – all but five countries' entitlements are in the range 50 per cent to 90 per cent of the adult entitlement. It is clear that even within the EU with its predominantly high-income countries (HICs) (except Romania), unemployment benefit entitlement for the youngest working-age group is almost certainly insufficient to sustain independent living. In only five countries do 15–24-year-olds receive more than half of the adult entitlement (reported as insufficient to sustain independent living in some or all of Romania, Lithuania, Spain, Denmark and the UK).

For 15–24-year-olds, in the period between 2009, when the first indications of an impending sovereign debt crisis were recognised in the Eurozone, and 2013, when the fullest effects of the Eurozone crisis (EzC) were felt in EU countries, benefit coverage increased in half of the 18 countries for which equivalent data was available, and declined in the other half.[11] For the most part benefit levels and eligibility tightened as the 'austerity' period in the EU advanced. Improvements in income security were typically contingent on participation in education and training, if offered at all. By 2013, comparing age groups across the EU27, on average 33 per cent of 15–24-year-olds who had been dismissed from jobs received unemployment benefits, compared to 52 per cent of 25–29-year-olds and 57 per cent of 30–64-year-olds (see Leschke and Finn, figure 5.4). Leschke and Finn (2019: 154) conclude that between 2010 and 2014 'younger and older youth [were] worse off than before the Great Recession [GFC]'.

Overall, the three studies indicate major differences at country level in unemployment benefit provision for young people in the EU. Covering the period well before the GFC, Gallie and Paugam's (2000) study found the UK, Ireland and the four southern European countries to be the weakest providers. At the earliest onset of the GFC, Scarpetta et al. (2010) found minimal social protection for school leavers, with only four European countries offering benefits equivalent to those of adults, but some movements towards more generous provision as the effects of the GFC took hold. Leschke and Finn's (2019) study encompassing the full GFC period found an extremely wide range of benefits between countries for 15–24-year-olds, with no benefits in some countries and rates higher than those for 25–29-year-olds in others. The advent of the EzC also produced polarised responses between countries – some substantially increasing benefits, others reducing them. By 2013 barely a third of 15–24-year-olds received unemployment benefits. Long-standing comparative generosity in benefits payments in this age group in the Scandinavian countries was also being substantially reined back (Lorentzen et al., 2014).

---

[10]   In descending order, Romania (122 per cent), Lithuania, Estonia, Denmark, UK (51 per cent), Belgium, Austria, Hungary, France, Greece, Czechia (31 per cent), Finland, Poland, Italy, Denmark, Slovakia, Slovenia (15 per cent), Spain, Cyprus, Portugal, Luxembourg and Latvia (0 per cent) (Leschke and Finn, 2019, figure 5.5).

[11]   In ascending order of percentage-point change, benefit coverage for 15–24-year-olds increased as approximate proportions of their 2007 value in Finland (10 percentage points), France, Slovenia, Slovakia, Romania, Denmark and in Greece (50 percentage points); and declined in Sweden (5 percentage points), the UK, Denmark, Hungary, Austria, Spain, Poland, Czechia, Portugal and in Cyprus (70 percentage points) (Leschke and Finn, 2019, figure 5.6).

We conclude that despite wide variation over time and between countries, by 2013 there were few if any EU countries in which unemployment benefit would allow independent living for 15–24-year-olds; the same was true for 25–29-year-olds in some countries. In effect, social protection in the EU as it was conceived after the Second World War no longer applies for younger would-be new entrants to the labour market.

2.4.2 Low-income and Lower Middle-income Countries

However severe the erosions of social protection for young unemployed people in European high- and upper-middle income countries, they describe connections between being unemployed and eligibility for income support that typically exceeds provision in almost all low(er) income countries. Chapter 1 emphasised the ways in which the scale, reach and meaning of EYU in low(er) income countries is to be understood in the context of nation states that have little or no fiscal capacity for social protection, in which unemployment is regarded as a luxury, and where the informal sectors of domestic agriculture in particular (and other forms of labour casualisation) absorb young people's labour as a necessary characteristic of subsistence.

Multiple studies confirm these claims. In a survey of 67 low-income countries (LICs) and lower middle-income (LMICs) countries Vodopivec (2006) found that no 15–29-year-olds would be eligible for social protection. Cho et al.'s (2012) major World Bank study of social protection and labour policies in middle- and low-income countries constructs four country clusters, each with different demographic, structural, employment and/or productivity profiles. Although none of the data are age-differentiated, it is of relevance that two of the clusters contained low-income countries with high-proportions of youth populations[12] and exhibited combinations of weak economic indicators, weak labour market regulation and poor or absent forms of social protection, amongst other related fields of poor provision. On almost all indicators, Cluster 3 countries show levels of risk that Cho et al. describe as 'serious', while Cluster 4 countries show mostly 'moderate' levels of risk. This indicates that a large number of LICs have very weak provision for mitigating unemployment risks generally, a situation that disproportionately impacts on young people due to the demographic profile of the countries (see also Chapter 3).

Data on how unemployed young people survive in the absence of state-provided social protection are extremely sparse. Betcherman and Khan (2015: 8) argue in respect of sub-Saharan Africa (SSA) that 'because household incomes are low and because unemployment insurance and safety nets are non-existent or very limited at best, few Africans can afford not to participate in the labour force at all, or to remain completely unemployed if they do want to work' (see also Fox et al., 2016; Fox and Thomas, 2016). Furthermore, surveys of youth jobs in Africa confirm that many of the formal indicators for SSA are misleading. 'Open' unemployment is 'relatively rare' (Betcherman and Khan, 2018: 5); YU rates are especially low, the youth–adult unemployment ratio is the lowest for all world-regions, and the ratio of young wage workers to all other forms of labour market participation amongst young people is very low – about 10 per cent (Filmer and Fox, 2014). In the same vein, Baah-Boateng (2016) draws

---

[12]   The 14 countries in Cluster 3 comprise very low-income countries (mostly African, plus Bangladesh, Cambodia and Tajikistan); 14 other countries in Cluster 4 comprise low-income countries (mostly sub-Saharan African, plus Nicaragua, Pakistan and Mongolia).

attention to two scenarios in respect of Africa. Where there is no social protection for the unemployed and informal labour markets proliferate, 'youth tend to seek refuge in the informal sector for survival rather than remaining unemployed' (p. 425). Obversely, where some protection is available, 'youth have no choice but to register as unemployed to enjoy social benefits, resulting in reported high [levels of] open unemployment' (p. 425). In countries in the former category, Baah-Boateng shows, informal labour accounts for as much as 90 per cent of the youth labour market and unemployment rates are below 5 per cent, while those in the latter category are typified by informal labour at less than 25 per cent of the youth population and YU rates above 25 per cent.

Such observations are generalisable beyond Africa. In Afghanistan, similar conclusions have been drawn:

> ... in the current circumstances, a rapid increase in [agricultural] production ... cannot be achieved through the existing practices. *The level of disguised unemployment in a subsistence economy like Afghanistan needs to be rectified by providing employment in other sectors, not by forcing the agricultural sector to remain at subsistence level for ever.* ... What the economy in general and the agriculture sector in Afghanistan in particular need is a sustainable and evolving indigenous agricultural development. (ActionAid Afghanistan, 2009: 23, emphasis added)

Evidence of this kind is compelling, but also difficult to interpret where data are uneven and unreliable, and outcomes are wholly determined by very variable and highly specific local and national circumstances. The use of different conceptions of unemployment and different criteria for counting or estimating different forms of labour market participation adds to the opacity of such data as are available. The use and application of overlapping categories like informal labour, open unemployment, vulnerably employed, contributing family worker and own-account worker can obstruct accurate comparisons over time and place (we return to this point in Chapters 3 and 5). For example, unwaged agricultural work in the informal or vulnerably employed sectors accounts for up to two-thirds of workers in SSA, on Betcherman and Kahn's (2018) calculations, whereas Hamaguchi et al.'s (2013) for LICs in SSA indicate that vulnerable employment encompasses *almost all* forms of youth employment. Even definitions of the commonly used category 'economically inactive' are liable to variable interpretation. Estimates of the extent of YU are therefore open to question in many LICs and LMICs.

Whatever the extent of these alternatives to waged work, unemployment benefits remain extremely rare in low(er) income countries.[13] We return to these issues in detail in Chapters 3 and 5, not only with regard to estimates of informal labour but to the construction of the categories of vulnerable as distinct from unemployed would-be workers and the existence of huge reserve armies of labour (RAoLs).

---

[13]   As the IGO with unique responsibility for defining and applying such categories in its own collection and analysis of definitive global data on YU, the ILO sets standards and criteria which have been adjusted over time to accommodate changing conditions in the nature and forms of employment. For a summary of ILO definitions and how they have evolved, see http://wiego.org/informal-economy/concepts-definitions-methods (accessed 23 August 2020); see also Fox et al. (2016).

2.5 MANAGING AND GOVERNING YOUTH UNEMPLOYMENT

Young people are not always passive recipients of the scarring effects of YU, or of home-lessness, or inadequate or absent social protection. Over the last decade, distinct recognisable social movements amongst young people have coalesced temporally, locally and globally, in multiple acts of dissent, protest, disorder and sometimes violent expressions of anger and resentment at perceptible injustices. States have responded – often harshly and violently – to such protest, but this has been the least prominent and least immanent manifestation of the direct exertion of physical power by states seeking to manage the consequences of scarring, homelessness and lack of social protection. In many countries across most world-regions successive governments have devised increasingly sophisticated ways of managing and governing the consequences of EYU that fall short of violent interventions but may call upon civil and criminal sanctions if the techniques of 'soft power' fail. Interventions of all these kinds significantly and symbolically further extend the complex institutional frameworks for addressing the downstream consequences of EYU across multiple policy sectors, involving 'special' schools, social workers and other state officials – and in extreme instances the police, lawyers and the judiciary.

The history of social unrest and breaches of social order amongst young people is long and extensive. Unemployment and its social consequences in conditions of economic uncertainty and decline have been frequent causes.[14] In 2011, in the wake of the GFC, youth protest movements spread in and beyond the advanced economies. The 'Arab Spring' protests in all the countries of Northern Africa, the Spanish 'indignados' (outraged young), the Portuguese 'Geração à Rasca' (desperate generation), Piratenpartei (Germany), the 'Occupy' movement that began in the USA, and the English August Riots were all emblematic of such youth protest movements (Sukarieh and Tannock, 2015).[15] The rapid spread of recessionary conditions resulting from the GFC became a particular centrepiece for challenges to civil and social order in the USA, the Middle East, Europe and beyond (Cairns et al., 2016).[16] In some countries, the absence of social protection for young people in periods when YU exceeded 40 per cent were specific drivers of conflict and protest – for example, in Greece (Papadopoulos and Roumpakis, 2012) and in Spain (Ramos-Díaz and Varela, 2012). Sloam's (2014) study of young Europeans' civic engagement in 2011 as the GFC was bedding in found that 'the out-raged young' in Germany, Italy, Portugal and Spain were successfully exploiting the capacity of 'new media' to speed political mobilisation and establish new protest movements:

> [C]rises have proved so effective in mobilizing young people, because they operate both on a personal (micro-) and a societal (macro-) level, connecting young people's individual experiences of youth unemployment, high university tuition fees, etc. to broader economic and political issues such as economic inequality. (Sloam, 2014: 227)

---

[14] Sukarieh and Tannock (2015) trace the history of youth as a revolutionary subject in considerable depth – organised early twentieth-century youth movements, global uprisings of the 1960s and reaction against neo-liberal policies.

[15] In addition, Sukarieh and Tannock (2015: 80) list protests in Bahrain, Canada, Chile, France, Greece, Kuwait, Saudi Arabia and Yemen in 2011, and later in Brazil, Sweden and Turkey in 2012–13.

[16] See Cairns et al. (2016) for extended analysis of the political impacts of YU and job insecurity.

To the extent that these movements have been internationally coordinated or mutually inspired, they represent a potentially important and informative aspect of the underpinning connectedness of the globalising dynamics of YU (Chapter 1). It is likely that they will revive if labour markets contract significantly.

One of many indices of the recognition of the huge impact of the GFC on young people is the response it elicited from the ILO, IMF and World Bank. In 2010, without precedent, the Directors-General of ILO and IMF co-chaired a special joint international conference in a rare display of common cause-making about the relationship between mass unemployment worldwide resulting from the GFC and threats to social order.[17] This was remarkable in itself in terms of joint action between two historically-counterposed international governmental organisations (IGOs) (see Chapter 8; see also Fergusson, 2021). A year later, at the annual summit of world leaders in Davos, the ILO Director-General reported youth protests in more than a thousand cities in 82 countries worldwide (Somavia/ILO, 2012a), following this up with more developed arguments that such protests were the direct result of 'the growth of inequality and intolerable levels of youth unemployment' (Somavia/ILO, 2012b). These interventions were based on the ILO's re-analysis of data from the Gallup World Poll's Social Unrest Index, which found that 'unemployment is most strongly associated with the estimated risks of social unrest, along with disposable income (figure 1.12)' (ILO/IILS, 2011: 17). Elsewhere, the same report clearly argues that, following the GFC, 'in advanced economies, the debate has often centred on fiscal austerity and how to help banks … in some cases, this has been accompanied by measures that have been perceived as a threat to social protection' (p. viii); and that 'during a crisis, a social protection floor can play a very important role in providing income security to vulnerable individuals and families' (p. 92).

Perhaps relatedly, in the following year the World Bank took the unprecedented step of acknowledging that 'lack of job opportunities can contribute to violence or social unrest' (World Bank, 2012: 12), and that 'frustration and even social unrest may develop when education and effort are not rewarded or when people perceive the distribution of jobs to be unfair' (p. 137). This was a relatively rare moment of alignment in the views and prognoses of these IGOs, indicative of rising levels of serious concern about the consequences of EYU. Of particular interest is recognition of the importance of social protection for those who are most exposed to global financial and economic crises, if social unrest is to be stemmed while economies 'recover'.[18] This is as relevant to the development of the global analytics of EYU we advocated in Chapter 1 as it is to the analysis of the causes of burgeoning EYU itself.

The social unrest that continued in the wake of the GFC epitomises the argument that YU is irreducibly and essentially a social policy issue. Far short of such extremes and long before them, though, the capacities of states for managing and governing YU have been approved, applied, developed and refined by governments worldwide. The speedy interventions of national and transnational actors in the early 2010s were in large part attributable to policy developments and reconfigurations of state infrastructures in contexts of rapidly evolving

---

[17] See https://www.ilo.org/global/about-the-ilo/newsroom/news/WCMS_144399/lang--en/index .htm (accessed 23 August 2020).

[18] See, for example, concern expressed by the OECD's Secretary-General with regard to Southern Europe that 'while social protection programmes helped soften the blow of the crisis for many people, others were left behind with little or no support' (OECD, 2014: 10).

deregulated and hyper-flexible labour markets – most notably but by no means exclusively in the North Atlantic alliance that pioneered the neo-liberalisation of labour markets and social protection in the 1980s and 1990s (see also Chapter 4). Understanding how extended periods of YU 'produce' social policy issues and problems for social policy therefore routes critical analysis towards the ways in which states, state agencies, state bureaucracies *and* leading IGOs recognise YU as a material source *of* strain, distress, despondency and vulnerability – or as an object *for* reform, management and governance.[19]

One set of policy responses is based on principles of care, support and mitigation, the other on principles of monitoring, correction and punitivity. For the first, the agencies that are able to provide monetary benefits, welfare support and housing, for example, remain cornerstones of the powers and virtues of welfare states that provide compassionate relief as a right of citizenship and a human right that references internationally recognised UN standards. In some countries, such states have never been fully established.[20] In others they have been radically eroded – not least as a response to episodes of mass YU, as in the UK (and sometimes the USA).[21] In yet others – notably the Eurozone – most governments maintained historic rights to unemployment and other benefits (notwithstanding the comments of the OECD, above).

For the second set of responses, an influential literature spanning political science, sociology, social policy and criminology provides a powerful analysis and critique of the ways in which states contrive to redefine the victims of labour market failures as idle, feckless or miscreant victims of 'dependency cultures' – in short, using Mills' (1959) terminology, as architects of their own 'private troubles'. In various ways this literature explores the ways in which state bureaucracies became reconstructed as agencies of managerialisation, behavioural reform, punitive correction and of 'governing the soul', as applied to 'the unemployed' and other 'deviants'.[22]

These two sets of responses to YU very clearly conceive the role of social policy in fundamentally conflicted ways. The first identifies the need for multi-sectoral policies of mitigation that traverse the complex interactions between institutions and agencies of education and training, employment, housing provision and social protection – and at its best adopts a life-course perspective that recognises the risks of the serial accretion of disadvantages that arise from early experiences of protracted YU. The second conceives of the key agencies of social policy as state actors whose principal responsibilities are to regulate social and economic behaviour in ways that minimise the alleged welfare dependency of those who resist and refuse allocation to precarious or dehumanising jobs that do not pay 'living wages' – at its worst a cluster of

---

[19] For example, Brown et al. (2014: 182–4) provide an insightful in-depth analysis of the ways in which UK social policy has responded to manifestations of vulnerability amongst young people living in difficult circumstances of many kinds, including the individualisation of their social problems.

[20] The OECD Secretary-General (quoted in footnote 18 above) went on to criticise the countries of Southern Europe that were and remain most beset by YU because their provision of social support 'often failed to reach the poor even before the Great Recession' (OECD, 2014: 10).

[21] The USA's response under the Obama presidency to the dramatic collapse of the youth (and adult) labour markets following the first shock-waves of the GFC in 2008 provided major temporary relief until the partial recovery (see Tooze, 2018).

[22] Most notably, see Rose (1989, 1999); Pollitt (1990); Pierson (1991); Osborne and Gaebler (1992); Clarke et al. (1994, 2000); Walters (2000); Garland (2001); Peck (2001); Wacquant (2009); Standing (2011); Tyler (2013). For an extended critical overview of the governance literature as applied to unemployed young people, see Fergusson (2016b: 177–88).

agencies that withhold social protection, enforce participation and deploy tactics that result in resented employment, 'self-invisibilisation' as a means of self-protection from punitive actors, or at the extremes civil or criminal records. The former set of responses typifies the social and political values of social democratic policy which would be expected to pursue a life-course perspective that secures the futures of nascent citizens. The second typifies neo-liberal values that prioritise the interests of business and 'enterprise' and minimise reliance on state benefits and high levels of taxation. While few regimes match these ideal-typifications, most are more closely aligned with one than the other as competing political positions are struggled over in democratic assemblies and state agencies. As Chapter 1 signalled, these issues are fundamental to questions about the ways in which the governance and policy of YU is (co-)produced and (co-)determined by national and transnational actors.

2.6   SUMMARY AND CONCLUSIONS

As Chapter 1 argued, awareness and knowledge of global social policy formation has recently developed significantly in many policy sectors but it has not done so in relation to young people and unemployment. This chapter has begun to chart how and why EYU urgently needs to be recognised as a matter of *social* policy, whether nationally or transnationally. As anticipated in the introduction, our focus has been primarily on the national level of social governance and policy in order to demonstrate the essentially *social* nature of YU and its complex multi-sectoral and life-long interfaces. We hope that this necessary approach has nonetheless also drawn clear attention to the indispensability of 'the global' for perceiving YU as a social policy issue. Indeed, not only are most of the issues which we have considered internationally ubiquitous – albeit in highly diverse manifestations – it is clear that many are also the outcomes of 'upstream' dynamics rooted in the world economy and trade and its governance globally. One dimension of this is seen in the distinctive alliances of a fast-expanding EU, and of the 'bloc' of anglophone countries that were most heavily influenced by neo-liberalisation during the 1980s and 1990s, which interpreted the causes of persistent and extensive YU very differently and pursued very different responses to it. Another dimension is the globalisation of the youth labour force, whose size, distribution and deployment can only be properly understood in global terms, in terms of how human labour is (re-)distributed across national and regional boundaries worldwide. This, too, has had major 'downstream' effects on the distributions and configurations of YU within national borders. Both dimensions and yet others are considered further in Chapters 3 and 4.

Our review of international literatures on the scarring effects of YU demonstrated the substantially-increased risks that unemployment subsequently affects young people's future employment, income, health and well-being. Our findings identify entrenched social policy problems that arise from ever-deepening social inequalities, exclusions and dissent amongst scarred generations temporarily or permanently shut out of waged work of a kind that provides socio-economic security. We argued that the extensive restrictions imposed on young people's development through unemployment doubly impede their progress towards adult independence because of the high cost and inadequate availability of accommodation in many countries. The causes of types of homelessness and of inadequate, unaffordable and unsafe housing cannot be extricated from delayed entry to youth labour markets and the consequent scarring effects. Obstacles to young people's access to housing independence and the incidence of youth homelessness are both primarily products of failing social policies and inadequate welfare states. In the face of these obstacles, the potential for social protection for young people that comes anywhere close to the levels of an actual 'living wage' is manifestly unavailable almost universally, being mostly out of reach for young people aged up to 21 and 24 years and above.

In all, it is through these conditions of scarring and cumulative disadvantages working their way across all aspects of young people's lives in many socio-economic strata that YU becomes a manifestly multi-dimensional social policy issue. Between the neo-liberal turn of the 1980s and the GFC, to varying degrees over this period, the state-induced dependencies of young people – themselves the direct products of labour market and related policies – on parents and more experienced others have been variously denigrated, denied, refused or ignored by successive governments of many political stripes. Globally, young people's responses in the form of mass protests gave serious – if momentary – cause for alarm. Some calls for strengthened social protection were met, often conditionally and temporarily; most were ignored, often despite the pleas of some leading institutions of global governance (including ILO's passing of the Social Protection Floor Recommendation in 2012 (Deacon, 2013)). Ten years after the GFC almost everyone with a job up to and beyond the age of 24 years in the UK was denied payment at the national minimum wage. Across Europe, huge numbers of young people aged 15–24 and above without jobs remain little better off financially than wholly dependent school children. In place of social welfare, in neo-liberal states and their keener imitators, YU has been incrementally reworked as an object of management often heralded in the rallying cry of 'engagement'. When necessary, wherever policies of quasi-enforced participation have been shown to be ineffective, YU has become an object of oppressive governance.

The tensions we identified between distinctive sets of responses to YU and the profoundly conflicted analyses they embody are inextricably linked to fundamental labour market issues that bear particularly heavily upon young people. Succinctly described, such tensions reside in equally fundamental questions as to whether the availability of paid labour for all workers should be determined by agreed public rights, standards and regulations; or whether by the processes of free markets and the forces of supply and demand through which they are said to be organised. We maintain a critical commentary on these and other key questions in the chapters that follow, through our focus on the rights of young people to decent work – most recently as set out in UN Sustainable Development Goals (SDGs) #1 and #8.[23]

---

[23] This book assigns particular importance to SDG 1.3: 'Implement nationally appropriate social protection systems and measures for all, including floors, and by 2030 achieve substantial coverage of the poor and the vulnerable'; and to SDG 8.5: 'By 2030, achieve full and productive employment and decent work for all women and men, including for young people and persons with disabilities, and equal pay for work of equal value'.

3.   The global youth labour force

3.1   INTRODUCTION

It is by now well established that the globalisation of economies and labour markets and the accompanying changes in production systems have profound social impacts on labour systems, workers and the employment relationship. A vast literature chronicling the growth of the industrial and service sectors, the impact of technological change in industry, and changes in product market conditions has helped elucidate the scale and nature of such changes. However, a full picture of their drivers must necessarily also attend to changes in labour forces, whose availability and organisation are vital to how transnational processes are concretely manifested. This is a point well understood by Critical Labour Studies. It has persuasively demonstrated that labour remains a major social force in ongoing processes of globalisation. Labour has not been denied agency by globalising processes; rather, its participation in shaping them (including resistance to them) has been vibrant and robust, and its responses to state and corporate internationalisation have conditioned their timing, pace, nature and effects (Munck and Waterman, 1999; O'Brien et al., 2000; Yeates, 2001, 2002; Munck, 2002; Taylor, 2011; Yeates and Pillinger, 2019).

The wide-ranging implications of global economic restructuring for labour forces and workers have, to date, been discussed predominantly in terms of social class and gender; age has been a tangential consideration. As a result, there is little dedicated research into how young people are (re)positioned within globalising labour systems, whether in terms of the types of employment (low- or high-skilled), quality of employment (wages and working conditions), or the distribution of employment and unemployment. We have been greatly surprised by this. Attention to young people and globalisation has been decidedly inflected by a curious combination of trade and cultural studies literatures heralding young people as the vanguard of major technological innovations and changing product markets, and of cultural shifts resulting from changing youth identities and consumer patterns. Insofar as these literatures come anywhere close to labour economics or sociology, they are concerned with the new economic opportunities that the global youth 'bulge' affords. IT sector advocates seem to be especially quick to note the business opportunities arising from the fact that 90 per cent of the largest populations of young people the world has ever seen reside in developing countries.[1]

---

[1]   Writing from a business perspective Hanna (2010) offers one such account of the opportunities demographic change presents to the IT sector: 'Investing in this "youth bulge" now is essential to succeed in an increasingly competitive and skill-intensive global economy .... [Y]outh use of ICT will increasingly matter for development outcomes and will have wide-ranging effects on youth transitions. ICT offers unprecedented opportunities to youth: harvesting worldwide knowledge, informing and education inside and outside schools, changing the environment for learning ..., and offering new employ-

In all of this, questions about how the restructuring of youth labour forces and labour markets underpin changes in product markets, production processes or employment structures are rarely asked. Even domestic and international actors, long attuned to the development and labour impacts of contemporary forms of economic globalisation, seem largely oblivious to the youth-specific aspects of labour markets as key institutions of global social organisation.

This chapter begins to scrutinise the transnationalising political-economic dynamics of youth unemployment (YU), which are continued in Chapter 4. Our starting point is that YU is analytically inseparable from the constitution of the global youth labour force more widely. This foundation routes our arguments towards young people's movements in and out of different categories of the labour force. It is worth emphasising at this point that our relatively extensive coverage of youth *employment* in relation to the world economy is not an end in itself, but a means of identifying the *transnational* structures and processes that are reshaping youth labour markets, and how some young people are drawn into global circuits of capital and labour while others are excluded from them. These global dynamics are essential to explaining the production, reproduction and underlying rapid and persistent growth of youth *unemployment* worldwide. In combination, these chapters underpin our focus on endemic youth unemployment (EYU) and the global financial crisis (GFC) (Chapters 5 and 6), and on global governance and policy responses to YU (Chapters 7 and 8).

The chapter is organised in four sections. Section 3.2 presents a close re-reading of classic studies in labour history through a youth labour lens. This directs us towards the pioneering work of Friedrich Engels and other works in similar vein to illuminate the labour condition of young people. The concepts of 'reserve army', relative surplus population and the international division of labour are assessed with an eye to their contributions to a *global* understanding of YU. Sections 3.3 and 3.4 present data on the size and composition of the global youth labour force, what we term the global reserve army of youth labour (GRAoYL), based on the first of the international datasets constructed for this book as described in Chapter 1. To this end, Section 3.3 describes our dataset, its scope, construction, strengths and limitations, and Section 3.4 presents and discusses the structure and composition of the GRAoYL at world level, disaggregated into country groupings. Section 3.5 draws conclusions and sets out bridges to Chapter 4, which elaborates on key propositions of this chapter through a focus on the relationship between youth labour and contemporary global economic restructuring.

3.2 THE NEW INTERNATIONAL DIVISION OF YOUTH LABOUR: NINETEENTH AND EARLY TWENTIETH CENTURIES

Young people are largely absent from political economy accounts of the relationship between population, labour, production and wealth. This is not to say no consideration has been given to this subject, however. Friedrich Engels' work is unique among political economists of the

---

ment opportunities and second chances .... ICT also broadens employment opportunities for youth and provides second chances for work for youth disabilities. IT-enabled services and business process outsourcing offers considerable scope for future growth in youth employment in developing countries. Offshore employment ... acts [as] an alternative to migration' (Hanna, 2010, p. 258). See also Oshri et al. (2011).

time for his detailed attention to the labour condition of young people in nineteenth-century English industrialisation (Engels, 2009). Primarily concerned with different forms of relative surplus population in the context of the wider thesis about 'how the bourgeoisie exploits the proletariat in every conceivable way for its own benefit' (p. 279), he showed that young people and women predominated among the reserve army of workers that is a *permanent* structural feature of the labour system so inherent to capitalist accumulation. Thus:

> English manufacture must have, at all times, save the brief periods of highest prosperity, an unemployed reserve army of workers, in order to be able to produce the masses of goods required by the market in the liveliest months. This reserve army is larger or smaller, according as the state of the market occasions the employment of a larger or smaller proportion of its members ... When they enter upon the more active branches of work, their former employers draw in somewhat, in order to feel the loss less, work longer hours, *employ women and younger workers*, and when the wanderers discharged at the beginning of the crisis return, they find their places filled and themselves superfluous – at least in the majority of cases. (Engels, 2009: 118–19, emphasis added)

We return to the gender aspects of these dynamics, but for now emphasise his key point that employers drew on unemployed youth labour in times of crisis and that young people (and children) offered employers two sorts of distinct advantage over adults: their physique and their cost. Regarding physique, in the 'light' manufacturing sector, Engels noted that young people's 'flexibility of finger' was a distinct advantage when it came to spinning and weaving, which required no muscular strength. Regarding cost, young people could be paid less than adults. This was not just a reflection of the 'skill' content of the work or their status as workers 'in training': it enabled employers to outsource the costs of social reproduction. As Engels argued, it was assumed that they could stay in the parental home, that they did not have an independent household to sustain, and that they were financially supported by their family. Of course, the wages they earned were never 'surplus' or 'pin' money: whether adults were employed or not, their wages were essential for family solvency; indeed, they were often sole 'breadwinners' of the family.[2] Young people paid the price of this outsourcing in other ways, notably through the toll of the work on their bodies. Engels' meticulous research into the consequences of the mass employment of young people in factory and mining settings amply revealed their age-specific vulnerabilities in the form of damage wrought by their working conditions to their physical constitution – their health (notably high rates of mutilation, deformity, disability, morbidity and mortality) and their 'moral development'. The effects of this damage were long-term and, in many cases, life-shortening.

Karl Marx (1887) echoed much of Engels' analysis of the English factory system. He reported extensively on the sizeable proportion of children and young people in the industrial workforce, noting they routinely comprised half of all employees, their hazardous working conditions, and the unique labour qualities that employers saw in them.[3] Regarding machine

---

[2]   Amongst Engels' concerns about the impacts of mass employment was the way it undermined working-class family life. One aspect of this was the impact of children and young people working to support their unemployed parents. This situation upended usual structures of family authority, and the young workers became 'the masters in the house' (Engels, 2009: 168–9).

[3]   Two examples stand out. One pertains to lucifer match manufacturing, half of the workforce of which was under 18 years old. The working conditions were so unhealthy and unpleasant that 'only the most miserable part of the labouring class, half-starved widows and so forth, deliver up their children

work, Marx commented, for example, that 'the quickness with which machine work is learnt by young people, does away with the necessity of bringing up for exclusive employment by machinery, a special class of operatives' (p. 285). Furthermore, such work allows 'a rapid and constant change of the individuals burdened with this drudgery' and reshapes the old system of division of labour. Machine work is, he argued,

> systematically re-moulded and established in a more hideous form by capital, as a means of exploiting labour-power. The life-long speciality of handling one and the same tool, now becomes the life-long speciality of serving one and the same machine. (p. 258)

Whereas Engels focused exclusively on the urban factory system, Marx was also concerned with rural agricultural work. He noted how the extraction of greatest value from peasant labour was from its young cohort (Marx, 1887: 468–81). Later studies put greater empirical flesh on the bones of this analysis. Vladimir Lenin's early twentieth-century empirical study of the German peasantry showed that capitalist agricultural production was underpinned, ultimately, by unwaged child and youth labour:

> In the busy season, the peasant suffers from a shortage of workers; he can hire workers only to small extent; he is compelled to employ the labour of his own children to the greatest extent. The result is that in German agriculture, in general, the percentage of children among family workers is nearly half as big again as that among wage-workers … The peasant has to work harder than the wage-worker. This fact is … now fully proved by statistics for whole countries. Capitalism condemns the peasant to extreme degradation and ruin. (Lenin, 1967: 37, emphasis in original)[4]

Such studies constitute early major landmarks for the way they understand the distinctive position of youth labour in processes of social and economic change. Capitalist industrialisation processes, they posit, depend on a renewable pool of adaptable, available and dispensable youth labour. Capitalist economics is a vital component of the permanency of this pool. Relative cost to the employer is a significant factor: young people can be taken on or shed easily and can be persuaded to work highly intensively while commanding lower wages. This points to a macro-economic dimension, in that the youth labour condition is pivotal in managing wage inflation. As Marx argued 'the general movements of wages are exclusively regulated by the expansion and contraction of the industrial reserve army and these again correspond to the periodic changes in the industrial cycle' (1887: 446). Wages are, therefore, determined 'by the varying proportions in which the working class is divided into active and reserve army' (p. 446). The concept of relative surplus population is 'the pivot upon which the law of demand and supply of labour works' (p. 448). At its simplest, the expansion of the

---

to it' (Marx, 1887: 170). A second referred to settings where 'young persons have to do heavy work in rope-walks and night-work in salt mines, candle manufactories, and chemical works [and] … turning the looms in silk weaving' (p. 306).

[4]   The extract is from *Pravda* in 1913, in which Lenin considered the case of peasant farming at some length. 'German [census] statistics show that among wage-workers the largest percentage of children (3.7 per cent …) is to be found in the big capitalist farms …. But among family workers the largest percentage of children is to be found among the peasants – about 5 per cent (4.9 per cent to 5.2 per cent). As many as 9 per cent of *temporary* wage-workers employed in big capitalist enterprises are children; but … among the peasants as many as 16.5 to 24.4 per cent of the temporary *family* workers are children!' (Lenin, 1967: 36).

reserve army *relative* to the active one depresses wages. Young people are a critical element of this relationship insofar as they form a disproportionate share of the expanding reserve army in periods of stagnation, over-production and lower demand for labour. Not only are their own wages held down when in work by the availability of even younger cheaper and more disposable others, but their own dispensability is a mechanism for wage depression of older others. In summary,

> the capitalist buys with the same capital a greater mass of labour power, as he progressively replaces skilled labourers by less skilled, mature labour power by immature, male by female, that of adults by that of young persons or children. (p. 446)

Furthermore, the youth 'reserve' labour force is no more monolithic than the 'active' one. Both are fragmented, by age, gender and social class; the dynamics of youth labour exploitation vary by sector and industry. This recognition holds out the prospect of multiple (intersecting) social *divisions* of youth labour and of structural differentiation *within* the youth labour force. Such plurality also opens up the prospect of reserve youth *armies* of labour operating in segmented labour markets. With this comes one possible explanation of why high levels of YU can co-exist with high levels of youth employment.

Engels' observations about how capital sought constantly younger and cheaper workers centred on English manufacturing because, as a frontier site of a high level of capitalist industrial development, England foretold, he argued, the social catastrophe awaiting Germany and other countries intent on following its model of development. However, his research was not confined to England: it extended to factory labour across the British Empire. In this regard, he noted the same preference for younger workers there. Notably, in 1839 nearly half (46 per cent) of factory operatives were under 18 years old, 58 per cent of whom were females (Engels, 2009: 165).[5] This employer propensity towards youth labour was, then, not a peculiarity of England but a far broader international tendency.

Marx and, later, Rosa Luxemburg, elaborated more systematically the international dimensions of the 'reserve army'. Marx was clear how important the expropriation of non-capitalist labour (for example, the peasantry) and the looting of colonised countries by European capital was in the genesis of capital and the English proletariat, but Luxemburg went even further. She argued that attending to this expropriation only in the initial appearance of capital and to primitive forms of accumulation relegated it to an incidental feature of accumulation rather than an integral one. Thus, not only does the recruitment of labour for the industrial reserve army of workers draw on enormous 'social reservoirs outside the dominion of capital' (for example, the peasantry) but '[c]apital needs the means of production and the labour power of the whole globe for untrammelled accumulation; it cannot manage without the natural resources and the labour power of all territories' (Luxemburg, 1951: 345–6).

Although little of Marx's or Luxemburg's work made explicit reference to young people, it helps to construct this study's global analytics of YU because of the centrality accorded to *global* and not just national modes of social organisation. In articulating how social divisions (of social class) inherent in production and accompanying systems of values and beliefs

---

[5]   He noted that '[o]f 419,560 factory operatives of the British Empire in 1839, 192,887, or nearly half, were under eighteen years of age, and 242,296 of the female sex, of whom 112,192 were less than eighteen years old' (Engels, 2009: 165).

are structured *globally*, and how these reflected one's place – literally and socially – in the world, Marx and Luxemburg drew attention to the *transnational* organisational features of capitalism as well as to the extensively international reach of the 'new' division of labour so associated with industrialisation. Highlighting that 'local' labour markets are interconnected internationally does not deny that local or national conditions influence the characteristics of labour systems in any given place. Rather, it points to a world economy in which centralising elements fuse with local conditions (Mittelman, 1995) and in which some places in poorer countries can be as if not more integrated with overseas economies than with the economic 'hinterlands' of their own countries (Wallerstein, 1974, 2004). Recognising, as both Engels and Marx did, that young people occupy distinctive positions within the labour force, it is but a short step to the conclusion (drawing on Marx's and Luxemburg's insights) that the youth workforce has global characteristics. Therefore, in principle, we can speak of international divisions of *youth* labour and *global* reserve armies of youth labour. This paves the way for probing questions about the characteristics of the global youth labour force, how it is consti-tuted and re-made, and with what effects and outcomes.

The concerns of this nineteenth-century theoretical tradition resonate with histories of YU in the early twentieth century. As an already highly internationalised economy (Hirst and Thompson, 1996), the UK provides a useful example of this. Amongst the first recorded indi-cations that YU was a systemic feature of the economy came in reports of what was known in the UK as 'the boy-labour problem' (Casson, 1979; see also Tawney, 1909; Gollan, 1937). William Beveridge (1909), a civil servant who is widely regarded as the architect of the British post-war welfare state, wrote:

> When [the boys] grow up and begin to expect the wages of grown people, they must go elsewhere to obtain these wages. They leave or are dismissed, and their places are taken by a fresh generation from the schools. (1909: 125–6)

The relationship between the condition of entry into employment and later experiences of unemployment among young men was in fact long known. Since the beginning of the nine-teenth century, 'trade unionists had complained about the "overstocking of trade with boys", and centuries earlier similar arguments were used when the statutes for the regulation of apprentices were introduced' (Casson, 1979: 127). This was not only about wages, though, but about costs that employers were not willing to bear. Thus, children who began their employment aged 14 years or under were routinely made redundant on or soon after their sixteenth birthdays so that employers could avoid the costs of paying unemployment and health insurance contributions to the state (p. 14). So ingrained was the desire by employers to minimise their labour costs that by the early 1930s employment among 14- and 15-year-olds remained much higher than that of 16-year-olds and older groups. Correspondingly, so low was the demand for 16-year-olds that those with the longest education were most likely to be unemployed. Even the 14- and 15-year-olds were 'discharged after two or three years, without having received any training', effectively leaving as unskilled as the day they started work (p. 9).

During economic turndowns, long-term YU was especially widespread in areas dominated by single industries, such as in Lancashire in the north of England, where the cotton industry competed internationally and in which long-term employment prospects were poor or absent (Casson, 1979, citing Jewkes and Winterbottom, 1933). This interpretation – that the comparatively lower cost of the youngest juveniles explains higher rates of unemployment among older juveniles – is further endorsed by Cameron et al.'s (1943) survey of 18–25-year-old males in Cardiff, Glasgow and Liverpool at the end of the Great Depression in 1939, which found that unemployment rates rose from about 10 per cent amongst 15-year-olds to 24 per cent amongst 22-year-olds.

As Casson's (1979) informative overview makes clear, age was a significant structural differentiator of younger labour cohorts, in that the greatest comparative advantage (such as it was) accrued to the very youngest groups of the industrial workforce, albeit for a very short time. Confirming the Marxist law of wage-setting, youth labour's low cost relied on ongoing mass supplies from a reserve pool (of school-age children) that bolstered the supply of workers overall:

> In most trades relying on young people it is cheaper to hire and fire casually than to screen job applicants carefully and to follow grievance procedures before separation. An employer can tolerate high wastage of labour if he can rely on a ready supply of new recruits from the next generation of school-leavers. So long as each new generation is happy to enter these trades, employers will have little incentive to improve their personnel policies. (Casson, 1979: 28)

Casson leaves no doubt that workers' organisations helped sustain younger workers' vastly inferior labour conditions:

> Trade unions have done little to promote the interests of young workers. It is far easier for an employer to dismiss a young worker than an older worker. Craft unions do not normally oppose the laying-off of apprentices when their training is complete, and have done little to improve their pay relative to other workers. (p. 28)

The relationship between the systematic expulsion of young people from employment and the global economy is also provisionally illustrated by international unemployment rates during the 1920s and 1930s. This is essentially a story of how successive economic crises in the forms of major recessions in the USA, the UK, Germany and beyond between 1919 and 1923, and the Great Depression of 1929–39 that followed the 1929 Wall Street Crash, were manifested in rising unemployment. Table 3.1 provides an overview of unemployment crises in seven European and two other anglophone countries.[6] It shows that, at different points between 1921 and 1939, these countries experienced record peaks, the highest of which was in 1932 when rates ranged between 19 per cent (Belgium) and 44 per cent (Germany). Seven of the nine countries had YU rates of 15 per cent or above for at least one in three years (meeting our EYU criteria) and this continued in some countries, notably Denmark, Sweden and Norway, over almost two decades up to the onset of the Second World War. Denmark and Norway stand out for having a 15–32 per cent rate for a remarkable 16 of 20 *continuous* years.

Data about young people's unemployment was much sparser than all-age unemployment during the interwar years, but was more regularly recorded by the mid-1930s. It provides further evidence of a relationship between YU and global economic crisis, with young people especially hard hit. In Germany, for example, a hyperinflation crisis that predated the Great

---

[6] Although standardised data on unemployment rates started to be produced by ILO in the 1920s, it was mostly confined to advanced economies (see Chapter 7).

Table 3.1   Unemployment rate, all ages, selected countries, 1920–1939

Year	Australia	Belgium	Canada	Denmark	Germany	Netherlands	Norway	Sweden	UK
1920	6	–	5	6	4	6	2	5	3
1921	10	10	9	20	3	9	18	27	17
1922	9	3	7	19	2	11	17	23	14
1923	6	1	5	13	10	11	11	13	12
1924	8	1	7	11	13	9	9	10	10
1925	8	2	7	15	7	8	13	11	11
1926	6	1	5	21	18	7	24	12	13
1927	6	2	3	23	9	8	25	12	10
1928	10	1	3	19	9	6	19	11	11
1929	10	1	4	16	13	6	15	10	10
1930	18	4	13	14	23	8	17	12	16
1931	27	11	17	18	34	15	22	17	21
1932	28	19	26	32	44	25	31	22	22
1933	24	17	27	29	36	27	33	23	20
1934	20	19	21	22	21	28	31	18	17
1935	16	18	19	20	16	32	25	15	16
1936	11	14	17	19	12	33	19	13	13
1937	8	12	13	22	7	27	20	11	11
1938	8	14	15	22	3	25	22	11	13
1939	9	16	14	18	1	20	18	9	11

Note: Figures are percentages (rounded).
Source: Adapted from Galenson and Zellner, 1957: 455, table 1.

Depression resulted in YU rates in Germany that spiralled to 23 per cent before comparable rates afflicted other countries, and peaked at 44 per cent in 1932 (Table 3.1) (Petzina, 1986). Of the six million people this represented,

> approximately one million, or one in six, were young men and women under the age of 25 years. The entire younger generation between the ages of 14 and 25 years, made up 24.1 per cent of the total male unemployed and 38.5 per cent of the total female unemployed in mid-1932 … Taking into account those not registered because of non-entitlement to benefits … youth unemployment *may have been in reality almost double the officially recorded levels* by the end of 1932. (Wiedwald, 1932, cited in Stachura, 1986: 123, emphasis added.)

Germany was not exceptional. Table 3.2 shows just how high YU rates were in many countries: excepting Switzerland, they ranged between 25 per cent (Czechoslovakia) and 42 per cent (Hungary). For the same reasons as Wiedwald noted, we must assume that all or most of these rates significantly underestimate the actual extent of YU. The gender-disaggregated data show that young women are consistently more likely to be unemployed than young men, and by very wide margins in some countries.

Of particular interest are the very large differences between the 15–24-year-old and 25–29-year-old groups during the Great Depression (Table 3.3), underscoring our earlier

Table 3.2   Youth unemployment rate, 15–24-year-olds, selected countries, early 1930s

Country	Year	Total	Males	Females
Czechoslovakia	1932	24.6	–	–
Denmark*	1933	28.1	27.9	29.3
Finland*	1933	33.3	–	–
Germany	1933	26.1	23.4	36.7
Great Britain	1930	31.4 (approx.)	25.4	44.2
Hungary	1930	42.0	–	–
Italy*	1932	41.5	32.7	57.6
Netherlands	1933	27.8	–	–
Norway	1933	27.0	–	–
Sweden*	1933	33.7	–	–
Switzerland	1934	15.0	14.0	17.0
United States	1930	28.5	24.8	42.4

Note: * Figures refer to young unemployed persons of less than 26 years of age. Figures are percentages.
Sources: ILO, 1934a: 33; ILO, 1935b: 6–18.

*Table 3.3   Unemployment rate by age range and gender, selected countries,
1930–1940s*

Age range (years)	Australia (1933)		Belgium (1937)		Canada (1931)		UK (1931)		USA (1930)		US (1940)		France (1936)	
	M	F	M	F	M	F	M	F	M	F	M	F	M	F
15–19	20	17	8	3	22	11	9	7	8	6	23	22	5	4
20–24	26	15	12	3	23	9	15	12	9	5	18	13	5	4
25–29	21	12	12	3	21	8	14	10	7	4	13	9	5	4
30–34	17	11	12	3	–	–	13	11	6	4	12	8	5	3
35–39	16	10	13	3	18	8	13	11	6	4	11	10	5	3

Note: Figures are percentages (rounded).
Source: Adapted from Eichengreen and Hatton, 1988: 31, table 1.9.

comments regarding the labour market disadvantages of the youngest age groups. But in contradistinction, the gender differences in Table 3.2 are not repeated here, albeit based on a very different dataset.

This brief review of nineteenth- and early twentieth-century histories of youth labour provides some important analytical tools for thinking about YU as a global phenomenon. While detailed evidence is sparser for the nineteenth century than the twentieth century, such data as are available show that the trends of disadvantages and discrimination in employment amongst young(er) people are consistent, if quite variable. First, the data highlight how young people have long been adversely incorporated into national and global labour forces. Such incorporation takes many forms, including a disproportionately large share absorbed into a permanent pool of 'reserve' labour – an intrinsic feature of the ordinary workings of globally-organised capitalist economies. Second, situating youth labour within a wider political-economic context draws attention to the existence of a pool of young workers to be used flexibly by employers for managing labour costs. At the same time, the fragmented, locally variable, age-stratified nature of youth labour forces and labour markets means that high levels of youth employment are frequently entirely consistent with high levels of YU across multiple scales and levels. Third, ideology is very powerful in the reproduction of the youth labour condition: ideas of young people's innate flexibility and availability are not mere epiphenomena – they are integral to justifying and maintaining the socio-economic relations and political-economic means of production. Fourth, data for the last three decades (and their relationships with financial crises) variously confirm and extend these arguments (see Chapters 5 and 6).

We build on these points throughout the book. The remainder of this chapter takes forward our proposition of the concept of a 'global reserve army of youth labour', and, in the first-ever calculation of the global youth labour force in these terms, we enumerate its size and composition (Section 3.4). Before that, we briefly describe the dataset on which this analysis is based.

3.3   THE GLOBAL YOUTH LABOUR DATASET: SCOPE, DEFINITIONS, LIMITATIONS

ILO global labour force data correspond quite closely to the main distinctions between Marx's concepts of the active labour army and the reserve labour army (Bellamy-Foster et al., 2011). Using ILO labour statistics (ILOStat), we identify for every country for which data was available the numbers of young people aged 15–24 years who are wage workers, vulnerably employed, unemployed or economically inactive. We aggregate these categories into group totals and an overall total. The global active army of youth labour is the category of youth wage workers, while the global reserve army of youth labour (GRAoYL) is the sum of the categories of unemployed, the vulnerably employed, and the economically inactive population. The broad composition of the reserve army for this analysis is an expansive one, and represents what might reasonably be termed a maximalist interpretation of the size of the GRAoYL (cf. Bellamy-Foster et al., 2011).

3.3.1   Definitions of Categories

We operate the same definition of each of the labour groups as Bellamy-Foster et al. (2011) to ensure broad comparability between the youth and adult workforces, but by including those of working age under the age of 25 we bring in a significant cohort which Bellamy-Foster et al. excluded.[7] This allows us to compare the structure of the youth and adult groups.

---

[7]   We build on Bellamy-Foster et al.'s (2011) analysis of the global workforce. Ours differs in two key respects. First, whereas they plotted global workforce trends annually, over 15 years from 1997 to 2011, we take a snapshot of the contemporary situation using ILO data from the most recent year available at the time of writing (2018). Second, they defined the global workforce as 15 years and over, and excluded all those classed as economically inactive who were less than 25 years and greater than 54 years of age. Their data on the economically inactive population's share of the reserve army 'include only prime age workers between 24 and 54 years of age without work, and exclude all of those ages 16–23 and 55–65' (p. 495). Despite the efforts of many governments to marginalise or exclude young people from unemployment counts, it is entirely appropriate to recognise that, as Bellamy-Foster et al. argue, 'from

3.3.1.1 Young people
ILOStat youth-specific indicators routinely give the range of 15–29, but we restricted our analysis to the 15–24 age group, as this is the standard definition of young people under-pinning UN data.[8] We selected the indicators 'Youth employment by sex, age and status in employment (thousands) – annual' and 'Youth working-age population by sex, age and labour market status (thousands) – annual', from which we drew the relevant data for our dataset.[9] We supplemented this dataset with additional data searches within ILOStat, and cross-classified the countries by World Bank income group for a sense of how the elements of the global youth workforce are distributed between and within these country income groups.

3.3.1.2 Labour/workforce components
Wage workers are defined in ILOStat as 'employed' (most are in the formal or organised sector of the economy). We do not distinguish between the nature of employment (full-time, part-time, under-employed, etc.) so as not to duplicate counts of national youth workforces, which could have led to overestimation of the numbers of those in employment. Working conditions of those in employment vary considerably. Many young wage workers are undoubtedly on temporary, short-term contracts, with few labour rights, and are poorly paid. Reflecting this, some labour lexicons refer to them as 'excluded workers' (Ofreneo, 2016) or 'the precariat' (Standing, 2011).

Bellamy-Foster et al. (2011: n.p.n) describe the vulnerably employed as 'a residual category of the "economically active population", consisting of all those who work but are not waged workers'. The 'vulnerably employed' category is essentially a measure of workers in the informal, subsistence and agricultural economies who are not wage workers but who are economically active. The group comprises 'own account workers' – essentially workers who are not employees (that is, self-employed)) and are engaged in subsistence (the production of goods exclusively for own final use by their household) and entrepreneurial activities (for example, street vendors) – and 'contributing family workers' (essentially unpaid family workers, as in persons contributing to a family business, often in agriculture). It includes those 'would-be wage workers' who are in practice 'peasant producers, traditionally thought of as belonging to non-capitalist production, including subsistence workers who have no relation to the market' (Bellamy-Foster et al., 2011: n.p.n). They are, in practice, underemployed.[10] They enter or leave this category when the wage economy is un/able to support them. Ofreneo

---

a practical standpoint, in most countries those in these age-[group]s too need and have a right to employment' (n.p.n). See also Appendix 5.1 for further discussion.

[8]   The UN defines 'youth' as those persons between the ages of 15 and 24 years old, and the ILO follows this convention. This definition is 'without prejudice' to any other definitions made by member states. See https://www.un.org/en/sections/issues-depth/youth-0/index.html (accessed 12 January 2020). ILOStat is based on national data sources (censuses, enquiries).

[9]   See   https://www.ilo.org/shinyapps/bulkexplorer57/?lang=en&segment=indicator&id=EMP_3EMP_SEX_AGE_STE_NB_A   and   https://www.ilo.org/shinyapps/bulkexplorer23/?lang=en&segment=indicator&id=EIP_2WAP_SEX_AGE_RT_A (both accessed 7 January 2020).

[10]   Note that ILOStat includes a measure of 'underemployed' which is very restrictive. Our use of the term is in a broader sense of those who would like to work more hours. Bellamy-Foster et al. (2011, n.p.n) note that this category 'includes the greater part of the vast pools of unemployed outside official unemployment rolls, in poor countries in particular'; and that they correspond to '"stagnant" and "latent" portions of the reserve army'.

(2016) refers to informal economy workers as 'excluded workers', because informality is part of the coping mechanism of workers who cannot get jobs in the formal sector of waged work.[11] Yates (2009, cited in Bellamy-Foster et al., 2011: n.p.n) strengthens the case for considering vulnerably employed workers as an inescapable part of a global reserve army because 'in most of the world, open unemployment is not an option; there is no safety net … underemployment means death' (see also Chapter 1, p. 5, and Chapter 2). In this sense, vulnerable employment is a necessity not a choice, and therefore is included as part of the reserve army of labour.

The unemployed category consists of all those who meet the criteria of being available and actively looking for a job in recent weeks. This is a highly restrictive category. It does not include those who are participants in or recipients of government-backed active labour measures.[12] In many countries many under-18-year-olds and some 18–21-year-olds are altogether excluded from unemployment counts on grounds that they are eligible to be in full-time education or training, or are required to be, up to the age of 18+; and/or are ineligible for unemployment benefits, either by virtue of being students (part-time or full-time), or because government policy denies their eligibility. This category does not include those who are unable to find work in the formal economy, retreat from unemployment and instead enrol in courses, or undertake some other activity that then becomes classed as economically inactive (see below).

The economically inactive category includes people who do not belong to the economically active groups (wage workers and unemployed) but are also 'would-be workers' – albeit of a different kind than the vulnerably employed category. The economically inactive category is a heterogeneous group, comprising, in the case of 15–24-year-olds, those who have been economically marginalised and wholly shut out of the labour force – discouraged workers (including full-time informal carers), prisoners, and pauperised parts of the working class, as well as students in further and higher education. Unavoidably, given the statistical bases of ILO data which start at age 15 for young people, this category also includes those who are still in compulsory education. It also excludes under-15s who are either child labourers in low-income and other countries, those who are statistically invisible vulnerably employed workers, and those who should properly be counted 'own-account' subsistence street workers.

It might be argued that those in compulsory education do not belong to the reserve army because they are outside the capitalist labour market and are not of working age. Indeed, historically, there has been a contraction in the use of youth labour by employers, due to the extension of compulsory schooling and raising of the school-leaving age alongside child labour laws, welfare provision, training and apprenticeship schemes and, of course, the expansion of higher education, all of which have removed cohorts of young people from the active army of labour (Braverman, 1974: 273; see also Chapter 7). But this inhibition or prohibition of some young people from joining the active army by the extension of social and educational training provision does not deny that they are part of the reserve army. Furthermore, changes to the extent of that provision have been part and parcel of managing crises and technological change. For example, raising the school-leaving age and the expansion of further and higher

---

[11] Indeed, as Ofreneo argues, '[i]nformal work, generally unprotected or not covered by the formal labour law system, is rooted in the joblessness or near joblessness in many Asian countries that forces many workers to accept substandard employment' (Ofreneo, 2016: 127).

[12] Illustrating this, Ireland's official unemployment rate of 9.5 per cent in 2015 would have doubled to nearly 20 per cent if participants in training courses and back to work schemes were included (Hennigan, 2015, cited in O'Leary and Negra, 2019: 136).

education have diverted school leavers from the active army, vulnerable employment and unemployment into education and, thus, into the economically inactive group. It is well known that education functions as a reservoir for discouraged would-be workers (see, for example, Biggart and Furlong, 1996), and that post-compulsory education has an absorptive function in times of impending or actual economic crisis, disguising the true extent of youth joblessness – sometimes referred to as 'warehousing', with the express intention of shrinking the pool of unemployed labour (see Heinz, 1987; Fergusson, 2014). At another level, the production and maintenance of a reserve army of (skilled) labour has been a major feature of the schooling system (Bowles and Gintis, 1976; Dale, 1989). Those in education can therefore legitimately be included in the reserve army of labour – those aged 15 are in the final years of the compulsory phase of education and will soon join the active army if not diverted to further education or training, while the expansion of further and higher education has, after all, been a major plinth of the management of youth labour formation and entry to the workforce.[13]

3.3.2   Dataset Scope and Limitations

Our dataset is comprised of the maximum number of ILO member countries and territories for which there is full youth workforce data available from ILOStat for our selected age groups. It incorporates more than 757 million 15–24-year-olds across 142 countries or territories.

This is an extensive dataset, but its coverage of the world is not comprehensive. It covers 74 per cent of the world's countries and 76 per cent of ILO countries and territories.[14] Forty ILO member countries and territories were excluded because of absent or incomplete data on the youth workforce in ILOStat.[15] Despite these limitations, our dataset covers 62 per cent of the world's total youth (15–24-year-old) population.[16] As such, as far as we are aware, it is the largest and most comprehensive such dataset on the global youth workforce.

---

[13]   From the perspective of high-income countries, the school-leaving age is generally 16, but from that of low- and lower middle-income countries it typically ranges between 12 and 15 years. In many countries across the full range of CIGs, the permitted age of employment is lower than the minimum age of compulsory schooling, and low-income countries may have no recorded minima for either, underscoring the point that many young people aged 15–18 are part of the reserve army of labour. The most comprehensive independent country listings on ages of education and employment are nevertheless incomplete. See https://www.right-to-education.org/sites/right-to-education.org/files/resource-attachments/RTE_IBE_UNESCO_At%20What%20Age_Report_2004.pdf (accessed 7 January 2020). See also Woodin et al., 2013 (chapter 2) for a full exposition of the complexities of defining these age minima at country level.

[14]   As at January 2020, when this calculation was carried out, there were 195 countries in the world, 193 of which are members of the United Nations, and 187 are members of the ILO. ILO country designations and rules for their use stipulate that Hong Kong, Macao, Taiwan, Palestine, and Kosovo should not ordinarily be referred to as countries, but as territories.

[15]   Among the countries excluded are some large populous countries (including China), some small (island) countries and some high-income countries (HICs) such as Germany, Australia, Japan and New Zealand. These exclusions were determined by the parameters we used to ensure consistency within the dataset. We recognise that the absence of China from our dataset is a significant limitation, given that it accounts for 19 per cent of the world's population.

[16]   There are 1.2 billion young people aged 15 to 24 years worldwide, accounting for 16.2 per cent of the global population. See https:// www.un.org/en/sections/issues-depth/youth-0/index.html (accessed 12 January 2020).

3.4   THE GLOBAL YOUTH WORKFORCE

This section provides an overview of the global youth workforce and the key results from our dataset analysis.

3.4.1   World Overview

Figure 3.1 shows the composition of the global youth and adult workforces. The left-hand column shows 15–24-year olds (column 1) and the right-hand column shows 25–54-year-olds (column 2). It shows the percentage share of the four labour categories that collectively constitute the global youth and adult workforces. Notably, the columns distinguish between wage workers (the 'active army') and vulnerably employed, unemployed, economically inactive labour (the 'reserve army'). These latter three categories constitute the fullest extent of the global reserve army of labour.

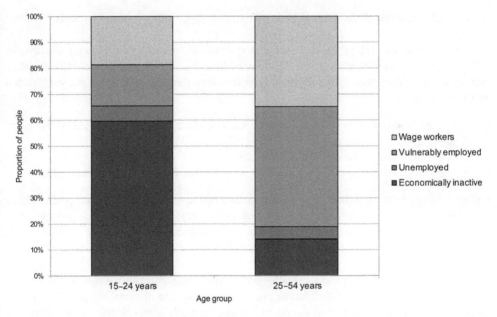

Note: 2018 signals the latest year for much of the available data from ILOStat at the time of constructing our dataset. However, ILOStat also draws on country-level data from earlier years.
Source: The authors, calculated from ILOStat, accessed 12 January 2020.

Figure 3.1   Global youth and adult labour forces (2018)

The proportion of young wage workers is less than a quarter (23 per cent) of that of the youth reserve army (column 1). Thus, most of the global youth workforce comprises the reserve army. Those officially designated as unemployed (open unemployed) form by far the smallest share, at 6 per cent of the total global youth workforce and 7 per cent of the reserve army. The vulnerably employed category is much larger, at 16 per cent of the global youth workforce and about one-fifth (19 per cent) of the reserve army. By far the largest category is the economically inactive, which makes up three-fifths (60 per cent) of the global youth workforce and three-quarters (74 per cent) of the reserve army. It is of great significance that this young reserve army is more than four times the size of the active youth army of wage workers.

This difference between the reserve and active armies of young people (column 1) is far greater than for the adult workforce (column 2).[17] The biggest difference between the youth and adult workforces lies in the magnitude of the vulnerably employed and economically inactive categories. Proportionately, the size of the vulnerably employed category is more than three times greater for adults than for young people. For the economically inactive, this difference is even greater: the economically inactive youth group is more than four times the size of the economically inactive adult group. Thus, the vulnerably employed category accounts for about 45 per cent of the total global adult workforce as compared with 15 per cent of the global youth workforce, while the economically inactive category accounts for about 15 per cent of the global adult workforce as compared with 60 per cent of the global youth workforce.

3.4.2   Distribution of the Global Youth Workforce: Country Income Groups

We now present the size of the total active and reserve armies of youth labour worldwide, differentiated by the World Bank's definitions of four country income groups (CIGs) (2018 classification).[18] They specify the mean daily gross national income (GNI) per person for each group as follows:

- 32 low-income countries (LICs) (also referred to as developing countries): less than $2.7;
- 47 lower middle-income countries: $2.7–$10.7;
- 60 upper middle-income countries: $10.8–$33;
- 79 high-income countries (also referred to as developed countries): more than $33.

Figure 3.2 depicts stark differences in the structure of the youth workforce across the richer and poorer parts of the world. The highest share of young wage workers as a proportion of the youth workforce is found in rich (high-income) countries. The highest share of the youth reserve army of labour (as a proportion of the youth workforce in those countries) is located in the middle- and low-income countries.

In HICs, two in every five (39.7 per cent) potential young workers are wage workers, while in low-income and lower middle-income countries almost nine of every ten potential young workers (87.1 per cent) is part of the reserve army of youth labour. Reciprocally, only one in ten (10.6 per cent) of the world's youth reserve army is located in HICs.[19] The world's poorest countries have the smallest absolute and proportionate counts of wage workers of all the CIGs. Just 8 per cent of the youth workforce in LICs are wage workers, accounting for one in twenty (5.4 per cent) of the world's young wage workers. In addition, LICs have by far the

---

[17]   Bellamy-Foster et al.'s (2011) data show that the adult reserve army is less than twice the size of the active adult labour army. Their data goes up to 2011, whereas ours is based on 2018 data.
[18]   For more detailed information on CIGs, see Table 5.5.
[19]   Of the global reserve army, 9.1 per cent is in HICs, 16.5 per cent is in UMICs, 60.3 per cent is in LMICs, and 14.1 per cent is in LICs.

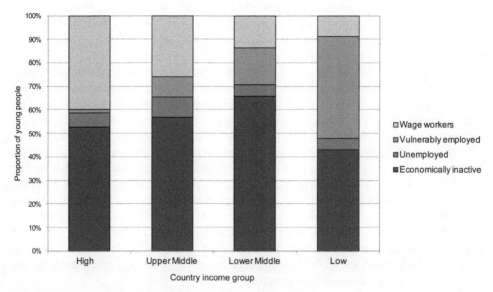

Source: The authors, calculated from ILOStat, accessed 12 January 2020.

Figure 3.2   *Global active and reserve armies of youth labour by country income group (2018)*

highest proportion of vulnerable workers of all country groups: the vulnerable worker category accounts for two in five (43.1 per cent) of the youth workforce in LICs. This proportion greatly exceeds those proportions in each of the higher-income country groups, which range between one in 50 (1.5 per cent) in HICs, one in 10 (8.6 per cent) in upper middle-income countries (UMICs), and three of every twenty young workers (15.5 per cent) in lower middle-income countries (LMICs).

In contrast, in comparison with the categories of wage worker and vulnerably employed (and to a lesser degree, the economically inactive group), there is a striking degree of consistency in the proportion of young unemployed people across the four country income groups. In descending order, the highest proportion of officially recognised unemployed youth is in UMICs (8.5 per cent), followed by high-income countries (6.2 per cent), LMICs (5.1 per cent), and LICs (4.9 per cent). In addition to near parity in unemployment rates between the four CIGs, unemployment accounts for the economic status of less than one in ten (8.5 per cent) young people – a relatively miniscule 44 million compared with the numbers of wage workers (142 million), vulnerably employed (118 million) or economically inactive (462 million).

In summary, in descending order across the four country income groups, from high-income to low-income, the proportion of young wage workers declines dramatically in steady increments from 40 per cent to 9 per cent while the proportion who are vulnerably employed rises even more dramatically and incrementally from 2 per cent to 43 per cent. The economically inactive populations differ much less between the three highest income groups (in ascending order, from 53 per cent (high income) to 57 per cent (upper middle-income) and to 65 per cent (lower middle-income)), while the low-income group has a notably smaller proportion of young people who are economically inactive (43 per cent). And, as noted, the proportionate differences between groups regarding the unemployed cohorts are negligible, in comparison. We also note that the group of countries with the lowest incomes also has the smallest cohort of young people who are unemployed.

Our focus has been on comparisons between country income groups regarding the proportions of young people in each of the four categories that describe their economic/employment status, highlighting marked differences. But maintaining attention on the relative size of each category in each country income group risks losing sight of the absolute size of the groups and the populations of 15–24-year-olds they encompass. There is, of course, great diversity among and within the CIGs, including in terms of the range of countries they include and the number and proportion of 15–24-year-olds each group encompasses.[20] It is worth noting that the HICs and UMICs (139 countries) comprise almost twice as many countries as the LMICs and LICs (79 countries), and that these two poorer groups, in terms of GNI per person, account for more than twice as many 15–24-year-olds (521 million: 69 per cent of the youth population) as the two wealthier groups (237 million: 31 per cent of that population). Put differently, the opportunities and prospects of about a third of 15–24-year-olds are determined by 139 governments of relatively affluent countries, while those of about two-thirds of this age group are determined by 79 governments of relatively poor countries.

This is significant in the analyses that follow in this and later chapters, and in two respects. First, in aggregate, the 79 LICs and LMICs each have responsibility for 6.6 million young people; the 139 HICs and UMICs are responsible for 1.7 million. That is to say, the governments of poor and poorer countries are responsible for populations of young people almost four times the size of those that live in rich and richer countries. Second, the differences in these youth population ratios as between high- and upper middle-income groups and low- and lower middle-income groups are likely to have significant implications for the extent to which governments can attune economic and social policies to the subtler and more fine-grained needs of larger (and so potentially more diverse) youth populations.

These differences notionally double the advantage of rich(er) countries over poor(er) because the former have infinitely greater economic resources to deploy *and* they are able to deploy them across youth populations averaging a quarter of those of the latter. As noted earlier, the mean GNI per person of the very wealthiest countries is up to 200 times greater than that of the very poorest. The GNI range of poor(er) countries spans a nominal range of less than US$3,500 (to a maximum of US$3,995), while that of rich(er) countries can be modestly described as spanning a US$46,000 range (not counting the very high incomes of the upper quartile of the high-income group). Many more poor(er) countries have huge populations, compared to those of rich countries, many of them with disproportionately large youth populations. The challenges they face are enormous, and their means to address them are in some cases very limited.

These disparities contribute substantially to accounting for the overwhelming size of the GRAoYL and for the ostensible anomalies which offer immediate explanations for it – that is, the low rates of unemployment and exceptionally low rates of economic inactivity in LICs, despite the diminutive proportion of young people who are wage workers and the huge proportion of young people who are vulnerably employed.

---

[20]   These and subsequent data are set out in full in Table 5.5.

3.4.3   Country-level Youth Workforce Profiles

In order to provide an even higher level of granularity as to international differences, we further disaggregate this data by country. Figure 3.3 exemplifies selected country-level profiles. It shows the country-level youth workforce profiles for two countries selected from each of the four World Bank CIGs. The countries are: for HICs, USA and Spain; for UMICs, Brazil and Namibia; for LMICs, Indonesia and India; and for LICs, Tajikistan and Sierra Leone (columns 1 to 8, reading left to right). The two countries selected for each group provide a reasonable illustration of the range of income, youth population and employment profiles within the CIGs.[21] Nevertheless, we recognise this is a very small selection of countries and we do not claim that our selection is representative or typical. However, it does facilitate an initial overview of the nature of profiles in eight countries. As well as being of interest in their own right, these data mark a crucial and important difference from data in Chapter 5, which is based on ILO classifications of (un)employment that 'undercount' YU rates, compared with Bellamy-Foster et al.'s (2011) classifications.

Figure 3.3 (p. 56) highlights the strikingly diverse composition of the youth labour force profiles of the eight countries. At the extremes of these examples, half of the potential youth workforce of the USA (column 1) are wage workers – almost twenty times the 2.6 per cent of 15–24-year-old wage workers in Sierra Leone (column 8). Equally notable is the 0.1 per cent of potential young workers in the USA who are vulnerably employed, compared with 38 per cent in Sierra Leone. The economically inactive fraction of each country's potential youth workforce is large, though it spans a narrower range (between 45 per cent in Brazil (column 3) and 73 per cent in India (column 6)). Consistent with our earlier observations above regarding the minimal differences in the unemployment category between the four country income groups, the differences in YU between the eight countries (ranging from a low of 3 per cent in Tajikistan (column 7) to a high of 16 per cent in Brazil (column 3)) are comparatively small. In summary, the starkest difference between these eight countries is, once again, in the size of the reserve army of youth labour. These countries are ranked as follows, in ascending order, from the smallest to the largest reserve armies as a share of the total youth workforce: USA (50 per cent), Brazil, Indonesia, Tajikistan, Spain, Namibia, India, Sierra Leone (97 per cent).

---

[21]   Our criteria for selecting the eight countries represented in Figure 3.3 are that they should:
- be reasonably representative of the range of annual GNI per person for all countries in the group (the marginal break lines that separate the four country income groups in some cases represent very small differences or temporarily overlap). All eight selected countries fall within the second and third quartiles of the range for each group; that is, they are no more than 25 per cent above or below the median income distribution for the group that they are part of;
- provide reasonably representative coverage of the parts of the world that predominate in each group. Thus the high-income group disproportionately comprises European countries, the low-income group is heavily dominated by sub-Saharan African countries, and so on;
- include a diverse profile of countries based on the size of their 15–24-year-old youth populations, which range between hundreds of millions and hundreds of thousands; and
- indicate the wide diversity of employment profiles as between the two selected countries in each group.

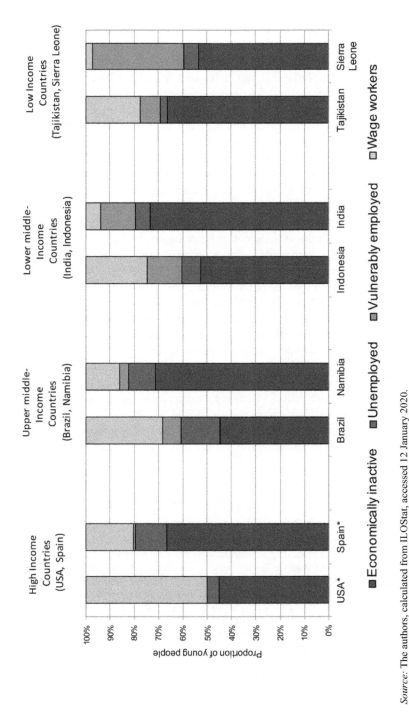

Source: The authors, calculated from ILOStat, accessed 12 January 2020.

Figure 3.3 Country youth workforce profiles by country income group classification (2018)

3.5   CONCLUSION

This chapter has begun our analytical and empirical connection of YU to ongoing processes of global economic restructuring. Identifying currents in early political economy that most directly and illuminatively 'speak' to youth-specific features of global social organisation led us to re-read Engels, Marx, Lenin and Luxemburg. In combination, their work amply revealed the pronounced youth attributes of manufacturing and agricultural workforces, and how labour forces internationally are interconnected through global economic structures. If age (like gender) is, in classical Marxist theory, secondary to social class as a historical force, it does not obviate our point that age is nevertheless a major social division of labour.

Drawing on Marxist analytical frameworks does not signal our uncritical acceptance of that doctrine, but it has to be recognised that the studies by Engels and his peers stand head and shoulders above the treatises of other classical political economists of the time for the compelling and lucid insights they afford into the condition of youth labour in a globalising world economy. They provide a firm foundation for a global analytics of YU because they offer lucid insights into: transnational modes of economic organisation, including among labour forces worldwide; the fluidity of movements between active and reserve elements of the youth workforce; and structural differentiation within youth labour forces and segmented labour markets in which these labour forces operate. Such perspectives add theoretical weight to the compositional structures of the youth labour force, and highlight fragmentation within it (including, importantly, by age – especially within youth cohorts) as well as *connections* between the fractions of it. This, in turn, opens up a vista onto the relationship on a worldwide basis between those with jobs and those without them; open and hidden unemployment; waged and unwaged work; formal employment, casualised and informal work; and formal and informal economies.

As a first step to taking these ideas forward in relation to YU, we have presented the first-ever calculation of the size and composition of the contemporary global youth labour force of which we are aware. Three key points from our empirical analysis stand out. First, the proportion of jobless young people (reserve army) is a massive four times greater than the active army of youth labour (waged workers). This differential is far greater for young people than for adults. Second, open (recorded) YU is a consistently small share of the jobless youth labour force irrespective of country grouping. Third, the greatest international variation between country groups is seen in the proportional size of the other three components of the youth labour force – wage workers, vulnerably employed and economically inactive. This variation *largely* corresponds with a country's position in world income rankings: *in general*, the proportion of young people in waged employment is greatest among richest countries – (the USA and Brazil in Figure 3.3), and this proportion reduces down the country income scale (India and Sierra Leone in Figure 3.3). Relatedly, the proportion of young people vulnerably employed or economically inactive is smallest in rich countries and larger further down the country income scale.

The data on which these findings are based provide a snapshot of the size and composition of this labour force in 2018. Trend data across several crucial dimensions of difference discussed in Chapters 5 and 6 will elaborate and nuance these findings, but for now we emphasise the following points. One is that the magnitude of the 'surplus' youth population is so great that existing development paths are clearly entirely unable to absorb it into wage employment under prevailing conditions of social organisation and social relations of labour: economic growth as we know it cannot solve the youth surplus problem. The second is that most of the world's young unemployed people, whether formally unemployed or economically inactive, live in upper middle-income and lower middle-income countries (respectively totalling 64 per cent and 68 per cent). Paradoxically, it appears to be the high- and low-income countries that have low recorded and 'hidden' YU (both at 52 per cent). We return to this issue in detail in Chapter 5.

These points carry through into the next chapter in which we consider how relationships between youth labour forces within and between countries are re-made through dynamics unleashed by contemporary globalising processes.

4. Global economic restructuring and youth labour markets

4.1 INTRODUCTION

This chapter takes forward our discussion of the relationship between youth unemployment (YU), global youth labour forces and the world economy that Chapter 3 began. We explore the qualitative, textual features of this relationship and how they structure young people's incorporation into waged labour or their exclusion from it. Underpinned by a critical re-reading of expansive literatures on the globalisation of production, global 'assembly lines', global labour forces and labour market restructuring, we make connections across data and literatures that have not given *systematic* consideration to young people, but which, taken together, provide key insights into how young members of the workforce are re-positioned within the ongoing restructuring of the world economy. Our temporal focus for the purposes of this chapter is the era of global economic liberalisms that took hold following the end of the Second World War and involved systemic tendencies towards greater international economic integration.[1]

Overall, we aim to draw out points of connection between globalising production and global youth labour forces. Specifically, we discuss the significance of young age and youth labour within global economic restructuring and reflect on how social divisions of labour revolving around (young) age are being reconfigured. In doing so, we take further steps towards fleshing out the new international division of youth labour (NIDYL) and global reserve army of youth labour (GRAoYL) concepts (Chapter 3), thereby advancing our wider aim of elaborating a truly global perspective on endemic youth unemployment (EYU). In this respect, we point to 'upstream' causes of scarring forms of YU, marginalisation and exclusion that take shape within countries, that have wide-ranging repercussions across the life course (Chapter 2), and that are inherently transnational in origin. Although this chapter is focused on youth labour and youth unemployment in the Global South that results from international outsourcing, wherever relevant we also endeavour to derive and interpret its impact on the advanced economies of the Global North. While direct evidence of this is remarkably difficult to gather, the ostensible effects are undeniable: almost by definition, offshoring productive labour to young workers typically precedes reduced employment opportunities for young people (and others) in the outsourcing country. In this sense, this chapter is concerned with two globally connected dynamics of mass and endemic youth unemployment (EYU): loss of jobs in the country of

---

[1] We write of liberalisms in the plural, cognisant that the 'embedded liberalism' (Ruggie, 1982) of the world order from the mid-1940s to the 1970s was distinct from the neo-liberalism that took hold from the 1970s, and from the dominant form of neo-liberalism after the global financial crisis (GFC) when the multi-polar geo-political and economic landscape further fragmented (Gallagher, 2011).

origin, and new modes of exclusion of young people from employment in countries to which labour has been outsourced. Affected most are those who cannot meet employer requirements – typically, good dexterity, linguistic skills and/or educational attainment.

The chapter is organised around three substantive sections, plus the conclusion. We start by re-reading 'classic' works on the globalisation of (manufacturing) production in the 1960s and 1970s (Section 4.2) and then turn to examine in greater depth the youth profile of global labour forces, the 'special features' attributed to young people in global assembly lines in manufacturing and services sectors, and the role of public policy in stabilising youth-specific forms of neo-liberal supply-side labour flexibility (Section 4.3). The themes of youth labour market segmentation and social inequality are taken up in Section 4.4, where we discuss the impacts of industrial relocation on youth labour markets in countries of origin and destination, and how these are repositioning the long-term relationship between young people and labour markets. Section 4.5 concludes the chapter, drawing together its key points, relating them to those from Chapter 3, and looking ahead to the chapters that follow.

4.2   THE 'NEW' INTERNATIONAL DIVISION OF YOUTH LABOUR: MID-TWENTIETH AND EARLY TWENTY-FIRST CENTURIES

Industrial restructuring since the 1960s has been an extensively internationalised process, involving globe-spanning firms levering comparative trading advantages in ways that have polarised wages, wealth and poverty on a worldwide scale. These are among the principal conclusions of a now-vast literature which has attended to the labour and wider social consequences of firms' accumulation strategies that have involved externalising parts of the production process (for example, Hymer, 1972, 1976; Cohen et al., 1979; Fröbel et al., 1980; Cowling and Sugden, 1987; Dunning, 1993; Gereffi and Korzeniewicz, 1994; Dicken, 2003; Bellamy-Foster et al., 2011).

Fröbel et al.'s (1980) study is a notable exemplar in this literature. It drew on industrial data and economic sector studies of German textiles and electronic assembly industries between the early 1960s and late 1970s and showed that capital-intensive and labour-intensive manufacturing was being relocated overseas. German industrial production was undergoing a process of rationalisation, whereby the more skilled work was broken up into simpler parts, automated where possible, and undertaken by labour forces with low(er) levels of skills and education. A dominant feature of this rationalisation was the fragmentation of the labour force, as jobs were relocated away from strongly unionised and protected workforces towards weakly organised, cheaper ones, especially in lower-cost countries. But not *all* jobs were relocated: lower-skilled work on assembly lines was most likely to be offshored, while white-collar work (marketing, research and development, finance and administration, proprietorship) was retained in the 'core'. Thus, the restructuring of production was premised on a significant labour shift from Germany to sites overseas (South-East Asia and Latin America were favoured then) to make goods for import into Germany.[2] This rationalisation was undertaken

---

[2]   By the mid-1970s, 45 per cent of employees of overseas German textile and garment industry firms producing overwhelmingly or exclusively for the German market were based in low-wage countries – nearly double that of a decade earlier (25 per cent in 1966) (Fröbel et al., 1980: 113).

'according to the dictates of optimal profitability' (Fröbel et al., 1980: 89), and created a 'new international division of labour' (NIDL) that structured relations between labour forces in Germany and newly offshored relocations.

This global labour force restructuring was profoundly aged and gendered. The labour forces of the offshored countries were much younger and more feminised than those in Germany; the offshored unskilled and semiskilled jobs were disproportionately occupied by young women. In Taiwan, for example, 'the majority of the women employed belong to the fourteen to twenty-four age group ... of the female production workers, 87 per cent were under twenty-five years of age' (Fröbel et al., 1980: 345), while in Malaysia, 'the proportion of workers in this age group who worked directly in production (operators) had reached a total of 100 per cent in many factories' (p. 346). Industrial sectors differed in the extent to which young female workers were concentrated in offshored labour forces: there were differences among free production zones in operation for several years and those established more recently (p. 344). In terms of age, in textiles, 22 per cent of employees were younger than 20 years old (8 per cent in Germany), while in the garment industries, this proportion rose to 43 per cent of employees (18 per cent in Germany). Female workers comprised the majority of the labour force in both industries (Table 4.1).[3]

Table 4.1   Distribution of foreign employees of the Federal German textile and garment industry by sex and age, 1974

	Employees covered	Female (%)	Below aged 20 years (% of total employees)
Textile industry	*5826*	*70*	*25*
Industrial, socialist countries	2901	64	26
Developing countries	2925	77	22
For comparison: Federal Germany (1970)	–	54	8
Garment industry	*4311*	*88*	*31*
Industrial, socialist countries	3081	86	25
Developing countries	1230	92	43
For comparison: Federal Germany (1970)	–	87	18

Source: adapted from Fröbel et al., 1980: 114: table I-14. Column 4: emphasis added.

Wages in the new industrial sites were between a tenth and a fifth of those in traditional sites (p. 360). Fröbel et al. (1980) summarise their findings thus:

As is evidenced by the ... statistics on age, sex and skill, the structure of employment in free production zones and world market factories is extremely unbalanced. One particular type of worker is

---

[3]   In this sector, '[T]ypically, an employee of a Federal German garment firm in a low-wage country is a young woman ... who has been trained by the firm and works as a seamstress, probably at a simple sewing machine, which may have already been scrapped in the firm's German plant, and then shipped to the low-wage country' (Fröbel et al., 1980: 115).

selected from the practically unlimited supply of unemployed labour and recruited into employment in the world market factories: young and female workers. The criteria for selection are quite clear. The workers who are chosen are those who (1) work for the lowest wages, (2) are the most productive … and (3) are unskilled and semiskilled. (p. 347)

Labour costs, they argued, were a decisive factor in offshoring processes. The primary reason for relocation was to take advantage of disparities in wages and working conditions between traditional industrial countries and low-wage countries. Government subsidies or the financial cost of fixed capital on the local market in countries to which production was relocated were at best secondary considerations (Fröbel et al., 1980: 177). The cost savings being sought could be realised by increasing the amount of time during which the existing productive equipment was used for production, and by relocating to 'sites with no or comparatively minimal limits of night work, shift work, and holiday work, and with a large reserve army of workers who are forced to work at any time dictated by the company' (p. 178). Savings in equipment costs were also important. Baerreson (1971) showed that a large supply of available Mexican workers was crucial in the US electronics sector relocation to Mexico because this meant access to a large pool of young women who could perform delicate assembly operations with unaided eyesight, whereas in the USA available workers were usually older women who needed microscopes and magnifying glasses (cited in Fröbel et al., 1980: 349 fn 2). With investment per such offshored workplace far lower in the site of relocation than in Germany, deep 'reservoirs' of available young people were decisive for firms looking to capitalise on differential advantages in wage and working conditions between sites. The comparative advantage of developing country sites was simply that acute poverty forced unemployed people to work at almost any wage (Fröbel et al., 1980: 341). The logics creating these employment structures were transnational because:

> Even in those regions in which a concentration of world market factories had developed to such an extent that the availability of young unemployed women has been drastically reduced, no change in the structure of employment occurs. Instead, the firms react almost without exception by relocating production to new sites where this particular type of worker can be easily hired. (p. 349)

Although the work was nominally 'equal' in the traditional and new industrial sites, the conditions in the latter were premised on anything but equality – characterised by low wages, long hours, high intensity of work, social insecurity, night work and lack of safety (p. 359). Competition in world markets was thus premised on 'harder, dirtier, more monotonous and more dangerous' work (p. 360). As Engels observed a century earlier (Chapter 3), the poverty of working conditions associated with production by 'modern' methods in 'free' production zones and world market factories in 'underdeveloped' countries constituted '*super-exploitation*' (p. 359) where 'the physical and mental recovery and reproduction of the labour-power expended in the labour process is not guaranteed or accomplished' (p. 359).

The globalisation of production and NIDL theses have been the subject of intense scrutiny over the years (Yeates, 2001) but they have continued to resonate strongly because they capture a major dynamic in the contemporary world economy, namely how firms relocate parts of the production process to countries with lower employer costs (regardless of skill) than those in which they are headquartered. This is not to say that wage costs are the sole determinant in such decisions. First, capital searches for sites of available surplus labour and seeks to maximise the extraction of value from that labour. Second, capital's vying for strategic or tactical trading advantages determines the scale and distribution of employment and unemployment within *and between* countries. Third, labour forces are inextricably connected around the world by virtue of capital accumulation strategies that have fragmented production internationally. Fourth, exploitation binds the experiences of workforces across highly divergent global development contexts. These points in no way contradict Fröbel et al.'s (1980) original conclusion that

> the new international division of labour is determined by the logic of the valorisation of capital and not the interests of those who work in the production processes, either in the industrial or the developing countries. (p. 181)

4.3 YOUTH LABOUR IN THE GLOBAL ASSEMBLY LINE

Subsequent decades have witnessed the proliferation of fragmentation processes identified by Fröbel (Tschang, 2011; ILO, 2015a) and, along with them, extensive impacts on labour systems and employment structures. Production systems have become organised around longer, more complex global supply chains (GSCs) than the simple North–South structures that were the subject of the Fröbel study.[4] Not only do they connect more countries, but a far greater range of goods and services is produced and traded within them, the number of production stages has increased, trade in intermediate products has increased, and supply relationships between firms are more numerous and complex (Meixell and Gargeya, 2005, cited by ILO, 2015a: 132; ILO, 2015a; Lambregts et al., 2016). The number of jobs affected have also increased. The ILO calculated that GSC-related jobs increased by about 50 per cent between 1995 and 2013, from 296 million to 453 million, and, correspondingly, accounted for a greater share of total employment (16.4 per cent (1995), 20.6 per cent (2013)) (ILO, 2015a).

Although the degree of dependence on such jobs varies between countries and sectors, the rise of global relocation of production is highly consequential for employment, unemployment and wider development.[5] Many governments in poorer parts of the world have seen the attractions of onshoring – more highly sought after formal-sector jobs, lower unemployment, greater prosperity – and have adopted export-oriented development strategies to encourage investment by firms seeking to relocate some of their operations overseas.[6] Middle-income

---

[4] We use the term GSCs to cover supply chains structured across different scales and proximities of distance. It therefore covers regional supply chains – that is, GSCs on world-regional scales.

[5] The ILO reports that the largest share of GSC-related jobs in total employment is in Taiwan (more than half of GSC jobs), followed by the Republic of Korea and the EU-27 (around one-third of GSC jobs). Among the least exposed are Japan and the USA. The proportion of GSC-related jobs increased in Taiwan, Korea and the EU27 since the GFC, but declined in emerging economies (Brazil, China, Indonesia, Mexico, the Russian Federation) and resource-driven advanced economies (Australia, Canada) (ILO, 2015a: 134–5).

[6] The IT sector exemplifies this point. IT has been at the foreground of the growing global services economy, underpinned by technological advances (incorporation of IT in business operations, economic liberalisation, demographic change). The development of service sectors was traditionally assumed to be confined to developed countries with mature markets and industrial sectors (Foray and Lundvall, 1996), but massive investment in education and infrastructure has enabled developing countries to achieve service sector expansion. For example, the Indian government's liberalisation reforms of the early 1990s pursued trade and education policies favourable to an export-orientation in science and technology (D'Mello and Sahay, 2008: 80). This is discussed further later in the chapter.

countries have been especially eager to participate in the global economy, many of which have large reserve armies of youth labour (see Chapter 3 and Section 4.4 below). One consequence is that the fortunes of economies and labour markets, regionally and globally, are far more intertwined than ever before. For example, the higher the proportion of GSC-related jobs in any country, the greater the degree of exposure of those jobs and the economy to international competition, international trade shocks, and recessions and financial and other crises in overseas economies that are a potential existential threat to jobs 'at home'. In addition, GSC jobs lower down the international chain are exposed to corporate strategies and decisions of firms further 'up' the chain.

The sheer complexity of economic globalisation prevents a totalising, definitive narrative about their relationship to global YU. International economic integration takes place across many different scales. Centralising elements fuse with distinctive local and regional conditions which mean that border-spanning processes continue to be mediated by and refracted through a range of political, social and cultural institutions and conditions that are not wholly reducible to corporate boardroom economics (Mittelman, 1995; ILO, 2015a; Yeates, 2018). With this in mind, it is nevertheless possible to identify some principal dynamics and 'logics' bearing on the (re)positioning of youth labour within the global economy, local youth labour markets and youth unemployment. Focusing on manufacturing and services industries at the frontline of the 'new' global economy – textiles, garments, electronics, and IT (especially information technology-enabled services (ITES)) – the remainder of this section reexamines data to show that young people are *selectively* incorporated into transnational circuits of production, and that this incorporation is structured by intersecting social divisions of age, gender and social class.[7] We draw out the implications of these dynamics for the reconfiguration of social inequalities among youth labour cohorts.

4.3.1   The Enduring Youth Profile of Offshored Labour Forces

Numerous worldwide studies of industrial composition confirm Fröbel et al.'s (1980) findings regarding the young age profile of world factory labour. Jenkins' (n.d.) study of Costa Rica's industrial zones in the 1990s is amongst the most extensive and detailed. He found that production zones with a greater proportion of export-oriented firms had a much greater share of workers under 25 years old in the labour force – at least half the firms' workforce, compared with one-third or less in the other activities in the zone, and over a quarter in exporting firms outside such zones. In export processing zone (EPZ)-based textiles, garments and electronics firms specifically, under 25s constituted 40 per cent of the firms' labour force and a further 25 per cent were aged between 25 and 30 years old (Jenkins, n.d.: 19).

As with light manufacturing, so too with services. In offshored IT services, especially the ITES and business process outsourcing (BPO) industries dominated by India and the Philippines, young people between 18 and 26 years hold the overwhelming majority of

---

[7]   ITES includes call centres providing 'voice services', business process outsourcing, back-office and technical support services, finance, etc. (Vasavi, 2008). The work is more routine, less technical, and entry-level qualifications are lower than in other parts of the IT industry. Jobs are more vulnerable to automation, and thus to outsourcing and offshoring.

these industries' jobs (Joshi, 2004; Fuller and Narasimhan, 2008; Vasavi, 2008).[8] Half of the respondents in Joshi's (2004) India study were 21–25 years old, and those aged under 20 were concentrated in call centres (8.5 per cent aged 20 or less, compared with 3.2 per cent for IT firms). The median age of the ITES/BPO labour force in India is 27.5 years (Fuller and Narasimhan, 2008: 190) and is younger still in the Philippines at 25 years (Remesh, 2008; D'Cruz and Noronha, 2010; Torres, 2014; Beerepoot and Vogelzang, 2015; Errighi et al., 2016; Marasigan, 2016). A similar youth workforce profile exists in the export-oriented informatics industry in the North Caribbean (Freeman, 2000). The strong preference for young workers stands out: equivalent operations in the West have mixed-age profiles (Vasavi, 2008).

What explains this employer preference for young workers in these industries? Is the labour costs thesis sufficient, or are other factors involved? What impacts do these preferences have on local youth labour markets and employment structures? The remainder of this section begins to answer these questions, starting by looking at other social attributes of youth workforces.

4.3.2 Other Social Attributes: Education, Gender, Family Status, Mobility

Industrial composition studies show that most export-oriented industries' workforces are not only preponderantly young, but well educated. The Indian and Filipino ITES youth workforces are drawn from highly educated segments of the middle-class, urban, privately educated youth population imbued with ample cultural capital suited to the markets the firms serve. Nearly all are university graduates, and many have a postgraduate qualification.[9] Having the required minimum two years of university education is not in itself sufficient, however: excellent command of spoken and written English is required (Errighi et al., 2016). Unsurprisingly, employees tend to have limited or no previous work experience (only a quarter of Filipino ITES workers had any such experience in Marasigan's (2016) study).

The ITES/BPO industries may be distinctive in their insistence on a university education, but they are not alone in their requirement for a minimum level of education. Many offshored industries at the upper tier of the export production sector require prospective employees to have completed secondary school. Country and sectoral differences are apparent. Export manufacturing firms' workforces tend to have lower levels of formal education: 54 per cent had not completed high school and 75 per cent had not received further education (Jenkins, n.d.: 20).

---

[8]   The ITES/BPO sector accounts for one-third of employment in the Indian IT industry (Fuller and Narasimhan, 2008). BPO in India employs 3.1 million workers, 30 per cent of them women (World Bank, 2016). The Philippines' industry employs over a million workers, and is 'the second-largest contributor … to the country's GDP' (Errighi et al., 2016; see also Torres, 2014). The growth and scale of the Indian ITES sector has '[given] rise to India's reputation as the "back-office of the world": most ITES companies cater to clients in the US and UK, Australia and beyond' (Vasavi, 2008: 214). Critics label ITES as 'the global beck and call service' and the workers as 'cyber coolies', underscoring the servile nature of the work and relations of subservience that it signifies (Vasavi, 2008: 215). The Philippines has become the world's second biggest outsourcing destination (Torres, 2014).

[9]   Joshi (2004); Fuller and Narasimhan (2008); Remesh (2008); Vasavi (2008); D'Cruz and Noronha (2010); Beerepoot and Vogelzang (2015); Errighi et al. (2016); Marasigan (2016). Over 90 per cent of those working in IT and call centres in Joshi's (2004) study of India were graduates, of which close to 40 per cent had a Masters' degree. In the Philippines, 80 to 90 per cent of employees in BPO companies are university graduates (Bird and Ernst, 2009, cited in Errighi et al., 2016: 14).

It is predominantly *young women* who are employed in export production: 80–90 per cent of export-labour forces are comprised of women aged 16–24 years old.[10] Selecting for young, educated women ensures that most recruits will be single and child-free (Freeman, 2000; Joshi, 2004; Stitcher, 2013). Such marital and parental statuses, together with their young age generally, confer comparative advantages in the eyes of employers over older, married women with children: they incur no maternity leave, sick leave or health care costs to employers. Tiano's study of Mexico's *maquiladora* garments, services and electronics workforces usefully illustrates the hierarchy of social attributes preferred by manufacturing employers:

> Competition for electronics jobs has traditionally been so intense that firms have been able to hire the 'most desirable' women workers – secondary school graduates who are single and childless .... Apparel firms, whose position in the international economy is weaker than that of the transnational electronics subsidiaries, are less able to recruit from the 'preferred' sector of the labour force; thus apparel assemblers tend to be less educated, are more likely to have children, and are more apt to have partners or to be single heads of households. (Tiano, 1990: 198)

Importantly, Tiano notes the conditions under which employers can realise their preferences. Conditions of relative surplus labour are a crucial explanator: high levels of open or hidden unemployment are associated with the employer-preferred social composition of the industrial workforce, namely young, female, educated, single with no dependants. Conversely, low levels of unemployment in a region or country produce a labour force composed of workers with supposedly 'less desirable' workforce attributes – older, less educated, married mothers or fathers. Having employer-preferred characteristics may well increase the chances of a relatively lucrative job in the formal economy, but, as Tiano makes clear, this is unlikely to be a stepping-stone to a better one. The electronics industry is ill-suited, she argues, for imparting transferable skills that might increase employees' chances in the job market following the average five years length of employment that prevailed in export-oriented manufacturing in Mexico at the time. In the absence of good quality jobs in the local area, employees are locked into poor working conditions, and, if their jobs have been relocated elsewhere or they are too old or costly, they are channelled into hidden unemployment in the informal economy or end up in economic inactivity as discouraged workers or mothers.

Any consideration of such global youth workforces and relative labour surpluses must take account of other labour reservoirs that can be drawn upon at times of expansion and expelled at times of contraction. A key such reservoir is comprised of migrant labour. Thus, Asian countries in the initial stages of industrial development notably relied on migrant workforces for continuous supplies of youth labour. Salaff (2013) found that migrant young women from rural areas featured predominantly in Taiwanese EPZ labour forces. Similarly, in China, light manufacturing industries (apparel, shoes, electronics, toys) and low-end services sectors employ young, female unmarried migrant workers from rural areas seeking to escape from poverty, unemployment and limited jobs availability (ILO, 2003: 61). Young men from rural areas also comprise a disproportionately large share of the migrant workforce in the construction sector (ILO, 2003: 61; see also Ofreneo, 2016).

---

[10] Jenkins (n.d.); Grossman (1979); Fröbel et al. (1980); Elson and Pearson (1981); Lim and Fong (1981); Enloe (1983); Ward (1984); Tiano (1990); ILO (2003, 2015a); Vasavi (2008); Domínguez et al. (2010); Safa (2013); Stitcher (2013).

The experience of China is a useful reminder of the importance of labour control within employers' calculations of labour costs (London and Ross, 1995) and of how the profile of global youth workforces is advantageous within this.[11] China's productive structure has mostly comprised labour-intensive light manufacturing and processing in which the foremost competitive advantage of EPZ-based firms has been achieved through high productivity based on high labour intensity and control over the labour force (ILO, 2003; Cantin and Taylor, 2008; Ofreneo, 2016).[12] High labour intensity has been achieved by dormitory labour regimes set up to maximise the application of employees' labouring capacities, including observing how employees act in their non-working day. Gendered forms of worker control and worker abuse are recurrent themes of those regimes (Cantin and Taylor, 2008: 62). Such conditions are also defining features of world market factory employment in non-manufacturing sectors elsewhere. For example, ITES/BPO sector employment in India and the Philippines is not only characterised by extreme labour insecurity (workers are hired on a project-by-project basis and are entirely dependent on business contracts won by service-providing vendors (Ofreneo, 2016)), but by high levels of labour control, especially in call centres. Night-time work, an unrelenting 24/7 work schedule, employer-imposed restrictions on worker movements during office hours, demanding performance targets, and physically uncomfortable working conditions are characteristic working conditions in that sector (Ofreneo, 2016).

Despite these conditions, ITES/BPO sector employment is sought-after because of the higher wages it commands. Such wages finance active participation in high-end Western consumerism. However, they also constitute the material (economic) basis of new forms of social inequalities related to expanding middle classes (Upadhya and Vasavi, 2008; Vasavi, 2008). By contrast, the low wages of their peers in Chinese and other Asian world market manufacturing industries prohibit incorporation into such transnational cultural circuits – at least, not those revolving around the high-end consumer products they assemble (iPhones, iPads, computers, digital chips) (Ofreneo, 2016: 127). Still, despite these differences between young employees in manufacturing and services industries, their material conditions as offshored workers in developing countries have much in common. In both industries, young people are drawn to off-shored jobs by the lack of viable better alternatives locally. However, although their wages tend to be higher than those of their counterparts in domestically facing firms, their labour is assigned far lower value and their working time is longer and more intense than if they were working in the offshoring country. Also, they are locked into relatively low-wage work often without the opportunity to build transferable skills, and work under precarious conditions on fixed contracts in unhealthy and unsafe environments, without collective representation due to anti-union restrictions (Pratap, 2014; Ofreneo, 2016). They have no recourse to occupational or state benefits should their employer 'sack' them (Chapters 1 and 2), at which point they are

---

[11]   London and Ross (1995) found 'constant support for that part of the theory [of capital flows from core to periphery] that emphasises the control of labour' (p. 212), arguing that '[t]he most favoured sites for mobile capital possess a certain combination of economic and social characteristics: acceptable market size, adequate infrastructure, and favourable balance of class forces ... [F]oreign capital ... was attracted to places with less protest and fewer strikes, and [to] states that were more repressive' (p. 212). Labour discipline in the country of investment and in the country of *dis*investment are at stake since prospective relocation of production means the abolition of jobs in the 'home country'.

[12]   Although this may be changing now to some extent, as China tries to upgrade to more capital-intensive production (Li et al., 2012; Lin and Yu, 2015).

invariably channelled into hidden unemployment in the informal sector. It is also crucial to register here that every young person who secures employment in these world market factories and offices helps create and define a new contradistinctive category of unemployed would-be workers in the offshoring 'home' country – especially those who lack requisite dexterity or linguistic, digital or other skills (a point to which we will return in Section 4.4 below).

Key questions arising from this are: What imagined or real qualities do employers project on to young people? What supposedly unique attributes are young people perceived as possessing that makes them such sought-after employees? Answering these questions routes our argument towards exploring the age ideology at work here. Section 4.3.3 scrutinises the features of age ideology as they appear in these industrial settings. Section 4.3.4 examines the wider institutional and regulatory environment of labour law and policy that produces and stabilises employer preferences for certain kinds of young worker.

4.3.3   Reinterpreting the 'Natural Skills' Thesis of Global Labour: Age Ideology

The pervasive influence of gender ideologies in the construction of global workforces has received considerable attention in academic literatures seeking answers to why it is that young women overwhelmingly constitute the labour force of world market factories, and what employer discourses and practices are used to manage these labour forces.[13] Elson and Pearson (1981) were among the first to problematise the construction of female workforces in these terms. Employer preferences, they found, invoked women's 'natural' skills, abilities and dispositions – their 'nimble fingers', their more docile, malleable dispositions, their willingness to accept tough work discipline, their suitability to tedious, repetitive work, and their disinclination to work full time or long term or to join trade unions. Gender ideologies based on essentialist notions of women as secondary wage earners were significant justifications for wage inequalities between female employees and their male counterparts and for super-exploitative wages that do not cover the full costs of reproducing their labour power on a daily or generational basis. Elson and Pearson (1981) explained such gender ideologies in terms of a reserve army: they are 'highly advantageous to firms which periodically need to vary the size of their labour force so as to adjust to fluctuating demand for their output in the world market' (p. 93). As one local female reserve army is called upon in a world factory of the Global South, so, reciprocally, the reserve army of youth and/or adult labour in the 'source' country of the Global North swells.

Carla Freeman's (2000) study of the Barbadian and Jamaican informatics industry found strong evidence for the 'young and malleable' 'docile girl' caricature in the services sector global assembly line workers. She, too, revealed familiar gender ideologies about femininity and domesticity underpinning the corporate construction of the ideal workforce, and how gendered discursive manipulations are a key part of the armour deployed by employers to make 'adjustments in response to fluctuations in the organised resistance of workers in the "supply and quality of available labor"' (Freeman, 2000: 137). Service-sector versions of 'flexible labour' and 'nimble fingers' arguments have also been detected in the feminised ITES/BPO industry (Taylor and Bain, 2005, cited in Vasavi, 2008: 214–215).

---

[13]   See, for example, Elson and Pearson (1981); Ong (1987); Eraydin and Erendil (1999); Freeman (2000); Domínguez et al. (2010); Safa (2013); Stitcher (2013).

Within this, we can discern a distinctive age ideology involved in constituting global work-forces. Foremost is employers' reluctance to meet the total costs of the reproduction of labour power. Thus, employer preferences for young, single women 'make sense' insofar as daughters and childless single women – above all *young* women – cost less than men. Furthermore, as Engels (2009) noted, physical attributes of young people are key considerations for employers (Chapter 3). In this regard, Stitcher (2013) noted that young workers only form a preponderant share of the workforce until their health deteriorates over time from poor working conditions.[14] Employers' use of temporary employment contracts provide them with sufficient flexibility to accommodate the risks of an ageing youth workforce while preventing their labour costs from rising (Safa, 2013; Stitcher, 2013). Employers' unwillingness to bear labour reproduction costs (sickness benefits, pensions, parental or other care benefits) is not fully explained by the gender ideology noted by Elson and Pearson (1981) and others, for it does not account for age-specific aspects of employer preferences and behaviours whose underlying assumptions are that young women are financially supported by their parents. Freeman's (2000) research showed that

> In the Barbadian informatics sector, employers say, on the one hand, that they hire young women because their subsistence needs are insured by the safety net of their families and they are 'secondary' earners with little financial responsibility. (p. 117)

Classing young workers' wages as 'pin money' is an age-based version of the secondary labour market thesis of social segmentation that Engels observed in the mid-nineteenth century (Chapter 3). The problem for workers is that now, as then, such employer assumptions are invariably incorrect. Safa's (2013) Caribbean study showed that family income relies on young single women making major financial contributions. In Puerto Rico, for example, such contributions constitute a minimum of 40 per cent of family income.

As will now be evident, the social and political relations of production of contempo-rary outsourcing mimic those of nineteenth-century child labour in the UK and Europe. Nineteenth-century age ideology is also apparent in contemporary employer arguments that young people fulfil the requirement of a cost-efficient workforce. Safa's (2013) study of manufacturing reported that 'management prefers to hire young women because they are sup-posed to be more efficient ... [and] have lower rates of absenteeism' (p. 77), while Freeman's (2000) study of informatics reported that young women are seen as ideal workers because they have an undivided sense of responsibility to work. In addition to gender ideologies, young people's exceptional labour discipline is an essential element of employers' cost calculation. Completion of the minimum period of education and no prior work experience signal to employers a set of dispositions that are as, if not more, important than subject skills.[15]

The now-massive literature charting the growth of the Asian ITES/BPO sector is in broad agreement that the plentiful supply of available, trainable English-speaking youth labour was a critical factor in the expansion of the sector and the competitive advantages youthful labour conferred in terms of lower wages and higher productivity (Goyal, 2006; Upadhya and Vasavi,

---

[14] See Baerreson (1971), who showed that job applicants with attitudes and physical skills that reduce equipment costs are prioritised by Mexican employers (see Section 4.2 above).

[15] See Freeman (2000: 124–5) and Section 4.2 (above) regarding IT employers' preference for edu-cated first-time employees. See also Tiano (1990), page 60, above.

2008; Vasavi, 2008; Majumder and Sharma, 2014). Despite extraordinary staff turnover rates – 70 per cent *per year* (Upadhya and Vasavi, 2006)[16] – employers still regard their preferred workforce profile as highly cost-efficient, so voluminous is the supply of youth labour in India, so deep is its youth labour reservoir (Chapter 3, Figure 3.3), and so great is the extraction of value from staff.

Youth signals the 'body' and 'mentality' of the ideal worker cherished by employers worldwide. The attributes and dispositions of such 'ideal types' are codified in young age. As Freeman (2000: 105) argued, 'their youth and recent completion of secondary school … implies that they are literate, disciplined to the rhythm of a regimented day, and first-time wage earners'. Literacy signals minimum educational levels required for successful training and performance of tasks. Being 'disciplined' to the school regimen signals a disposition towards authority that is transferable to the work environment. Being a first-time wage earner signals to prospective employers both a lack of work experience and that low wages are more likely to be accepted. We conclude that age ideology is an essential element of employers' pursuit of the flexible worker ideal. Distinct from gender ideology (but often pursued in tandem with it), the ideal young worker construct mobilises an age-specific ideology of trainability.

Our observation stands in stark contrast to the inverse view of some early would-be entrants to employment in 'core' countries that outsource labour: in these advanced economies, young people are less and less attractive to employers especially when labour markets are over-subscribed, and their applicants' qualifications and skills offer weak or absent fits to specific required productive tasks. In effect, high-income countries' employers are incentivised to look to the youth of middle-income countries for labour. They employ their newest, higher achieving, adaptable school leavers in preference to HIC early leavers lacking further or higher education. In doing so they employ capable and adaptable fresh-to-market school- or college-leavers at a fraction of the wage that their rich-world counterparts would command.

At the other end of the 'cycle', employer powers to enforce workforce expulsion lead us to conclude that the intensive use of young labour is an essential element of the latency of mass youth employment that so relies on the easy imposition of YU. Young people have few legal defences when faced with unemployment; they constitute much more accommodating, 'docile', flexible reserve armies than adults. It is the *bi-directional fluidity of movement* of large populations of potential young workers between employment and unemployment that makes young people such an attractive potential labour force for employers in high-income and middle-income countries alike. The explicit lack of employment security, or the informality of employment in other modes, reflect a particular set of working conditions. These conditions interact with the structure of the prospective labour force, either in the form of surplus labour or a reserve army of labour – the two are not easily separated. In other words, young unemployed people are always available as a latent workforce; and, reciprocally, all young people employed under insecure conditions are always available as a latent cohort of unemployed youth, in the Global South and Global North alike – but in very different contexts of social protection and employment rights. From this vantage point, the NIDYL is no longer so highly differentiated between country income groups, and young people's job insecurity

---

[16] This is attributed to the onerous and repetitive nature of the jobs for which employees are technically over-qualified and which most employees regard as good enough for a 'first job' but as ultimately transient (Vasavi, 2008; Joshi, 2004).

and exposure to unemployment are no longer as wholly dissimilar as they once were across the three high(er) income groups (as Chapter 5 shows). Perhaps the greatest change alongside offshoring of labour is that exposure to summary dismissal without compensation is becoming normalised in the Global North where social protection for young workers has been partially (sometimes completely) eroded (Chapter 2; see also 4.3.4 below), especially in contrast to lower middle-income countries in which jobs in outsourced industries may be scarce but are also attractive and comparatively well paid by local standards, and in which unprotected short-notice dismissal is unquestioningly normalised.

4.3.4 Enabling and Stabilising Employer Preferences: Flexibilising Youth Workforces

Much of the socio-economic change attributed to the global fragmentation of production and the accompanying reconfigurations in the international division of youth labour would not have taken place or been sustained had it not been for institutional environments enabling these global workforce characteristics. The practices of employers could not have been achieved on the international scale over (very) many years without the support of state measures reshaping youth labour around a flexible ideal. Indeed, constructing a reliably 'safe' set of institutions conducive to ensuring continuous supplies of ideal flexible workers has been a public policy priority for many governments over many decades.

Indeed, since the 1980s, there has been a widespread international effort to redesign youth labour market institutions in high-income countries to make them more 'flexible', a project often justified on the grounds of needing to become or remain 'globally competitive'. Pools of unemployed labour have long been present in many youth labour markets, but they were greatly expanded by supply-side measures which shifted towards labour contracts making labour cheaper and more flexible rather than increasing demand for it. Such policies typically took the form of government-driven erosion of wage controls, changes to employment law that empowered employers to recruit and dismiss employees at much lower cost, and the erosion of rights to state support when unemployed, primarily in the USA, Canada and the UK but also elsewhere (Standing, 1999; Peck, 2001; Bukodi et al., 2008; Van Berkel, 2010). 'Re-gearing' education systems has been a critical part of this project due to their capacities to hold or release whole age-cohorts of young people into active labour pools. When labour availability is surplus to demand, adaptive changes on the parts of educational providers and of employers enable fluid overlaps between the end of juvenile dependency and the attempted beginnings of adult financial independence. Schools, colleges and universities identified the revenue benefits offered by developing part-time, stretched, flexible-entry, out-of-hours and online educational and training programmes leading to qualifications. Employers were quick to take advantage of de-regulatory zero-hours, flexible and minimal-commitment modes of employment and capitalise upon opportunities to greatly reduce labour costs while enhancing their ability to expand and contract their own labour forces at will. Such measures performed a key macro-economic role, to absorb surplus labour by 'warehousing' students (Chapters 2 and 3) when necessary, or to facilitate the rapid availability of surplus labour in response to fluctuations in demand and to manage-down worker demands for increased pay.

Across the dimensions of 'flexibility', once again, the most useful labour market segment is the youth cohort. Every year, a significant fraction of an entire birth-cohort seeks entry to labour markets. As business and economic cycles and market conditions dictate, employers can employ or ignore whatever fraction of each cohort they deem appropriate. Those young people whose availability as prospective employees is not taken up must choose between resuming full-time education or training, joining work-experience and training schemes that are nominally voluntary/compulsory, or becoming formally unemployed or 'economically inactive' (whether recorded as such or not). In many countries the category 'unemployed' is no longer available for young people (typically aged 15 up to 18–21 years) since they 'elected' to attempt to join the labour force when other options (education, training, apprenticeship) are on offer. The hitherto relatively sharp distinctions between studenthood and employee status have in effect been reconstructed in the form of new categories and conditions of engagement in the interstices between the two, within and beyond high-income countries (HICs).

The pursuit of flexible labour paradigms (pioneered in the UK and USA in varying evolving forms between the 1980s and 2000s) fell most heavily on young workers, but was also evident in institutionally divided labour markets (such as Germany, Japan, and South Korea) in which one segment of 'insiders' enjoys secure higher paid jobs in strained co-existence with another segment of 'outsiders' occupying more casualised forms of work with lower rates of pay and higher rates of unemployment. This structure, too, has a demonstrably clear age profile (and ideology), with younger workers unsurprisingly prevalent in the lower, casualised, tier.[17]

The most comprehensive international study to have examined the impacts of such flexi-bilisation policies (Blossfeld et al., 2005, Blossfeld et al., 2008) confirmed that, irrespective of welfare or labour regime type, the overall shift towards supply-side flexibility instituted across employment law, in social security, vocational systems, and labour market programmes impacted disproportionately upon young people.[18] As labour market 'outsiders', young people are more exposed to economic 'turbulence' due to a combination of labour force (in)expe-rience, internal labour markets, and power structures, and are employed in more precarious and lower-quality employment (Kurz et al., 2008). A partial, uneven flexibilisation has thus taken place, impacting mainly on young people, compounded by segmentation among youth cohorts that, together, has directed most of the risks of corporate restructuring and the shift in bargaining power of labour towards the youngest and most vulnerable groups 'at the bottom' (Bukodi et al., 2008: 3; Kurz et al., 2008).

In terms of these impacts on YU specifically, these latter studies did not find a trend towards precarious first jobs in all countries (Bukodi et al., 2008; Kurz et al., 2008), but in almost all countries '[t]he school to work transition has become increasingly difficult ... and flexible and precarious forms of work are more common in the first job after leaving the educational system' (Kurz et al., 2008: 352). This greater likelihood of experiencing insecure forms of first employment (stop-gap, casual, seasonal, part-time) is also more likely to 'generally induce

---

[17]   See Thelen and Kume (1999); Palier and Thelen (2010); Emmenegger et al. (2012); Song (2012); Crouch (2015); Watanabe (2018).

[18]   *flexCAREER: Flexibility Forms of the Labor Market – a Cross-national Comparison of Social Inequality* undertook initial analysis of retrospective and panel data covering most of the 1990s (and earlier) for Canada, Estonia, France, Germany, Great Britain, Hungary, Ireland, Italy, Mexico, the Netherlands, Norway, Spain, Sweden and the USA (Blossfeld et al., 2005). The project subsequently analysed panel data from eleven countries (excluding Canada, Ireland, Mexico and Norway and adding Denmark) from 1994 to 2001, studying labour market entry and early careers of young adults (Blossfeld et al., 2008).

more turbulence in the [subsequent] employment careers of young people' (p. 350). Even so, there was no clear convergence of experience: in three countries the risks of unemployment were found to be increasing, in two they were declining, one showed no discernible trend, and there were cohort divergences in other countries. Such variations did not correspond with the type of welfare regime or the degree of labour protection afforded to young people. In fact, the only clear relationship the study found was 'between macro-economic developments in the respective countries and the trend in the risk of unemployment' (p. 348). This relationship is a key focus of Chapter 6 (below) which advances this observation by developing a new and much larger dataset. Kurz et al.'s (2008) study also pointed to a ratchet or path dependency effect, whereby '[o]nce certain forms of flexible work have become established as an important route into the labour market, there is a tendency to maintain them *even when the macroeconomic situation changes*' (p. 352, emphasis added). In effect, macro-economic changes consolidate and fix trends – a similar finding to that of David Autor and other labour economists (see Section 4.4 below). Notably, the Blossfeld study pointed to: *greater* flexibility as a structural feature of youth labour markets internationally; how the socio-economic costs of economic turbulence are most borne by young people; and to forms of employment insecurity prone to fostering repeated or prolonged periods of unemployment in early years in the labour market.

4.4 WIDER LABOUR FORCE IMPACTS OF GLOBAL ECONOMIC RESTRUCTURING

As Section 4.3.4 suggests, the impacts of economic globalisation on young workers are not confined to which groups of young people are recruited into global factory workforces and the terms and conditions of their employment: they also cover impacts on local labour forces and youth labour markets. In this section we look at these impacts at both ends of the production chain. What little evidence exists can be gleaned from industry-specific qualitative studies. These invariably show that although unemployment is not a feature of the working lives of most employees in export-oriented industries (Section 4.3.2), it is nevertheless a feature of the lives of some of them and, importantly, that the already fragmented labour markets in which active and reserve armies of youth labour operate are reconfigured to the detriment of the most marginalised cohorts of young unemployed.

Tiano's (1990) Mexico study (see Section 4.3.2 above) is one of the few that have investigated employees' personal experience of unemployment prior to global factory work. She found that although '[w]omen who have completed secondary school, involving three years of education beyond the six years of primary school, are ... in an advantaged position in the labour market' (p. 198), and one in three had experienced unemployment lasting 1–6 months. Furthermore, the maquila programme favoured the young but – crucially – failed to persuade chronically unemployed men and older women or their sons and daughters to participate in these workforces. These findings give good insights into the local impacts of the arrival of a global factory, and how processes of international economic integration solidify extant forces of socio-economic exclusion. To be sure, export production factories create new jobs locally for certain sections of the labour force, primarily young and relatively well-educated people, and thus divert the most 'employable' from unemployment, but the most marginalised groups of the labour force, the already long-term unemployed of whatever age, do not benefit

(Tiano, 1990: 222–3). In this, export-oriented industrial strategies propel *greater* local labour force differentiation revolving around age, gender and social class.

The arrival of global factories in the services sector in low-income countries (LICs) is similarly accompanied by promises of significant numbers of new jobs, which are not typically offered to the most marginalised *young* people. Both India and the Philippines welcomed the promised prized ITES/BPO sector white-collar jobs. In India, the prospect of employing some of the 16 million 15–24-year-olds projected to be unemployed in 2020 proved irresistible to the Indian government, keen to 'leapfrog' into a post-industrial service economy (Goyal, 2006; D'Mello and Sahay, 2008; Upadhya and Vasavi, 2008; Vasavi, 2008; Majumder and Sharma, 2014). This was further enhanced by the promise that inward investment would benefit disadvantaged members of the youth labour force as well as English-speaking young people. Government backing for the ICT industry would '[broaden] employment opportunities for youth and provide second chances for work for youth disabilities' since many ICT jobs can harness possibilities for telecommuting.' (Hanna, 2010: 258). In practice, this industry did little to resolve mass YU. Planned efforts to systematically overhaul vocational education, training and employment generation systems were absent (Vasavi, 2008: 216). Only six per cent of 18–24-year-olds could access higher education. This limited the industry's capacity to absorb large numbers of educated young unemployed people and opened up a gulf with the unemployed – mostly non-English educated youth from rural areas 'without the cultural capital to gain entry into such work' (Vasavi, 2008: 216).

These social divisions were built on entrenched structural inequalities of class and caste. The English-speaking skills required by the ITES industry are typically available 'only to those who studied in private schools (where English is the medium of instruction)', meaning that 'such jobs then become by default, available primarily to the higher socio-economic group' (Vasavi, 2008: 220). Most of the young unemployed population is thereby excluded, fostering even greater inequality. In Mumbai, the epicentre of the Indian ITES industry, middle classes are pulling away from low-income classes, with a large section of youth labour excluded from the opportunities enjoyed by its peers. Upward mobility is predominantly from the lower-middle class to the middle-middle class (Beerepoot and Vogelzang, 2015: 202).

In the face of the difficulties in attracting sufficient numbers of young people and rising costs of city living, it is unsurprising that industry advocates have considered other pools of reserve labour in small cities and rural locations. Citing a 2011 NASSCOM Strategic Review, Majumder and Sharma (2014) comment favourably on the advantages of urban to rural relocation in India: advantages include low-end work like data entry being easily done anywhere, and rural labour costs being significantly lower than urban.[19] But, they argue, there is also an important 'social cause' to be considered, namely 'access to female employees' (p. 83). Here, well-worn gender ideologies re-surface in the authors' emphasis on how '[n]ot only are women equally adept at handling IT tasks but they have proved to be more loyal employees' (p. 83). By 'loyal' the authors presumably mean super-exploitable, due to even fewer alternative jobs being available to women outside of the informal economy in these areas.

---

[19]   Majumder and Sharma (2014: 79) argue that 'In rural BPOs the attrition rate is only 3–5% compared to urban BPOs where this figure stands at 50%. The operational expenses are 30–40% lower than the major cities. … a person working in rural BPO is paid 30–40% less than what is paid in urban areas'.

Other Asian countries' cities with large English-speaking populations have offered a viable alternative labour reserve for the industry. The growth of the industry in the Philippines is, like India, a story of a successful state–capital alliance to re-gear formal education and training systems to support that expansion. It is an alliance that has led to increased differentiation in local labour markets and wider socio-economic inequalities (Ofreneo, 2016). There, YU rates remain high, vulnerable work in the informal economy persists, and the region has the highest concentration of the working poor (ILO, 2011, cited in Ofreneo, 2016). Inequality is spurred by a new 'elite' of urban middle-class youth working in global factories rapidly pulling away from young unemployed people excluded from the new jobs.

The labour-differentiating and inequality-reconfiguring impacts of these development strategies are also felt reciprocally in the countries from which production has been offshored. The altered labour market structures into which young people are to integrate are structurally different from those of previous generations. Globalisation and technological changes have polarised demand for skills, such that predominantly service-based high-income economies now produce high-paid jobs for those with high skills and low-paid jobs for those with low skills (Autor and Dorn, 2013). Such polarisation in the general labour market has a stark effect on wages, inequality and employment of young people. In countries of the European Union, for example, where about 30 per cent of graduates are over-qualified for their jobs (Cedefop, 2010), the routinisation and polarisation effects of information technologies combined with the impacts of globalisation processes on job employment, earnings and social inequality are 'particularly relevant to the youth population' (Bheemaiah and Smith, 2015: 33). Cedefop (2014) predicted a loss of one-fifth of all jobs requiring low-level qualifications in the European Union by 2025, while deskilling of such jobs as remain has already resulted in some low-skilled workers being pushed out of the labour force altogether (Beaudry et al., 2013). In parallel, about one-third of service-sector graduates are over-qualified for the jobs they do (Cedefop, 2010), and the erosion of skilled work in this sector by automation and routinisation has made many of those jobs vulnerable to being outsourced. It is but a short step to more jobs being offshored by the growth of the highly qualified youth-labour hungry ITES sector in India, the Philippines and other countries.

Furthermore, recent studies of developed/developing country international trade competition have highlighted the 'dis-employment' effects and deindustrialisation dynamics in high-income countries that foreclose once-secure pathways to employment for subsequent generations of young people. One focus of attention is China's growing dominance in manufacturing on employment in developed countries. Such effects include large reductions in average wages, especially among workers in the bottom 40 per cent of the initial wage distribution where young people tend to be concentrated; increased unemployment and labour force non-participation within the same local labour markets; and the non-materialisation of employment gains in other industries in the regions affected that might have offset these losses (Autor et al., 2013; Autor, 2014; Autor et al., 2014; Murray, 2017). The scale of long-lasting 'dis-employment' effects for such generations is illuminated by Acemoglu et al. (2016), who calculated that 2.4 million jobs in the USA were lost to the rise in import competition from China during the 2010s, and by Murray (2017) who put these job losses at 150,000–170,000 in Canada. Canada saw a greater proportion of the overall decline in manufacturing employment over that period than the USA (21 per cent vs. 10 per cent, respectively), reflecting the degree of exposure of Canadian manufacturing to international trade competition from China

(Murray, 2017). Of interest is that most of this employment reduction took place *prior* to the GFC and resulted in a *permanent* loss of comparative advantage in the sectors in which China had become more dominant (Acemoglu et al., 2016).

4.5   CONCLUSION

This chapter's 'reading' of evidence regarding the relationship between contemporary global restructuring, the 're-making' of global youth labour forces and YU has routed our discussion towards the position of youth labour within state and corporate strategies over the last five decades. Drawing on extensive literature and a wide range of development contexts, in the periphery as well as the core, we have considered youth labour impacts of corporate offshoring in 'frontier' global industries and of states' export-oriented development strategies and policies to engineer flexible labour markets. Instantiated micro-settings (notably firms' workforce recruitment and management practices and their relationship to local labour markets) and macro-settings (notably the role of YU in realising 'national development') have helped elucidate where and how the construction and institutionalisation of young people as archetypal global flexible workers is unfolding. In doing so, we fleshed out the argument that young people occupy a distinct place within the global labour force and the social edifices on which it is built and that structure it.

Our findings point to the overall conclusion that, globally, contemporarily as historically (Chapter 3), no other age group is so flexible, cheap to hire, open to accepting disadvantageous conditions of work, pay or contracts, lacking in collective action and support, or easily disregarded or dismissed as young people. As was the historical norm before child labour was outlawed, young people remain the most flexible and exploitable section of the labour force, whether because of their inexperience, their lack of labour organisation and associated bargaining tactics and powers, their ignorance of their rights, or as a result of deeply institutionalised age discrimination between youth and adult labour forces and between sections of the youth labour force. Either way, the flexible, fluid, adaptive, absorptive attributes that employers project on to young people are remarkably well-aligned to public policies to re-engineer youth labour markets and depress wages. The pools of reserve youth labour that have grown deeper over time are vital to preventing wage inflation: so long as they can be rapidly mobilised as circumstances and conditions require, their availability and willingness to work prevents pay rates rising (as employees make use of staff shortages to make the case for better pay), supported by the threat of collective withdrawal of labour without the risk of the youth reserve army being called upon (just as organised labour sought to limit the use of youth labour in the nineteenth century (see Chapter 3)). Correspondingly, just as easily, ill-protected 'surplus' youth labour can be removed from active employment and channelled into overt or hidden unemployment. As we argued, the *bi-directional fluidity of movement* of young workers between employment and unemployment makes young people an attractive and highly flexible labour force for employers seeking to manage the ebb and flow of supply and demand for labour and ensure continuing capital accumulation and wealth creation.

Young age is, therefore, a significant factor of global labour force formation and management. Three main elements stand out. First is the age composition of global workforces: in the frontier outsourced global industries we examined, there is a pronounced employer preference for young people, especially those without labour market experience, including of unemployment. The second element is ageist ideologies: employers project onto young people qualities that constitute their own vision of ideal workers, namely available, trainable and dispensable. The third element is fragmentation within the youth labour cohort: inequalities *among* youth cohorts as well as *between* youth and adult cohorts are an indelible feature of the global youth labour force. Public policies have encouraged fragmentation, stabilising that labour force through an array of interlocking education, training, social security, employment, trade and development measures. Such policies have institutionalised that fragmentation in ways that are conducive to economic growth strategies, of which the construction of offshored export-oriented labour forces and the flexibilisation of youth labour markets are archetypal examples.

So ingrained and powerful are social divisions of age within processes of restructuring of global production and labour, that we affirm they warrant dedicated, systematic attention in their own right. Youth is a significant structural differentiator of global labour forces. Youth labour ideology is remarkably consistent, between countries, industries, development contexts, and is enduring over time. It might be said to be universal. The preponderance of young people within the workforces we have examined is a strong indicator of wage depression and poor working conditions. Other social attributes of workforces can be read-off from their young age structures. We have been truly surprised at how little change national institutional differences in welfare and labour seem to make regarding the conditions of offshored work in middle-income countries – work that is carried out under conditions largely controlled by 'parent' companies based in HICs. This is not to say, however, that youth labour is undifferentiated or that the incorporation of young people into global labour forces is fixed. As we saw, sector- and industry-specific requirements can change the social composition of youth workforces, while 'contingent' local labour conditions affect the extent to which employers can realise their ideal worker preferences. Such factors impact upon which social groups are drawn into waged labour in the formal economy and which are relegated to residual labour markets and/or to long-term (usually hidden) unemployment in the informal sector, education or economic 'inactivity'. These are universal social laws, and enduring features of social processes of industrial workforce composition, as first documented by Engels in the nineteenth century (Chapter 3).

If age merits attention in its own right, it is also clear that it is conditioned by gender and social class. We found an especially close relationship between age and gender ideologies regarding secondary (offshored) labour force status, 'natural skills' and amenability to labour discipline. Youth is such a strong code for these that employing young people often means in practice employing single women without care responsibilities. There is a similar affinity between age and social class. Recruitment policies of global industries are particularly instructive in this regard, be it ITES' recruitment of graduates straight from university or the informatics industry's recruitment straight from school. For employers, completion of education is code for trainability and possession of industry-appropriate cultural capital. In sum, the global youth labour force is fragmented and structurally differentiated by age, education, social class, and gender, within and between countries.

The dynamics of the inclusion and exclusion of youth labour in globalising economies are unsurprisingly complex. The creation of mass employment opportunities occasioned by the arrival of a global factory on the shores of poorer countries of the world diverts some young people from open or hidden unemployment and supports the *possibility* of an independent income and transition to adulthood. However, this comes at a price, adversely impacting as it does upon other fractions of the youth labour force. First, the working conditions of young employees in 'enclave' economies give tangible meaning to the term 'indecent' work. Second, extant structures of uneven development are accentuated due to the tendency of world market factories to site themselves in already more-developed regions and zones, while labour market segmentation among youth cohorts, as well as between younger and older workers, is further cemented. Third, unemployment among young people without sufficient capital (cultural, parental or proxy economic – see Chapter 2) remains hidden in the informal sector or in economic inactivity. Fourth, a deindustrialisation dynamic in the 'outsourcing' country of disinvestment can foreclose on once-secure paths to employment for new cohorts and future generations. What we see, then, is that global economic restructuring re-positions youth labour within national labour markets; such markets are connected internationally by global dynamics that refract across the global labour force in myriad complex interactions and configurations.

At another level, catastrophic youth welfare outcomes from unemployment (Chapter 2) are a logical consequence of capital valorisation strategies seeking to take advantage of voluminous supplies of youth labour in order to enhance comparative advantages, securing the highest possible labour productivity at the lowest possible cost. This is unsurprising, but our research has specifically highlighted a novel point: it is *not only* that young people are more vulnerable to predatory practices by employers in offshored global industries, but *also* that zones with a plentiful supply of available young workers offer distinct advantages to corporations seeking more favourable trading returns by offshoring parts of the production process. The depth of youth labour reservoirs in countries and regions identified as possible relocation sites has been a key 'competitive advantage' in developing nations' attempts to gain a stronger foothold in the global economy. All these are capable of generating catastrophic welfare outcomes in terms of decent work and sustainable pay. But these massive global transformations of the distribution and participation of global youth labour pay little if any attention to the social organisational and social relations of welfare that are fundamental to young people's security. YU, we have argued, is a social policy issue, and is central to interpreting the NIDYL across complex bi-lateral and multi-lateral business deals that export demand for young labour and import its products and services at 'cut-price' rates (Chapter 2). Those enterprises that offshore their labour, and the governments that support them in doing so, also offshore the welfare responsibilities of employers towards employees.

The evidence we reviewed strongly suggests that the voluminous availability of (unemployed) young people in a locality or region *indicates* conducive production conditions for capital and adverse conditions for young people. We surmise, therefore, that high rates of YU (open or hidden) in a plentiful youth population signal high potential returns on capital valorisation strategies. To repeat: if capital valorisation leads firms to seek out areas of labour surplus, then young people are at once an indicator of that surplus *and* a target for employers seeking to reconstitute their global workforce in the areas in which new production is established. Testing the salience of YU in labour components of siting decisions must be the subject of further research beyond the scope of this book. For now, we are content to note that we disagree with the argument that high levels of YU disprove Marx's argument that capitalism demands more youthful workers and fewer adult workers (Mayer et al., 2019: 3). As we have shown, high levels of YU are *entirely consistent with* capital's demand for more youthful workers, and these dual processes unfolding within the global youth labour force are closely interconnected. The next two chapters map the extent of these high and generally rising rates of YU, first by setting them in the context of global financial crises, differentiating between trends of rising YU, and examining the scope and depth of EYU across different country income groups (Chapter 5); then by examining the statistical relationships between economic growth and contraction worldwide and changes in YU rates, and those between YU and health and education indicators, using original datasets constructed for this project (Chapter 6).

5. Financial crises and endemic youth unemployment

5.1 INTRODUCTION

Our analysis of the position of youth labour within the global economy in Chapters 3 and 4 accounts for a crucial aspect of the destabilising volatility of the global dynamics of youth unemployment (YU) and the constantly shifting patterns of its global distribution. These dynamics do not occur in isolation, however: other major, and often determining, factors prevail upon and alter them. Foremost among these are the cyclical conditions of the global economy (Aruoba et al., 2010; Bayoumi and Bui, 2010; Kose et al., 2012; Ductor and Leiva-Leon, 2016) and the stability of global finance (Danielsson et al., 2018). Whatever the prospective monetary gains of the now-longstanding 'new' international division of youth labour (NIDYL) for corporations, and whatever the consequences for young people and others in the shifting transnational dynamics of employment and unemployment, international economic and business cycles sometimes alter employers' scope for manoeuvre in business development. But economic cycles are normally relatively predictable and easy to adapt to. In contrast, changes in the stability of global financial systems are considerably more likely to disrupt production in almost all economies, because of their high degrees of internationalisation, especially where production has been relocated to economic environments in which the robustness of altered business models (Chapter 4) has yet to be tested under adverse and crisis conditions. Financial crises are inherently difficult to predict, whether in terms of their magnitude, their impacts on employment, or how they are experienced and responded to across politically and economically diverse nation states and administrations.[1]

Transnational financial crises in which national crises interact and become deeper and more prolonged (and sometimes global in scale) are historically common. Since the Long Depression that spanned the last three decades of the nineteenth century, there have been at least six major transnational or global financial crises.[2] All have had major and often devastating impacts on human lives and livelihoods and the material and financial security of affected populations. Most have, to varying degrees, been associated with extremes of unemployment

---

[1] For example, in 2018, predictions of a global recession in 2021 were widely and confidently held, but were pre-empted in 2020 and 'realised' under entirely unpredictable conditions: see Chapter 9.

[2] For the Long Depression, see, for example, Rosenberg (1943) and Musson (1959). Subsequent financial crises included the Wall Street Crash and the Great Depression of 1929–39, the Latin American debt crisis (1981–82), the early 1980s and 1990s recessions, the Scandinavian crises of 1991–92, and the Asian financial crisis of 1997–8 (see Bordo and Murshid, 2000; Reinhart and Rogoff, 2008a, 2008b, 2009; Choudhry et al., 2012), as well as the global financial crisis of 2008.

in some or all affected countries, often and especially amongst young people, and often at overwhelming scales and over prolonged periods. Chapter 3 (Section 3.2, pp. 43–47) considered the causes and effects of the early twentieth-century global economic and financial crises of 1919–21 and 1929–39 and their effects on YU across and beyond the economies of the Global North, for example.

In what follows, in Section 5.2 we begin by reviewing financial crises and their effects on YU rates in groups of countries after the Second World War, followed by the global financial crisis (GFC) that began in 2007/08. We briefly consider its origins and causes, and outline initial evidence of its impact on YU across groups of countries. Section 5.3 describes worldwide YU trends amongst 15–24-year-olds over the period 1991–2019. It differentiates between the numbers and rates of young people who constitute the active and inactive labour force and compares YU rates with those of adults. It compares different definitions and criteria for determining who is included in the labour force and who is not, and builds on this to clarify the nature and size of the global reserve army of youth labour (GRAoYL), introduced in Chapter 3. Section 5.4 elaborates the concept of endemic youth unemployment (EYU) as proposed in Chapter 1 and provides prominent examples of its global distribution at national and world-regional levels, also identifying multiple representations of gender differences in global, regional and national labour forces. Section 5.5 reviews the global distribution of YU according to economic differences, using the classification of all countries into four ranked World Bank (WB) country income groups (CIGs). The closing section (5.6) briefly summarises key findings and draws interim conclusions that make the case for the statistical analyses in Chapter 6.

5.2 TWENTIETH-CENTURY FINANCIAL CRISES AND YOUTH UNEMPLOYMENT

5.2.1 Post-war Financial Crises and Youth Unemployment

At national level, since 1975, an average of 13 countries per year have experienced banking crises.[3] Here we focus on multi-national and transnational crises. Reinhart and Rogoff (2008b) identified what they term the 'Big 5 Crises' between 1977 and 1992, in Finland, Japan, Norway, Spain and Sweden. Verick (2011) draws attention to OECD-wide increases in YU rates in these crises of between 10 and 40 percentage points over periods of 2–12 years. In Finland, Japan, Spain and Sweden, YU had not returned to pre-crisis rates 15–20 years later. The Asian financial crisis of 1997 also had a huge adverse impact on YU rates (Knowles et al., 1999). Historically, YU rates have been more sensitive to downturns in the economic cycle following financial crises, compared to adult rates, and the negative effects on YU are typically longer-lasting. Choudhry et al. (2012), for example, model the impact of several crises on YU between 1980 and 2005, across 70 countries in Latin American (1981–82), Scandinavia and Japan (1991–92), Europe (1991–92), and Asia and Russia (1997–98). All had repercussions on YU rates far beyond the regions and countries of origin. Crisis conditions were associated with increased YU rates in all countries, but were statistically significant only in high-income

---

[3]   Behavioural Finance and Financial Stability Project, Harvard University (*The Economist*, 13–19 October 2018).

countries (HICs), where the impact was also more severe. In similar vein, Bruno et al.'s (2017) study of youth and adult unemployment between 1981 and 2009 across 27 OECD countries examined the impact on YU rates of systematic banking crises.[4] All OECD countries except Australia, Canada and New Zealand experienced at least two crises, with several having up to seven.[5] The authors' key finding was that *YU rates are primarily sensitive to the economic cycle and to the impact of the financial crisis itself.*

5.2.2   The Global Financial Crisis

The GFC (2007/08) was the first crisis of comparable scale to the Great Depression of 1929–39. It had an unprecedented impact on youth labour markets worldwide, principally as a result of its scale, as its consequences ricocheted between extensively connected economies knitted together by global supply chains – themselves the products of global economic restructuring and the global transformation of production (Chapter 4). The immediate origins of the GFC can be traced to a major boom in the credit available to would-be US homeowners, to the financial securities that supported it, and to the associated boom in house-building in the USA and parts of Europe that began in the 1990s and early 2000s.[6] The trigger to the global crisis is widely viewed to be the collapse of Lehman Brothers bank in the USA in 2007. By autumn 2008 the USA's Federal Reserve Bank had put US$800 billion into bank recapitalisation to secure and revive mortgage and other lending. In the UK, as a result of financial practices broadly similar to those in the USA, the UK's Northern Rock bank was forced to take the extraordinary step of seeking emergency funding from the Bank of England (BoE). A series of other banks and lenders were variously broken up, underwritten by the BoE, or otherwise recapitalised at a total cost to the UK Treasury of £37 billion. The UK Chancellor of the Exchequer described the world banking system as 'standing on the very brink'.[7] In Ireland and continental Europe, between 2007 and 2009 numerous banks faced similar collapse. France and Germany issued loan guarantees totalling €720 billion, and the European Commission committed a €600 billion recovery package. Much of Eastern Europe was even more severely affected and Western European banks' claims on many of these countries ran to hundreds of billions of dollars. Across Asia, the Americas, Northern Africa and beyond, by 2009 almost all of the 60 countries that register regular gross domestic product (GDP) statistics with the International Monetary Fund (IMF) were facing, or already in, recession.

The societal impacts of these unfolding crises were far-reaching. In 2012 the president of the European Central Bank argued that the European social model of job security and social welfare had 'already gone' (Tooze, 2018: 420). In the same year, the US Treasury estimated losses to US household wealth at $19 trillion. US house prices had fallen by a third and nine

---

[4]   Defined as multiple defaults and failures to meet financial obligations to time (Honohan and Laeven, 2005).

[5]   Up to nine econometric models in Bruno et al.'s (2017) study took account of variations in the sizes of the age group, GDP growth, number of financial crises, inflation rates, interest rates, part-time employment, and labour market differences, comparing duration effects of crises on unemployment, and on YU versus total unemployment rates.

[6]   This and the following summary in this section are drawn from Tooze's (2018) authoritative account of the crisis and its inherently global nature.

[7]   See http://news.bbc.co.uk/1/shared/bsp/hi/pdfs/221208_darling.pdf (accessed 23 August 2020).

million families lost their homes to foreclosure. The IMF estimated UK household wealth losses to equate to 50 per cent of GDP (Tooze, 2018: 42–3, 156). Furthermore, the GFC exposed the weakness or absence of effective global financial governance. In 2007 there was no effectively functioning international financial regulatory framework, still less any form of coherent and robust global governance to protect against further financial crises that were transnational in character (see Chapter 8).

The global impact of the GFC on YU rates worldwide over more than a decade was unprecedented. In Chapter 6 we critically review and extend the accumulating contemporary literature that seeks to explain these effects using economic data on changing annual national GDP rates and corresponding changes in YU rates, and test the relationships between them using a dedicated extensive dataset newly constructed for this study. In what follows here, in order to contextualise the analyses of Chapter 6, we describe and depict some key YU trends over the past three decades that signal the changes associated with the GFC.

5.3 GLOBAL YOUTH UNEMPLOYMENT TRENDS

5.3.1 Global Youth Unemployment: Rates and Totals

As Figures 5.1 and 5.2 show, between 1991 and 2003 the world YU rate increased by almost four percentage points, raising unemployment levels amongst 15–24-year-olds by more than 20 million. From 2003, the rate began a steady decline over five years to approximately 12 per cent, taking six million young people out of unemployment. The impact of the GFC beginning in 2007/08 was an immediate and sharp increase in YU rates to 13.5 per cent, returning almost six million young people to unemployment over two years. Globally, total YU numbers declined steadily after the peak period of the GFC, taking almost 10 million out of unemployment by 2018. However, although the unemployment count fell, the rate of unemployment between 2009 and 2016 continued to rise to almost 14 per cent, exceeding the initial 2009 GFC peak. Projections to 2021 anticipated an underlying continuation of this upward trend in the rate and the count.[8] Almost continuously, before as well as after the GFC, YU rates have risen for 29 years and are expected to continue to do so, *despite* the constant decline in the YU count since the GFC.

---

[8]   What may appear at first sight as a discrepancy between Figures 5.1 and 5.2 is a function of changes in the size of the youth labour force. In 2005 for example, it reached a peak at almost 587 million (not shown), and YU was 78 million, representing an unemployment rate of 13.3 per cent. Corresponding data for 2014, at the trough in YU levels after the peak period of the GFC, was 518 million (not shown) and 69 million, giving an unemployment rate of 13.4 per cent. Thus, the reduction in the numbers employed over nine years was seven million, but it coincided with a 58 million reduction in the numbers of young people in the labour force, most of which occurred in the years following the onset of the GFC (Figure 5.3). Numerically, this accounts for the imperceptibly small decline in the unemployment rate.

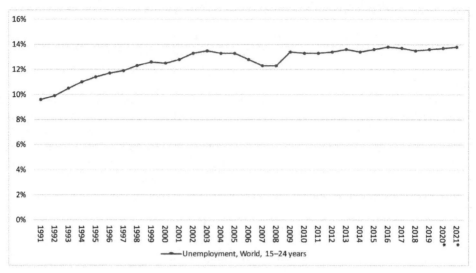

Note: * Indicates projected data.
Source: ILOSTAT, WESO Data Finder, 2020, accessed 12 January 2020.

Figure 5.1   World unemployment rate, aged 15–24 years, 1991–2019

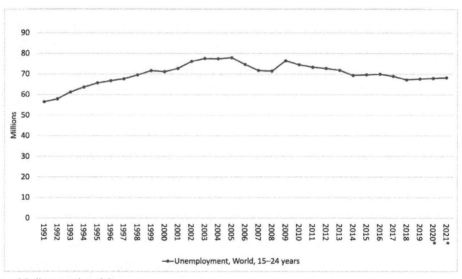

Notes: * Indicates projected data.
This dataset includes both real and imputed data from 1991–2019, as well as projections for 2020–2021. Estimates may differ from official national sources.
Source: ILOSTAT, WESO Data Finder, 2020, accessed 12 January 2020.

Figure 5.2   World unemployment totals, aged 15–24 years, 1991–2019

5.3.2 Young People 'in' and 'not in' the Labour Force

Amongst 15–24-year-olds the global proportion in the labour force has declined dramatically over three decades (from 58 per cent to 41 per cent) with a corresponding increase in the proportion that is not in the labour force (from 42 per cent to 58 per cent) (Figure 5.3). Numerically, Figure 5.3 represents a sharp decrease in the numbers of young people in the labour force of 92 million to 497 million (not shown in the graphic) – a decline of 16 per cent. Figure 5.3 also reflects a corresponding extraordinary 60 per cent increase in the number of young people not in the labour force (from 427 million in 1991 to 709 million by 2019).

Authors' note: In Figures 5.1–5.8, for each YU cohort for which data was sourced from ILOSTAT WESO Data Finder, in addition to the annual figures shown, the ILO's World Economic and Social Outlook (WESO) data provides upper and lower Error Bounds between which the calculations of the data shown may have varied in each year, allowing that some data sources are estimated or derived, rather than drawn from national surveys and statistical sources. The Error Bounds typically indicate variations above and below the specified data-point for each year within a range of one to two percentage points.

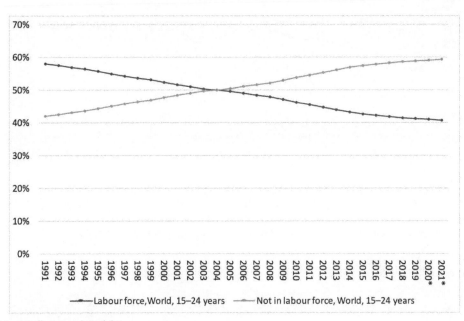

Note: * Indicates projected data.
Source: ILOSTAT, WESO Data Finder, 2020, accessed 12 January 2020.

Figure 5.3   Proportion 'in' and 'not in' the labour force, aged 15–24 years, 1991–2019

5.3.3   Comparing Youth and Adult Unemployment (Rates and Totals)

Seen in this context, comparison with the trajectory of adult global unemployment rates is salutary. It has long been unremarkable that YU rates universally greatly exceed adult rates. The original six percentage point difference between them in 1991 had already grown to nine points by 2003 (Figure 5.4). The upturn in adult unemployment rates from 3.8 per cent to 4.4 per cent following the onset of the GFC in 2009 was relatively minor and was in turn followed by a slow but consistent decline, whereas the YU rate continued to climb consistently between 2009 and 2016 (as noted above). On almost all available economic and related indicators worldwide, the adverse employment effects of the GFC had levelled off by the late 2010s. For adults, not only did unemployment rates remain typically seven to ten percentage points below YU rates, they were relatively constant (never differing by more than a small fraction of one percentage point year-on-year except in 2008–09) compared to percentage changes spanning an almost constantly rising four-point range for young people between 1991 and 2019. For 15–24-year-olds, the legacy of the GFC has been persistently increasing rates of YU world-wide *despite* a shrinking youth labour force and despite the global recovery from the financial and economic conditions that prevailed during the crisis.

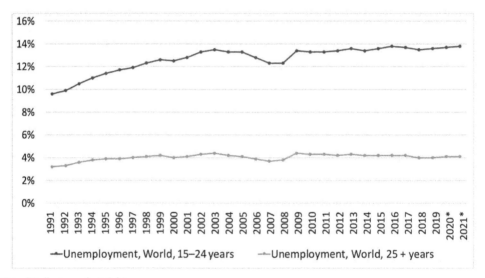

Note: * Indicates projected data.
Source: IOSTAT, WESO Data Finder, 2020, accessed 12 January 2020.

Figure 5.4   World unemployment rates, aged 15–24 years and 25+ years, 1991–2019

5.3.4   Comparing Young People and Adults not in the Labour Force (Rates and Totals)

These observations are even more striking if we compare the proportions of adults and of young people who are classified as 'not in the labour force'. Figure 5.3 (above) has shown that the share of young people who are not in the labour force has been growing constantly (at a steady average of about half of one percentage point per year) throughout the period under scrutiny. Figure 5.5 juxtaposes this against the adult rate.

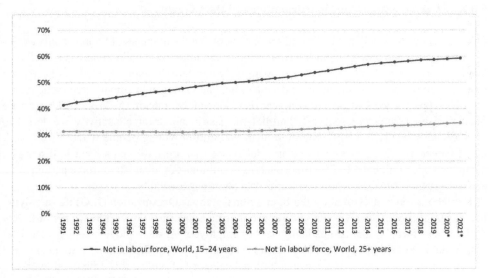

Note: * Indicates projected data.
Source: ILOSTAT, WESO Data Finder, 2020, accessed 12 January 2020.

Figure 5.5   World 'not in labour force' rate, aged 15–24 years and 25+ years, 1991–2019

The difference is once again striking. Not only is the rate of non-participation amongst adults much lower, it has increased by barely one tenth of a percentage point annually. By 2019, whilst only 34 per cent of adults were not in the labour force, 59 per cent of young people were not in the labour force. This approximate 25-percentage-point difference throws into sharp relief the high rate of young people who are 'non-participant'. If the steady current trajectory of non-participation continues, by 2030, almost two-thirds of 15–24-year-olds will be outside the labour force. The current and projected rates of their non-participation give intrinsic cause for major concern, as does the total number of young people not in the labour force (709 million in 2019). Many young people who are registered as unemployed may have some undeclared informal and/or irregular paid work. It is likely that greater proportions of this age group who are recorded as not being in the labour force undertake productive work within their households and immediate communities, whether or not they are paid (see also

Chapter 3, Section 3.4, esp. pp. 40–41, 48. Also pp. 69, 88 (below)). However, while these alternative legitimate and 'hidden' forms of labour would substantially deflate this 59 per cent figure, some other forms of genuine unemployment are also invisible and pass unrecorded, especially in developing countries with weak state infrastructures for gathering data of this kind, or at the other end of the spectrum in countries in which the state infrastructure for monitoring unemployment amongst welfare claimants and enforcing (sometimes unsuitable) employment is sufficiently hostile to deter registration. We follow up on these points later in the next sub-section.

5.3.5   Labour Force (Non-)participation and Data Quality

Other analyses suggest that it is beyond serious doubt that the numbers of young people world-wide who seek paid employment but cannot find it are to be counted in hundreds of millions. While adult unemployment has been comparatively constant throughout, YU rates have risen despite declining youth populations and a major decline in the youth labour force participation rate. The apparently relentless year-on-year rise in the global rate of 15–24-year-olds who are not in the labour force represents a 282 million increase in labour force inactivity over less than three decades to 2018, constituting more than 700 million young people without paid work (see Chapter 3). This raises two fundamental issues that are rarely addressed in discussion about the scale of global YU. The first concerns definitions of global labour force participation and non-participation, the second concerns data sources and quality.

The labour force is defined by the International Labour Organization (ILO) as 'supplying labour for the production of goods and services during a specified time-reference period'. 'Not in the labour force' is defined as being neither employed nor unemployed. As Chapter 3 set out, Bellamy-Foster et al.'s (2011) definitions reject the sharp distinction between 'in' and 'not in' the labour force, to include an additional category of 'vulnerably employed' workers. These are the 'own account workers' and 'contributing family workers' who are also part of the ILO's classification. Appendix 5.1 sets out detailed definitions of both sets of categories and provides a tabulated comparison of the two classifications. These distinctions are impor-tant because the two vulnerably employed groups are not wage workers. Those who work on their 'own account' cannot be assumed to receive monetary remuneration: in many (not only lower-income) countries, payment in kind in the form of services or domestically produced goods would be accepted. Where waged employment is scarce or absent, young people have little choice but to become 'contributing family workers', typically as members of subsistence farmers' families, most of whom work as an absolute necessity in order to be able to eat. Even the youngest children, those without schooling and early school leavers would also be expected to contribute. Where this occurs, it is extremely unlikely that any official account of these young people's contributions would or could be recorded at state level. So long as young people have reached eligibility for formal employment, they can be deemed wage workers or part of the labour force.[9] Otherwise, their presence in the labour force as workers, or their absence from it as unemployed or informal workers, passes unrecorded.

---

[9]   Where schooling is a legal requirement, school-leaving ages continue to vary from as low as 12 years to more typically 15–18 years.

With regard to concerns about the sources and quality of YU data, we are in no doubt about the ILO's assiduous maintenance of data to international standards. But there are many obstacles to acquiring sound, reliable and standardised country-level data that can be used internationally. Research by Jerven (2013) on GDP and income data in sub-Saharan Africa (SSA) casts light on the extraordinarily low rates of YU in low-income countries (LICs).[10] For both GDP and income he finds 'huge discrepancies and alarming gaps' (p. 5) in available data and argues that publicly available rankings of African economies according to GDP are misleading. Of particular interest, he argues that the expanded capacity for producing sound data during the later colonial era was reversed during the African economic crises of the 1970s, and then – quite remarkably – neglected during the 'structural adjustment' period of the 1980s and 1990s, in which informal markets grew as public spending was held back, as required by the IMF and WB. More generally, poor funding resulting from inadequate taxation regimes, inadequate staffing, inconsistent methodologies used by different states, and discrepancies between nationally developed accounts and corresponding records on international databases were found to have contributed to the paucity of comparable national data.

In all, high levels of labour informality and poor data infrastructure (and some probably unintended irregularities) undoubtedly account for what appear to be implausibly low under-estimated YU rates in many LICs, as Section 5.6 below shows.[11]

5.3.6 The Global Reserve Army of Youth Labour

However high these unemployment rates may seem, they nevertheless present a comparatively modest account of the ILO's dataset and its classifications and definitions (Appendix 5.1). If we follow the equivalent classifications and definitions used by Bellamy-Foster et al., as Chapter 3 and Figure 3.1 have shown, YU rates for comparable but different categories of (un)employment are often much higher. Recalling our data for 15–24-year-olds and for the total 'all-age' population (25–54-year-olds) from Figure 3.1 highlights some very informative differences, using Bellamy-Foster et al.'s categories.[12] Our data revealed that open unemployment accounts for a very modest 6 per cent of 15–24-year-olds globally, and 5 per cent of all ages. Sixteen per cent of the younger age group is classified as 'vulnerably employed' compared to a very much higher 46 per cent of 25–54-year-olds. These are the 'own account workers' and 'contributing family workers' referred to above, whom Bellamy-Foster et al. co-classify as 'vulnerably employed'. 'Wage workers' (who along with the unemployed make up the whole of the 'economically active population' in this classification) constitute the next largest category, at 19 per cent of the young population and 35 per cent of 25–54-year-olds. By far the largest category for the younger population is therefore the 'economically inactive' group, who make up a huge 60 per cent of 15–24-year-olds and a very modest 14 per cent of

---

[10] Jerven's main findings were from Ghana, Kenya, Malawi, Nigeria, Tanzania, Uganda and Zambia.
[11] This account does not attribute these difficulties to African states. Jerven (2013) found the IMF and WB to have been less than transparent about their methodologies for generating statistical series, and to have neglected the development of statistical services during the 'structural adjustment' period (pp. xvii, 35, 98–99). World Development Indicators, too, were found to lack consistency with country-level data (pp.23–28, 97–98).
[12] See Appendix 5.1 and Chapter 3 for detailed definitions.

25–54-year-olds.[13] This group is described by Bellamy-Foster et al. as 'would-be workers'. As Chapter 3 (Sections 3.2 and 3.4.1) emphasised, the difference between the data for 15–24-year-olds and 25–54-year-olds is remarkable. While the unemployment rate for both is almost identical, three times the all-age population is vulnerably employed, compared to young people, and more than four times as many 15–24-year-olds are economically inactive, compared to the older age group.

These comparisons highlight the pertinence of Bellamy-Foster et al.'s category 'vulnerably employed' to the study of youth economic participation. It is clear that there is very extensive recognition of 'own account workers' and 'contributing family workers' amongst adults and very little recognition of them amongst 15–24-year-olds who work but do not meet the criteria for being classified as wage workers. This is consistent with our observations in sub-section 5.3.5 that a great deal of young people's contributory family labour is unpaid, unrecorded, or both. This is particularly prevalent in contexts of subsistence production in informal econo- mies. 'Poor work', insecure, intermittent, transient and 'zero hours' (un)employment as well as various forms of forced labour all prevail with ever greater ease the greater the level of informality, whether motivated by subsistence and survival or by the exploitation of juveniles by adults, within families or otherwise.

Bellamy-Foster et al. regard all categories of workers except wage workers as being part of the global reserve army. This includes the vulnerably employed. Seen in the context of the total population, this indicates that 65 per cent of workers of all ages are part of that reserve army, the remaining 35 per cent being wage workers. Amongst 15–24-year-olds, this means that the reserve army is made up of a huge 81 per cent of young people, while only 19 per cent are wage workers (Chapter 3). The comparable data using the ILO classifications would be that (in 2019) 59 per cent of young people were not in the labour force and 41 per cent were in the labour force. But if we were to view this 59 per cent as a reserve army, it would be one that had not taken into account the unemployed (who are neither in the labour force nor outside it according to the definitions in Appendix 5.1) and the vulnerably employed (who are included in the labour force irrespective of their actively employed status).

In our view, the constituent categories of what we have termed a global reserve army of youth labour (GRAoYL) (Chapter 3) offer a more inclusive *and more accurate and realistic* definition of youth unemployment. We therefore propose that the GRAoYL be taken to mean: 'the labour pool of young people who can be drawn upon by employers when required and returned to the pool as the labour market dynamics of demand and supply dictate'. The size of and inclusionary criteria for the GRAoYL will undoubtedly continue to be further refined, but it is evident that most of the world's population of 15–24-year-olds exist without jobs or inde- pendent means of subsistence, contrary to their own needs and preferences. Even if as little as a notional half of 81 per cent of young people are accepted to constitute the GRAoYL (as noted in the previous paragraph, based on the calculations in Chapter 3), it would still account for 486 million 15–24-year-olds worldwide.[14] A more realistic estimate would probably be closer to 900 million – not much greater than the combined 709 million who are not in the labour force plus the 68 million recorded as unemployed in 2019. Whichever of these readings

---

[13]   The excess sum of the percentages for each category is due to rounding.
[14]   The global population of 15–24-year-olds in 2019 was 1.2 billion. Data sourced from https:// population.un.org/wpp (accessed 23 August 2020).

offers the best approximation, it represents a major cause for global concern – highlighting the significance of the concept 'endemic youth unemployment', to which we now turn.

5.4 ENDEMIC YOUTH UNEMPLOYMENT

5.4.1 Defining Endemic Youth Unemployment

In pursuit of a workable means of identifying protracted extremes of YU in diverse contexts, Chapter 1 proposed the concept of *endemic youth unemployment* (EYU) to facilitate a functionally useful mode of differentiation between places that experience occasional or recurrent episodes of high YU rates, as well as identifying places in which it is persistent or protracted. A number of the standard categories provide international currencies for capturing differences in rates and levels of YU, but none capture or categorise its persistent, protracted extremes in specific locations or at specific scales. The concept 'endemic' deliberately references the epidemiological meaning of prevalence or extended persistence of disease in populations which become locally permanent. Our usage of 'endemic' is intended to convey the sense of an economically and individually harmful phenomenon capable of traversing borders that is reproduced, sustained and endures over time, with no predictable end-point in some localities or at some scales.

Operationalising the concept of EYU requires specifying a 'standardised' rate and duration of YU that is appropriate to the global range of YU rates amongst 15–24-year-olds for the period 1991–2019. In terms of duration, we propose that ten years of YU at or above the specified threshold is a reasonable indicator of persistence/prevalence. This represents more than one year in every three of this period for which reliable standardised YU data are available for almost all countries. In terms of what should constitute a high rate of YU, since the global average has been between 12 per cent and 14 per cent for all except the first six years of this period but has yet to exceed it, we propose that YU rates at or above 15 per cent can reasonably be regarded as high. Our choice of this threshold is normative, in that we estimate that most societies would regard as excessive national YU rates that exceed the global mean (thereby affecting one in seven 15–24-year-olds), especially if this rate was recurrent or persistent. Our combined criteria are therefore that *YU rates should be at or above 15 per cent for at least ten years between 1991 and 2019 (or more generally one year in every three), for the purposes of defining a YU profile as endemic.*

5.4.2 World-regions and Countries and Endemic Youth Unemployment

Here we apply these EYU criteria to selected ILO world-regions and countries. Between 1991 and 2019, peak world-regional YU rates reached means of 33 per cent (Northern Africa in 1995), and have exceeded 50 per cent over extended periods in several countries. The YU profiles of seven of the 11 world-regions can be described as endemic for the period 1991–2019 (Table 5.1).[15]

---

[15] The ILO identifies 11 world-regions (the Arab states; Central and Western Asia; Eastern Asia; Eastern Europe; Latin America and the Caribbean; Northern Africa; Northern America; Northern, Southern and Western Europe; South-eastern Asia and the Pacific; Southern Asia; and sub-Saharan

Table 5.1   ILO world-regions with YU rates of 15 per cent and above, 1991–2019

Rank	ILO world-region*	No. of countries	YU rate at or above (%)	Years at this rate	Total years (of 29)
1	Northern Africa	7	15	1991–2019	29
			20	1991–2019	29
			30	1993–96, 2000–01, 2003, 2011–12, 2015–19	14
2	Northern, Southern and Western Europe	40	15	1991–2019	29
			20	1993–97, 2009–15	12
3	Arab states	12	15	1991–2019	29
			20	2004–05, 2013–19	9
4	Eastern Europe	10	15	1991–2007, 2009–18	27
			20	1996–2004	9
5	Southern Asia	9	15	1999–2019	21
6	Central and Western Asia	11	15	1996–2005, 2011, 2017–19	14
7	Latin America and the Caribbean	50	15	1998–2005, 2009, 2016–19	13

Notes: The ILO constantly updates underpinning data and adjusts it in ILO data tools such as WESODATA. We extracted the underpinning data from this source in January 2020.
* In addition, four excluded world-regions do not meet our proposed EYU criteria: Eastern Asia, Northern America, South-eastern Asia and the Pacific, and sub-Saharan Africa.
Source: ILO WESODATA, 1991–2019 (accessed 23 August 2020).

In the three first-ranked world-regions the '15 per cent x 10+ years' criterion has been met in every year, and has also exceeded the 20 per cent threshold in the two first-ranked world-regions. These data reflect averages across a total of 59 countries in the three first-ranked world-regions and 80 countries in the four lower-ranked world-regions.[16] In Northern Africa mean YU rates across seven countries were sustained at 30–40 per cent for almost half of this period. In all world-regions, the period following the onset of the GFC contributed to the recurrent high YU rates at and above the 15 per cent threshold. These four regions encompass approximately 20 per cent of all countries included in the ILO's global dataset. EYU has affected a substantial proportion of countries worldwide over almost three decades.[17]

Africa). See https://ilostat.ilo.org/resources/methods/classification-country-groupings/ (accessed 23 August 2020).
[16] We stress that these are aggregated data across all countries in each world-region: they are intended to provide a broad overview of the number of countries in scope as meeting the EYU criteria. (Country-level rates for some countries are included in Appendices 6.1–6.4.) Regularly updated comprehensive rate and count data can be found at https://www.ilo.org/wesodata (accessed 23 August 2020).
[17] Categorisations of countries into 11 world-regions when applying the EYU criteria generate some puzzling findings at first sight. When grouped and aggregated in this way, some of Europe has EYU profiles broadly similar to the profiles of Northern Africa, while the profile of sub-Saharan Africa is most closely comparable to that of parts of Eastern Europe, for example. This is inevitable – and not as counterintuitive as it may first seem – at this high level of aggregation: viewing distributions of unemploy-

Table 5.2   *Selected countries by world-region with YU rates at/above 15–60 per cent, 1991–2019*

Rank	ILO world-region/country*	Number of years at/above					
		15%	20%	30%	40%	50%	60%
1	**Sub-Saharan Africa**						
	Gabon	29	29	29	6	0	0
	Namibia	29	29	29	19	0	0
	South Africa**	29	29	29	29	26	2
2	**Eastern Europe**						
	Bosnia and Herzegovina	29	29	29	25	16	7
	Bulgaria	25	21	3	0	0	0
	Georgia	25	24	11	4	0	0
	Greece	29	29	11	7	3	0
	Montenegro	29	29	27	18	15	0
	North Macedonia	29	29	29	28	24	11
	Serbia	29	29	21	11	2	0
3	**Northern, Southern and Western Europe**						
	France	29	21	0	0	0	0
	Italy	29	29	15	3	0	0
	Spain	29	26	19	11	3	0
4	**Arab States**						
	Jordan	29	29	17	0	0	0
	Lebanon	18	18	0	0	0	0
	Occupied Palestinian Territory**	29	19	19	3	0	0
	Saudi Arabia	29	29	6	0	0	0
5	**Northern Africa**						
	Algeria**	29	29	14	13	2	0
	Egypt**	27	27	8	0	0	0
	Morocco	11	11	0	0	0	0
	Sudan**	27	27	9	0	0	0
	Tunisia**	27	27	9	1	0	0
6	**Latin America and Caribbean**						
	Argentina	28	21	8	1	0	0
	Colombia**	28	16	2	0	0	0
7	**Southern Asia**						
	Iran	29	22	0	0	0	0

Notes: * Four excluded world-regions do not meet our proposed EYU criteria: Central and Western Asia, Eastern Asia, Northern America, and South-eastern Asia and the Pacific.** Indicates war or armed conflict zone.
Source: ILO WESODATA, 1991–2019, accessed 23 August 2020.

Table 5.2 explores some illustrative examples at country level across the more severely affected world-regions. We stress that the countries included in Table 5.2 do not include all of the countries that meet our EYU criteria. The 24 countries shown are a reasonably typical distribution across the most severely affected world-regions. Almost all have also had rates at and above 20 per cent for more than 20 years, and 13 countries' rates reached or exceeded 30 per cent for at least ten years. Fourteen had rates at or above 40 per cent (seven meet the 10-year criterion). Seven countries have had rates above 50 per cent for periods between two and 26 years. Taken together they represent the more extraordinary and higher extremes of persistent, prevalent YU.

In an indicative ranking, the greatest extremes appear to be in sub-Saharan Africa and Eastern Europe, followed by Southern Europe and the Arab states. Most of the countries of Northern Africa, and a small number in Latin America and the Caribbean and in Southern Asia have also been badly affected, based on this selection. Table 5.2 also identifies past and current war zones and other persistent forms of armed conflict within nation states. Both typically have extremely adverse effects on young people's employment, save for the opportunities they offer for recruitment into military organisations or state-imposed military conscription (see Rosen, 2005, for a detailed account). However, reliable data are extremely sparse in these zones, including in ILO data.[18]

5.4.3   Gender and Endemic Youth Unemployment

Young women predominantly fare less well than young men in securing employment, including in the most depressed labour markets that meet our EYU criteria. The size and gendered composition of the global youth labour force has changed significantly over the last three decades, as between the proportions of both genders who are in the labour force and not in the labour force. Figure 5.6 describes the steady decline in the sizes of male and female youth labour forces (reflecting the data in Figure 5.3 above), particularly since the onset of the GFC in 2008, and the corresponding rise in the numbers of both sexes not in the labour force.

---

ment through the lens of EYU aligns some of the world's poorer world-regions with some of the poorer countries of the Global North.

[18]   For example, in the Middle East and Northern and sub-Saharan Africa, only very sporadic ILO data on YU rates are available for Libya (39 per cent in 2012), for Syria (35 per cent in 2011), and for Yemen (34 per cent in 2010), and no data are available for South Sudan. Yet continuous data from 1991 are available for Afghanistan, Iraq, Myanmar, Niger, the Occupied Palestinian Territory, Rwanda, Senegal and Sierra Leone. Only in Afghanistan, Iraq and the Occupied Palestinian Territory were YU levels recorded as exceeding 15 per cent (probably attributable to military conscription and/or local militia and mercenary activity involving under-25-year-olds). Exceptionally, continuous ILO data are available for the Yugoslav Wars of 1991–99. Kosovo and South Sudan remain amongst the few countries suffering armed conflicts for which no YU data are available for this period. It is not clear why such data are so uneven and unpredictable. Some ILO estimations (Myanmar, Rwanda, Senegal and Sierra Leone) model minimal annual variation in YU.

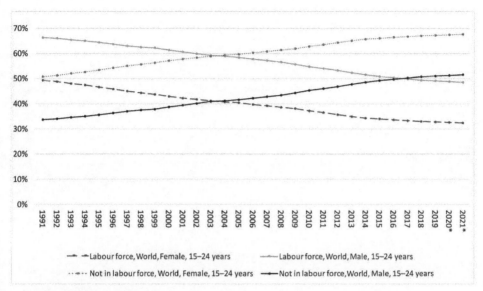

Note: * Indicates projected data.
Source: ILOSTAT, WESO Data Finder, 2020, accessed 12 January 2020.

Figure 5.6   Gender and labour force: men and women aged 15–24 in/not in labour force, 1991–2019

Table 5.3 shows that there has been a marked decline in the proportion of young women in the labour force between 1991 and 2019, while the proportion not in the labour force increased substantially. For young men, there was also a substantial reduction in labour force participation by 2019 and a corresponding increase in the proportion not in the labour force. But Figure 5.6 shows that in every year to 2019 the proportion of young men in the labour force is always between 16 and 18 percentage points greater than the proportion of young women, and the proportion of young women not in the labour force has also been consistently greater by a similar margin in each year.

Table 5.3   Proportion of young men and women in/not in labour force aged 15–24, world, 1991 and 2019 (per cent)

	Female		Male	
	1991	**2019**	**1991**	**2019**
In labour force (%)	49	33	66	49
Not in labour force (%)	51	67	34	51

Source: ILO WESODATA, 2020, accessed 12 January 2020.

In contrast, the unemployment rate amongst young women and men has been strikingly similar over the same period: in terms of total global YU rates, it is young men who are more

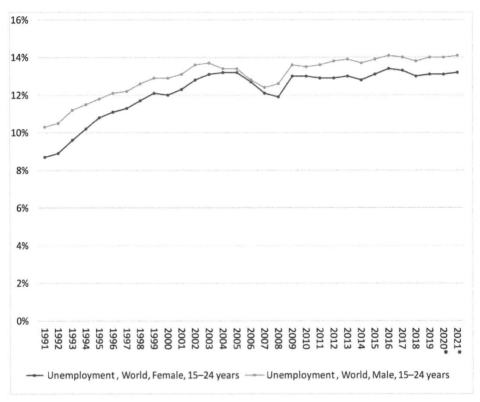

Note: * Indicates projected data.
Source: ILOSTAT, WESO Data Finder, 2020, accessed 12 January 2020.

Figure 5.7   *World unemployment totals, men and women aged 15–24, 1991–2019*

likely than young women to be unemployed. The range of differences in their YU rates varies minimally, however, between zero (in 2006) and 1.5 percentage points (in 1991) (Figure 5.7).

However, the global distribution of male and female unemployment amongst 15–24-year-olds varies greatly between countries and between world-regions. The YU rates of young women have exceeded those of young men in six of the 11 world-regions in most years since 1991. Table 5.4 compares the number of years in which young women exceed multiple YU rate thresholds for each of three decades to 2019 with the number for young men, across eight world-regions.

Once again, extreme differences prevail between world-regions. Gender differences in YU rates are substantial in five of the eight world-regions in which aggregate YU rates have reached or exceeded 15 per cent since 1991. Worldwide, on average, female YU rates tended to exceed male in more years for which YU rates of 12 per cent and 13 per cent prevailed. But at world-regional levels the differences are hugely increased, especially in the first three

Table 5.4   *World YU rates and world-regions with YU rates at/above 15 per cent,*
             1991–2019, male (M) and female (F)

Rank*	World/ILO world-region	YU rate (at and above)	Number of years at or above specified YU rates, by decades								Number of years in which female (F) YU exceeded male (M) YU
			1991–2000		2001–10		2011–19		Total (29 years)		
			M	F	M	F	M	F	M	F	
		11%	10	10	10	10	9	9	29	29	*0*
	World	12%	3	5	6	10	9	9	18	24	*6*
		13%	0	2	0	7	9	6	9	15	*6*
		15%	10	10	10	10	9	9	29	29	*0*
1	Arab states	20%	0	2	1	10	0	9	1	21	*20*
		30%	0	0	0	10	0	9	0	19	*19*
		40%	0	0	0	0	0	3	0	3	*3*
		15%	10	10	8	10	9	9	27	29	*2*
2	Northern Africa	20%	10	10	8	10	9	9	27	29	*2*
		30%	2	10	0	10	0	9	2	29	*27*
		40%	0	3	0	6	0	4	0	13	*13*
3	Latin America and the Caribbean	15%	0	7	0	10	3	9	3	26	*23*
		20%	0	3	0	5	0	4	0	12	*12*
4	Eastern Europe	15%	10	10	8	9	7	9	25	28	*3*
		20%	4	10	3	4	0	0	7	14	*7*
5	Central and Western Asia	15%	2	5	10	10	1	6	13	21	*8*
6	Southern Asia	15%	4	3	8	10	9	9	21	22	*1*
7	Northern, Southern and Western Europe	15%	10	10	9	10	9	7	28	27	*−1*
		20%	5	7	0	2	6	4	11	13	*2*
8	Northern America	15%	1	0	2	1	3	1	6	2	*−4*
		20%	0	0	1	0	0	0	1	0	*−1*

Note: * World-regions are ranked on number of years in which female (F) YU rates exceeded male (M) rates.
Source: ILO WESODATA, 1991–2019, accessed 12 January 2020.

ranked regions. In the Arab states, although young men and women experienced unemployment almost equally year by year at the 15 per cent+ rate, at the 20 per cent and 30 per cent rates more young women were unemployed than young men in two of every three years. The number of years in which female YU exceeded male for ten or more years at all rates at and above 15 per cent indicates that EYU was considerably more prevalent amongst young women than young men (applying the '10+ years at or above 15 per cent' criterion).[19] In Northern

---

[19]   Between 2001 and 2019, young women's YU reached and exceeded the 20 per cent, 30 per cent and 40 per cent thresholds in every year, whereas this occurred for one year only (in the 2001–10 period) amongst young men.

Africa, female rates rarely exceeded male rates at the 15 per cent and 20 per cent levels and both sexes met the EYU criteria throughout. But young women were unemployed in almost every year at the 30 per cent plus rate, and in almost every other year at the 40 per cent plus rate, and young men were not: EYU was much more prevalent amongst young women than young men. In Latin America and the Caribbean, more young women experienced unemployment than young men in almost every year at the 15 per cent rate, and in more than one in three years at the 20 per cent rate. In Eastern Europe and in Central and Western Asia, young women were unemployed slightly more often than young men, year for year at the 15 per cent and 20 per cent rates. Differences in Southern Asia, Northern, Southern and Western Europe and Northern America were small or inverted.[20]

By some measure, the greatest extremes of young women's exposure to rates of YU at or above 15 per cent have occurred in the Arab states, Northern Africa, and Latin America and the Caribbean over the last three decades. Some persistent elevated rates and frequencies of exposure also continue in Eastern Europe and Central and Western Asia (in the latter case including in the last ten years). In the other six world-regions, at aggregate level, differences are diminutive and, more recently, mostly inverted, with young men being more likely to have been unemployed.

In all, the changing global profile of gender differences in the labour force and labour market has been substantial and largely continuous since 1991. Recalling Figure 5.6, the stronger proportionate male presence in the labour force over the female presence has been sustained over three decades. The continuous decline in young women's and young men's presence in the labour force and the corresponding gender-differentiated increase in the proportion of all young people not in the labour force has been extreme and remarkable. Young women are at unequivocal disadvantages with regard to being available for employment and gaining employment, compared to young men, when viewed globally and in five of the 11 world-regions, irrespective of the decline in labour force participation rates for both sexes. While the extreme YU rate differences between them give major cause for concern, in terms of the principles of gender equality specified in SDG 5, across the board in most of the Arab states and Northern Africa, and in much of Latin America and the Caribbean (but also in Eastern Europe and Central and Western Asia), the trend towards parity has been slow, faltering and incomplete. Even in the other world-regions in which parity has appeared to stabilise or has been inverted in favour of young women workers, the high level of aggregation in world-regional groupings conceals great diversity in rates of progress towards equality. Underlying all this, perhaps the greatest cause for concern is the almost unerring 17-percentage-point gap over three decades between young women's declining presence in the labour force and the increasing numbers of them who were not in the labour force, compared to the trends for young men.

---

[20]   In the other three of the 11 world-regions (not included in Table 5.4), mean YU rates were consistently below 15 per cent for 1991–2019 and comparable differences between male and female rates were absent or inverted. Thus, in South-eastern Asia and the Pacific, rates ranged between 6 per cent and 13 per cent and were almost equal for males and females in all years. In sub-Saharan Africa, male and female YU rates ranged between 8 per cent and 11 per cent and were again equal in almost all years. In Eastern Asia, average YU ranged between 4 per cent and 11 per cent, and young men had consistently higher YU rates than young women in all years.

5.5 YOUTH UNEMPLOYMENT ACROSS COUNTRY INCOME GROUPS

Differentiating distributions of the extremes of YU geographically and by gender highlights major differences and inequalities. It would also be reasonable to infer that the economic status of countries would be associated with differences in extremes of YU worldwide. The standard reference point for differentiating between countries economically is the WB's country classificatory system. This classifies 218 countries on the basis of each country's gross national income (GNI) per person into four country income groups (CIGs): low (also sometimes labelled 'developing' countries), lower-middle, upper-middle, and high (also sometimes labelled 'developed' countries). Table 5.5 (p. 101, below) provides multiple detailed descriptors of each group.

We draw attention to some key aspects of these data. First, there are huge differences in income across CIGs (Columns 2 and 3). LICs exhibit a very narrow $2 range of mean daily incomes and LMICs and UMICs also exhibit modest ranges of $8 and $22, respectively. HICs cover a very wide range ($258). Mean daily GNI in HICs is 129 times greater than in LICs: at the greatest extreme there is an approximate 600-fold difference in GNI between Bermuda (US$415 per person per day) and Burundi (US$0.7 per person per day). Second, the total youth labour forces (15–24-year-olds 'in' and 'not in' the labour force) of the CIGs are very variable in size (Column 5): the youth population of LMICs (555 million) is almost four times that of HICs (141 million). The two middle-income groups account for three-quarters of the world's young workers and LMICs have by far the largest mean youth populations (Columns 6 and 7). Third, the ten birth-cohorts that span the 15–24-year-old age group represent very different proportions of the total adult labour force aged 25 years and above as between the four CIGs. Thus, on average, in LICs there are half as many young workers as adult workers (ratio 0.5:1), whereas UMICs and HICs there is only one young member of the total labour force for every five adult members (ratio 0.2:1) (Column 8). Fourth, as a consequence, it might reasonably be expected that the youth labour force in LICs (and in LMICs) face much higher risks of unemployment (including when competing with adult workers) compared to their counterparts in wealthier countries (UMICs and HICs). But Figure 5.8 shows that this is not so.

On first sight, the most counterintuitive observation is that, although the size of the youth labour force of LICs is half that of the adult labour force (a very much higher youth-to-adult ratio than for the other country income groups), YU rates in LICs are by far the lowest of the four groups and the least variable over three decades (compare Columns 7 and 8 of Table 5.5 and developing countries in Figure 5.8). But as Section 5.3.5 on labour force participation and data quality argued, this is in part because the ILO modelled data for many, if not most, of the countries in the LIC group are not the product of reliable source data. This is in part because of poor or absent local data infrastructure and other obstacles identified by Jerven (2013) in his analysis of data-sourcing problems in LICs in sub-Saharan Africa; and in part because of the differing meanings and statuses of the ILO category 'contributing family workers', who may be at least nominally 'in the labour force' *or outside it* as hidden and invisible workers in the informal economy.[21]

---

[21]   Of 25 African LICs, the YU profiles of all but four for 1991–2019 are modelled, in the absence of nationally reported data. Nineteen of these countries show YU rates that change very little each year, *all* of which are in the implausibly low range of 1–8 per cent. Sub-Saharan Africa accounts for 25 of the

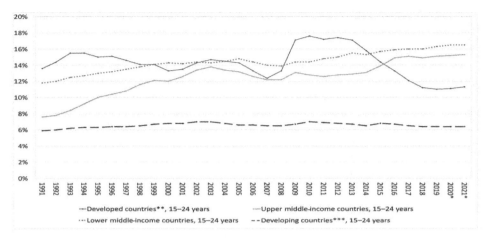

—Developed countries**, 15–24 years   —Upper middle-income countries, 15–24 years

··· Lower middle-income countries, 15–24 years   – – Developing countries***, 15–24 years

Notes:
* Indicates projected data; ** Also known as high-income countries (HICs); *** Also known as low-income countries (LICs).
Source: ILOSTAT, WESO Data Finder, 2020, accessed 12 January 2020.

Figure 5.8   Unemployment rates by country income group, 15–24-year-olds, 1991–2019

The other counterintuitive observation that becomes evident when juxtaposing these two sources of data is that 'developed' rich economies (the HICs) have exhibited by far the most volatile YU profiles over the last three decades. This volatility appears to follow global economic cycles, in the face of which HICs have ostensibly lacked resilience – at least in terms of protecting the livelihoods of young workers. Just like LMICs, HICs experienced ten years of YU rates in HICs at and above 15 per cent since 1991 (Table 5.5, Column 9) – marking them as exhibiting EYU. The rising YU rate to 1993 (Figure 5.8) coincided with the early 1990s' recession that affected most of the major anglophone economies of the Global North (a significant element of the HIC group). The huge leap in YU rates in HICs in 2007 which continued until 2013 coincided with the GFC. This relationship between changes in economic strength and patterns of YU growth and contraction is the principal focus of further exploration in Chapter 6.

There is less dissonance between the data in Table 5.5 and Figure 5.8 with regard to the other two country income groups. They have much in common. LMICs and UMICs have experienced strong underlying increases in YU rates since 1991. UMICs have experienced by far the greatest increase, doubling to 15 per cent by 2019. LMICs have maintained the highest YU rates of all four groups throughout this period (apart from the HICs in 2009–14), peaking at 16 per cent in 2019. As home to more than half a billion 15–24-year-olds, LMICs, as we noted, account for almost half of young people in the global labour force (an average of 12 million per country (Column 7)). Young people make up a very substantially larger proportion of the global labour force in LMICs than they do in UMICs and HICs (Column 6). LMICs

WB's 32 LICs. Between 2000 and 2010, ILOStat data suggests that about half of these countries began to return reliable annual YU data.

Table 5.5 Country income groups, 15–24-year-olds in labour force by GNI per person; size of youth labour force; youth–adult ratio of labour force; mean years of YU at 15%+ (2020)

Country income group	1 Number of countries in this group[a]	2 Mean daily GNI per person (US$)[b]	3 Min. & max. mean daily GNI per person (US$)[c]	4 Range (max. minus min.) (US$)	5 15–24-year-olds in in- and not-in labour force	6 15–24-year-olds as a proportion of global youth labour force (%)	7 Mean size of total labour force aged 15–24 per country (millions)	8 Ratio of young people to adults in labour force[e]	9 Years in which YU rate is at/above 15%* (1991–2019)
Low-income (LICs)[f]	32	Less than 2.7	0.7–2.7	2	146	12	5	0.5:1	0
Lower middle-income (LMICs)	47	2.7–10.7	2.7–10.7	8	555	46	12	0.3:1	10
Upper middle-income (UMICs)	60	10.7–33.0	10.7–33.0	22	363	30	6	0.2:1	4
High-income (HICs)[g]	79	More than 33.0	33.0–415.0	258	141	12	2	0.2:1	10

Notes:

[a] Country income group classification is revised annually by the WB in line with enduring changes in countries' GNI per person. Data from https://datahelpdesk .worldbank.org/knowledgebase/articles/906519-world-bank-country-and-lending-groups (accessed 1–28 February 2020).

[b] Data derived from WB data annual GNI per person for 2018–19 (divided by 365 to give daily income). See https://blogs.worldbank.org/opendata/new-country -classifications-income-level-2018-2019 (accessed 23 August 2020).

[c] Derived from data for 2013 (the most recent year for which the fullest range of country data are available). See https://data.worldbank.org/indicator/NY.GNP.PCAP.CD ?name_desc=false (accessed 23 August 2020).

[d] Data derived from ILO WESODATA, as the sum of all 15–24-year-olds in 2019 who were in the labour force and all who were not. See https://www.ilo.org/wesodata (accessed 23 August 2020).

[e] Data derived from ILO WESODATA: total 15–24-year-olds who were in workforce (active and inactive labour force) divided by the total aged 25 years and above in 2019 who were in workforce. See https://www.ilo.org/wesodata (accessed 23 August 2020).

[f] Low-income countries are also referred to as developing countries in Figure 5.8 below and subsequently

[g] High-income countries are also referred to as developed countries in Figure 5.8 below and subsequently.

Sources: Complied by the authors from WB and ILO WESODATA databases (see notes a–e).

have experienced ten years of EYU (Column 9). And yet the trajectory of YU in UMICs is currently on a par with that of LMICs (Figure 5.8). It is also possible that many if not most 'developing' (low-income) countries would show comparably high rates of YU if their surveys of youth labour in the formal versus informal sectors of economies (and their data-gathering capacity) were the equal of other country groups. Whether or not this is so, the only CIG that has *sometimes* been immune to a constant upward trajectory of YU over the last three decades is the high-income group. In short, relative poverty and rising YU rates tend to be associated, and relative affluence tends to provide some protection against them, viewed over the long run.

5.6   SUMMARY AND CONCLUSIONS

This chapter has extended previous chapters' mapping of key historical and contemporary manifestations of YU and the political, economic and social processes that give rise to them. Our principal focus has been on patterns of synchronicity between major disruptions in global financial systems, and trends and changes in the trajectories of YU at global, world-regional, and selected national levels. This focus has maintained particular attention to EYU, building on its introduction in Chapter 1 and operationalising it in this chapter in order to concentrate attention on those regions and income-based country groupings that have experienced the greater extremes of YU.

We have identified a great many instances of YU that have been endemic, according to our criteria, although our selection is by no means exhaustive. Building on Chapter 3, we have also indicated the growing aggregate size of reserve pools of youth labour along steady upward trajectories for most of the last 30 years, at scales that should give significant cause for concern if based on YU rates alone. The growing reserve pools should also give cause for alarm if we include the huge proportions of the 15–24-year-old age group designated as 'not in the labour force' and hidden or invisible, especially in and beyond LICs whose means of meeting standard international data-gathering protocols and procedures are substantially impaired. Significant fractions of young people in LICs, and of those who are recorded as not in the labour force, would undoubtedly value decent work with fair remuneration as specified in the SDGs, or indeed any form of quality employment that took them out of the GRAoYL and into the formal economy.

These mappings have demonstrated strong patterns of association between multiple varia- bles in worldwide and sub-global levels of YU. In the context of the GFC, in particular, the association between specific periods of economic decline and rising rates of YU has been so clearly synchronous as to refute any reasonable doubt that the sudden collapse of financial stability in many economies has been associated with major decline or partial collapse of some youth labour markets, locally, nationally and regionally. In other contexts, while the coincidental decline in some economies and the capacity of labour markets to absorb would-be young workers have been clearly evident, some regional and national economies and labour markets have been notably less adversely affected than others. In yet other contexts, the associ- ation is too weak to deduce that a slump in YU has been the sole or primary result of financial or economic disruption at whatever level. Understanding whether and how economic condi- tions might be related to underlying YU trends over the last three decades requires statistical modelling and analyses. This is the subject of Chapter 6.

APPENDIX 5.1   THE ILO'S AND BELLAMY-FOSTER ET AL.'S CATEGORIES OF LABOUR FORCE PARTICIPATION

Chapter 3 introduced Bellamy-Foster et al.'s (2011) classification of the size and composition of the global workforce. Their definition of the active labour force consists of wage workers and the global reserve army which comprises the vulnerably employed, the unemployed and the economically inactive population. The reserve army is an expansive category, in that it includes people who are employed but not in secure waged work. Bellamy Foster et al.'s data are derived from ILO data and re-classified according to these three new categories that comprise their global army reserve.

The principal categories used by ILOStat (ILO's major statistical portal concerning all aspects of employment) differ somewhat from those used in Bellamy-Foster et al.'s classification.[22] ILOStat uses the active labour force, consisting of the employed and the unemployed, and those 'not in the labour force' – that is, not including the economically inactive population. The relevant verbatim ILO definitions are as follows:

- The **labour force** comprises all persons of working age who furnish the supply of labour for the production of goods and services during a specified time-reference period. It refers to the sum of all persons of working age who are employed and those who are unemployed.
- **Persons in unemployment** are defined as all those of working age who were not in employment, carried out activities to seek employment during a specified recent period and were currently available to take up employment given a job opportunity.
- **Persons outside the labour force** comprise all persons of working age who, during the specified reference period, were not in the labour force (that is, were not employed or unemployed). The working-age population is commonly defined as persons aged 15 years and older, but this varies from country to country. In addition to using a minimum age threshold, certain countries also apply a maximum age limit.[23,24]

In summary terms, Bellamy Foster et al.'s four classifications, described in detail in Chapter 3, are:

- **Economically active population**: wage workers *and* unemployed;
- **Vulnerably employed**: a residual category of the economically active population, who work but are not waged workers, comprising 'own account workers' and 'contributing family workers' (described as 'in practice, underemployed');
- **Unemployed**: available and actively looking for a job in recent weeks (a sub-group of the economically active population);
- **Economically inactive**: those who are not economically active, i.e. are not wage workers *and* who are not classified as unemployed (described as 'would-be workers').

---

[22] See https://ilostat.ilo.org/data/.

[23] See https://www.ilo.org/wesodata/definitions-and-metadata.

[24] 'Persons outside the labour force' are also described elsewhere by the ILO as 'not in the labour force'.

The equivalence and difference between the two classifications can be summarised and mapped, as shown in Table 5A.1.

Table 5A.1   ILO and Bellamy-Foster et al. classifications compared

ILO	Bellamy-Foster et al.	Equivalence	Comment
Labour force ('in labour force') (includes ILO's 'own account workers' and 'contributing family workers')	**Wage workers**	Not equivalent	ILO's category includes groups not included by Bellamy-Foster et al.
Persons in unemployment	**Unemployed***	Equivalent	Actively seeking work and available to accept a job
[No equivalent]	**Vulnerably employed*** (includes 'own account workers' and 'contributing family workers' from ILO's classification)	Not equivalent	An additional 'underemployed' category, separated out from ILO's 'Labour force'
Persons outside the labour force ('not in labour force')	**Economically inactive*** ('would-be workers')	Equivalent	

Note: * These three categories combine to constitute Bellamy-Foster et al.'s global reserve army (GRA).
Source: The authors.

6. Youth unemployment, economic crises and human development, 1991–2018

with Sarah Tipping

6.1 INTRODUCTION

This chapter explores further the observed associations in Chapter 5 between national and transnational economic cycles and rising rates of youth unemployment (YU), the degrees of variability in that association across economies and labour markets, and the ostensible absence of an association in others. It focuses on the extent and nature of the association between changes in rates of YU and changes in rates of economic growth and contraction over extended time periods, and tests the degree to which combinations of other development factors (notably educational provision and health) might be associated with trajectories of YU worldwide.

We analyse the relationship between YU and these economic and social variables, using standard tests of statistical significance to address some key points of interest. Central to our analysis is to establish the extent to which fluctuating YU rates are associated with economic change, and differences in the extent to which unemployment affects young people and adults. Our second interest is in whether and how any such association altered during the global financial crisis (GFC). Our third interest is in whether changes in YU rates are associated with changes to welfare systems, as indicated by health and in educational provision.

In pursuit of these points of interest, our datasets enable us to consider the extent to which differing patterns of association are visible across distinctive groups of nations, according to their relative mean wealth and poverty, as classified by the World Bank's (WB) four country income groups (CIGs). Specifically, we constructed two new bespoke datasets that were capable of revealing the relationship between YU and economic and social changes at country level using internationally available data that spans almost three decades to 2018. The datasets combine: ILO unemployment data for 15–24-year-olds and 25–54-year-olds for all countries and all years for which reliable data are available; WB data on national gross domestic product (GDP) for economic variables across 74 countries; and the United Nations Development Programme's (UNDP's) Human Development Index (HDI) based on life expectancy at birth, expected and actual years of schooling, and gross national income (GNI) per person across 73 countries. Our datasets have greatly extended the scope of existing analyses of the relationship between unemployment and other variables. They also extend the geographical reach of analyses, which have hitherto been heavily dominated by high-income countries (almost exclusively OECD and EU), to include lower-income country groups.[1]

Our analysis builds on, tests, and greatly extends some observations from Chapter 5. Of particular relevance are that: financial crises have been associated with rising YU rates for several decades before the GFC; YU rates are more susceptible to crisis conditions than adult unemployment rates (aged 25 and above); declining GDP is the most powerful driver of increasing YU (alongside the crisis conditions themselves); Okun's Law regarding the relationship between declining GDP rates and increasing YU rates appears to be as relevant to youth as to adult unemployment; and unemployment crises continue beyond peak financial and economic crisis conditions, and are typically longer-lasting for young people than adults. Chapter 5 concluded by noting that for some countries, the effects of the GFC on YU have been so great as to leave little doubt that it was in part causal. In other countries, youth labour markets appeared to be less adversely affected, while in yet others the association between the two is too weak to claim any connection between them. It was not possible to generalise about the common characteristics of these different groups of countries with any confidence. These limitations are inherent in the data on which Chapter 5 drew. In recognition, in what follows in this chapter, our methodology allows us to test the significance of the trends to provide a quite different interpretation of the relationship between YU and economic status at country and CIG levels (wherever adequate data were available) than has hitherto been possible.

We approach our analysis from three perspectives, organised into three substantive sections. In Section 6.2 we review a set of studies that have tested the relationship between YU and economic trends at country level. These studies establish the validity of Okun's Law for the 15–24-year-old age group in relation to the effects of the GFC on YU. In Section 6.3 we present the results of our own analysis of the relationship between changes in GDP and changes in YU between 1991 and 2018 at country income group levels. We also differentiate between the pre-GFC and GFC periods in order to test the GFC's effects on YU.[2] Section 6.4 presents our analysis of a second global dataset that facilitates interpretation of the relationship between YU rates and social change (education and health) indicators as well as economic ones. Section 6.5 discusses the findings, and draws conclusions.

6.2   GDP GROWTH AND YOUTH UNEMPLOYMENT: OKUN'S LAW

Chapter 5 introduced 'Okun's Law'. This law identifies a strong association between changes in unemployment rates and changes in national economic output (Okun, 1962). Initially analysed using Gross National Product (GNP), Arthur Okun's pioneering study identified patterns of association that are now widely accepted and tested. Okun's Law has been succinctly described as follows:

> ... the rate of unemployment can be expected to drop (rise) by one-third of 1 percent for each positive (negative) 1 percent by which actual GNP exceeds potential GNP. ... Some Keynesian economists

---

[1]   See Appendices 6.1–6.4 for detailed information on all data used and their sources.

[2]   We identify the pre-GFC period as before 2009. We do not speak of a post-GFC period since the extreme effects of the GFC ended at different times in different countries. See Chapter 1 Section 1.7 for further discussion of this point.

have suggested that Okun's Law continues to hold, though at a 2 to 1, rather than a 3 to 1 ratio. (Hobbs, 2013: n.p.)

Most recently, Okun's Law has generated particular interest in the effects of the GFC internationally, especially in relation to YU. In what follows we briefly review 14 studies that test and refine Okun's Law, covering up to 35 years of data for periods ending between 2011 and 2015 across four continents, with an emphasis on Europe and Africa. They indicate a largely consistent, stable and generally strong relationship between changing rates of GDP growth and changes in YU rates at country level. Summarily, as GDP grows year-on-year, there is a corresponding decline in YU rates. Inversely, when GDP growth declines, YU rates increase. The most comprehensive study finds that approximately half of the increase in YU rates following the GFC can be attributed to changes in GDP. Where age differences were analysed, the greatest difference was between the greater sensitivity of 15–24-year-olds to changes in GDP growth compared with the lesser sensitivity of 25–34-year-olds. Differences between 35–64-year-olds were comparatively (very) small. Where estimates are provided, the effects of GDP change on YU rates for the youngest age group are between two and three times as great as for other age groups. In general, the most marked changes in GDP rates and in corresponding YU rates occurred after the onset of the GFC.

6.2.1 The Youth Unemployment–GDP Relationship: the EU and OECD

We summarise the key findings of studies that seek to interpret the relationship between GDP growth and change in YU rates. Most of the following analyses focus on Europe and include the years after the onset of the Eurozone crisis (EzC). The earliest was Hutengs and Stadtmann's (2013) analysis of five age-cohorts from 11 Eurozone countries for 1983–2011. They conclude that 'the relationship between business cycle fluctuations and the unemployment rate is the strongest for the youngest members of the labour force' (pp. 821–3). They also note that although the relationship between changes in GDP and YU rates differs greatly between countries, the association proposed by Okun's Law remains valid across the countries analysed.[3] In Germany, for example, there was little variation between age groups, while in Spain there were major variations. On average, 15–24-year-olds were most affected by downturns in the business cycle. Hutengs and Stadtmann's (2014) subsequent study analysed age- and gender-differentiated unemployment in relation to GDP in the five Scandinavian countries and the aggregated EU15 countries for 1984–2011. Rising YU rates in response to declining GDP were much greater for 15–24-year-olds than for all other age groups, and at the highest levels of statistical significance.

Zanin (2014) analysed 14 cohorts in five age groupings between 1998 and 2012 across the 32 OECD member countries. His general findings are, with exceptions, supportive of 'a significant inverse relationship between changes in unemployment rates and economic growth' (p. 244). Without exception 'the youngest cohort … are [sic] more sensitive to business cycle fluctuations than [other cohorts]' (p. 247). Banerji et al.'s (2015) study for the International Monetary Fund (IMF) is uniquely extensive, covering as it does 22 European countries,

---

[3] Note that changes in GDP are often referred to in the literature in terms of changes in the 'business cycle'.

most for the period 1980–2012. The analysis unambiguously validates Okun's Law, which 'explains' about 50 per cent of the increases in YU rates including during the GFC (pp. 15–18).

Marconi et al. (2016) focused on the EU28 countries (plus Iceland and Norway) for 2002–14, and marked an important difference between the YU rate and ratio. This recognises ambiguities in young people's employment statuses: exclusion from unemployment data because of short-time working, traineeships or part-time study, however brief or infrequent, 'dramatically affects the unemployment rate by reducing the size of the labour force' (Marconi et al., 2016: 580). Fifteen- to nineteen-year-olds were significantly more adversely affected by negative economic growth compared to adults (aged 25–64), but were sufficiently less adversely affected if the analysis was based on the YU ratio. The outcomes for 20–24-year-olds using the YU rate and the ratio were very similar, and were approximately twice as adversely affected by declining GDP as adults aged 25–64. More generally, the study demonstrates the methodological limitations of ignoring underemployment.

Dunsch's (2016) study is confined to Germany and Poland plus aggregated data for 15 EU countries for 1992–2014, including the GFC and EzC periods. Once again, for the EU15 countries this study finds that 15–24-year-olds were most adversely affected, although these results were not replicated in Germany or Poland. This signals caution about the risks of over-generalisation of the universality of Okun's Law, and over-simplified applications of it. This observation is also pertinent to our findings in Section 6.3. Dunsch's (2017) subsequent study focused on similar age groupings in ten Central and Eastern European countries (including comparison with the EU15), for periods varying between 1993–2015 and 2001–15. Once again she finds that the 'youngest cohort (15–24-year-olds) … regardless of gender, are the ones most affected by business cycle fluctuations' (p. 391).

Dixon et al.'s (2017) study covers 20 OECD countries between 1985 and 2013. It refines analysis by taking into account institutional labour market factors and labour market flexibility – particularly cognisant of the high proportions of young workers in temporary employment. Their key finding with regard to age is that 'when [the rate of productive] output changes, the effect on unemployment rates is more than twice as large for young workers [as] it is for older workers' (p. 2760).

6.2.2   The Youth Unemployment–GDP Relationship: Africa, Asia and Latin America

The findings of a number of other multi-country studies correspond with those reported above. Bölükbaş' (2018) inter-continental study of 20 emerging economies (mostly upper middle-income countries (UMICs)) between 1991 and 2016) examines the relationship between YU, economic growth and inflation, and finds that both inflation and negative GDP growth substantially increase youth unemployment. Two major studies that include Africa further extend the study's coverage. Ebaidalla (2016) confirms the validity of Okun's Law for the 32 member states of the Organisation of Islamic Cooperation (mostly Middle Eastern and African states) for the period 1993–2012. Inverting the norm of these studies by focusing on rising GDP growth rates and declining YU rates, Abé Ndjié et al. (2019) find a strong and highly significant relationship across 29 African countries between 2009 and 2016.

In striking contrast, however, three other Africa studies bring the predominant evidence of Okun's Law into question. Ihensekhien and Asekome (2017) analysed panel data for 1991 to 2013 in 23 low-income countries (LICs) in sub-Saharan Africa (SSA). In 18 countries economic growth over time was not related to declining YU rates. Prince et al.'s (2018) study of YU in Egypt, Morocco, Jordan and Tunisia found that from the early to mid-2000s to 2014, as GDP growth increased sharply, labour force participation rates amongst 15–24-year-olds plummeted, levelling off from about 2010, but not recovering. Ihensekhien and Aisien's (2019) later study analysed the YU–GDP relationship in Botswana, Equatorial Guinea, Gabon, Namibia, Mauritius and South Africa for 1991–2017, concluding that Okun's Law is not sustained by their findings.

These three studies, and Dunsch's (2016) study with regard to Germany and Poland, bring into question the universality of Okun's original proposition. Unsurprisingly, the other EU/OECD studies summarised above also found significant variations in results while continuing to confirm Okun's Law. As detailed readings of these studies show, differences in labour market institutions, structures and policies appear to explain many of the variations between countries, in the depth and nature of the relationships between changes in GDP growth and change in YU rates. The notable difference between the results of studies of first-world countries and others summarised in this small sample suggests that Okun's Law is most pertinent in high-income countries (HICs). The impacts of economic crises on the structures and distribution of paid employment for young people vary greatly in ways that are not represented in the studies summarised here. As the following findings reported in Section 6.3 indicate, significant variations occur between countries, and within and between CIGs, including in the periods before and after the onset of the GFC.

6.3   THE RELATIONSHIP BETWEEN YOUTH UNEMPLOYMENT AND GDP

In this section we outline the results of our analysis of the relationship between changes in GDP and changes in YU between 1991 and 2018 at country and CIG levels. We differentiate between the pre-GFC and GFC periods in order to test the effects of international financial and economic crisis on YU.

6.3.1   The Relationship between Unemployment and GDP Growth

Our dataset combined annual GDP growth and unemployment rates for two cohorts, aged 15–24 years and 25–54 years. The dataset runs from 1991 to 2018, although some countries have missing data. It contains 74 countries in total; 42 high-income, 19 upper middle-income, and 13 lower middle-income countries.[4] No low-income countries were included in the dataset owing to severe data limitations. More information about the data sources used in the analysis is provided in Appendix 6.1.

Figure 6.1 shows year-on-year changes in national unemployment rates plotted alongside annual GDP growth for the period 1991–2018. The two trends are 'in sync': increases in unemployment tend to coincide with decreases in GDP growth, whilst decreases in unemployment tend to accompany increases in GDP growth. Separate lines show changes in YU and in unemployment amongst older people (aged 25–54 years). Whilst the overall trends for the two age groups are very similar, the younger age group experiences sharper spikes and drops

---

[4]   See Table 5.5 for CIG definitions.

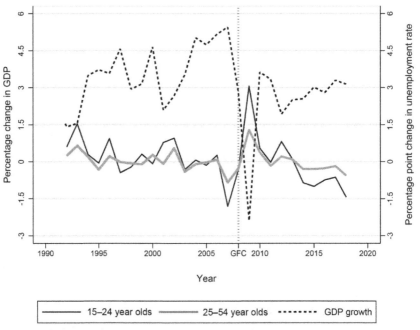

Note: the dataset from which Figure 6.1 is drawn begins in 1991 and records annual changes from then until 2018. Thus the first year for which the change is recorded is 1992.
Sources: Annual national unemployment rates (International Labour Organization); GDP growth data (annual %) (World Bank, national accounts data); OECD (national accounts data).

Figure 6.1   *GDP growth and change in unemployment rate, aged 15–24 and 25–54 years, 1991–2018*

in the trend line, indicating that unemployment rates generally increase and decrease more frequently, and more rapidly, for this age group than for the older one. The trend line for older people is less volatile by comparison.

A vertical dash line indicating the 2008 GFC is marked on the x axis of the illustration. There are differences in the relationship between unemployment and GDP growth before and after this point, which occur in both age groups. Before this point, there are fluctuations in GDP followed by a period of growth through the 2000s. This growth is accompanied by drops in unemployment. Shortly after 2008 there is a sharp drop in GDP growth, which coincides with a steep increase in unemployment, particularly amongst younger people. Post-2008, unemployment rates for young people increase on average by three percentage points, whereas unemployment rates for the older age group increase by one percentage point.[5] Our finding of a marked impact of the GFC on YU means we treat the two time periods separately throughout the rest of the chapter when analysing the relationship between GDP growth and unemployment.

In addition, the relationship between unemployment and GDP growth differs by CIG. Figures 6.2a and 6.2b show yearly changes in YU and annual GDP growth split by CIG for the

---

[5]   See Chapter 1 for a full explanation of this specification of the two time periods.

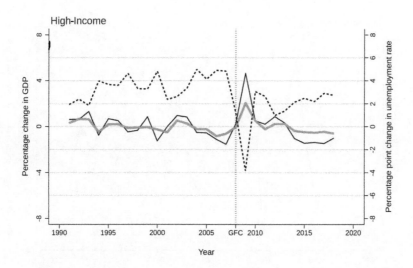

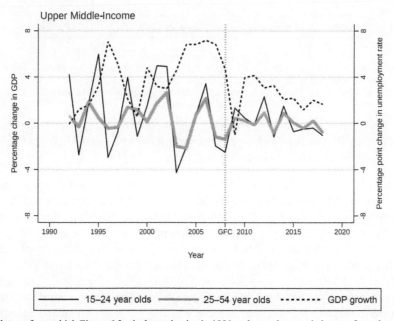

Note: the dataset from which Figure 6.2a is drawn begins in 1991 and records annual changes from then until 2018. Thus the first year for which the change is recorded is 1992.
Sources: Annual national unemployment rates (International Labour Organization); GDP growth data (annual %) (World Bank, national accounts data); OECD (national accounts data).

Figure 6.2a   GDP growth and change in unemployment rate, aged 15–24 and 25–54 years, by country income group, 1991–2018 [A]

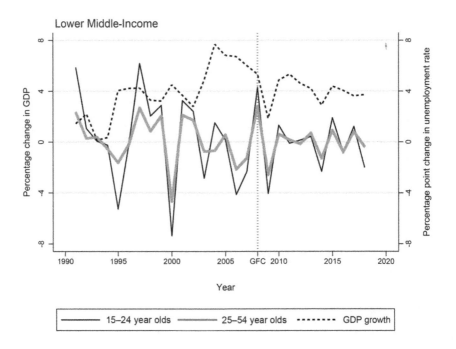

Lower Middle-Income

Note: the dataset from which Figure 6.2b is drawn begins in 1991 and records annual changes from then until 2018. Thus the first year for which the change is recorded is 1992.
Sources: Annual national unemployment rates (International Labour Organization); GDP growth data (annual %) (World Bank, national accounts data); OECD (national accounts data).

Figure 6.2b   *GDP growth and change in unemployment rate, aged 15–24 and 25–54 years, by country income group, 1991–2018 [B]*

period 1991–2018. For the HICs, the relationship between GDP growth and unemployment changes over time. Pre-2009 unemployment rates are generally stable, with a number of small peaks that reflect periods where GDP growth drops. However, after 2008 there is a large drop in GDP growth accompanied by a large rise in unemployment that amounts to an average increase in unemployment rates of nearly five percentage points for young people, compared to around two percentage points for older people. This reflects the extremes of YU in 2010 (see Figure 5.8).

A different pattern is seen for UMICs (Figure 6.2a). The larger number of peaks and troughs in the illustration suggest there is more volatility in GDP growth and unemployment for UMICs in both age groups. Prior to 2009, GDP growth had a loose relationship with changes in unemployment; drops in GDP growth are generally, but not always, accompanied by increases in unemployment. Post-2008, the pattern that we see amongst HICs is also visible amongst the UMICs, but in a less exaggerated form. Here, a dip in GDP growth is accompanied by a more moderate spike in unemployment, although the spike is again larger for young people than for the older cohort. This pattern corresponds to aggregate YU rates well below the rates for HICs and lower middle-income countries (LMICs), post-2008 (see Figure 5.8).

There is notably less evidence of a relationship between GDP growth and changes in unemployment amongst the LMICs (Figure 6.2b); the year-on-year changes in unemployment rates for both younger and older individuals appear unrelated to fluctuations in GDP growth. Post-2008 there are indications that unemployment in both age groups tends to *decline* when GDP declines, contrary to trends in HICs and UMICs. In contrast, recall from Chapter 5 that Figure 5.8 showed the overall YU average for *all* LMICs (many more countries than were included in our GDP–YU analysis) has been rising steadily since 2008, to become the highest for all CIGs since 2012. In addition, as Figure 6.2a shows, both GDP growth and the unemployment trends for both age groups follow each other very closely in the period immediately after the GFC, declining and rising again in unison before reverting to their erratic relationship from 2010 onwards.

6.3.2   Modelling the Relationship between Unemployment and GDP Growth

The relationship between unemployment and GDP growth, the central premise of Okun's Law, was formally tested using a set of statistical models. Such models summarise the relationship between unemployment and GDP growth mathematically. This allows us to quantify the change in unemployment rate associated with a percentage point change in GDP. The dataset described above was used to run a set of models to test the application of Okun's Law to different countries and CIGs. To recap, Okun's Law states that

the rate of unemployment can be expected to drop (rise) by one-third of 1 percent for each positive (negative) 1 percent by which actual GNP exceeds potential GNP. (Hobbs, 2013: n.p.)[6]

Different versions of Okun's Law exist.[7] The analysis we present here focuses on the 'difference' version of Okun's Law, which measures the relationship between growth, measured using GDP, and changes in the unemployment rate.[8]

The first step in our analysis was to explore the relationship between GDP growth and unemployment for the period after the onset of the GFC (2009 onwards), since the data for this

---

[6]   GNP is a different measure of a country's economic output as measured by GDP (see footnote 8).

[7]   Okun posited different versions of the law, each summarising different empirical relationships between unemployment and growth. The *difference* version focuses on how changes in the unemployment rate are related to growth (now GDP growth). It can be written as an equation, allowing quantification and formal testing of the relationship between growth and unemployment using statistical tests (see Appendix 6.2). The equation includes a coefficient ('Okun's coefficient'), which summarises the scale and direction of the relationship between change in unemployment rates and GDP growth. The value of this coefficient is estimated using a statistical model. The *gap* version measures the relationship between deviations in the unemployment rate and deviations from potential growth. The latter can be more problematic to estimate, since potential growth can be difficult to define and measure (see Okun, 1962; Chamberlain, 2011).

[8]   Okun's original work focused on GNP, rather than GDP. Both are measures of the national output and income of an economy; however, GNP includes net income produced by residents of the country who are based abroad. GDP specifically measures the income of the national economy, i.e. the total value of goods and services produced within a country's borders (Chamberlain, 2011). This makes GDP correspond more closely to the definitions for unemployment within a nation.

time period are more complete.We compare the pre-2009 and post-2008 periods in Sections 6.3.3 and 6.3.4.

We estimated Okun's coefficient for 74 countries for which we had data on GDP growth and unemployment for the period 2009–2018.[9] This coefficient summarises the scale and direction of the relationship between change in unemployment rates and changes in GDP (Appendix 6.2). For each country, we estimated two sets of Okun's coefficients: one that summarises the relationship between GDP growth and changes in the unemployment rate for young people (aged 15–24 years), and a second that summarises the same relationship for people aged 25–54 years. We used these estimated coefficients to test whether there was evidence for Okun's Law, that is, whether this relationship exists for different countries, and whether it exists for both younger and older workers.

The full output for the analysis is presented in Appendix 6.2. These coefficients show what percentage point change in unemployment rate is associated with a percentage point change in GDP growth, year-on-year for each country. The coefficient also indicates whether the relationship is positive or negative.[10] We expect the coefficients to be negative, since negative GDP growth is expected to be associated with an increase in unemployment. A coefficient of −0.25, for example, indicates that a percentage point increase in GDP growth would correspond to a 0.25 percentage point *reduction* in the unemployment rate. A larger coefficient indicates that a percentage point change in GDP growth would be associated with a larger change in unemployment. Large coefficients therefore indicate a stronger relationship between GDP growth and unemployment, suggesting that unemployment rates in those countries are more susceptible to changes in GDP.

For the proportional increases described by Okun between GDP growth and unemployment to be evident (i.e. for a percentage increase in growth to coincide with a decrease of one-third of a percentage point in unemployment rates), Okun's coefficients would need to be in the realm of −0.33. As quoted above, Hobbs (2013) notes that 'some Keynesian economists have suggested that Okun's Law continues to hold, though at a 2 to 1, rather than a 3 to 1 ratio'. For this updated proportionality to hold, Okun's coefficients would need to be around −0.5.

Table 6.1 shows the mean values of model coefficients by age and CIG that are presented in Appendix 6.2. These summary statistics enable trends to be identified across CIGs.

The data in Table 6.1 confirms Okun's Law. The mean coefficients provide evidence of a negative relationship between GDP growth and unemployment that holds for both age groups and all CIGs, as stated by Okun's Law; as GDP growth increases, unemployment falls.

For each of the three CIGs the mean coefficients for the younger age group are larger, generally more than twice the size of those for older people (ranging from 2.4 times the size of the coefficients for the older age group in HICs to 2.2 times the coefficient for the older age group in LMICs). This indicates YU has a stronger relationship with GDP growth than unemploy-

---

[9]   A separate model was used to estimate the value of Okun's coefficient for each country. The models were fitted using Ordinary Least Squares regression.

[10]   Two measures have a positive relationship if they move in the same direction; A and B have a positive relationship if the value of A increases as the value of B increases; similarly, the relationship is positive if the value of A decreases when the value of B decreases. In either of these situations the relationship is positive, regardless of inferred causality. A relationship is negative if the reverse happens and the two measures move in opposite directions; value A decreases as value B increases, or value A increases as value B decreases, again, regardless of inferred causality.

Table 6.1   Summary statistics of Okun's coefficients for post-2008 models, by country income group and age, 2009–2018

| Country Income Group | 2009–18 | | Proportional difference in mean coefficients 15–24 vs. 25–54* |
	15–24 years	25–54 years	
High income			
Mean coefficient	−0.747	−0.312	2.4
Standard deviation	0.471	0.217	
Number of countries	*42*	*42*	
Upper middle-income			
Mean coefficient	−0.607	−0.266	2.3
Standard deviation	1.014	0.362	
Number of countries	*19*	*19*	
Lower middle-income			
Mean coefficient	−0.511	−0.235	2.2
Standard deviation	0.660	0.392	
Number of countries	*13*	*13*	

Note: * The proportional difference in the mean coefficients is calculated as the mean coefficient for 15–24-year-olds divided by the mean coefficient for 25–54-year-olds. It shows how many times larger the coefficient for younger people is relative to that for older people.
Sources: Authors' calculations based on ILOStat and World Bank data (see Appendix 6.1 for source details).

ment amongst people aged 25–54, since a percentage point change in GDP growth is expected to have a larger impact on unemployment rates for younger people. For example, for HICs, the mean coefficient for the post-2008 period is −0.747, which indicates that, across all HICs, on average, a percentage point increase in GDP growth during this period would be associated with a 0.747 percentage point decrease in YU. However, since GDP was generally declining post-2008, this is better expressed as each percentage point drop in GDP being related to a 0.747 percentage point *increase* in YU. This represents a strong relationship between changes in GDP and YU, considerably above the 0.33 and 0.5 reference points outlined above. The smaller coefficient for the older age group indicates that a percentage point drop in GDP has a weaker association with changes in unemployment for the HICs. The coefficients for the older age group are more in line with the expected size of coefficients postulated by Okun's Law (i.e. around −0.33), providing evidence that Okun's law generally holds for older people in HICs for the period 2009–2018.

Table 6.1 also shows evidence of differences between CIGs in ways that corroborate Okun's Law. HICs have larger coefficients than UMICs and LMICs, and this is true for both age groups. For the younger age group, the average Okun's coefficients for HICs are 23 per cent higher than UMICs and 46 per cent higher than those in LMICs.[11] Similarly, for the older age

---

[11]   Calculated as the coefficient for the high-income group (−0.747, taken from Table 6.1) divided by its upper middle-income group equivalent (−0.607) = 1.23 = 23 per cent. The other percentages in this

group, the average Okun's coefficients for HICs are 17 per cent and 32 per cent larger than those in UMICs and LMICs, respectively. In addition, the values of the coefficients for the UMICs and LMICs are both smaller than the values suggested by Okun's Law, suggesting each percentage point change in GDP growth amongst these countries is met with a smaller change in unemployment than we would expect under Okun's Law.

6.3.3 The Impact of the GFC on the Relationship between GDP Growth and Unemployment

Further analysis explored whether the nature of the relationship between GDP growth and unemployment changed as a consequence of the GFC. We estimated separate Okun's coefficients for the pre-2009 and post-2008 time periods by age group and by country (see Appendix 6.3). A comparison of these coefficients allows us to comment on whether the relationship between GDP growth and changes in unemployment appeared to alter over time, and to identify the direction and nature of any such changes.

The comparison includes only countries for which we had sufficient pre-2009 data. A number of countries, specifically those in the upper middle- or lower middle-income groups, had to be excluded for this reason. This means the number of countries in this comparison is smaller than the comparisons in Section 6.2. Results for UMICs should be interpreted with some caution and we do not present results for LMICs.[12] The average coefficients for this analysis are presented in Table 6.2 (full output is presented for each country in Appendix 6.3, Table 6A.3). It should be noted that the post-2008 figures for the UMICs are different to those presented in Table 6.1 as they are based on the sub-set of countries for which there is information available for both time periods.

The figures for the HICs suggest a strengthening of the relationship between GDP and unemployment post-2008, since the average Okun's coefficients for the post-2008 period are larger than the average coefficients for the pre-2009 period. Whilst this is the case for both age groups, the increase is marginally higher for the older age group. The average coefficients for the younger age group were 24 per cent higher post-2008 than before, whereas the average coefficients for the older age group were 35 per cent higher.

Comparison of the coefficients for both time periods for the UMICs is hampered by the small number of countries included in the analysis, compared to the HICs. The coefficients for UMICs suggest the relationship between GDP growth and unemployment has also strengthened post-2008, indicated by the larger coefficients for this time period. However, amongst these countries the increase in the size of the coefficient was greater amongst the younger age group. The average coefficients for the younger age group were 14 per cent higher post-2008 than before, whereas the average coefficients for the older age group were 8 per cent higher.

---

paragraph are calculated in the same way.

[12] Only four LMICs had sufficient data points both pre-2009 and post-2008 to allow comparison between the two time points. Consecutive years of unemployment data were needed for each age group in order to calculate trends in unemployment rates. In addition, many LICs had missing years of unemployment data such that changes in unemployment rates could not be calculated for both age groups. See Appendix 6.1 for more information about the data.

Table 6.2   *Summary statistics of Okun's coefficients by country income group and age, pre-2009 and post-2008*

Country income group	1991–2008 (pre-2009)		2009–18 (post-2008)		Proportional difference in mean coefficients pre-2009 vs. post-2008*	
Age (years)	15–24	25–54	15–24	25–54	15–24	25–54
High income						
Mean coefficient	−0.604	−0.231	−0.747	−0.312	24%	35%
Standard deviation	0.471	0.195	0.471	0.217		
Number of countries	*42*	*42*	*42*	*42*		
Upper middle income						
Mean coefficient	−0.339	−0.167	−0.386	−0.179	14%	8%
Standard deviation	0.564	0.300	0.280	0.111		
Number of countries	*9*	*9*	*9*	*9*		

Note: * The proportional difference in the mean coefficients is calculated as the mean pre-2009 coefficient divided by the mean post-2008 coefficient. It indicates how large the pre-2009 coefficient is relative to the post-2008 value.
Sources: Authors' calculations based on ILOStat and World Bank data (see Appendix 6.1 for source details).

6.3.4   Discussion

Our analysis confirms Okun's Law in showing a negative relationship between GDP growth and unemployment rates. This is true, on average, for both age groups and across different CIGs. It also holds for both the pre-2009 and post-2008 time periods.

Our analysis also indicates that the association between GDP growth and unemployment rates is stronger for younger people than older people. Again, we see this across CIGs, where the average estimated Okun's coefficients for the younger age group are more than twice as large as those for the older age group, for each CIG. This implies that changes in GDP growth will, on average, result in percentage point increases in unemployment that are twice as large for younger people as for older people in all CIGs except LICs (for which sufficient data were unavailable).

The results show that the relationship between unemployment and GDP growth is strongest for HICs and weakest for LMICs, again, evidenced by the HICs having, on average, the largest Okun's coefficients and the LMICs having the smallest. This is clearly seen for young people, but is also in evidence, albeit at lower levels, for older people.

In addition to these findings, the results also indicate that the relationship between GDP growth and unemployment has not been stable over time for any CIG, although declining GDP growth continued to be associated with increasing unemployment. For HICs, the Okun's coefficients were generally higher post-2008 than pre-2009, meaning a percentage change in GDP growth post-2008 was associated with a larger change in unemployment than previously. The difference in the size of the coefficients was larger for the older age group than the younger age group. So whilst the relationship between GDP growth and unemployment remained considerably stronger for young people, the results suggest that, for HICs, the GFC had a proportionally greater impact on adult unemployment between the two time periods, compared to younger people.

The results for UMICs were less conclusive due to smaller numbers of them being available to include in the analysis. Our analysis suggests the (negative) direction of the relationship remained the same over the two time periods and that the size of the Okun's coefficients increased marginally over time. This indicates that a percentage point change in GDP growth had a larger impact on unemployment post-2008 than it had previously.

Okun's Law is a useful means of summarising and explaining the relationship between economic growth and employment rates. It describes a negative relationship between growth and unemployment, whereby increasing economic growth is associated with falling unemployment. This relationship has been identified in our analysis. We show how negative GDP growth is associated with larger increases in unemployment amongst younger people than older people, and with larger changes in unemployment (for both age groups) in HICs, compared to countries in the lower-income country groups. For HICs and UMICs we also show that, whilst the GFC did not change the *direction* of the relationship between economic growth and unemployment (increasing growth was still associated with decreasing unemployment), it appeared to strengthen the relationship – meaning changes in GDP growth were associated with larger changes in unemployment post-2008 than they had been before. Hence Okun's Law continues to be a very relevant means of describing the nature of the relationship between economic growth and unemployment for these various sub-groups and different time points, even if the typical 3:1 or 2:1 relationship between unemployment and negative economic growth is not always maintained. It also provides a useful frame for drawing comparisons between different CIGs.

6.3.5   Selective Country-level Analysis

Table 6.1 summarised the findings from a number of models for three CIGs. However, when looking at the experiences of individual countries a much greater range of differences can be seen than the distinction between CIGs suggests. We provide the full results for all countries in Table 6A.3 (Appendix 6.3); however, in this section the results for a few purposively selected countries are highlighted to demonstrate the range of differences in the relationship between GDP growth and unemployment that exists *within* two of the CIGs.

Table 6.3 summarises the results from five countries, three HICs (UK, Greece, and New Zealand) and two UMICs (Turkey and Mexico) for which there were data both pre-2009 and post-2008. The table provides Okun's coefficients for both age groups pre-2009 and post-2008, and indicates whether the change in the Okun's coefficients due to the GFC is significantly large.[13]

For most countries the Okun's coefficients for young people are higher than those for older people, with the exception being Turkey (this is true for both time periods).[14]

---

[13]   This is determined by testing the interaction term in the model using a t-test. A test with a p-value smaller than 0.05 is said to be statistically significant. Such a result indicates that the size of the coefficient changes substantially post-2008, and that the amount of change is more than would be expected to occur by chance.

[14]   For Turkey, the coefficients for young people are smaller than those for the older people in the period pre-2009, although this is reversed post-2008.

Table 6.3   Okun's coefficients for selected countries by country income group and age, pre-2009 and post-2008

Country	Country Income Group	Okun's coefficients (15–24 years)			Okun's coefficients (25–54 years)		
		1991–2008 (pre-2009)	2009–18 (post-2008)	P-value (significant?)	1991–2008 (pre-2009)	2009–18 (post-2008)	P-value (significant?)
Greece	High	−0.469	−1.620	0.000 (Yes)	−0.090	−0.777	0.000 (Yes)
New Zealand	High	−0.670	−1.522	0.009 (Yes)	−0.332	−0.466	0.332 (No)
UK	High	−0.678	−0.880	0.438 (No)	−0.284	−0.388	0.650 (No)
Mexico	Upper middle	−0.337	−0.296	0.787 (No)	−0.188	−0.165	0.695 (No)
Turkey	Upper middle	−0.077	−0.378	0.049 (Yes)	−0.096	−0.256	0.025 (Yes)

Sources: Authors' calculations based on ILOStat and World Bank data (see Appendix 6.1 for source details).

All countries see some degree of change in the Okun's coefficients in the pre-GFC and GFC periods in both age ranges. For the majority, the coefficients are larger post-2008. In Greece, New Zealand and Turkey the post-2008 coefficient for young people is substantially, and significantly, larger than the pre-2009 coefficient. This means that, in these countries, the GFC resulted in a far closer association between GDP growth and unemployment for young people than in the UK and Mexico. In Greece and Turkey this was also true for older people; however, for New Zealand the change in Okun's coefficient for older people is moderate and not statistically significant. In the UK the GFC also resulted in a moderate strengthening of the association between GDP growth and unemployment for both age groups; however, this change is not statistically significant. In Mexico the GFC caused a weakening of the relationship between GDP growth and unemployment, although this is again by a moderate amount and not statistically significant.

These observations are intrinsically interesting, but their principal purpose is to emphasise the very diverse versions of the relationship between GDP growth and change in YU that exists *within* CIGs, and how relatively arbitrary are the divisions between groups. The pre-2009 coefficients for Greece and Mexico in both age groups are quite similar, despite one country being high-income, the other upper middle-income; but their post-2008 coefficients differ dramatically, to the disadvantage of the HIC (Greece). Viewing findings by country income group can therefore be informative as it allows us to identify overarching patterns, but it can also mask major differences within groups.

6.4   ANALYSIS OF THE RELATIONSHIP BETWEEN YU AND HDI

6.4.1   Introduction

The findings of our uniquely extensive study of the relationship between GDP and YU using Okun's Law provokes important questions about whether shifting trends in YU are best understood through analyses using purely economic variables like GDP. We do not doubt that a wide range of other factors are both relevant and common to shaping YU profiles across countries, whether grouped according to their mean income, geo-political factors or other indicators and criteria. However, identifying these factors in a large-scale international analysis, particularly one that utilises statistical modelling, is hampered by the available data. There are very few sources of national data that are comparable across countries, fully available for a wide range of countries, and cover extended time periods. Data that enable us to explore the impact of countries' investment in the welfare of their citizens are of especial value in testing the limits of economic change-focused explanations of YU. The only dataset of which we are aware that can claim to meet this criterion on an extensive international scale is the Human Development Index (HDI). The HDI was developed with the aim of shifting attention from economic growth to human development outcomes. As the United Nations Development Programme (UNDP) states, 'people and their capabilities should be the ultimate criteria for assessing the development of a country, not economic growth alone'.[15]

We hypothesised that, like the GDP–YU growth relationship, there would be a negative relationship between changes in HDI and YU rates. That is, as HDI scores increase, YU rates decrease, since a higher index might indicate that a country is more invested in its citizens' welfare if it guarantees good educational opportunities and good health care, as well as maintaining a strong economy. We were keen to know if this social investment bears upon YU trajectories in any way for a wide range of countries for multiple aspects of development.

6.4.2   The Human Development Index and its Component Indices

The HDI was designed to capture (albeit in a necessarily simplified manner) different key elements of human development and combine them into a single summary score. It comprises information from three areas; health, education, and standard of living (specifically, gross national income, or GNI).[16]

In this section we are interested in the dynamic relationship between HDI and YU, meaning we are focusing on the relationship between *change* in HDI scores and *change* in YU rates, rather than the actual HDI scores and YU rates. This is analogous to the analysis previously presented that explores the relationship between GDP growth and changes in unemployment rates. This section differs from previous ones in that it focuses on unemployment amongst 15–24-year-olds only: the aim is to compare the relationship between HDI and YU to the relationship between GDP and YU, rather than drawing a comparison between youth and older age groups.[17]

---

[15]   See http://hdr.undp.org/en/content/human-development-index-hdi (accessed 23 August 2020).

[16]   GNI measures the total income of a country including foreign investments; this differs from GDP (the economic measure used so far in this chapter) which measures the total value of goods and services produced in a specific country. Each of the three measurements – health, education and national income – has been standardised to create indices ranging from zero to one. The HDI score is then calculated as the geometric mean of the three standardised indices. The HDI score takes values between zero and one, with a value closer to one indicating a higher measure of human development. Each component makes an equal (one-third) contribution to the calculation of the HDI score for each country, for each year (the two elements of the education score are combined so that together they contribute a third of the overall composite HDI score). Further information can be found on the Human Development Reports website, http://hdr.undp.org/sites/default/files/hdr2019_technical_notes.pdf (accessed 23 August 2020).

[17]   In the previous section (6.3), and consistent with other research using Okun's Law, annual change in YU rates have been measured as the difference in YU rates between consecutive years (that is, as measured in years *t* and *t-1*). Annual change in HDI has been calculated in the same way; the difference

Figure 6.3 shows annual change in HDI and the three component indices for the period 1996–2018 for 73 countries for which reliable continuous data were present.[18] The first point of note is that the average change in each index is consistently larger than zero, meaning HDI was, on average, increasing each year, albeit with some fluctuations in the rate of growth. The rate of growth of HDI depends on the behaviour of its three component indices – large changes in the rate of growth of any one of the three components are reflected in HDI growth as smaller changes. The dotted vertical line at 2008 in Figure 6.3 flags the onset of the GFC. In the period after 2008 there is a noticeable drop in the income index that causes growth in the overall HDI to slow. The life-expectancy index changes very little year-on-year: it is an almost-straight horizontal line. This is because life expectancy is a slow-moving metric: leaving aside large-scale wars or pandemics, it takes years or decades for life expectancy to be affected by changes in health/society/policy/etc.

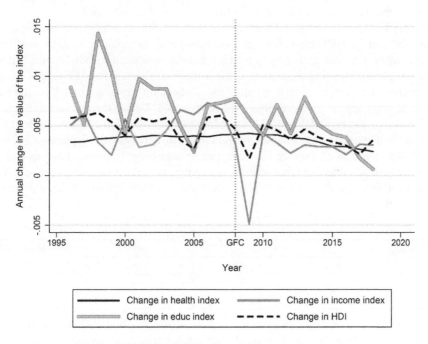

Source: Human Development Index (United Nations Development Programme).

Figure 6.3   *Annual change in HDI and in GNI, life-expectancy and education indices, 15–24-year-olds, 1996–2018*

---

in HDI scores is between years *t* and *t-1*. Annual rates of change have also been calculated for each of the three component indices, following the same formula.

[18]   Unlike the GDP analysis, a number of countries did not have HDI scores pre-1996, hence the analysis covers the time period 1996–2018 to ensure fuller data are available.

In the following section we first explore the relationship between overall HDI and YU, before moving on to look at the relationships between the different component indices and YU. We draw on findings from both analyses to fully understand what aspects of HDI are driving its relationship with YU.

6.4.3   The Relationship between HDI and Youth Unemployment Rates

The unemployment data used in the analysis of the relationships between changing youth and adult unemployment rates and GDP growth in the previous section were used again here to explore the relationship between YU rates and changes in HDI in the period from 1996 to 2018.[19] The analysis covers 73 countries for which we have both HDI scores and sufficient information on unemployment rates for that time period.[20] The dataset contains 41 high-income, 19 upper middle-income, and 13 lower middle-income countries. No low-income countries were included in the dataset due to data limitations.[21]

Table 6.4 shows the average HDI values for the start- and end- points of this time period. It shows the average HDI score increases over time for all three CIGs, but also how the score starts at a lower point and increases by a larger amount amongst the UMICs and LMICs.

The aim of the analysis was to identify whether there was a relationship between changes in YU over time and changes in HDI, whether the relationship varied across CIGs, and whether the GFC in 2008 appears to have altered the relationship. Unlike the analysis in Section 6.3, the relationship between HDI and YU is not framed by an economic theory, such as Okun's Law. Our focus nevertheless remains on relationships between social phenomena, and we use analytical methods to explore how changes in unemployment are related to changes in HDI, and where possible, how this relationship compares to the relationship between YU and GDP growth. Because the relationship between YU and GDP growth differed according to

Table 6.4   Summary statistics of HDI over time by country income group

Country Income Group	1996			2018			Mean increase 1996–2018
	Min.	Mean	Max.	Min.	Mean	Max.	
High Income	0.68	0.81	0.89	0.81	0.90	0.95	0.09
Upper Middle Income	0.62	0.66	0.70	0.71	0.78	0.83	0.12
Lower Middle Income	0.43	0.54	0.61	0.56	0.68	0.75	0.14

Sources: Authors' calculations based on ILOStat and UNDP data (see Appendix 6.1 for source details).

countries' incomes (Section 6.2), we analysed the relationship between YU and changes in HDI by CIG. Figures 6.4a and 6.4b show year-on-year changes in national YU rates plotted

---

[19]   To recap, the unemployment rates were based on real unemployment rates taken from the ILO; see Appendix 6.1 for more information about the data used in this analysis.

[20]   There was no HDI data for Macao, SAR China, hence this country was included in the GDP analysis but excluded from this analysis.

[21]   See Appendix 6.1.

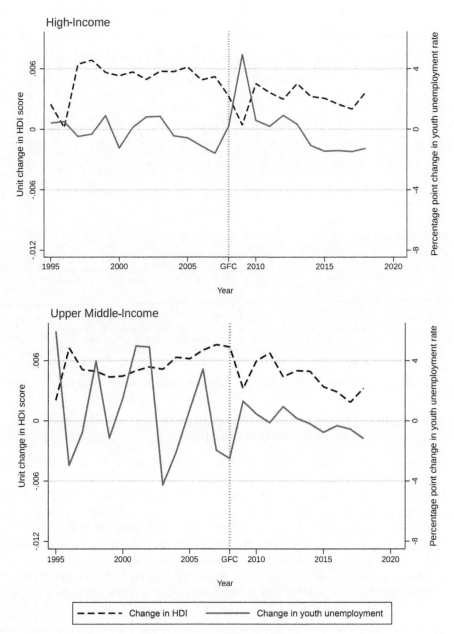

Sources: Human Development Index (United Nations Development Programme); unemployment rates, ILOStat.

Figure 6.4a   *Annual change in HDI and in unemployment rates, 15–24-year-olds, by country income group, 1996–2018 [A]*

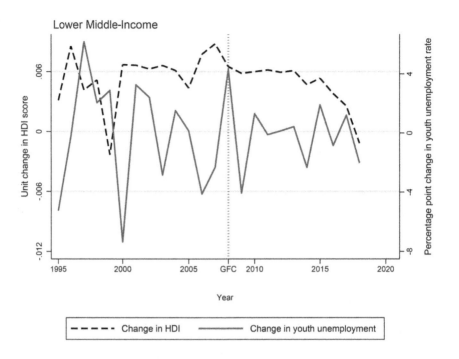

Sources: Human Development Index (United Nations Development Programme); unemployment rates, ILOStat.

Figure 6.4b   *Annual change in HDI and in unemployment rates, 15–24-year-olds, by
country income group, 1996–2018 [B]*

alongside annual changes in the value of the HDI score for the period 1996–2018 for each of
the country groups.

The data provide little evidence of a strong relationship between change in HDI and change
in YU rates during the period 1996–2018. Average annual change in HDI amongst the 41 HICs
is consistently greater than zero (the axis for HDI is on the right-hand side in the illustrations),
meaning HDI was, on average, increasing each year, albeit with some fluctuations in the rate
of growth.[22] On the other hand, changes in unemployment rates for the HICs (the axis on the
left-hand side) were both positive and negative, indicating that YU both rose and fell over the
same time period. There is a pause in HDI growth amongst HIC in 2009 (immediately after the

---

[22]   The vertical axis on the left shows year-on-year change in HDI score measured as the difference
in HDI score for two consecutive years; the axis ranges from −0.012 to 0.009, with a negative value
meaning the HDI score decreased between any two years. The axis on the right shows the same for unemployment amongst people aged 15–24; change is measured as the difference in employment rates for two
consecutive years. The mean change in unemployment ranges from −8 percentage points to 6 percentage
points. Again, a negative value means the unemployment rate fell between any two years.

GFC), which is accompanied by a rapid increase in YU. At this point the annual change in HDI from 2008 to 2009 was 0.0004, very close to zero but indicating that HDI scores were still, on the whole, increasing incrementally amongst these countries.

For the UMICs, the peaks and troughs in the illustrations are larger, suggesting more volatility in HDI and in YU rates. However, there is again no clear evidence of a relationship. The change in HDI remains above zero for the period 1996–2018. This means the HDI score for UMICs was increasing steadily over this period (although the rate of increase varies year-on-year), whilst the YU rates both increase and decrease. HDI growth appears to slow around 2009, but never reaches zero growth, suggesting the GFC had less impact on HDI in UMICs. The year-on-year changes in HDI amongst LMICs also appear unrelated to changes in YU rates. Unlike the HICs and UMICs, the average HDI growth amongst LMICs is negative in both 1999 and 2018. In other years HDI generally increases, although with large annual fluctuations. In the immediate post-2008 period, YU rates decline quite sharply, and then recover and fluctuate between 2010 and 2018; however, this is not accompanied by changes in HDI.

6.4.4   The Relationship between HDI Components and YU

Figures 6.4a and 6.4b suggest changes in the overall HDI score are not related to changing YU rates in any of the three CIGs: an increase in one is not generally accompanied by a decrease in the other. This suggests that there is no perceptible relationship between change in YU rates and the combined elements of the HDI (growth or decline in income, in school attendance or in longevity, when conflated as a single HDI value). However, we further investigated the component indices to get a fuller picture of what might be driving the relationship (or lack of relationship) between HDI and YU, and to help us better understand why sometimes a slowdown in HDI growth coincides with an increase in YU and other times it does not.

Figures 6.5a and 6.5b show annual change in each of the three components of HDI and in YU for the period 1996–2018. As with overall HDI, change for each component is simply measured as the difference between the value of the index in year t and its value in the preceding year. As before, there is a separate illustration for each of the three CIGs for which sufficient data were available.

Figures 6.5a and 6.5b suggest that, of the three indices, any association between changing HDI and changing YU is driven by an underlying relationship between changes in the country income index and changing YU, especially for the HICs. In particular, in the immediate post-2008 period a large increase in YU amongst HICs coincides with a similarly sudden and sharp decline in the income index (GNI) (even though overall HDI growth slows but does not decline, as shown in Figures 6.4a and 6.4b). Similar trends in YU and the income index respectively recur and then 'tail off' during the 2010s. Annual fluctuations in the education index and health index appear to have no association with any increase or decline in YU rates.

The figures suggest that some relationship exists between some of the component indices and YU. This warranted further investigation. We tested this potential relationship more formally using models similar to those used to test the relationship between GDP growth and changes in unemployment in Section 6.3. These models were used to investigate the relationship between changes in YU and changes in each of the three component indices.

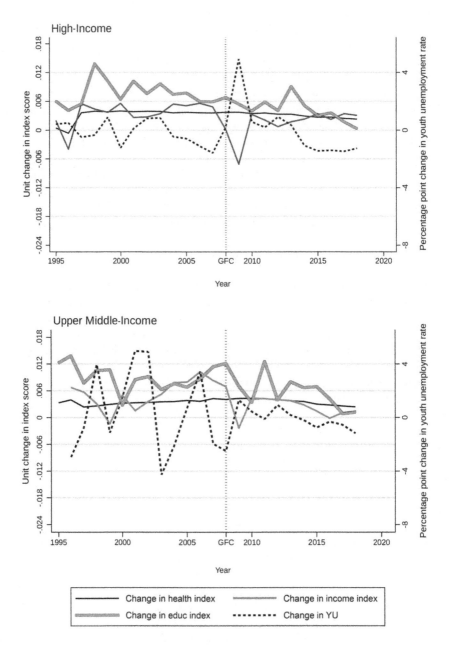

Sources: Human Development Index (United Nations Development Programme); unemployment rates, ILOStat.

Figure 6.5a   *Annual change in GNI, life-expectancy and education indices and in unemployment rates, 15–24-year-olds, by country income group, 1996–2018 [A]*

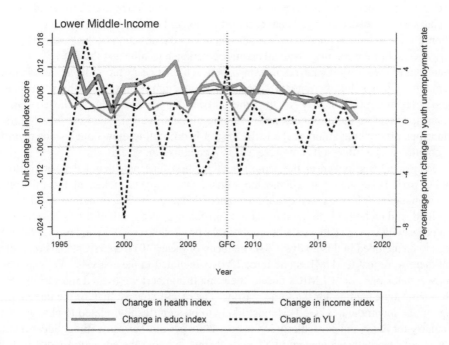

Sources: Human Development Index (United Nations Development Programme); unemployment rates, ILOStat.

Figure 6.5b   *Annual change in GNI, life-expectancy and education indices and in unemployment rates, 15–24-year-olds, by country income group, 1996–2018 [B]*

Two analyses were run for countries with data on both YU and the indices, replicating the two sets of analysis carried out on GDP growth and YU.[23] The first analysis looked at the post-2008 relationship between annual change in YU rates and annual change in the income index, annual change in the education index, and annual change in the health index.[24]

A total of 73 countries had sufficient post-2008 data for YU and the three component indices to be included in this analysis.[25]

The results confirmed that, of the three indices, change in the income index was more likely than change in the other indices to have a significant relationship with a change in YU, particularly amongst HICs. Around half the HICs included in the analysis had a significant negative

---

[23] As with the GDP analysis, to be included in the modelling, a country needed both HDI and YU data for a number of consecutive years in order to calculate annual differences. Data preparation is discussed in Appendix 6.1.

[24] Annual change being defined as the difference in the value of the index at times *t* and *t-1*. The relationship was then tested using a set of linear regression models. These are outlined in Appendix 6.4.

[25] More information about the data used in the analysis is given in Appendix 6.1.

relationship between change in the income index and change in YU, whereby YU increased as the income index decreased, and vice versa. A far lower proportion of these HICs had a significant relationship between change in either the education or health indices and change in YU. In addition, for these indices, there was less consistency in the direction of the relationship, with a fairly even split between negative and positive relationships amongst the HICs.[26]

There were fewer significant relationships between change in the indices and change in YU amongst UMICs, but, here again, there were more significant relationships between the income index and YU than between the other indices and YU. In addition, those significant relationships between income index and YU were all negative.[27] There were few significant relationships of any kind amongst the LMICs, so it is difficult to draw conclusions regarding these countries. The full results are presented in Appendix 6.4.

A second analysis looked at the same set of relationships but included an indicator for the GFC period, beginning in 2008. Once again, this analysis looked at the relationship between change in YU and change in the income, education and health indices for the period 1996–2018, and looked at whether the relationship changed as a result of the GFC. There were 53 countries with enough data available for both the pre-2009 (pre-GFC) and post-2008 (GFC) periods to be included in this analysis. The majority of these (40) were HICs. Data restrictions meant there were just ten UMICs and three LMICs included in the analysis. We were unable to draw conclusions about LMICs due to their small number; we treated the results for the UMICs with some caution for the same reasons. The results suggest that, of the three indices, change in the income index (GNI) is most likely to be significantly related to change in YU, particularly for HICs and particularly in the post-2008 period. The same direct linear relationship was not seen between change in YU and change in either the education index or health index. The results of these models are presented in Appendix 6.4.

6.4.5   Discussion

In this section we have investigated the dynamic relationship between HDI and YU with the aim of identifying whether changes in wider measurements of a country's development as indicated by index values for education and life expectancy as well as mean country-level income were related to changes in YU. The question we highlighted earlier (Section 6.4.1) was whether there was evidence that the economy might be the most powerful and most immediate driver of change in rates of YU, or whether social investment factors had an impact.

On the basis of this investigation of change in HDI over time, we conclude there is no discernible relationship between HDI and YU. On average, HDI was growing over the period of interest, albeit with some fluctuations in the rate of growth. However, the YU rate both increased and decreased over this period. There were time points where HDI and YU grew simultaneously, and other times at which the direction of change diverged. This led us to

---

[26] Change in the income index was significantly related to change in YU in 21 out of 41 HICs, far higher than the proportion for change in the education index (the education coefficient was significant for two of the 41 countries) or health index (the health coefficient was significant for three of the 41 countries): see Table 6A.4.1 in Appendix 6.4.

[27] Change in the income index was significantly related to change in YU in six of the 19 UMICs, whereas the education coefficient was significant for only one of the 19 countries and the health coefficient was significant for only three of the 19 countries.

investigate the component indices of the HDI, namely national income, education, and health, and the results of this analysis showed that the income index was the key to understanding any link between HDI and YU. Changes in this index were found to have a significant negative linear relationship to change in YU: as the income index increases, YU decreases, and vice versa. This relationship was most in evidence amongst HICs, but also evident in the other two CIGs in the analysis.

The results of modelling the relationship between the components and YU largely corroborate the models of economic growth and YU, and thus we conclude on this basis that economic growth is the strongest predictor of declining YU rates. There are some differences between the two sets of models at a country level, and these are likely to be due to the fact that GNI and GDP measure different aspects of economic growth. However, the differences between the outcomes of the two measures are relatively small, and the overall picture for each is the same, with regard to the nature of the relationship between the changing economic indicator and changing YU rates.[28] We do not suggest that changes in education and health indices are unimportant, only that there is no direct linear relationship between changes in these indices and changes in YU.

These findings and the absence of any evident statistical relationship between changes in the rates of YU and changes in the health and education indices of HDI leave no doubt about the strength of the relationship between the economic profiles of a great many countries and their rates of YU. We return to this point in Section 6.5 below. However, these findings and observations should not be taken to imply that the data provided by the HDIs regarding education and health has no impact on or relationship to employment and unemployment rates. The relationship between individual nations'educational success and the quality and reliability of employment, for example, is the subject of an extensive international literature too copious to reference here. The beneficial economic effects of highly developed education systems are by some measure too complex, diverse and diffuse to reduce to analyses of change in one measure of (un)employment and one age group that simply compares a single index of change in one with change in the other, year for year. Similar arguments apply to the complex relationship between health and employment. And as Chapter 2 stressed, the impact of economic factors on employment and unemployment are also significantly mitigated by the social policies of each country – including health and education policies – that cannot be reduced to a single numerical correlate. When seeking to analyse YU at country level across the maximum possible number of countries worldwide beyond annual measures of economic growth and contraction, the HDI is the only available comprehensive longitudinal global database of which we are aware that includes a single indicator for variables other than those of economic growth. The findings that it has facilitated are unambiguous, but it is beyond the scope of this study to pursue them further.

6.5   SUMMARY FINDINGS AND CONCLUDING COMMENTS

International research literatures (summarised in Section 6.2) have highlighted how, across much of Europe, and in several countries of Africa, Asia and South and Central America,

---

[28]   The 'match' between the two can be seen country by country in the results in Tables 6A.2.1 and 6A.2.2 (Appendix 6.2) and 6A.4.1 (Appendix 6.4).

rising YU rates are associated with declining GDP to differing degrees and over differing time-frames, at high levels of statistical significance. Other country studies have provided notable exceptions. In general, the most marked increases in YU occurred after the onset of the GFC. In many cases YU rates amongst 15–24-year-olds were found to be between two and three times as great as for older age groups.

Using a much more extensive dataset covering 74 countries across all continents, at most levels of development, spanning three CIGs, covering the pre-2009 and GFC periods (1991–2018) and two age groups (15–24 years and 25–54 years), our findings confirm, qualify and substantially extend the findings of that literature. The analyses undertaken for this study and its findings are the single most comprehensive published international analysis of its kind to date of which we are aware. Nevertheless it is important to recall the inherent limitations of the available datasets on which this study has drawn (see Appendix 6.1).

6.5.1   The Relationship between Change in GDP and Change in Unemployment Rates

As we indicated in the introduction to this chapter, the central purpose of our analyses was to establish the extent to which fluctuating YU rates are associated with economic change, taking into account differences between CIGs, and between young people and older adults aged 25–54 years.

In summary, our findings are as follows. First, there is clear evidence that the recurrent and generally strong association between declining economic trajectories and rising YU is statistically significant – that is, it cannot be explained solely by chance. Second, across the board, the association between year-on-year changes in GDP and in YU is clear, but strongly differentiated by CIG and by age. Overall, the relationship is twice as strong for 15–24-year-olds as for adults, on the average of all countries and across all CIGs over this period. Third, the relationship is strongest amongst HICs, less strong for UMICs, and weakest for LMICs. This is apparent when looking at the evidence for young people. In all but seven of the 42 countries covered in the analysis, there is a statistically significant relationship between change in unemployment rates amongst 15–24-year-olds between 2008 and 2018 and GDP growth. Amongst UMICs, the association between YU and GDP over the same period was statistically significant for just under half the countries covered in the analysis, whilst amongst LMICs there is evidence of a statistically significant relationship between YU and GDP growth for this period for only a third of the 13 LMICs covered by the analysis.

6.5.2   The Relationship between GDP and Unemployment Rates after 2008

We also aimed to establish whether and how the nature of any association between change in GDP and change in unemployment was altered after the onset of the GFC, once again taking into account differences between CIGs and between young people and adults aged 25–54 years.

The degree of association between changing YU rates and changes in GDP altered significantly during and after the GFC. Almost universally, young people aged 15–24 were very significantly more likely to be at risk of being unemployed than adults (25–54 years), in many cases by substantial or very substantial margins. However, although the relationship was always stronger for the younger group across HICs, the older group experienced a proportionately greater adverse impact on its unemployment rate when comparing its profile for the pre-2009 and post-2008 periods. Amongst UMICs, the association between YU and GDP was less strong for both age groups, considerably stronger for the younger than the older group, and stronger after 2008 than before.

In summary, changes in GDP growth were associated with larger changes in unemployment post-2008 than before. Okun's Law therefore remains very relevant to the relationship between economic growth and unemployment, especially amongst young people and especially after the onset of the GFC. But it is also clear that the association it predicts falters significantly and progressively in UMICs and LMICs, with no reliable data being available for LICs. More generally, beyond the differences in the association between CIGs, considerable diversity in the relationship prevails, as exemplified in the more detailed review of the findings for Greece and Mexico before and during the GFC period. This demonstrates that CIG classifications provide no more than broad-brush guides to the relationship between GDP trends and YU trends; that there are numerous examples in each CIG that are counter-typical; and that other factors than GDP continue to be important in interpreting unemployment rates at country level.

To place this summary of our findings regarding the GDP–YU relationship in a wider context, it is instructive to note the clear alignment between much of the descriptive data in Chapter 5 (especially Tables 5.4 and 5.5; and Figures 5.7 and 5.8) and the outcomes of the statistical modelling in this chapter. For example, the early decline in YU rates in some HICs following the onset of the GFC from 2013 onwards (Figure 5.7) coincides with the speedy recovery from recession, although high YU rates persisted in other countries listed in Appendix 6.2.[29] Similarly, the delayed response to the GFC of rising YU rates in UMICs between 2009 and 2014 (Figure 5.7) is largely visible in the low negative coefficients.[30] But, in contrast, the steady persistent rise in YU rates amongst LMICs from 2008 to 2019 (and beyond) in Figure 5.7 is much less clearly aligned with the coefficients for this group – indicating the strong influence of other variables in those countries.[31]

---

[29] A broad indication of this can be derived from the Okun's coefficients (Appendix 6.2), which show that, for the period 2009–18, about a quarter of HICs (Germany, Macao, Singapore, for example) had low negative coefficients below −0.400, while a quarter (Belgium, Greece, Italy, for example) had coefficients above −1.000. Overall, the speediest recoveries were typically in Eastern Asia and Northern Europe (Japan, Korea, Luxembourg, Switzerland, for example); the slowest occurred across almost all countries of Southern Europe.

[30] It is nevertheless important to note that the statistical significance indicators are below the standard thresholds for almost half of these countries. This group also includes the most extreme negative coefficients in the whole dataset (Bosnia and Herzegovina (−3.400); Jamaica (−3.286)).

[31] The coefficients are variable and do not meet standard statistical significance levels for most countries in this group. However, it is important to note that less than a third of LMICs could be included in the dataset because of limitations of data availability to the standard required for inclusion in the modelling for Appendix 6.2.

6.5.3   The Relationship between Change in HDI and Change in Youth Unemployment Rates

Our third area of interest has been in whether changes in YU rates are associated with changes in health and in educational provision. The HDI provides data for life expectancy (health) and for educational provision and take-up, as well as a measure of mean gross national income (GNI) per person. We found little evidence of a relationship between annual changes in countries' composite HDI values and annual changes in YU rates in the period 1996–2018.

Separate analyses of the three component indices of HDI took account of annual changes in the data for each of life expectancy, educational provision and take-up, and mean GNI per person; and year-on-year changes in YU rates for each country. The results of the analysis for the post-2008 period show that changes in GNI were more likely to have a statistically significant relationship with changes in YU rates from year to year: as changes in GNI increased, changes in YU rates declined, and vice versa. These results corroborate the results of the previous analysis of the relationship between changes in GDP and changes in YU from year to year. Once again, this was most evident in HICs, but also in countries in other CIGs. In contrast, we identified far fewer cases of significant associations between annual changes in the life-expectancy and education indices and changes in YU rates. Amongst HICs the relationships were both negative and positive, in approximately equal numbers. This pattern recurred in UMICs, but significant relationships between changes in the three components of HDI and in YU rates were fewer, especially for the education and life-expectancy indices.

A second set of analyses that examined separate results for the pre-2009 and post-2008 periods did not suggest significant differences in outcomes for the two periods in either the HICs or UMICs. Neither were there statistically significant relationships for these two time periods between annual changes in the education or life-expectancy indices and changes in YU rates. This implies that the GFC was not influential in shaping the relationship between annual changes in HDI components and changing YU rates. Across the piece, and irrespective of time period, we found no consistent or significant association between changes in the education or health components of the HDI and changing YU rates – while also observing that it should not be deduced from this that education and health factors have no positive bearing on young people's employment status, as noted above.

6.5.4   Concluding Comments

Our findings cast a clear light on the extent and consistency of strong and significant patterns of association between declining GDP (and GNI) and escalating YU rates across countries and CIGs over almost three decades. Some of the studies summarised in Section 6.2 indicate the probability that these associations are directly causal, especially during periods of extreme economic disruption, but they do not facilitate interpretations of the effects of such extremes on the basis of changing GDP and GNI rates alone. While it is beyond reasonable doubt that the effect of economic decline on rising youth and adult unemployment rates has in practice been causal, the influence of many other distinctive local economic and non-economic factors will have been significant in countries in which the association was found to be below standard thresholds for statistical significance (or missing, or negative). Early policy interventions on the part of states to ameliorate rapidly declining GDP rates, for example, alter patterns of association at country level. Country level and world-regional differences (see Tables 5.2 and 5.4) indicate the possibilities for further analysis towards understanding the specificities and distinctiveness of youth labour markets in contexts of economic decline. Detailed country-level analyses of how trajectories of economic decline play out in youth labour markets are beyond the scope of the present study, although many of the country-specific studies referenced in Chapters 3–5 contribute to interpreting some of the greater and lesser extremes of YU in the wake of the GFC and over longer periods.

APPENDIX 6.1   DATASET CONSTRUCTION

GDP and Unemployment Data, 1980–2018

The aim was to assemble, for as many countries as possible, a file containing annual gross domestic product (GDP) data, and annual unemployment rates by age group, for as many years as possible in the period 1980–2018. The file also needed to include the country income group of each country, as determined by the World Bank (WB).

GDP growth data (annual %) based on the WB national accounts data and OECD national accounts data files were downloaded from the WB website: https://data.worldbank.org/indicator/NY.GDP.MKTP.KD.ZG.

Annual national unemployment rates (%) for two age groups (15–24 years and 25–54 years) were taken from the International Labour Organization (ILO) website: https://www.ilo.org/shinyapps/bulkexplorer11/?lang=en&segment=indicator&id=UNE_TUNE_SEX_AGE_NB_A.

Real (i.e. not modelled) unemployment rates were used. Not all countries could be included in the analysis. Countries were excluded if they did not have available GDP growth data or unemployment data (the latter being more frequent). All available unemployment rates for each country were extracted, although there were no unemployment data available for some countries in some years. The analysis relied on being able to calculate changes in unemployment rates, hence consecutive years of data were needed for each country and age group. The consecutive years allowed us to calculate trends in unemployment rates.

There were 74 countries – 42 high-income, 19 upper middle-income, and 13 lower middle-income – with sufficient data post-2008 to be included in the analysis. Of these, 55 countries also had sufficient data both pre-2009 and post-2008 to allow comparisons to be drawn between those two periods. Table 6A.1 lists all countries included, with their first and last year of available consecutive data and a flag indicating whether they had been included in the pre-2009/post-2008 analysis. The analysis of GDP and unemployment was conducted on these countries. The final analysis dataset focused on the more recent period 1991–2018. This helped to ensure fuller data.

Table 6A.1   List of countries included in the analysis, and years of unemployment data included

Country	Country Income Group	First Year	Last Year	Total Years	Sufficient data for comparison of pre-2009 and post-2008?
Argentina	Upper middle	2009	2014	6	No
Australia	High	1980	2018	39	Yes
Austria	High	1982	2018	37	Yes
Azerbaijan	Upper middle	2009	2018	10	No
Belgium	High	1983	2018	36	Yes
Bhutan	Lower middle	2009	2015	7	No
Bolivia	Lower middle	2011	2018	8	No
Bosnia and Herzegovina	Upper middle	2009	2018	10	No

Country	Country Income Group	First Year	Last Year	Total Years	Sufficient data for comparison of pre-2009 and post-2008?
Bulgaria	Upper middle	2000	2018	19	Yes
Cambodia	Lower middle	2009	2016	8	No
Canada	High	1980	2018	39	Yes
Chile	High	1988	2018	31	Yes
Colombia	Upper middle	2009	2018	10	No
Croatia	High	2002	2018	17	Yes
Cyprus	High	2000	2018	19	Yes
Czech Republic	High	1993	2018	26	Yes
Denmark	High	1983	2018	36	Yes
Ecuador	Upper middle	2003	2018	16	Yes
Egypt, Arab Republic of	Lower middle	2009	2017	9	No
El Salvador	Lower middle	2009	2018	10	No
Estonia	High	1994	2018	25	Yes
Finland	High	1986	2018	33	Yes
France	High	1983	2018	36	Yes
Germany	High	1983	2018	36	Yes
Greece	High	1981	2018	38	Yes
Honduras	Lower middle	2009	2018	10	No
Hong Kong SAR China	High	1982	2016	35	Yes
Hungary	High	1992	2018	27	Yes
Iceland	High	1991	2018	28	Yes
Indonesia	Lower middle	1999	2018	20	Yes
Ireland	High	1983	2018	36	Yes
Israel	High	1980	2018	39	Yes
Italy	High	1980	2018	39	Yes
Jamaica	Upper middle	2012	2018	7	No
Japan	High	1980	2018	39	Yes
Korea, Republic of	High	1980	2018	39	Yes
Kyrgyz Republic	Lower middle	2009	2018	10	No
Latvia	High	1996	2018	23	Yes
Lithuania	High	1997	2018	22	Yes
Luxembourg	High	1983	2018	36	Yes
Macao SAR China	High	1992	2017	26	Yes
Malaysia	Upper middle	2009	2016	8	No
Malta	High	2000	2018	19	Yes
Mexico	Upper middle	1991	2018	28	Yes
Moldova	Lower middle	2002	2018	17	Yes
Netherlands	High	1987	2018	32	Yes
New Zealand	High	1986	2018	33	Yes
North Macedonia	Upper middle	2009	2018	10	No

Country	Country Income Group	First Year	Last Year	Total Years	Sufficient data for comparison of pre-2009 and post-2008?
Norway	High	1982	2018	37	Yes
Peru	Upper middle	1994	2018	25	Yes
Philippines	Lower middle	1987	2018	32	Yes
Poland	High	1996	2018	23	Yes
Portugal	High	1984	2018	35	Yes
Romania	Upper middle	1995	2018	24	Yes
Russian Federation	Upper middle	1992	2018	27	Yes
Serbia	Upper middle	2009	2018	10	No
Singapore	High	1982	2016	35	Yes
Slovak Republic	High	1994	2018	25	Yes
Slovenia	High	1994	2018	25	Yes
South Africa	Upper middle	2000	2018	19	Yes
Spain	High	1980	2018	39	Yes
Sri Lanka	Upper middle	2009	2016	8	No
Suriname	Upper middle	2009	2015	7	No
Sweden	High	1989	2018	30	Yes
Switzerland	High	1990	2018	29	Yes
Thailand	Upper middle	2003	2018	16	Yes
Trinidad and Tobago	High	1985	2016	32	Yes
Turkey	Upper middle	1988	2018	31	Yes
Ukraine	Lower middle	2009	2018	10	No
United Kingdom	High	1983	2018	36	Yes
United States	High	1980	2018	39	Yes
Uruguay	High	1998	2018	21	Yes
Vietnam	Lower middle	2009	2018	10	No
West Bank and Gaza	Lower middle	2000	2018	19	Yes

Data on Human Development, 1996–2018

The United Nations Development Programme's (UNDP's) Human Development Index (HDI) was devised with the aim of shifting attention from economic growth to human development outcomes. In our analyses, we have used the overall index and its three component indices: the health index, which is based on life expectancy at birth; the education index, which is based on expected years of schooling and mean years of (actual) schooling; and the income index, which is based on gross national income (GNI) per capita. The overall HDI is the geometric mean of the three component indices. All four of these measures take values between zero and one, with a higher score indicating higher levels of development. The data were downloaded from the Human Development Reports website: http://hdr.undp.org/en/content/human -development-index-hdi.

The aim of the analysis was to assess whether there existed a dynamic relationship between changes in unemployment rates amongst people aged 15–24 years and changes in the HDI score. This meant that countries were excluded if they did not have both HDI scores and data on youth unemployment (YU). The 74 countries for which we had sufficient data to calculate change in unemployment rates over time for young people (listed in Table 6A.1) were therefore used as a starting point when assembling the data. The unemployment data that were used for the GDP growth and YU analysis was also used for the analysis of HDI and YU. HDI data were extracted for all but one of these 74 countries (HDI scores were not available for Macao SAR China and this country had to be excluded). As with the GDP and YU analysis, the focus was on change over time; hence, it was important that consecutive years of HDI data were available to allow this. Fortunately, HDI data are generally complete for most countries; once a country has been given an HDI score, it tends to remain in the HDI dataset in subsequent years. The HDI and YU analysis focuses on the period 1996–2018 as fuller data are available for this period.

Data Coverage

One of the original intentions of this analysis was to compare the relationship between economic growth and YU within high-income, upper middle-income, lower middle-income, and low-income countries. However, the requirement for consecutive years of data meant countries with a high proportion of missing years or inconsistent data entries (overwhelmingly lower middle-income or low-income countries), could not be included.

Of the 79 high-income countries listed by the WB, 42 (53%) were included in the GDP–YU post-2008 analysis, compared with 19 out of 60 (32%) upper middle-income countries and 13 out of 47 (28%) of lower middle-income countries. The income data were very sparse, such that none of the 31 low-income countries could be included in the analysis for the reasons outlined above. For the high-income group, the excluded countries were overwhelmingly smaller in terms of population (for example, in the high-income group, the exclusions include St Kitts and Nevis, Barbados, and the Northern Mariana Islands). The 42 countries included in the analysis contain 94 per cent of the total population of high-income country group, based on population figures from 2018.[32] However, the respective proportions for the upper middle- and lower middle-income groups were lower as the excluded countries were not consistently smaller than the countries that could be included. The total population coverage for the upper middle-income group was 22 per cent, whilst that for the lower middle-income group was 28 per cent.

---

[32] Population figures were taken from the World Bank website: https://data.worldbank.org/indicator/SP.POP.TOTL?end=2018&start=2018.

APPENDIX 6.2   OUTPUT FROM MODELLING OKUN'S COEFFICIENTS, 2008–2018

Okun's coefficients for the 74 countries for which we had post-2008 data are presented in Tables 6A.2.1 (young people, 15–24 -year olds) and 6A.2.2 (older people, 25–54-year olds).

The coefficients are generated using a set of linear regression models (estimated using Ordinary Least Squares). These models were used to assess whether there was an underlying linear relationship between GDP growth and changes in YU and to quantify and test the relationship using statistical tests. The model equation is:

$$u_t - u_{t-1} = \alpha + \beta \, G_t + \varepsilon_t$$

Where u_t is unemployment at time t, G_t is GDP growth at time t (measured as $(GDP_t - GDP_{t-1})/GDP_{t-1}$, where GDP_t is real GDP at time t), and ε_t is an error term. The parameter β is the model coefficient, known as Okun's coefficient, which measures the size and direction of the relationship between changes in the unemployment rate and GDP growth.

The coefficient shows the impact on unemployment rates associated with a unit change in GDP growth and the direction of that relationship – a negative coefficient indicates an inverse relationship where the value of unemployment reduces as GDP growth increases, and vice versa. A positive coefficient means GDP growth and unemployment rates will increase or decrease in tandem. A larger coefficient implies that a unit change in GDP growth will result in larger changes in the unemployment rate.

The value of this coefficient is tested in the model using a t-test. The resulting p-value indicates whether, for each specific country, GDP growth is significantly related to changes in unemployment. The relationship is deemed to be significant at the 90% level if the p-value is smaller than 0.1, significant at the 95% level if the p-value is smaller than 0.05, and significant at the 99% level if the p-value is smaller than 0.01 (marked in the table with asterisks). P-values are probabilities; a small p-value indicates that there is a very small probability that the findings we are testing occurred purely by chance. The model output also includes the R-squared. This is a value ranging between 0 and 1 that measures the amount of variation in unemployment that is summarised using GDP growth. This statistic is used to measure whether the model is a good fit. A value close to one indicates a better fit, whereas a value close to zero indicates a poor fit.

Table 6A.2.1   Okun's coefficients for young people (aged 15–24 years) in the period post-2008, by country income group and country [A]

Country		Model output for 15–24-year-olds				
	Country income group	Okun's coefficient	Standard error for Okun's coefficient	T-test for Okun's coefficient	P-value for t-test	Model R-squared
Australia	High	−0.560	0.583	−0.960	0.365	0.103
Austria	High	−0.445	0.107	−4.152	0.003***	0.683
Belgium	High	−1.302	0.545	−2.389	0.044**	0.416

Country		Model output for 15–24-year-olds				
	Country income group	Okun's coefficient	Standard error for Okun's coefficient	T-test for Okun's coefficient	P-value for t-test	Model R-squared
Canada	High	−0.703	0.107	−6.549	0.000***	0.843
Chile	High	−0.798	0.297	−2.690	0.027**	0.475
Croatia	High	−1.113	0.540	−2.062	0.073*	0.347
Cyprus	High	−1.097	0.273	−4.015	0.004***	0.668
Czech Republic	High	−0.921	0.170	−5.421	0.001***	0.786
Denmark	High	−0.514	0.209	−2.456	0.040**	0.430
Estonia	High	−0.971	0.195	−4.991	0.001***	0.757
Finland	High	−0.529	0.154	−3.434	0.009***	0.596
France	High	−1.204	0.141	−8.536	0.000***	0.901
Germany	High	−0.177	0.043	−4.150	0.003***	0.683
Greece	High	−1.620	0.113	−14.356	0.000***	0.963
Hong Kong SAR China	High	−0.571	0.185	−3.081	0.022**	0.613
Hungary	High	−0.887	0.188	−4.706	0.002***	0.735
Iceland	High	−0.565	0.157	−3.599	0.007***	0.618
Ireland	High	−0.331	0.162	−2.047	0.075*	0.344
Israel	High	−0.624	0.253	−2.464	0.039**	0.431
Italy	High	−1.084	0.364	−2.977	0.018**	0.526
Japan	High	−0.216	0.114	−1.900	0.094*	0.311
Korea, Republic of	High	−0.056	0.100	−0.561	0.590	0.038
Latvia	High	−1.173	0.141	−8.350	0.000***	0.897
Lithuania	High	−1.016	0.166	−6.132	0.000***	0.825
Luxembourg	High	−0.046	0.457	−0.102	0.921	0.001
Macao SAR China	High	−0.024	0.032	−0.768	0.468	0.078
Malta	High	−0.220	0.091	−2.406	0.043**	0.420
Netherlands	High	−0.597	0.141	−4.247	0.003***	0.693
New Zealand	High	−1.522	0.262	−5.801	0.000***	0.808
Norway	High	−0.430	0.291	−1.480	0.177	0.215
Poland	High	−0.645	0.713	−0.904	0.393	0.093
Portugal	High	−1.552	0.347	−4.470	0.002***	0.714
Singapore	High	−0.382	0.092	−4.151	0.006***	0.742
Slovak Republic	High	−0.717	0.443	−1.619	0.144	0.247
Slovenia	High	−0.641	0.163	−3.939	0.004***	0.660
Spain	High	−2.245	0.252	−8.926	0.000***	0.909
Sweden	High	−0.599	0.144	−4.166	0.003***	0.685
Switzerland	High	−0.349	0.083	−4.230	0.003***	0.691
Trinidad and Tobago	High	−0.440	0.098	−4.475	0.004***	0.769
United Kingdom	High	−0.880	0.223	−3.955	0.004***	0.662

Country		Model output for 15–24-year-olds				
	Country income group	Okun's coefficient	Standard error for Okun's coefficient	T-test for Okun's coefficient	P-value for t-test	Model R-squared
United States	High	−1.082	0.220	−4.926	0.001***	0.752
Uruguay	High	−0.517	0.183	−2.835	0.022**	0.501
Argentina	Upper middle	−0.098	0.103	−0.943	0.415	0.229
Azerbaijan	Upper middle	0.053	0.056	0.947	0.375	0.114
Bosnia and Herzegovina	Upper middle	−3.400	1.085	−3.133	0.017**	0.584
Bulgaria	Upper middle	−1.041	0.453	−2.297	0.051*	0.398
Colombia	Upper middle	−0.383	0.138	−2.779	0.027**	0.525
Ecuador	Upper middle	−0.115	0.106	−1.090	0.308	0.129
Jamaica	Upper middle	−3.286	2.510	−1.309	0.261	0.300
Malaysia	Upper middle	−0.152	0.378	−0.402	0.704	0.031
Mexico	Upper middle	−0.296	0.059	−4.979	0.001***	0.756
North Macedonia	Upper middle	−0.139	0.558	−0.249	0.811	0.009
Peru	Upper middle	−0.077	0.328	−0.234	0.821	0.007
Romania	Upper middle	−0.328	0.113	−2.910	0.020**	0.514
Russian Federation	Upper middle	−0.478	0.050	−9.469	0.000***	0.918
Serbia	Upper middle	−0.697	0.771	−0.905	0.396	0.105
South Africa	Upper middle	−0.455	0.374	−1.216	0.259	0.156
Sri Lanka	Upper middle	−0.474	0.216	−2.198	0.079*	0.491
Suriname	Upper middle	0.517	0.616	0.839	0.449	0.150
Thailand	Upper middle	−0.307	0.109	−2.822	0.022**	0.499
Turkey	Upper middle	−0.378	0.116	−3.255	0.012**	0.570
Bhutan	Lower middle	−0.509	0.235	−2.164	0.096*	0.539
Bolivia	Lower middle	0.579	0.663	0.873	0.423	0.132
Cambodia	Lower middle	−0.103	0.564	−0.183	0.862	0.007
Egypt, Arab Republic of	Lower middle	−1.423	0.688	−2.068	0.084*	0.416
El Salvador	Lower middle	−0.608	0.934	−0.651	0.536	0.057
Honduras	Lower middle	−2.117	0.975	−2.171	0.066*	0.402
Indonesia	Lower middle	−0.728	0.730	−0.997	0.348	0.110
Kyrgyz Republic	Lower middle	−0.360	0.116	−3.102	0.017**	0.579
Moldova	Lower middle	−0.239	0.192	−1.249	0.247	0.163
Philippines	Lower middle	−0.101	0.070	−1.447	0.186	0.207
Ukraine	Lower middle	−0.179	0.183	−0.976	0.362	0.120

| Country | Model output for 15–24-year-olds | | | | | |
	Country income group	Okun's coefficient	Standard error for Okun's coefficient	T-test for Okun's coefficient	P-value for t-test	Model R-squared
Vietnam	Lower middle	−0.503	0.423	−1.189	0.273	0.168
West Bank and Gaza	Lower middle	−0.350	0.220	−1.590	0.151	0.240

Notes: * p-value < 0.1, ** p-value < 0.05, *** p-value < 0.01.

Table 6A.2.2　Okun's coefficients for older people (aged 25–54 years) in the period post-2008, by country income group and country [B]

| Country | | Model output for 25–54-year-olds | | | | |
	Country income group	Okun's coefficient	Standard error for Okun's coefficient	T-test for Okun's coefficient	P-value for t-test	Model R-squared
Australia	High	−0.179	0.301	−0.595	0.568	0.042
Austria	High	−0.248	0.047	−5.328	0.001***	0.780
Belgium	High	−0.209	0.163	−1.283	0.236	0.171
Canada	High	−0.394	0.050	−7.823	0.000***	0.884
Chile	High	−0.409	0.063	−6.496	0.000***	0.841
Croatia	High	−0.388	0.152	−2.553	0.034**	0.449
Cyprus	High	−0.436	0.089	−4.902	0.001***	0.750
Czech Republic	High	−0.278	0.053	−5.243	0.001***	0.775
Denmark	High	−0.353	0.096	−3.675	0.006***	0.628
Estonia	High	−0.479	0.083	−5.760	0.000***	0.806
Finland	High	−0.185	0.048	−3.835	0.005***	0.648
France	High	−0.300	0.068	−4.439	0.002***	0.711
Germany	High	−0.114	0.027	−4.183	0.003***	0.686
Greece	High	−0.777	0.093	−8.357	0.000***	0.897
Hong Kong SAR China	High	−0.260	0.029	−9.111	0.000***	0.933
Hungary	High	−0.266	0.083	−3.203	0.013**	0.562
Iceland	High	−0.278	0.086	−3.229	0.012**	0.566
Ireland	High	−0.176	0.077	−2.278	0.052*	0.394
Israel	High	−0.545	0.132	−4.138	0.003***	0.682
Italy	High	−0.280	0.100	−2.792	0.023**	0.494
Japan	High	−0.135	0.045	−2.985	0.017**	0.527
Korea, Republic of	High	−0.083	0.054	−1.550	0.160	0.231
Latvia	High	−0.541	0.051	−10.543	0.000***	0.933
Lithuania	High	−0.477	0.086	−5.568	0.001***	0.795
Luxembourg	High	−0.004	0.066	−0.061	0.953	0.000
Macao SAR China	High	−0.016	0.006	−2.570	0.037**	0.485
Malta	High	−0.049	0.034	−1.464	0.181	0.211
Netherlands	High	−0.298	0.103	−2.908	0.020**	0.514
New Zealand	High	−0.466	0.077	−6.044	0.000***	0.820
Norway	High	−0.130	0.115	−1.130	0.291	0.138
Poland	High	−0.310	0.239	−1.299	0.230	0.174
Portugal	High	−0.628	0.160	−3.923	0.004***	0.658
Singapore	High	−0.188	0.042	−4.532	0.004***	0.774
Slovak Republic	High	−0.212	0.146	−1.457	0.183	0.210

Country	Model output for 25–54-year-olds					
	Country income group	Okun's coefficient	Standard error for Okun's coefficient	T-test for Okun's coefficient	P-value for t-test	Model R-squared
Slovenia	High	−0.252	0.076	−3.332	0.010**	0.581
Spain	High	−1.062	0.124	−8.585	0.000***	0.902
Sweden	High	−0.175	0.059	−2.957	0.018**	0.522
Switzerland	High	−0.086	0.101	−0.857	0.416	0.084
Trinidad and Tobago	High	−0.163	0.050	−3.275	0.017**	0.641
United Kingdom	High	−0.338	0.050	−6.788	0.000***	0.852
United States	High	−0.765	0.125	−6.103	0.000***	0.823
Uruguay	High	−0.172	0.021	−8.220	0.000***	0.894
Argentina	Upper middle	−0.086	0.014	−6.240	0.008***	0.928
Azerbaijan	Upper middle	−0.031	0.014	−2.284	0.056*	0.427
Bosnia and Herzegovina	Upper middle	−0.767	0.447	−1.716	0.130	0.296
Bulgaria	Upper middle	−0.413	0.211	−1.954	0.086*	0.323
Colombia	Upper middle	−0.233	0.053	−4.377	0.003***	0.732
Ecuador	Upper middle	−0.145	0.056	−2.603	0.031**	0.459
Jamaica	Upper middle	−1.586	0.691	−2.295	0.083*	0.568
Malaysia	Upper middle	−0.215	0.056	−3.841	0.012**	0.747
Mexico	Upper middle	−0.165	0.031	−5.395	0.001***	0.784
North Macedonia	Upper middle	−0.175	0.219	−0.799	0.451	0.084
Peru	Upper middle	−0.043	0.111	−0.389	0.708	0.019
Romania	Upper middle	−0.132	0.032	−4.069	0.004***	0.674
Russian Federation	Upper middle	−0.215	0.020	−10.714	0.000***	0.935
Serbia	Upper middle	−0.242	0.366	−0.661	0.527	0.052
South Africa	Upper middle	−0.180	0.122	−1.468	0.180	0.212
Sri Lanka	Upper middle	−0.102	0.074	−1.377	0.227	0.275
Suriname	Upper middle	−0.231	0.148	−1.568	0.192	0.381
Thailand	Upper middle	−0.062	0.021	−3.017	0.017**	0.532
Turkey	Upper middle	−0.256	0.056	−4.538	0.002***	0.720
Bhutan	Lower middle	0.008	0.108	0.075	0.944	0.001
Bolivia	Lower middle	−0.117	0.256	−0.456	0.668	0.040
Cambodia	Lower middle	−0.303	0.475	−0.637	0.552	0.075
Egypt, Arab Republic of	Lower middle	−0.705	0.289	−2.437	0.051*	0.498
El Salvador	Lower middle	−0.076	0.399	−0.191	0.854	0.005
Honduras	Lower middle	−1.335	0.525	−2.543	0.038**	0.480
Indonesia	Lower middle	−0.046	0.293	−0.158	0.878	0.003

Country	Model output for 25–54-year-olds					
	Country income group	Okun's coefficient	Standard error for Okun's coefficient	T-test for Okun's coefficient	P-value for t-test	Model R-squared
Kyrgyz Republic	Lower middle	0.043	0.061	0.712	0.499	0.068
Moldova	Lower middle	−0.105	0.079	−1.330	0.220	0.181
Philippines	Lower middle	−0.039	0.026	−1.531	0.164	0.227
Ukraine	Lower middle	−0.085	0.045	−1.874	0.103	0.334
Vietnam	Lower middle	0.078	0.225	0.347	0.739	0.017
West Bank and Gaza	Lower middle	−0.372	0.107	−3.484	0.008***	0.603

Notes: * p-value < 0.1, ** p-value < 0.05, *** p-value < 0.01.

APPENDIX 6.3   OKUN'S COEFFICIENTS FOR PRE-2009 AND POST-2008 PERIODS

Okun's coefficients for 55 countries for which data were available for both the pre-2009 (1991–2008) and post-2008 (2009–18) periods were estimated using linear regression equations (fitted using Ordinary Least Squares) that used data covering the period 1991–2008 and an interaction term to identify the pre-2009 and post-2008 time periods. The interaction term was used to test whether the relationship between GDP growth and changes in unemployment pre-2009 was different to that post-2008. The model equation is:

$$u_t - u_{t-1} = \alpha + \beta_1 \, G_t + \beta_2 \, G_t {}^*GFC + \beta_3 \, GFC + \varepsilon_t$$

Where u_t is unemployment at time t, G_t is GDP growth at time t (measured as $(GDPt - GDP_{t-1})/GDP_{t-1}$, where GDP_t is real GDP at time t), and ε_t is an error term. *GFC* is a dummy variable indicating whether the data came from pre-GFC (1991–2008) or after (2009–18). Specifically, the dummy variable was 1 = post-2008 period, 0 = pre-2009 period. Okun's coefficient for the pre-2009 period is therefore β_1. The coefficient for the interaction ($\beta2$) measures the difference in size between the pre-2009 and post-2008 time periods. Okun's coefficient for the post-2008 period is therefore $\beta_1 + \beta_2$, the sum of the coefficient for the pre-2009 period and the difference between the two time periods.

As with Appendix 6.2, the coefficient shows, for each time period, the impact on unemployment rates associated with a unit change in GDP growth and the direction of that relationship.

The value of the interaction term is tested in the model using a t-test. The test result, and its associated p-value, indicate whether the relationship between GDP growth and change in unemployment is different for the two time periods. The difference is deemed to be significant at the 90% level if the p-value is smaller than 0.1, significant at the 95% level if the p-value is smaller than 0.05, and significant at the 99% level if the p-value is smaller than 0.01. These are indicated in Table 6A.3 using asterisks.

Table 6A.3   Okun's coefficients for country income group and country, by age group and time period

Country	Country income group	Okun's coefficients for 15–24-year-olds			Okun's coefficients for 25–54-year-olds		
		1991–2008 (pre-2009)	2009–18 (post-2008)	P-value for difference between coefficients	1991–2008 (pre-2009)	2009–18 (post-2008)	P-value for difference between coefficients
Australia	High	−0.858	−0.560	0.622	−0.412	−0.179	0.403
Austria	High	−0.098	−0.445	0.220	−0.039	−0.248	0.089*
Belgium	High	−0.914	−1.302	0.582	−0.322	−0.209	0.566
Canada	High	−0.609	−0.703	0.588	−0.313	−0.394	0.433
Chile	High	−0.496	−0.798	0.399	−0.237	−0.409	0.182
Croatia	High	−0.171	−1.113	0.540	0.087	−0.388	0.294
Cyprus	High	0.169	−1.097	0.384	−0.168	−0.436	0.546

Global youth unemployment

Country	Country income group	Okun's coefficients for 15–24-year-olds			Okun's coefficients for 25–54-year-olds		
		1991–2008 (pre-2009)	2009–18 (post-2008)	P-value for difference between coefficients	1991–2008 (pre-2009)	2009–18 (post-2008)	P-value for difference between coefficients
Czech Republic	High	−0.566	−0.921	0.339	−0.199	−0.278	0.519
Denmark	High	−0.931	−0.514	0.165	−0.403	−0.353	0.709
Estonia	High	−0.353	−0.971	0.087*	−0.090	−0.479	0.008***
Finland	High	−0.853	−0.529	0.418	−0.457	−0.185	0.035**
France	High	−0.923	−1.204	0.589	−0.167	−0.300	0.451
Germany	High	−0.455	−0.177	0.124	−0.273	−0.114	0.149
Greece	High	−0.469	−1.620	0.000***	−0.090	−0.777	0.000***
Hong Kong SAR China	High	−0.430	−0.571	0.593	−0.253	−0.260	0.945
Hungary	High	−0.106	−0.887	0.055*	−0.107	−0.266	0.270
Iceland	High	−0.510	−0.565	0.820	−0.139	−0.278	0.131
Ireland	High	−0.523	−0.331	0.258	−0.244	−0.176	0.430
Israel	High	−0.416	−0.624	0.656	−0.138	−0.545	0.137
Italy	High	−0.222	−1.084	0.050**	0.008	−0.280	0.035**
Japan	High	−0.071	−0.216	0.146	−0.068	−0.135	0.109
Korea, Republic of	High	−0.381	−0.056	0.264	−0.175	−0.083	0.522
Latvia	High	−0.445	−1.173	0.019**	−0.281	−0.541	0.019**
Lithuania	High	−0.224	−1.016	0.126	−0.253	−0.477	0.179
Luxembourg	High	−0.314	−0.046	0.444	−0.089	−0.004	0.234
Macao SAR China	High	−0.103	−0.024	0.125	−0.072	−0.016	0.036**
Malta	High	−1.595	−0.220	0.008***	0.229	−0.049	0.030**
Netherlands	High	−0.697	−0.597	0.748	−0.314	−0.298	0.915
New Zealand	High	−0.670	−1.522	0.009***	−0.332	−0.466	0.332
Norway	High	−0.332	−0.430	0.860	−0.115	−0.130	0.934
Poland	High	−1.768	−0.645	0.347	−0.757	−0.310	0.358
Portugal	High	−0.706	−1.552	0.035**	−0.253	−0.628	0.007***
Singapore	High	−0.221	−0.382	0.288	−0.093	−0.188	0.366
Slovak Republic	High	−1.313	−0.717	0.189	−0.509	−0.212	0.103
Slovenia	High	−0.613	−0.641	0.949	−0.181	−0.252	0.706
Spain	High	−2.210	−2.245	0.910	−0.846	−1.062	0.235
Sweden	High	−1.240	−0.599	0.076*	−0.406	−0.175	0.084*
Switzerland	High	−0.335	−0.349	0.951	−0.181	−0.086	0.483
Trinidad and Tobago	High	−0.433	−0.440	0.979	−0.115	−0.163	0.601
United Kingdom	High	−0.678	−0.880	0.438	−0.284	−0.338	0.650
United States	High	−0.640	−1.082	0.010**	−0.373	−0.765	0.001***

Country	Country income group	Okun's coefficients for 15–24-year-olds			Okun's coefficients for 25–54-year-olds		
		1991–2008 (pre-2009)	2009–18 (post-2008)	P-value for difference between coefficients	1991–2008 (pre-2009)	2009–18 (post-2008)	P-value for difference between coefficients
Uruguay	High	−0.626	−0.517	0.670	−0.261	−0.172	0.517
Bulgaria	Upper middle	−1.661	−1.041	0.615	−0.945	−0.413	0.347
Ecuador	Upper middle	0.163	−0.115	0.389	0.014	−0.145	0.215
Mexico	Upper middle	−0.337	−0.296	0.787	−0.188	−0.165	0.695
Peru	Upper middle	−0.228	−0.077	0.718	−0.081	−0.043	0.798
Romania	Upper middle	0.194	−0.328	0.013**	−0.016	−0.132	0.147
Russian Federation	Upper middle	−0.217	−0.478	0.116	−0.134	−0.215	0.221
South Africa	Upper middle	−0.712	−0.455	0.820	−0.072	−0.180	0.833
Thailand	Upper middle	−0.176	−0.307	0.586	0.018	−0.062	0.126
Turkey	Upper middle	−0.077	−0.378	0.049**	−0.096	−0.256	0.025**
Indonesia	Lower middle	−1.205	−0.728	0.679	0.290	−0.046	0.330
Moldova	Lower middle	0.413	−0.239	0.322	0.302	−0.105	0.159
Philippines	Lower middle	−0.294	−0.101	0.859	−0.124	−0.039	0.814
West Bank and Gaza	Lower middle	−0.469	−0.350	0.748	−0.398	−0.372	0.908

Notes: * p-value < 0.1, ** p-value < 0.05, *** p-value < 0.01.

APPENDIX 6.4   CHANGES IN YOUTH UNEMPLOYMENT AND THE HUMAN DEVELOPMENT INDEX, 1996–2018

Table 6A.4.1 shows model coefficients for the 73 countries (41 high-income, 19 upper middle-income, and 13 lower middle-income) for which we had post-2008 data on both the Human Development Index (HDI) and YU. These models were used to assess whether there was an underlying linear relationship between HDI and YU and to quantify and test the relationship using statistical tests.

The HDI is a composite score that combines information from three indices, each of which is aligned with one of the UN Sustainable Development Goals (SDGs). The health dimension is measured by life expectancy at birth (SDG 3); the education dimension is based on expected years of schooling (SDG 4.3) and mean years of (actual) schooling (SDG 4.6); and the income dimension is based on gross national income (GNI) per capita (SDG 8.5). The final HDI score is the geometric mean of these three (normalised) indices.

The coefficients are generated using similar models to those outlined in Appendix 6.2. A set of linear regression models was run at country level and fitted using ordinary least squares. The relationship between change in YU and change in each of the three components was summarised using the equation:

$$u_t - u_{t-1} = \alpha + \beta_I I_t + \beta_H H_t + \beta_E E_t + \varepsilon_t$$

Where u_t is unemployment at time t, I_t is *change* in the income index at time t (measured as the value of the income index at time t minus the value of the income index at $t-1$), E_t is change in the education index and H_t is the change in the health index (both measured in the same way as the income index), and ε_t is an error term. The parameters β are the model coefficients for each respective index. These measure the size and direction of the relationship between change in that particular index and changes in YU.

The coefficients show the impact on YU rates associated with a unit change in each index, whilst holding the other two indices constant. They also show the direction of that relationship – a negative coefficient indicates an inverse relationship where YU reduces as the growth in the index increases, and vice versa.

The value of the coefficients is tested in the model using a t-test. The table contains the p-values from these t-tests. The p-values indicate whether, for each specific country, a change in that specific index is significantly related to changes in YU. The relationship is deemed to be significant at the 90% level if the p-value is smaller than 0.1, significant at the 95% level if the p-value is smaller than 0.05, and significant at the 99% level if the p-value is smaller than 0.01 (marked in the table with asterisks). P-values are probabilities; a small p-value indicates that there is a very small probability that the findings we are testing occurred purely by chance. Table 6A.4.2 shows the model coefficients for 53 countries (40 high-income, ten upper middle-income, and three lower-middle income) for which data were available for both the pre-2009 (1996–2008) and post-2008 (2009–18) periods. The coefficients were estimated using linear regression equations (fitted using Ordinary Least Squares) using data covering the period 1996–2008 and an interaction term to identify the pre-2009 and post-2008 time periods. The interaction term was used to test whether the relationship between each indicator and YU pre-2009 was different to that post-2008. The model equation is:

$$u_t - u_{t-1} = \alpha + \beta_{I1} I_t + \beta_{H1} H_t + \beta_{E1} E_t + \beta_{I2} I_t{*}GFC + \beta_{H2} H_t{*}GFC + \beta_{E2} E_t{*}GFC + \beta_3 GFC + \varepsilon_t$$

Where u_t is unemployment at time t, I_t is *change* in the income index at time t (measured as the value of the income index at time t minus the value of the income index at t-1), E_t is change in the education index and H_t is the change in the health index (both measured in the same way as the income index). *GFC* is a dummy variable indicating whether the data came from pre-GFC (1996–2008) or after (2009–18). Specifically, the dummy variable was 1 = post-2008 period, 0 = pre-2009 period, and ε_t is an error term.

As with the models presented in Appendix 6.3, the model coefficients for each index in the pre-2009 period are β_1. The coefficient for the interaction (β_2) measures the difference in size between the pre-2009 and post-2008 time periods. The model coefficient for the post-2008 period for the education group is therefore $\beta_{E1} + \beta_{E2}$, the sum of the coefficient for the pre-2009 period and the difference between the two time periods.

Once again the value of the coefficients is tested in the model using a t-test. The table contains the p-values from these t-tests. The p-values indicate whether, for each specific country, a change in that specific index is significantly related to changes in YU (significances and probabilities are as for Table 6A.4.1).

Table 6A.4.1   Model coefficients for change in unemployment rates amongst young people (aged 15–24 years) in the period post-2008 by country and country income group

Country	Country income group	Coefficient for income index	Coefficient for education index	Coefficient for health index	P-value for income index coef.	P-value for education index coef.	P-value for health index coef.
Australia	High	196.7	7.3	735.0	0.596	0.895	0.532
Austria	High	−289.6	−14.5	−345.7	0.007***	0.602	0.282
Belgium	High	−92.9	443.3	−342.9	0.755	0.391	0.888
Canada	High	−479.4	49.2	443.9	0.000***	0.063*	0.017**
Chile	High	−260.4	90.4	−487.3	0.024**	0.001***	0.380
Croatia	High	511.2	622.2	4,232.9	0.238	0.054*	0.176
Cyprus	High	−541.9	−15.4	1,040.8	0.048**	0.945	0.765
Czech Republic	High	−676.1	−103.8	204.5	0.002***	0.230	0.850
Denmark	High	−299.8	−11.0	659.0	0.104	0.852	0.144
Estonia	High	−693.8	201.3	−399.9	0.001***	0.406	0.418
Finland	High	−433.7	−11.4	−617.2	0.010**	0.881	0.511
France	High	−705.2	−2.0	350.3	0.000***	0.962	0.144
Germany	High	−143.1	38.1	−88.4	0.010**	0.396	0.862
Greece	High	−1,219.9	43.6	−3,096.8	0.001***	0.699	0.266
Hong Kong SAR China	High	−392.1	−68.2	441.3	0.036**	0.511	0.697
Hungary	High	−575.2	88.8	40.5	0.026**	0.276	0.967
Iceland	High	−82.9	−90.4	7,159.9	0.313	0.266	0.003***
Ireland	High	−440.1	−112.8	391.9	0.000***	0.064*	0.727
Israel	High	−364.0	20.4	834.7	0.071*	0.903	0.304
Italy	High	−807.4	132.1	−2,481.9	0.003***	0.558	0.114
Japan	High	−145.0	−31.2	−220.8	0.133	0.739	0.649
Korea, Republic of	High	−256.3	64.2	15.0	0.346	0.442	0.927
Latvia	High	−719.5	−264.2	−429.5	0.048**	0.442	0.693

Country	Country income group	Coefficient for income index	Coefficient for education index	Coefficient for health index	P-value for income index coef.	P-value for education index coef.	P-value for health index coef.
Lithuania	High	-809.8	9.0	-930.2	0.004***	0.946	0.329
Luxembourg	High	-91.0	7.1	-131.5	0.559	0.986	0.927
Malta	High	-171.6	-4.1	-224.0	0.014**	0.911	0.648
Netherlands	High	-222.1	-66.4	993.2	0.165	0.280	0.150
New Zealand	High	-66.5	26.0	1,743.8	0.901	0.948	0.280
Norway	High	-112.0	94.3	-39.0	0.703	0.278	0.952
Poland	High	-419.2	6.2	1,371.3	0.409	0.939	0.420
Portugal	High	-704.8	230.3	1,461.2	0.084*	0.324	0.484
Singapore	High	-106.8	-23.5	939.5	0.483	0.799	0.232
Slovak Republic	High	-670.6	54.0	3,118.4	0.059*	0.799	0.053*
Slovenia	High	-201.3	-72.0	1,236.1	0.236	0.292	0.201
Spain	High	-1,307.3	-1.4	1,366.9	0.008***	0.996	0.570
Sweden	High	-371.8	13.8	-486.8	0.023**	0.697	0.735
Switzerland	High	1.6	102.8	-322.1	0.957	0.005***	0.237
Trinidad and Tobago	High	-244.5	-8.2	-2,368.0	0.084*	0.931	0.166
United Kingdom	High	-334.0	-30.6	1,095.7	0.032**	0.130	0.009***
United States	High	-654.7	-10.2	302.0	0.013**	0.932	0.407
Uruguay	High	-173.9	-30.8	-1,053.4	0.218	0.506	0.595
Argentina	Upper middle	-106.1	-11.1	1,666.4	0.089*	0.891	0.102
Azerbaijan	Upper middle	4.5	-55.8	5.0	0.712	0.003***	0.955
Bosnia and Herzegovina	Upper middle	502.2	-89.8	12,801.8	0.447	0.286	0.024**
Bulgaria	Upper middle	-569.7	-83.3	2,037.0	0.129	0.472	0.151
Colombia	Upper middle	-229.2	11.4	-343.3	0.025**	0.804	0.592
Ecuador	Upper middle	-145.3	5.9	-1,772.3	0.065*	0.626	0.026**
Jamaica	Upper middle	-2,185.1	-636.7	3,379.5	0.032**	0.074*	0.101

152

Country	Country income group	Coefficient for income index	Coefficient for education index	Coefficient for health index	P-value for income index coef.	P-value for education index coef.	P-value for health index coef.
Malaysia	Upper middle	−135.8	−103.9	−630.3	0.719	0.560	0.875
Mexico	Upper middle	−158.6	10.3	−303.3	0.011**	0.752	0.371
North Macedonia	Upper middle	54.0	−271.3	926.9	0.870	0.225	0.385
Peru	Upper middle	−108.7	67.1	−3,059.4	0.477	0.169	0.017**
Romania	Upper middle	71.3	80.6	1,132.2	0.674	0.276	0.072*
Russian Federation	Upper middle	−332.6	13.3	−143.0	0.001***	0.794	0.239
Serbia	Upper middle	464.3	−102.0	5,549.9	0.526	0.624	0.143
South Africa	Upper middle	−488.2	−0.4	149.0	0.248	0.995	0.285
Sri Lanka	Upper middle	−274.8	−136.0	110.8	0.227	0.708	0.934
Suriname	Upper middle	43.9	379.7	1,954.8	0.956	0.290	0.487
Thailand	Upper middle	−206.1	58.5	−364.2	0.023**	0.051*	0.164
Turkey	Upper middle	−319.6	52.8	−1,041.0	0.015**	0.377	0.219
Bhutan	Lower middle	−214.2	−346.0	760.9	0.332	0.208	0.761
Bolivia	Lower middle	395.0	57.0	−282.0	0.173	0.617	0.535
Cambodia	Lower middle	−72.2	64.1	−298.3	0.496	0.345	0.236
Egypt, Arab Republic of	Lower middle	−633.4	88.1	2,651.1	0.182	0.637	0.383
El Salvador	Lower middle	−1,001.3	−61.2	97.0	0.002***	0.014**	0.817
Honduras	Lower middle	−108.8	132.9	−286.1	0.642	0.396	0.862
Indonesia	Lower middle	−418.9	62.6	−945.3	0.336	0.623	0.316
Kyrgyz Republic	Lower middle	−172.3	56.3	−230.7	0.372	0.756	0.496
Moldova	Lower middle	−107.2	−213.5	355.7	0.374	0.385	0.386
Philippines	Lower middle	−75.8	−0.4	227.1	0.411	0.989	0.542
Ukraine	Lower middle	−40.7	384.4	309.6	0.804	0.492	0.433
Vietnam	Lower middle	63.4	78.4	−679.6	0.316	0.018**	0.158
West Bank and Gaza	Lower middle	−218.4	−78.3	2,398.9	0.466	0.707	0.489

Table 6.4.4.2   *Model coefficients for change in unemployment rates amongst young people (aged 15–24 years), pre-2009 and post-2008*

Country	Income group	Income pre-2009 coef.	Education pre-2009 coef.	Life pre-2009 coef.	Income post-2008 coef.	Education post-2008 coef.	Health post-2008 coef.	P-value for difference between income coefs	P-value for difference between education coefs	P-value for difference between health coefs
Australia	High	−270.3	13.3	201.7	196.7	7.3	735.0	0.179	0.905	0.609
Austria	High	−201.7	−13.5	174.5	−289.6	−14.5	−345.7	0.810	0.987	0.592
Belgium	High	−765.2	−122.0	−1413.2	−92.9	443.3	−342.9	0.273	0.298	0.726
Canada	High	−178.2	18.0	−533.2	−479.4	49.2	443.9	0.016**	0.513	0.053*
Chile	High	−255.6	63.1	10.5	−260.4	90.4	−487.3	0.983	0.704	0.752
Croatia	High	−544.9	34.2	−960.6	511.2	622.2	4232.9	0.288	0.306	0.114
Cyprus	High	338.9	−122.6	−2021.2	−541.9	−15.4	1040.8	0.420	0.781	0.637
Czech Republic	High	−392.1	18.5	201.9	−676.1	−103.8	204.5	0.447	0.519	0.999
Denmark	High	438.5	164.8	2415.6	−299.8	−11.0	659.0	0.041**	0.021**	0.098*
Estonia	High	−485.8	−88.8	−2938.3	−693.8	201.3	−399.9	0.408	0.435	0.212
Finland	High	−530.1	28.6	2807.6	−433.7	−11.4	−617.2	0.761	0.749	0.146
France	High	−143.3	159.1	465.2	−705.2	−2.0	350.3	0.185	0.361	0.932
Germany	High	−413.2	16.8	−143.9	−143.1	38.1	−88.4	0.328	0.909	0.980
Greece	High	51.8	10.1	−1534.3	−1219.9	43.6	−3096.8	0.000***	0.734	0.478
Hong Kong SAR China	High	−251.8	26.5	942.6	−392.1	−68.2	441.3	0.527	0.532	0.791
Hungary	High	452.0	−80.6	−1513.2	−575.2	88.8	40.5	0.005***	0.203	0.205
Iceland	High	−111.3	132.3	417.9	−82.9	−90.4	7159.9	0.864	0.264	0.042**
Ireland	High	−301.8	−27.7	437.7	−440.1	−112.8	391.9	0.109	0.077*	0.961
Israel	High	−178.9	56.7	−227.0	−364.0	20.4	834.7	0.549	0.885	0.506
Italy	High	−270.1	−160.7	436.3	−807.4	132.1	−2481.9	0.055*	0.373	0.055*
Japan	High	−118.9	−8.0	622.5	−145.0	−31.2	−220.8	0.823	0.829	0.073*
Korea, Republic of	High	−447.2	74.0	184.8	−256.3	64.2	15.0	0.702	0.953	0.770

Country	Income group	Income pre-2009 coef.	Education pre-2009 coef.	Life pre-2009 coef.	Income post-2008 coef.	Education post-2008 coef.	Health post-2008 coef.	P-value for difference between income coefs	P-value for difference between education coefs	P-value for difference between health coefs
Latvia	High	−331.7	89.2	52.6	−719.5	−264.2	−429.5	0.310	0.258	0.740
Lithuania	High	20.9	−71.7	1735.7	−809.8	9.0	−930.2	0.182	0.821	0.299
Luxembourg	High	−122.6	−90.2	−2351.8	−91.0	7.1	−131.5	0.912	0.786	0.455
Malta	High	560.4	28.0	−3015.1	−171.6	−4.1	−224.0	0.168	0.781	0.259
Netherlands	High	−217.7	15.3	465.0	−222.1	−66.4	993.2	0.986	0.498	0.605
New Zealand	High	−291.6	39.9	−511.3	−66.5	26.0	1743.8	0.615	0.962	0.137
Norway	High	112.5	−28.3	−369.5	−112.0	94.3	−39.0	0.534	0.205	0.749
Poland	High	−610.1	−125.9	3331.2	−419.2	6.2	1371.3	0.780	0.450	0.363
Portugal	High	−191.1	−142.7	2596.7	−704.8	230.3	1461.2	0.407	0.066*	0.678
Singapore	High	−142.1	215.0	620.3	−106.8	−23.5	939.5	0.876	0.310	0.774
Slovak Republic	High	−297.6	−349.8	256.4	−670.6	54.0	3118.4	0.288	0.104	0.206
Slovenia	High	−316.1	95.4	306.1	−201.3	−72.0	1236.1	0.773	0.122	0.434
Spain	High	−1064.5	−173.1	2145.3	−1307.3	−1.4	1366.9	0.568	0.585	0.764
Sweden	High	−386.1	−43.8	−1977.1	−371.8	13.8	−486.8	0.966	0.458	0.648
Switzerland	High	50.8	−38.8	438.6	1.6	102.8	−322.1	0.661	0.156	0.595
United Kingdom	High	−116.5	−45.3	1208.3	−334.0	−30.6	1095.7	0.172	0.745	0.831
United States	High	−365.0	35.2	−464.6	−654.7	−10.2	302.0	0.247	0.679	0.212
Uruguay	High	−208.4	208.6	871.0	−173.9	−30.8	−1053.4	0.885	0.238	0.505
Bulgaria	Upper middle	783.9	458.0	−2451.3	−569.7	−83.3	2037.0	0.080*	0.259	0.271
Ecuador	Upper middle	473.3	26.9	−3100.5	−145.3	5.9	−1772.3	0.009***	0.686	0.171
Mexico	Upper middle	−112.0	154.5	−138.2	−158.6	10.3	−303.3	0.668	0.117	0.741

Country	Income group	Income pre-2009 coef.	Education pre-2009 coef.	Life pre-2009 coef.	Income post-2008 coef.	Education post-2008 coef.	Health post-2008 coef.	P-value for difference between income coefs	P-value for difference between education coefs	P-value for difference between health coefs
Peru	Upper middle	-64.3	35.0	-552.7	-108.7	67.1	-3059.4	0.817	0.563	0.040**
Romania	Upper middle	40.5	-101.2	822.6	71.3	80.6	1132.2	0.921	0.245	0.798
Russian Federation	Upper middle	-250.8	-106.1	-17.0	-332.6	13.3	-143.0	0.606	0.567	0.703
South Africa	Upper middle	-119.3	19.5	-285.2	-488.2	-0.4	149.0	0.581	0.818	0.041**
Thailand	Upper middle	-54.7	-6.1	223.4	-206.1	58.5	-364.2	0.520	0.075*	0.496
Turkey	Upper middle	-180.5	-191.3	343.4	-319.6	52.8	-1041.0	0.306	0.092*	0.158
Indonesia	Lower middle	-663.6	31.3	-558.7	-418.9	62.6	-945.3	0.711	0.862	0.769
Moldova	Lower middle	215.6	-9.3	-1166.2	-107.2	-213.5	355.7	0.446	0.845	0.734
Philippines	Lower middle	302.1	264.3	2803.9	-75.8	-0.4	227.1	0.824	0.611	0.668

7. Historical origins and early development of global youth unemployment policy, 1919–1979

There is yet another provision in the Treaty of Versailles of which the full value has not yet been appreciated. That is the great labour provision which has been introduced in order to improve the conditions of labour by international co-operation. As you know, the difficulty was that whenever there was any proposal to improve the conditions of labour in this country we had to bear in mind the fact that we had to compete in the markets of the world, with countries that had no provisions of that character; but when you get the nations marching together to raise the standard, the nations working side by side to improve the conditions, the nations co-operating to lift the toilers, that difficulty disappears, that excuse vanishes, and by that you will greatly improve the conditions of the worker throughout the world by the process of international confidence.

David Lloyd George (UK Prime Minister, 1916–22), speech in Leeds, 20 October 1922
(ILO, 1931: 4 fn 1).

7.1 INTRODUCTION

No discussion of global youth unemployment (YU) can afford to ignore the institutional 'architectures' and the political practices of policy-making that contribute substantially to producing and reproducing it. Chapters 3–6 have highlighted the contemporary structure of global YU, and signalled the extent to which this is the result of national-level public and private policy decisions internationally. This chapter and the next (Chapter 8) move our discussion squarely on to a different institutional terrain – that of global governance – examining closely its key historical and current forms, and its achievements and limitations. As a concept, global governance has suffered almost as much as 'globalisation' in becoming an all-encompassing phrase rather than a clearly defined descriptor, but at its heart are 'formal institutions and regimes empowered to enforce compliance, as well as informal arrangements that people and institutions either have agreed to or perceived to be in their interests' (Commission on Global Governance, 1995: 2). Our interest for the purpose of this book lies squarely with the making of YU policy in multi-lateral spheres of governance.

Our comprehensive examination of global YU policy as a long-standing field of inter-governmental practice in spheres of cross-border governance has not hitherto been attempted (Chapter 1). This chapter and Chapter 8 begin to rectify that omission by opening up a panoramic window onto the constitution of this global policy field and, in turn, in the words of Lloyd George in the epigraph above, onto a century's worth of international cooperation regarding the labour conditions of the world's young 'toilers'. For this, we examine the historical origins and development of global policy on YU in some depth, from 1919 to the present day. This history is organised pragmatically, in chronological order. We start with the League of Nations (LoN) system which took forward nineteenth-century labour and trade union activism into codified norms on youth (un)employment and – as we shall argue – laid the pathway for initiatives across the twentieth century. We trace the development of this evolving policy field in relation to the growing hold of the Keynesian economic paradigm from the 1930s and of the international social development paradigm at the UN and other multilateral organisations, ending in the late 1970s when neo-liberalism ushered in a new set of political priorities in global policy-making. Chapter 8 picks up the story from the 1980s to the present day. Together, the chapters chart the scope and 'textures' of the policy field together with its dominant institutional, ideological, agentic and programmatic features. They cover a century's worth of global policy initiatives (1919–2021) that lie at the heart of the legal-administrative and political construction of YU as a global policy field (see Appendix 7.1 for a detailed time-line of initiatives corresponding with the timeframe of this chapter).

This long temporal range provides a vista onto major aspects of contemporary global policy-making on youth (un)employment, and their relationship to major shifts in economic and development thought and practice. Although transnational labour activism long pre-dates the establishment of international governmental organisations (IGOs) at the start of the twentieth century (Kirk, 2003; Silver, 2003; Van der Linden, 2003, 2008; Kirk et al., 2009; Reinalda, 2009; Hobsbawm, 2014; Maul, 2019), that activism, and the claims it articulated, became a significant factor in the international arena after the First World War – starting in the work of the LoN and continuing throughout the United Nations (UN) era. It is this fraction of the global history of labour internationalism that we trace. Through this, we discuss the tensions in ensuring that international competition and the rights of capital and employers do not preclude the rights of young workers, and in ensuring that young workers are sufficiently available to replenish workforces. How these tensions between protective, competitive and exploitative currents were reconciled helps shed light on the ideological and institutional contours of the policy field, and, in turn, on the compromises between capital and labour that formed around youth labour – a 'global youth labour compact'. Thus, we situate global YU policy in the context of the historic movement to fix international labour standards to counter the negative consequences of global economic dynamism (Reinalda, 2009; Maul, 2019).

In unpacking the emergence and development of YU as a global social policy field, we work between macro and micro aspects of global power relations shaping its development. This brings into focus conjunctions of ideas and practices, and of political-economic constraints and opportunities, that structure problem-definition (what are the dominant definitions of the underlying causes and effects of YU that are to be addressed?), response-definition (what sorts of responses are deemed warranted and feasible? Which are resourced?), and policy timing (what prompts significant global responses to YU at certain times but not others?). Identifying key milestones in the institutionalisation of global YU policy, we trace the constitution of the policy field – its major participants, structural features, and relational qualities. In this, we attend both to significant changes in the field's scope, orientation and emphasis over time, and to its enduring continuities.

The chapter is organised around four main sections. Section 7.2 traces the contours of the youth labour aspects of the International Labour Organization (ILO) Constitution, and how the ILO enacted its mandate through the first decade of its existence. We show that the ILO only very tangentially addressed YU but that its work on minimum working age and unemployment defined when and how young people could be employed (and were prepared for employment) as much as it defined the prohibition on employing them. These measures laid the normative and institutional 'floor' on which later initiatives on global YU built. Such initiatives are the subject of Section 7.3, which focuses on the ILO's first initiatives on global YU during the 1930s, when it produced the first-ever global policy instrument in this field in 1935, in the form of a Recommendation. The section discusses the conditions that gave rise to the Recommendation, the actors involved, its policy approach and content, and its institutional passage into global labour 'law', and the outturn from that initiative. We argue that although the Recommendation was facilitated by Keynesian economic theory, its content reflected little if any of the theory's hallmarks, instead inscribing a clear focus on supply-side approaches to YU – that is, approaches that are concerned with the adequacy of the supply of labour (for example, the available skills and predispositions of young people). Section 7.4 resumes coverage of the ILO's YU-related work after the Second World War, tracing the development of global YU policy during the UN/Bretton Woods era at a time when full employment was high on the UN's policy agenda. We show the degree of continuity with pre-war approaches to global YU, and how the ILO increasingly emphasised not just vocational training but education – not least to shelter 'surplus' youth labour. In this regard, it saw the emergence of the first inter-IGO working partnership between ILO and UNESCO, that picked up on pre-war networks and continued over the remainder of the century, together with an emphasis within the UN more widely on how YU was an inseparable element of wider social and economic development issues that in turn required a multi-faceted response. Throughout the period we cover in Section 7.5, the signs of growing neo-liberalisation of global policy were becoming increasingly evident. Tracing these signs as they manifested in global YU policy, we emphasise the dualisation of ILO's response to global YU – a division that distinguished between 'developing' and 'developed' countries. This dualisation was, we argue, part of a wider shift in the global political economy of global policy-making, ushered in by the reordering of global political and economic priorities and the return to monetarism as a bedrock of global economic governance. Section 7.6 ties together the main findings of the chapter in an overall conclusion that provides a bridge to Part II of this long history of global YU policy, taken up in Chapter 8, which picks up from the late 1970s and the fall-out from the ILO's World Employment Programme.

7.2   FIRST PRIORITIES: ADULT UNEMPLOYMENT AND MINIMUM WORKING AGE

Historically, the International Labour Organization is the organisational centre of global policy on YU. Article 23 of the Treaty of Versailles (1919) that founded the LoN committed members to 'endeavour to secure and maintain fair and humane conditions of labour for men, women, and children, both in their own countries and in all countries to which their commercial and industrial relations extend'.[1] The Treaty's labour clause was elaborated in the Preamble of the ILO's Constitution which stated that improvement of labour conditions

> is urgently required; as, for example, by the regulation of the hours of work, including the establishment of a maximum working day and week, the regulation of the labour supply, *the prevention of*

---

[1]   Forty-three founding members of the LoN represented about half of the world's sovereign states. A further 21 countries subsequently joined the LoN in the 1920s and 1930s. Over the lifetime of the LoN (1920–46), 18 states withdrew from it, mostly during the 1930s, and one (the Soviet Union) was expelled. African and South-East Asian colonies were not members in their own right (with the excep-

unemployment, the provision of an adequate living wage, the protection of the worker against sickness, disease and injury arising out of his [sic] employment, *the protection of children, young persons and women*, provision for old age and injury, protection of the interests of workers when employed in countries other than their own, recognition of the principle of equal remuneration for work of equal value, recognition of the principle of freedom of association, the organization of vocational and technical education and other measures. (ILO, 1919a, emphases added)

In many ways, the Constitution reflected the ideas and (some) demands of an already-established epistemic community of reformist trade union and progressive industrialists, and built on pre-ILO labour movement activity campaigning around the abolition of child labour and the protection of young people and women (Maul, 2019). It also reflected the *minimal* consensus that could be achieved at the time, namely that the survival of open markets and international economic competition ultimately depends upon the *gradual* de-commodification of labour through national social reforms (ILO, 1919a: 29). At another level, the Constitution can be read as the outcome of a major rift in the institutional architecture of global economic and social governance. Although the Constitution highlighted the ILO's mandate in the prevention of unemployment, its powers were in practice limited to dealing with the consequences of unemployment through palliative 'social' policy measures. The wider economic mandate that would have enabled it to address the causes of unemployment through macro-economic, finance and trade policy was vested in the League's Economic and Financial Section (ILO, 1919a: 2019) and a relatively powerful Financial Committee. The former was no more than an administrative arm of the executive, and had no powers independent of the League's members, while the latter was run by bankers and used central bank cooperation guided by monetarism as the principal means of international economic management (Mazower, 2012). This separation of economic from social aspects of unemployment in the LoN system and the retention of full sovereignty over all matters 'economic' was insisted upon by the majority of League governments.[2] It was a fragile settlement, however, and the separation remained an ongoing axis of contestation that periodically erupted over the years as the contradictions arising from this institutional bifurcation became all too apparent. As becomes clear in this chapter and the next, the consequences of restricting the ILO's mandate to 'social' policy matters were also very apparent in its work on youth labour and unemployment.

The ILO did not explicitly address YU until the early 1930s (see Section 7.3), but some of its Conventions during the first decade applied to young workers as part of the general labour force and/or helped lay the foundations for later responses to YU. Key Conventions in this regard were, first, the Unemployment Convention (1919, C002) which committed members to establish 'a system of free public employment agencies' (Article 2) to prevent and protect against unemployment (ILO, 1919b). Second, a suite of Minimum Age Conventions defined the minimum working age as 14 years and above, and stipulated principles governing labour market entry, access to employment and working conditions of the youngest cohorts of the

---

tion of selected members of the British Empire). The USA and countries of the Saudi peninsular were never members. Membership of LoN and of the ILO were separate, as the ILO was an autonomous organisation.

[2]   Early proposals for a permanent body to oversee equitable international distribution of raw materials that would help revitalise production and address unemployment was rejected by governments on the basis that they deemed it an infringement of their national sovereignty (Pedersen, 2015; Maul, 2019: 56 fn 147).

labour force.[3] Third, the Night Work of Young Persons (Industry) Convention (C006) was the first ILO instrument to address the working conditions of young people (16–18 years old), which set the minimum age of employment in certain industrial processes involving night-time work (ILO, 1919c).[4]

The international standards these Conventions defined were far from universally applicable, however. This was not only because only a minority of the world's countries were ILO members, but also because 'special treatment' provisions for some countries were inscribed in the Conventions. For example, the Minimum Age (Industry) Convention (C005) made special provisions for Japan and India, permitting some forms of employment of children at a lower age (12 years old) and, in India's case, allowing child employment in small manufacturing enterprises (ILO, 1919d). For ILO members' colonies, protectorates and possessions which were not fully self-governing, a 'local conditions' clause granted the colonial powers the ability to adapt the Convention's provisions to local conditions or determine that local conditions rendered the provisions inapplicable (ILO, 1919d, Article 8). Even in countries that were full members of the ILO, some sorts of child labour were expressly permitted. For example, the Minimum Age (Industry) Convention exempted work by children in technical schools providing the work is 'approved and supervised by public authority' and in undertakings in which only members of the same family are employed (ILO, 1919d). The Night Work Conventions for women (C004) and young persons (C006) similarly exempted young people working in family businesses from the general prohibition of night work, and defined a range of circumstances and industrial undertakings where night work was permitted (ILO, 1919c, 1919e).

If the Conventions carved out a wide range of territories, industries, circumstances and conditions in which international standards were *not* expected to be met, they also elaborated health, education and welfare principles for how youth labour *could* be used. For example, the Minimum Age (Agriculture) Convention (ILO, 1921a) clarified that child education and vocational training took precedence over child employment. The Minimum Age (Non-Industrial Employment) Convention, passed a decade later, did similarly (ILO, 1932). Although the minimum age Conventions recognised that employment, training and education of young people are interlinked, they expressly defined young workers aged 14 years or older as outside the Conventions' scope and left it to national-level policy to define the principles guiding the use of youth labour. Still, by articulating the relationship between supporting compulsory school attendance and supporting preparation for the 'adult' life of work, they gave meaning to Article 4 of the Geneva Declaration of the Rights of the Child which stipulated that '[t]he child must be put in a position to earn a livelihood, and must be protected against every form

---

[3]   These were agreed on a sector-specific basis between 1919 and 1965. Notably, the 1919 Minimum Working Age in Industry Convention excluded family undertakings (dealt with in the Minimum Age (Family Undertakings) Recommendation, 1937). These Conventions were replaced by the Minimum Age Convention and Recommendation, both 1973. As Chapter 3 showed, this sector is an important source of work and income for a significant proportion of young unemployed people worldwide, especially in lower-income countries.

[4]   Article 1: 'Young persons under eighteen years of age shall not be employed during the night in any public or private industrial undertaking …'. Article 2: 'Young persons over the age of sixteen may be employed during the night in the following industrial undertakings on work which, by reason of the nature of the process, is required to be carried on continuously day and night'.

of exploitation' (League of Nations, 1924).[5] They also gave meaning to peace education work going on elsewhere in the League's International Committee on Intellectual Cooperation whose concerns included YU and the defence of human rights (Hermon, 1987). Vocational education sat uneasily in this mix and nearly two decades elapsed before the ILO turned its full attention to this matter.[6]

Developing institutional machinery for collecting and reporting social statistics became a priority because meaningful policy implementation, intervention and problem-solving depended on it. Many ILO instruments stipulated administrative and statistical apparatuses, not least for monitoring employers' adherence to agreed standards and working conditions, but there was as much work to be done to develop better labour force data. Indeed, the ILO was all too aware of the rudimentary nature of unemployment data, and it knew that strengthening the statistical infrastructure was vital to fulfilling its role as the guardian of the labour clauses of the Treaty of Versailles.[7] Alongside setting up ILO-level institutional machinery in the form of an Unemployment Committee and a Mixed Committee on Economic Crises, it initiated work on unemployment statistics through an International Economic Conference (1928). This statistical work came together with work on national measures in its 1928 International Labour Conference (ILC), at which a special report *Unemployment: Some International Aspects, 1920–1928* (ILO, 1929) was presented. The report was vital for visibilising the scale and distribution of YU internationally, but it also underpinned a policy articulation revolving around interventions to remedy deficiencies in the numbers or capabilities of young unemployed people.[8]

During its first decade (1919–29), the ILO's busy programme hardly broached YU directly, but its work on minimum working age and unemployment laid a normative 'floor' defining the policy principles guiding the employment of young people, their preparation for work and their education, as well as the foundations of a statistical infrastructure. These gave meaning to a fledgling international human rights framework. These 'floors' were a formative influence in the making of the youth workforce because they delineated the inactive youth workforce (unavailable for work because in full-time training/education) from the active one (available for

---

[5]   The Declaration was the first human rights document approved by an inter-governmental institution, and the first to specifically address children's rights. It was non-binding. The General Assembly of the LoN re-approved it in 1934, though the signatories were not legally bound to incorporate it into national laws (Buck, 2014).

[6]   The 1921 Vocational Education (Agriculture) Recommendation (No. 15) was the only instrument of this period addressing vocational education. It recommended that members 'endeavour to develop vocational agricultural education and in particular to make such education available to agricultural wage-earners on the same conditions as to other persons engaged in agriculture' (Article I) (ILO, 1921b).

[7]   It commented that: 'Information in regard to unemployment [that is] at present available is not adequate. ... *although various kinds of unemployment are recognized to be international in character, both because they appear in every industrial country and because they are due to international causes*, nevertheless it is impossible to arrive at any exact and statistical view of the problem on an international scale' (ILO, 1919f: 239, emphasis added).

[8]   The following quote gives a flavour of those discussions: 'Other problems closely associated with the specialisation of employment exchanges are those of vocational guidance and the re-training of adults for work in occupations other than those in which they have hitherto been engaged. In Great Britain, a great deal is being done on these lines. The Industrial Transference Board ... recommended the extension of instructional centres for juveniles unemployed and the development of practical industrial training for adults' (ILO, 1929: 202).

work having completed full-time training/education). Such distinctions helped 'make sense' of who should count as unemployed and who shouldn't; as such, they were bedrocks of social reformism because they provided the basis for intervention. At another level, this work was without a doubt an important step in the construction of the global policy field, but its scope was far from universal: not only did the concept of 'YU' reflect the prevailing circumstances and economic structures of the minority of the countries of the world that were full members of the ILO, but the international standards under construction were deemed not applicable to the majority of the world's youth workforce which resided in ILO members' colonies.

7.3   DEFINING THE GLOBAL POLICY FIELD: ILO, YOUTH UNEMPLOYMENT AND THE GREAT DEPRESSION

YU came to feature prominently in the ILO's work in the 1930s as the material and political impacts of the 1929 financial crisis became all too apparent. Not only did unemployment rocket, but more and more governments and civil society youth, labour and peace groups pressed forcefully and publicly for responses to it other than supply-side measures. A good part of this activism comprised demands for international-level action, but a shift in thinking about the role of the state in tackling unemployment in open economy contexts was also becoming apparent. Indeed, by the early 1930s, proto-Keynesianism became increasingly dominant in discussions about unemployment.[9]

7.3.1   Galvanising the ILO into Action: Policy Responses

Despite only rudimentary unemployment statistics being available, they were nevertheless sufficiently advanced by the period of the Great Depression for an ILO international study of YU to proceed. Covering Europe, the USA, Canada, New Zealand and Japan, the study showed that one in four of the 25 million unemployed people worldwide were under the age of 25, amounting to 'about 6 or 7 million' young people (ILO, 1935b: 16) (see also Tables 3.1–3.3, Chapter 3). This was acknowledged as a likely underestimate of YU, due to, for example, the lack of contact of young people with unemployment institutions (ILO, 1935b: 20–22). The study found mixed evidence that young people were more seriously affected by unemployment than other age groups of the working population, but showed that women were consistently disproportionately represented among the young unemployed.[10]

In many ways, the report confirmed what youth groups had been highlighting for some time: that young people were especially seriously affected by the economic crash and the crisis that

---

[9]   We use this term because Keynes' *General Theory of Employment, Interest and Money* was not published until 1936. ILO economists had endorsed the basic ideas of Keynesian thought in the 1920s, and were members of an epistemic community of economists working with Keynes directly or indirectly (Maul, 2019: 86). The ILO's support for public works and reduced working hours are tangible examples of the influence of Keynesian thought. See, for example, *Unemployment and Public Works* (ILO, 1931).

[10]   The ILO report (ILO, 1935b: 17) noted that 'unemployment among young persons forms a higher percentage of total unemployment among women than among men, the difference being sometimes a very substantial one (Germany, Great Britain, Italy, United States)'. It explained this difference thus: this 'higher rate of unemployment among girls and young women is nothing but a direct consequence of the fact that there are more young persons among women workers than among men' (p. 17).

followed, and that the ILO should adopt a more assertive position on unemployment in general and YU in particular. In one respect, this was pushing an open door. The ILO was already forging alliances with the international educational communities on minimum age of entry to employment, with international Keynesian communities on demand-led approaches, and with international health communities on the psychological effects of unemployment on young people.[11] Although the ILO's work raised the profile of YU as a global policy issue, it proved far more difficult, it seems, to get this issue onto the ILO's own formal agenda. Our scrutiny of archival records shows that socialist civil society advocacy had, since the early 1930s, been critical to pressing this case in the face of systematic objections by the ILO Governing Body.[12]

In any case, it was not until 1933 when unemployment was at an all-time high (see Table 3.2 above), and the world employment position had already massively deteriorated, that an ILO response to YU became apparent. This year was the first that ILC discussion time on YU had been scheduled, and it enabled workers' organisations and some governments to demand international action (ILO, 1934a). The ILO's response (ILO, 1934a, 1935a, 1935b) evidenced diverse sources of economic and social thought. The first of these was the influence of Keynesianism. The Director's Annual Report that year invoked YU as part of a wider argument about the intolerable consequences of a lack of state economic planning:

> Nothing is more responsible for the bitter feeling of frustration experienced by millions of young men and women all over the world than the knowledge that they are condemned to want and idleness at a time when greater plenty is within easier reach than their fathers ever knew. *The assumption… that the consumers would automatically come forward to absorb all that new productive equipment could create, has been signally falsified by the event. Hence the demand for a systematic effort to adapt consumption.* (ILO, 1933: 69, emphasis added)

The ILO had already argued for the use of demand-side economic measures to address 'surplus' numbers of workers and/or their underexploited skills and capabilities, but this was the first time it applied this argument to young people. The strong influence of Keynesian 'aggregate demand management' labour economics on ILO thinking became apparent two years later as it rejected wage deflation as a strategy to reduce industry costs (ILO, 1935a: 34) and strongly argued for expansionist, demand-stimulating measures to reduce unemployment. Expansionist forms of state intervention in economies were shown to have demonstrated 'the power of Governments to influence the course of recovery …. There is less and less willingness to accept the thesis that all human agencies are impotent to control the fluctuations of economic fortune' (ILO, 1935a: 35–6).

---

[11]   Maul (2019: 70) notes that '[t]hroughout the interwar period, the ILO and the LNHO [League of Nations Health Organization] cooperated on a series of committees and conferences, which examined the relationship between health and general living conditions, rural hygiene, and child welfare. … The ILO's cooperation with the LNHO reflected more than anything a renewed sense of concern with the socio-economic bases of health'.

[12]   For example, '[T]he impulse to consider the expediency of international regulations on the subject was given by a proposal made by the Socialist Youth International on 23 August 1932. This suggestion was submitted to the Governing Body at its Session in October of the same year, but … the question of unemployment among young persons failed to secure a majority of the votes of the Governing Body …. In October 1933, however, the Governing Body reconsidered the matter and decided to place the question of unemployment among young persons on the agenda of the Nineteenth Session of the Conference' (ILO, 1935b: 1).

In considering how changes in the structure of economic organisation and industrial production affected overall demand for youth labour and its distribution, the ILO recalled the programme of economic measures it advocated in the previous two years to remedy economic depression and reduce YU, for example restoration of stable monetary conditions, international cooperation to prevent price fluctuations, re-circulation of 'idle' capital, and increased community purchasing power – though all but the last lay outside ILO's constitutional mandate (ILO, 1935b: 162).

The second element of the ILO's response was its support for extending the period of compulsory education. The Director-General's Report argued that courses of technical instruction and voluntary labour camps had been shown to maintain the development of the young unemployed but that 'it must be recognised that at best they are unsatisfactory palliatives' (ILO, 1934a: 32). Only the prospect of work or extended schooling could prevent the undermining of the younger generation.

The idea that lengthening compulsory education and extending vocational and professional training could keep young people out of the labour market and thus out of unemployment reflected a convergence of educational and labour market thinking about YU.[13] Moreover, it was one that resulted from epistemic linkages already forged between the international labour and educational communities. For example, the first International Conference on Public Education (ICPE) in Geneva in 1934 was on 'compulsory education and the raising of the school-leaving age'. Organised by the International Bureau of Education (IBE) and supported by the ILO, the conference strengthened international support for creating and extending secondary education up to the age of 14 at least (Woodin et al., 2013: 19). Foreshadowing an issue of major concern eight decades hence (see Chapters 2 and 8), the IBE's Recommendation on 'Admission of Secondary Schools' read: 'the overcrowding of institutions of higher education and the extent of unemployment among the intellectual classes, are *likely to cause dangerous unrest among young people*' (IBE/UNESCO, 1934: 3, emphasis added). At another level, the education perspective on unemployment is also evident in a substantial ILO report on YU (ILO, 1935b).[14] This made crystal clear the ILO's close tracking of research and debates in international educational, teacher and student associations, and in other parts of the LoN (such as the Child Welfare Committee, UNICEF's precursor), as well as the ILO's support for extending the period of compulsory education, vocational guidance and training as a solution to 'overcrowded' labour markets and unemployment (ILO, 1935b). The 1935 Annual Report of the Director-General unequivocally argued the labour market case for extending time spent in education and out of the active labour force, by relieving over-subscribed labour markets and improving intellectual and physical development (ILO, 1935a: 41–2):

> 'Raising of the School-leaving age' (RoSLA) represented the key strand of ILO's approach to YU. It reflected an understanding that the imperative went beyond issuing unemployment relief to preventing YU and with it the 'intellectual, physical and moral deterioration to which the youthful unemployed are exposed'. (ILO, 1935a: 42)[15]

---

[13]   International Bureau of Education 'Compulsory Education and the Raising of the School-leaving age (1934)' (UNESCO, 1979).

[14]   The Director-General's report (ILO, 1935a) was underpinned by an extensive research report, *Unemployment Among Young Persons* (ILO, 1935b). This report was one of the most substantial ever produced by the ILO on YU. It comprised a review of research evidence and the scope of international action already taken to address YU. Topics included statistical data on youth employment and unemployment, the school-leaving age and age of admission to employment, among many others.

[15]   '… [i]t can hardly be expected that young persons thrown on their own resources at a tender age will be able to offer much resistance to the demoralising influence of prolonged unemployment .... [They] may easily be driven to the verge of despair and to a complete loss of personal dignity' (ILO, 1935b: 64–5).

RoSLA was, in effect, a matter of national economy *and* of youth protection. ILO argued that unemployment relief was of no help to a young man [*sic*] for learning towards a productive job and a career 'if the springs of his ambition are dried up' (ILO, 1935a: 12, 41).

In highlighting the acute vulnerability of young people, the ILO was following a tradition of thinking on youth protection that sees employment as the best way of preventing their delinquency and 'moral decay'. In this, it prefigured debates about the scarring effects of unemployment on young people by some five decades (Chapter 2). If this was a pronounced demoralisation discourse, it was much more than a dog-whistle for social conservatives or proto neo-liberals, for it framed YU not so much as personal misfortune as a matter of the maldistribution of social rights:

> In times of economic depression, ... the adjustment of the available possibilities of employment between the various age groups becomes a most pertinent question. ... At certain times [a number of] factors may produce vast upheavals in the social structure by giving the eternal rivalry between 'young' and 'old' the character of a fight for *the right to work*. (ILO, 1935b: 138, emphasis added)

This latter reference is an early exemplar of the emergent rights discourse that became so central in post-Second World War global YU policy. For all its emphasis on longer periods of compulsory education and improved vocational training, the ILO was above all aware of their limitations as effective solutions to YU:

> Whatever their value, measures for the general and vocational education of young unemployed persons and their temporary occupation in labour centres are, after all, mere palliatives ... reincorporation in normal employment is the only lasting solution of the problem of unemployment. (ILO, 1935b: 137–8)

The essence of the ILO's approach may be characterised as stimulating demand for youth labour overall and diverting surplus youth labour into education, training and public works schemes.[16] Taking this agenda forward into practical policy entailed two sorts of response. One was through Conventions on working hours.[17] These were not specific to young people, though lower YU was cited as a potentially beneficial effect of measures to reduce working hours and share out available work.[18] A second response covered other measures through what eventually became the Unemployment (Young Persons) Recommendation, 1935 (No. 45) (ILO, 1935d). A draft Recommendation, annexed to the ILO's *Unemployment Among Young Persons* (ILO, 1935b), covered general and vocational education, recreational and social

---

[16]   The ILO (1935a) floated a range of ideas to reduce the youth labour supply and steer it towards education and/or vocational training (p. 152).

[17]   C047 – Forty-Hour Week Convention, 1935 (No. 47) and C051 – Reduction of Hours of Work (Public Works) Convention, 1936 (No. 51). They supplemented those already passed in specific industries and occupations (Industrial sector 1919, Commerce and Offices 1930, Coal Mines 1931), and their provisions were subsequently extended to additional occupations.

[18]   These proposals were debated at the ILC. For example, 'a distribution of the available employment among young unemployed persons ... might aim at reducing full-time unemployment, either by organising a system of rotation for young workers (point 38) or by applying more especially to young workers (point 39) the reduction in the normal hours of work which has already been recognised by the Conference as being, in principle, desirable as a remedy against unemployment generally' (ILO, 1935c: 179).

services, employment placing services, centres and public works, the role of trade unions and private organisations, as well as the improvement of YU statistics (see Appendix 7.2, p. 182).

The Recommendation showed clear signs of a collectivist ethos in the organisation of services for young unemployed people and arguably brought together a set of best practice models of services for young unemployed people. It was an important milestone in efforts to ensure that countries reliably provided unemployment benefits *and* further education or training for young people without work. However, it also foreshadowed more punitive responses to YU that became a marked feature of neo-liberal responses later in the century, and there was no escaping that it was primarily concerned with remedial measures rather than with preventing YU (see Chapter 2). The role of economic planning in preventing YU was confined to the Preamble and just one article of the draft Recommendation was given over to how employment is distributed among the working-age population.[19] Thus, Article 43 states: '[p]resent attempts to promote re-employment by a reduction in ordinary hours of work should be pursued with special vigour in respect of employment in which young persons engage'. *How* this might be done was not specified, though. This vagueness contrasts with extensive treatment of such matters in the ILO report (ILO, 1935b) and with the highly detailed prescriptions in the Recommendation of Special Employment Centres.

7.3.2   The Politics of Global Consensus: the Passage of the Recommendation

The Draft Recommendation was passed unanimously by 106 delegates (ILO, 1935c: 686). Its passage was a feat of international diplomacy. First, there was the question of which instrument would be used. The rationale for working through a Recommendation rather than through a Convention was procedural and tactical (ILO, 1935b: 156), but this choice was controversial since an ILO Recommendation is a much less powerful instrument than a Convention.[20] The Spanish government, for example, much preferred a Convention because it would make it 'more compulsory for Governments to adopt measures to remedy unemployment among young persons' (ILO, 1935c: 604).

The substantive work on the content of the Recommendation entailed a complex process of consultation and negotiation that saw the Committee on Unemployment Among Young People devoting 12 sessions to progressing the work, in addition to several ILC plenary sessions. Attesting to the vibrancy of civil society organisations revolving around services and advocacy on YU, dozens of diverse recognised reputable national bodies (religious, workers, academic, educational and unemployed groups) and international associations made representations during the process in the form of petitions, resolutions, memorandums, appeals, communications and addresses to the Committee (ILO, 1935c: 828ff.). Each of these organisations commanded significant support from affiliated or subsidiary member organisa-

---

[19]   This was noted by the Spanish government which argued that the Recommendation 'has one grave fault: that it omits reference to several fundamental problems with which all Governments are faced and with which the Conference will undoubtedly have to deal in a later Session. These are problems which relate to unemployment in general, but which must be solved' (ILO, 1935c: 604).

[20]   ILO Conventions mandate action by member states, whereas Recommendations are non-binding guidelines. They do not need to be ratified to be applicable, and member states are not required to report progress in implementing them. Indeed, ILO supervisory machinery does not normally track implementation of its Recommendations.

tions; some submitted petitions with thousands of signatures. They proved influential: their submissions were cited during debate on the draft Recommendation, and the final version of the Recommendation stated that '[t]he public authorities should assist educational and other social services for the young unemployed organised by trade organisations and other associations' (Article 18).

Two questions gave rise to extended discussion among delegates on matters of principle. The first was the proposal to raise the school-leaving age to 15. Details of the debates are not available in the archives, but references to differences of opinion within the negotiating Committee were diplomatically reported by ILO (1935c) thus: opponents argued that it 'would give rise to difficulties resulting from the budgetary situation in certain countries', while advocates 'were of [the] opinion that the social consequences of the measure were such as to render it eminently desirable' (ILO, 1935c: 593). Employers eventually supported the motion, though they 'doubted the competence of the International Labour Organization to deal with the question of raising the school-leaving age' (ILO, 1935c: 595). In the end, the Committee decided to recommend the raising of the school-leaving age to 15 years.

The second point of contention revolved around special employment centres for unemployed young people. One question was whether or not they should be included in a Recommendation that highlights best/ideal models of provision or practice. This point drew 'lengthy discussion' (ILO, 1935c: 593). Many ILO countries, such as those which already had such provision, wished to see such centres included in the Recommendation. Opponents argued these centres were little more than labour camps that might compete on unfair terms with industry, and that they were amenable to being used for political indoctrination and military purposes; they opposed including such centres in the Recommendation. Rather than delete the section dealing with this subject, delegates took a pragmatic response: recognising that because such centres already existed in a large number of countries that included Roosevelt's USA and Nazi Germany, 'it was therefore necessary to insert in this Recommendation certain safeguards against the dangers to which allusion had been made' (ILO, 1935c: 593). The section dealing with special employment centres was retained and elaborated highly detailed standards.

A further question revolved around compulsory attendance. The issue was whether governments could require young unemployed people in receipt of benefits to attend these centres. An Employers' group amendment to strengthen wording in the Recommendation to this effect, if passed, would have significantly extended governments' powers to coerce young unemployed people.[21] Unsurprisingly, the Workers' Group delegates objected to the proposed amendment, arguing that '[i]f [young people] receive no allowances unless they attend the camps, this is the very strictest form of coercion which can be laid upon them. The Workers' Group cannot accept this measure of coercion' (ILO, 1935c: 625), and that voluntary attendance at employment centres 'is the only condition on which we can accept the principle of employment centres' (p. 626). That battle may have been won in relation to employment

---

[21] The 1934 Unemployment Provision Convention stipulated that 'the right to receive benefit or an allowance may be made conditional upon attendance at a course of vocational or other instruction' (Article 8) (ILO, 1934b).

centres, but the Recommendation did not shy away from the use of compulsion for young unemployed people in other respects.[22]

The initiative commanded overwhelming support from delegates, all of whom recognised the urgent need for an ILO instrument in this area. For many, though, the initiative was a pale shadow, either because it took the form of a relatively weak Recommendation (government of Spain), or because there had not been sufficient discussion of particular issues (UK government viz. special employment centres, public relief works for young people), or because the Recommendation was not sufficiently specific (UK government viz. maintenance allowances) or did not go far enough (Dutch Workers group which wanted to return young unemployed mothers to their homes; the USA government which wanted to return young unemployed people to school, and exclude general reconstruction and recovery measures). The unease of many delegates with the overall weakness of the Recommendation was palpable and fully recorded (ILO, 1935c: 595–606).

Clearly relieved, the ILO Director's closing speech reiterated the symbolic and material significance of having successfully concluded the Recommendation in a way that recognised its limitations in dealing with the effects rather than the causes of YU, and its downstream risks of scarring (see Chapter 2):

> We have adopted a Recommendation with regard to juvenile unemployment, which deals with the effects of the great change that has taken place in the basis of our economic life and which affects young persons. That is of immense importance, in my opinion .... The effects of this loss [of discipline] may colour the whole of their lives for ill. (ILO, 1935c: 700)

The ILO was hopeful that the Recommendation was just a starting point, a basis for future Conventions 'dealing not only with young unemployed persons but with young workers in general' (ILO, 1935b: 156). The following year's ILC saw the *prevention* of 'complete idleness' briefly mentioned in the Director-General's address (ILO, 1936), but no further action was committed. In fact, no further Conventions specific to young unemployed or employed people were passed. The ILO's youth-specific initiatives over the next decade covered vocational guidance, training and apprenticeships[23]; these dealt with vocational training of workers in all its aspects but were merely returning to unfinished work that had stalled after the 1921 Vocational Education (Agriculture) Recommendation (R015). YU was not specifically addressed in the Apprenticeship Recommendation, while the Vocational Training Recommendation only advised that schools and other providers of special courses should be supported 'to make good the loss of opportunities for training caused by unemployment' in the event of economic depression or financial difficulty that might reduce facilities for technical and vocational education' (ILO, 1937: 5(2)).[24]

---

[22] For example, Article 9.1 stated that 'Where such attendance is not compulsory for all juveniles it should at least be made compulsory for unemployed juveniles, who should be required to attend for a prescribed number of hours every day or ... every week' (ILO, 1935d).

[23] Recommendations on Vocational Education (Building) (1937), Vocational Training (1939, R057), Apprenticeship (1939, R060), Vocational Guidance (1949, R087).

[24] Both Recommendations were replaced by the Vocational Training Recommendation, 1962 (No. 117). R177 was later replaced by the Human Resources Development Recommendation, 1975 (R150).

In spite of increased inter-state tensions in the 1930s, the labour movement had not given up on its objectives. Unemployment was at the centre of ILO work, and the package of measures the ILO had put together on public works, labour migration, unemployment insurance, working hours and paid holidays amounted to a state-led active employment creation and incomes stabilisation programme. Certainly, it reflected an integrative conception of social and economic policy, signalling that the ILO had entered into a 'quasi-symbiotic' relationship with Keynesianism (Maul, 2019: 86) that was to last until the 1970s. Although this relationship strengthened the hands of those seeking to reorganise capitalist economies along social liberal democratic premises (Maul, 2019; see also Reinalda, 2009), it hardly seemed to reflect the realities of young people's labour position.[25] Often overlooked by ILO measures in practice, what attention they did receive invariably led the ILO to palliative measures to mitigate the consequences of prolonged spells of joblessness.

This 'expansionist' phase – such as it was – in the early development of the ILO's mandate on YU was short-lived. The efficacy of the ILO as a LoN organisation was straining under the weight of weakening commitment to economic and political internationalism by its member governments, many of whom withdrew or were expelled from it. Whatever the prospective achievements of the 1935 Recommendation, in that year YU in advanced economies was running at rates between 16 per cent (Australia, Germany, UK), 20/25 per cent (Denmark and Norway, respectively) and 32 per cent (the Netherlands). In most of these countries rates were a little lower by 1938, on the eve of the Second World War, but there is little reason to attribute this improvement to the ILO's work. Rather, it was mainly a function of the steady continuing recovery from the alarming YU rates in the wake of the 1929 financial crash: in most advanced economies in 1932–33 YU varied between the lower 20 per cent and lower 40 per cent ranges (see Tables 3.1 and 3.2, Chapter 3).

The outbreak of the Second World War radically changed the dynamics of YU. At the level of labour markets, military conscription and the human carnage of the war itself 'solved' the problem of surplus youth labour, in and far beyond the world's advanced economies.[26] The war also changed the dynamics of global policy-making. Many states no longer participated in the ILO and LoN (see footnote 1, p. 158–9) and whatever claims the ILO had to being a platform for labour internationalism receded. More immediately, the ILC was suspended during the war and the ILO's work all but ceased as all attention was directed towards war and planning for its aftermath.

---

[25] Maul (2019) argues that the ILO's embrace of Keynesianism had a discernible geo-political dimension: it (re-)oriented ILO towards the West. This [was] inseparable from the growing influence within ILO of the USA's New Deal, the expulsion of USSR, Italy's withdrawal from ILO, and a turn away from authoritarian alternatives to the open economy more generally.

[26] In the very specific context of German expansionist ambitions, under 'Hitler's solution of Germany's unemployment problem ...' it was the introduction of universal male military conscription in 1935 that emerged as 'the primary factor which substantially reduced unemployment' (Stachura, 1986: 23). In 1933, total unemployment in Germany had peaked at 44 per cent (Table 3.1, Chapter 3).

7.4   NEW BEGINNING OR FALSE START? YOUTH UNEMPLOYMENT IN GLOBAL POLICY 1945–70

The outcome of the Second World War fundamentally changed the geo-economic, -political, and -institutional dynamics of the global governance of YU. The pre-war preoccupation with YU in the context of economic depression and rudimentary public services gave way to the realities of war-time economies: de facto full employment and shortages of labour and raw materials. As the UN reported, '[n]ot only did unemployment disappear but the war effort led simultaneously to an increase in hours of work and to an increase in the labour force' (UN 1949: 8). Institutionally, the ILO was in a very different place in this new global policy-making landscape. On the one hand, the Declaration of Philadelphia strengthened its economic mandate (Article 2 stipulated it would address 'all national and international policies and measures, in particular those of an economic and financial character') in step with 'the right to pursue both their material well-being and their spiritual development in conditions of freedom and dignity, of economic security and equal opportunity' (ILO, 1944a). At the same time, having narrowly retained its status as an autonomous UN agency (Maul, 2019: 108), the ILO was now but one agency within a wider UN system committed to promoting 'higher standards of living, full employment and conditions of economic and social progress and development' (UN Charter Article 55). Unlike the LoN, however, the UN was not equipped with the means to enforce implementation of any of its agreements.[27]

Additionally, the ILO was embedded in a system of multilateral governance in which non-UN organisations bore on youth (un)employment. The mandates of powerful new institutions of global economic governance in the realms of international development (International Bank for Reconstruction and Development (IBRD)), finance (International Monetary Fund (IMF)) and trade (General Agreement on Tariffs and Trade (GATT)) incorporated full employment objectives and their interventions had a significant bearing on worldwide unemployment.[28] Despite the ILO's new-found economic mandate, the separation of institutions of global economic and global labour governance postponed its ambition to be the 'social guardian' of the world economy. In a context in which the Keynesian paradigm reigned, among certain rich countries controlling those new global institutions at least, the conflict that such a separation gave rise to was at least containable.

A further aspect of this new institutional settlement was that the ILO's membership was far more extensive than during its LoN-era incarnation, and over the coming decades the victories of national liberation movements brought many more independent self-governing nations into

---

[27]   LoN provisions for members to be able to apply economic sanctions against one another were abolished in 1946 (Mazower, 2012; Maul, 2019: 27).

[28]   Article I (iii) of the Articles of Agreement of the IBRD refers to the objectives of 'assisting in raising productivity, the standard of living and conditions of labor in [members'] territories': see https://www.worldbank.org/en/about/articles-of-agreement/ibrd-articles-of-agreement/article-I (accessed 15 January 2020). Article I (ii) of the IMF's Articles of Agreement refers to the IMF's objective as 'the promotion and maintenance of high levels of employment and real income and to the development of the productive resources of all members as primary objectives of economic policy': see https://www.imf.org/external/pubs/ft/aa/ (accessed 15 January 2020). The Preamble of GATT refers to 'raising standards of living, ensuring full employment and a large and steadily growing volume of real income and effective demand …'.

this international community of states and civil society. This expansion of Global South membership drew the ILO into the emergent 'international development' apparatus and brought in countries with markedly different histories, economic and employment models, and social structures from those of its founding members, most especially the advanced industrialised countries.

The opening years of the ILO's UN-era programme saw it still preoccupied with LoN-era business. One priority was vocational training. Its approach shifted away from the 'problem' of surplus youth labour and towards the harmful effects of mass youth employment on young people's education and training (ILO, 1944b: 57). It also embodied a new emphasis on supporting industrialisation in 'developing countries'. Vocational training accounted for about half of the ILO's technical assistance programmes at this time (Maul, 2019: 155). A new instrument in the form of a Vocational Guidance Recommendation was concluded in 1949. But its continued focus on palliative measures was notable, ironic even, given that the ILO had ten years earlier criticised them as wholly inadequate responses to YU. By the late 1940s, though, countries again needed to concern themselves with unemployment and the ILO was gearing up for a policy on full employment[29] that would give meaning to the UN Charter (articles 55[30] and 56) (UN, 1945) and the Universal Declaration of Human Rights (UDHR) (UN, 1948).[31]

The pursuit of full employment was the most significant element of global YU policy at this time. An expert group report (UN, 1949) cogently argued the case for full employment as essential to global prosperity, peace and development.[32] Mass unemployment and its obverse, full employment, were 'simple' matters of political priorities: 'the choice for a country is not between more or less efficient uses of available resources but between employing some resources or leaving them idle' (UN, 1949: 7). Its report stands as one of the most comprehensive demand-side analyses of mass unemployment ever to have come from an IGO.[33] Running centrally throughout the report was an argument for stronger institutions of global *and* national economic governance capable of supporting more effective cooperation and coordination in the context of an integrated international economic order. As it argued, 'a complete solution'

---

[29] UN General Assembly Resolutions on Full Employment in 1949 (A/RES/308(IV)), 1950 (A/RES/405(V)), and 1954 (A/RES/829(IX)).

[30] Article 55: 'the United Nations shall promote: a. higher standards of living, full employment and conditions of economic and social progress and development; b. solutions of international economic, social, health, and related problems; and international cultural and educational co-operation; and c. universal respect for, and observance of, human rights and fundamental freedoms for all without distinction as to race, sex, language, or religion. Article 56: 'All Members pledge themselves to take joint and separate action in co-operation with the Organization for the achievement of the purposes set forth' (UN, 1945).

[31] The UDHR specified 'the right to work, to free choice of employment, to just and favourable conditions of work and to protection against unemployment' (Article 23). Adopted by UNGA December 1948, A/RES/217(III) A.

[32] 'The importance of full employment policies [is] among the conditions necessary for the smooth working of an international economic system, for the attainment of convertibility of currencies, and for the development of multilateral trade' (UN, 1949: 7).

[33] See, for example: 'the major cause of unemployment in industrialized countries is the insufficiency and instability of effective demand. … Under normal conditions, any unemployment exceeding the amount which is due to the frictional and seasonal factors to which we have referred above is a clear indication of a deficiency in effective demand' (UN, 1949: 13).

to the problem of full employment necessitated it being 'dealt with on a world basis' (UN, 1949: 9).

Its recommendations are by today's standards strikingly statist and the antithesis of market control (UN, 1949, Part III, p. 73). They included all countries adopting a full employment target suitable to their own circumstances. Such a target would define the standard of attainment of national employment stabilisation measures (for example, fiscal and monetary policies; investment and production planning; wages and prices). The report also recommended a system of compensatory measures to expand effective demand that would come into effect if unemployment exceeded the limit prescribed by the full employment target for three successive months (UN, 1949: 73).[34] It further recommended international-level measures to eliminate the structural disequilibrium in world trade, create a stable flow of international investment to meet the needs of 'underdeveloped' areas, and stabilise international trade. Such measures would be rolled out under the auspices of a powerful Economic and Social Council (ECOSOC) (pp. 87–8), with which the IBRD and the IMF would work closely to realise full employment (p. 88).

This global full employment programme was not implemented but it was remarkable for the scale of its ambition for what coherent global economic and social governance could achieve and for the holism of its internationalist analysis of unemployment. From the vantage point of our focus on global YU, we highlight the following points. First, mass unemployment was defined as a core issue of global governance in a way that focused attention on full employment of a quality that would end underemployment and enable socially acceptable standards of living.[35] From today's vantage point, this is a salutary reminder that (youth) unemployment can be disguised through forms of insecure or poverty-level forms of underemployment. Second, the goal was not just full employment, but full employment as an *integral* part of a programme to expand world trade 'of which the economic development of underdeveloped countries would form the most important single element' (UN, 1949: 12).

The ILO's new emphasis was not only on vocational training, but on education – not least to shelter surplus youth labour. This drew it into alliance with UNESCO, now the UN agency specialising in matters of education and youth, and an inter-IGO partnership that revolved around the question of compulsory education. Scrutiny of key Resolutions shows the extent to which both organisations were closely aligned, and how closely they worked on joint projects.[36] In this respect, we cite an ILO report on child labour and compulsory education that

---

[34]   Notably, the report advocated that for industrialised countries full employment targets should be defined in terms of unemployment and as a range rather than a precise figure. The report stood back from suggesting indicative targets for different country circumstances, instead contenting itself with specifying that national targets 'should be expressed in terms of the smallest percentage of unemployment of wage-earners which the country in question can reasonably hope to maintain in the light of seasonal movements and in the light of structural changes in the economy, which inevitably give rise to some temporary unemployment that could not be eliminated through public policy' (UN, 1949: 74).

[35]   As the ILO's Director-General stated, the issue of unemployment was that 'there is unemployment, and underemployment in the sense that employed workers are not used as productively as possible, arising from the scarcity of the complementary resources and industrial capacity which are necessary to employ workers at a socially acceptable standard of living' (ILO, 1950: 12).

[36]   The 1945 ILO Resolution on the protection of children and young workers recommended that 'the gradual raising of the minimum age should be accompanied by simultaneous measures for assuring the maintenance of children, such as *policies to secure full employment*, the provision of a living wage for

was presented under the joint auspices of UNESCO and the IBE to the 14th ICPE (1951) and later published by UNESCO (IBE/UNESCO, 1951; ILO, 1951: 462). Such cooperation was clearly mutually beneficial to both organisations' campaigns. It complemented UNESCO's campaign to extend 'free and compulsory education' (UNESCO, 1951: 3), not only in the rich countries but also in the poorer ones.[37] The ILO's interest in compulsory school attendance continued to centre on ensuring that the school-leaving age coincided with the minimum age of admission to work (ILO, 1951).[38] Although these goals and the discourses underpinning them were continuous with those of the pre-war decades, what *had* changed was that the work–education nexus was now framed as a matter of human rights (UN, 1948): from an educational perspective, the right to quality educational and vocational provision; from an (un) employment perspective, the right to work under conditions of freedom. This education–work nexus was a defining feature of the UN's approach to YU and has remained so ever since.

The ILO's shift in emphasis on the right to work and full employment while preventing 'premature unemployment' and underemployment was consolidated in the UN Declaration on Social Progress and Development (UN, 1969)[39] and through the ILO World Employment Programme (WEP).[40] Both of these built on an international human rights regime strengthened by the Declaration on the Rights of the Child (UN, 1959) and by the 1966 International Covenant on Economic, Social and Cultural Rights which incorporated full employment (UN, 1966). Such developments were part of a growing emphasis on young people within the UN more generally, which launched initiatives on juvenile delinquency (1959), education (1962, 1963, 1965, 1968), and dependence-producing drugs (1971). But progress was uneven, and the first UN Development Decade (1960–69) passed entirely without any substantial progress on YU. The 1959 Declaration of the Rights of the Child, for example, did not extend what was already enshrined in ILO LoN-era frameworks regarding minimum working age and the con-

---

all employed persons, family allowances, etc., and that, in order to aid in the simultaneous raising of the school-leaving age, economic assistance should be provided …' (ILO *Official Bulletin*, Vol. XXVIII, 15 December 1945, 31, p. 472). UNESCO Recommendation No. 21 regarding the free provision of school supplies, took a similar approach, and was adopted in 1947 by the ICPE (UNESCO-IBE: Int. Conf. on Pub. Ed.: Collected Recommendations, 1934–1950, p. 58) (ILO, 1951).

[37]   Amongst the features of UNESCO's compulsory education plans were RoSLA, educational and vocational guidance, and compensation to the parents of children obliged to remain at school. ICPE urged the IBRD (World Bank) to make long-term loans to countries for the purpose of implementing compulsory education enforcement plans (UNESCO, 1951: annex II, p. 17).

[38]   An ILO report highlighted the dual goals as being to 'protect the child against the harmful physical and moral effects that premature full-time employment may have …' and to avoid children being 'left without useful occupation during the transitional period and exposed to the dangers of the street or to illegal exploitation' (ILO, 1951: 463). The desire to avoid such a period appears in IBE Recommendation No. 32: 'The age at which children are authorised by law to take up employment and the school-leaving age should be fixed in accordance with each other' (para. 19) (IBE/UNESCO, 1951).

[39]   The Declaration affirmed that everyone has the right to work and the free choice of employment (Article 6), that '[t]he rapid expansion of national income and wealth and their equitable distribution among all members of society are fundamental to all social progress' (Article 7), and that 'full productive employment and elimination of unemployment and under-employment' were central to this (Article 10a) (UN, 1969).

[40]   The concepts of 'productive employment' and 'basic needs' used in the WEP helped the ILO engage with debates about the impoverishing effects of shifting terms of production and trade between 'developed' and 'developing' countries (see Section 7.5 and Chapter 4).

ditions under which YU was prohibited (UN, 1959). A UNESCO Recommendation on technical and vocational education (TVE) made no reference to the youth labour worlds for which TVE was supposed to prepare children (UNESCO, 1963).[41] And the ILO, for its part, converted provisions of earlier Recommendations on aspects of youth employment (education and training) into the Social Policy (Basic Aims and Standards) Convention (C117, 1962). There was no substantive development of the ILO's approach, however: C117 simply reaffirmed earlier ILO Recommendations' emphasis on broad systems of education, vocational training and apprenticeship, the school-leaving age and minimum employment age.[42] Whatever this 'interlude' in the ILO's and UNESCO's longstanding cooperation over the inseparable issues of education, training, secure employment and the harms of unemployment for young people, their shared values and alliance were to come to the fore once again, discursively at least, in the face of the 2008 global financial crisis (GFC) (see Chapter 8).

7.5   THE REAPPEARANCE OF YOUTH UNEMPLOYMENT: THE ONSET OF NEO-LIBERAL GLOBAL ECONOMIC RESTRUCTURING

If youth (un)employment had in effect receded into the background of international social and economic policy, it returned with a vengeance in the 1970s: the 1973 oil crisis and recession surfaced 'grave crises' facing the world economy. Mass YU reappeared as a lived phenomenon, as a matter for all governments, and as an item on the UN agenda (UNGA, 1971; see also Appendix 7.1). Indeed, it became very clear early in the decade that youth (un)employment was increasing at a rapid rate, and that young people (young *women* in particular) were disproportionately adversely impacted by the recession (UN, 1971a, 1971b, 1972; Turnham, 1973; Gallis, 1977). The UN's *1970 Report on the World Social Situation* highlighted increasing unemployment as amongst the serious problems facing youth worldwide (UN, 1971a). Its World Economic Survey review of developing country research showed 'a much higher rate of unemployment among young people: in the 15–24 age group, for example, rates commonly ran double those for the whole adult population' (UN, 1971b: 127 fn 11).

Youth employment and unemployment featured as a global issue in 1971 for the first time in UN history and the UN General Assembly (UNGA) urged government action.[43] But, despite the universalist language of human rights, the UN's response set out on a well-trod path. Its International Development Strategy for the Second UN Development Decade covering the 1970s (A/RES/2626(XXV)) was only able to pledge that '[p]articular attention will be devoted to technical training, vocational training and retraining' (para. 67) and that

---

[41]   This was revised in 1973 as Recommendation No. 68 (UNESCO, 1973).
[42]   The most relevant article to YU stated this: 'Adequate provision shall be made to the maximum extent possible under local conditions, for the progressive development of broad systems of education, vocational training and apprenticeship, with a view to the effective preparation of children and young persons of both sexes for a useful occupation' (Article 15.1).
[43]   UNGA Resolution 'Youth, its problems, needs and its participation in social development' (A/RES/2770 (XXVI)) (1971). This was followed up in 1973 when UNGA urged member countries to 'adopt all possible means to increase work opportunities in order to reduce or eliminate unemployment among young people' and to take 'concerted action … to meet the needs and aspirations of youth' (A/RES/3140(XXVIII)).

'developing countries will adopt suitable national policies for involving [young people] in the development process and for ensuring that their needs are met in an integrated manner' (para. 70). This was a pitiful response at the best of times, but one whose paucity was all the more apparent given the strategies' fanciful attachment to well-worn and utterly unrealistic supply-side solutions in the face of the unfolding economic crash, falling demand for youth labour, and the pronounced youth profile of rising unemployment. In an all-too-similar vein, the ILO continued to emphasise developing broad education and vocational training systems in the context of Special Youth Schemes,[44] programmes for people with disabilities[45] and an emphasis on 'human resources' development systems.[46] The ILO also continued its work on the minimum working age, revising earlier Conventions on Minimum Age and consolidating them into a single 1973 Minimum Age Convention which raised the recommended standard for employment in developing countries from 14 to 15 years, or the age at which compulsory education ended, whichever was the higher (Woodin et al., 2013: 23). In the midst of this, light was hardly ever directed at the structural economic and social causes of YU.[47]

The UN's Second Development Decade strategy omitted reference to full employment as a goal, but the ILO continued to press it as an overriding objective (ILO, 1976).[48] Young people were identified as one social group for whom 'special measures' were recommended 'to provide the young with productive employment, equal opportunity and equal pay for work of equal value, vocational training and working conditions suited to their age' (ILO, 1976). YU featured in the ILO's follow-up employment research programme. We identify two strands to this. A first strand, focusing on Western industrialised countries (Freedman, 1977; Gallis, 1977; Melvyn, 1977; Schneider, 1977; ILO, 1978), highlighted palliative measures to manage YU. The research backed away from any analysis of the globalising dynamics of (un) employment, but alluded to a qualitative shift in economic structures underway that meant that high levels of YU would not be resolved by cyclical upturns after the recession ended.[49] A second strand focused on (un)employment in general outside the industrialised countries

---

[44]   The Special Youth Schemes Recommendation (1970) (R136) defined international labour standards for 'special' youth schemes that 'meet needs for youth employment and training' not met by existing educational or vocational training programmes or through the labour market, and which enable unemployed young persons to use their qualifications in the service of the community.

[45]   The provisions of earlier ILO Recommendations were 'converted' into a Convention (C142 1975) emphasising life-long vocational training and provisions for people with disabilities.

[46]   ILO C142 – Human Resources Development Convention, 1975 (No. 142): Article 1 'Each Member shall adopt and develop comprehensive and co-ordinated policies and programmes of vocational guidance and vocational training, closely linked with employment, in particular through public employment services'.

[47]   Exceptionally, a 1970 ILO report, *Towards Full Employment: A Programme for Colombia*, located unemployment as a cause of social and economic inequalities linked to land tenure, income distribution and international trade (Maul, 2019: 177).

[48]   The ILO's World Conference on Employment, Income Distribution, Social Progress and the International Division of Labour (1976) reaffirmed 'the maintenance of as high a demand for labour as is necessary in order to achieve full employment' as a priority (ILO, 1976: 14). The Conference was a milestone in the New International Economic Order initiative (UNGA, 1974a, 1974b) and particularly attended to 'developing' countries that were worst affected by global economic crises.

[49]   Melvyn (1977: 56), for example, argued that 'In many countries programmes and measures to alleviate youth unemployment have the support … of both employers' organisations and trade unions. Yet what has been undertaken so far is still in the nature of a palliative. The problem, however, is a long-term

(Sabolo, 1975; Lydall, 1977) from which some incidental observations were made about the position of young people. This strand was far more attuned to global economic restructuring already underway by that time (Chapter 4), at least in terms of the jobs waiting to be created in developing countries, and recommended that all social partners support national strategies to increase labour-intensive export-oriented industrialisation as part of efforts to address high levels of unemployment and underemployment. Despite the different emphases and perspectives within this research programme, the papers invariably drew the overall conclusion that unemployment in developed and developing countries could no longer be regarded as a temporary problem arising from some cyclical or other imbalance in the economy; rather, it was a structural problem necessitating a medium-term perspective *to plan for and respond to unemployment as a permanent feature* of the world economy.

As far as global YU policy is concerned, we note two main outcomes of the ILO programme. First, youth employment was identified as a priority area for a new UN Taskforce on Youth. This provided a 'permanent' institutional home within a UN-wide youth programme. Second, the ILO re-positioned itself within a shifting global political economy of global policy-making. While its labour standards departments were preoccupied with palliative 'social' measures for YU in the rich countries, its development-focused ones were bolstering arguments *supportive* of labour-intensive export-oriented industrialisation as a job creation strategy in developing countries.[50] Its backing for export-oriented industrialisation was in practice a further nail in the coffin of the Keynesian consensus and helped unleash a new round of global restructuring made possible by fundamental changes in labour systems (see Chapter 4). In arriving at this conclusion, we do not doubt that the ILO was feeling the chill of changing political priorities and dynamics globally. By the mid-1970s, neo-liberalism was beginning to be felt in national policy-making across many of the world's richest countries, prefacing an all-out attack on the Keynesian paradigm that crashed through what was left of the UN's Second Development Decade and the ILO's World Employment Programme (ILO, 1976). As a response to its increasing marginalisation in a neo-liberalising global political space, the ILO and its labour standards agenda were under immense pressure to adapt, if only to retain some influence to try to ensure that the global reorganisation of labour would proceed in an 'orderly' manner – issues to which we return in Chapter 8.

7.6   CONCLUSIONS

This chapter has charted the range and nature of initiating actions on YU that were developed in the multilateral sphere of global governance from 1919 to the late 1970s. It has covered

---

one and calls for new and imaginative approaches to employment, the organisation of work, education and leisure'.

[50]   The ILO's follow-up action programme from the Conference highlighted how 'appropriate intensified capital movements and transfers of technical knowledge [could] promote a reciprocally advantageous international division of labour' (p. 9). The Declaration on Multinational Enterprises and Social Policy was adopted in 1977, and has been revised periodically since. The most recent revision (ILO, 2017c) affirms: 'With a view to stimulating sustainable economic growth and development, raising living standards, meeting employment requirements and overcoming unemployment and underemployment, governments should declare and pursue, as a major goal, an active policy designed to promote full, productive and freely chosen employment, and decent work' (para. 13).

six decades, from the first days of the ILO in the democratic structures of the LoN that brought social consciousness of YU and public deliberation about it into international politics; through the establishment of the UN and Bretton Woods systems in the 1940s that provided the institutional basis of a global governance founded on 'embedded liberalism' and saw a growing emphasis on palliative measures to address YU alongside a formal commitment to full employment; to the late 1970s and the rise of neo-liberalism that upended the post-war geo-economic liberal world order and the development prospects of the newly independent nations and which led to historic rises in YU worldwide. The universe of IGOs we examined provides one reading of the global institutional history of YU, but it is a very significant one, for these were pre-eminent forums for elaborating a method to develop international social standards, so that matters of potential international conflict could become a *regular and continuous feature* of impartial international dialogue and policy-making, rather than being left to the chance, randomness and partisan nature of individual governments' predilections. In this context, YU became a coherent global policy field in which socially liberal claims, practices and norms were elaborated and codified in international labour law and norms, and through which wider contestation about the nature of social justice in globalising open economies was manifested. There are three respects in which we deploy the adjective 'coherent' here.

First, diverse initiatives on YU *recurred* over a long period of time. They were neither one-off nor ad hoc but were repeated and resourced; they were connected, ideationally and institutionally. Their effects accumulated over time and proved influential in the longer term, outliving the LoN and underpinning UN-era initiatives. Indeed, the present-day global institutional regime governing YU discussed in Chapter 8 owes much to the early decades covered in this chapter, for they laid the international legal and normative foundations that imparted meaning to young people's 'right to work'.

It is notable that most global policy responses addressed YU from the perspective of developing employment, unemployment, education or vocationalism more generally. In essence, this global policy field unfolded within emergent and evolving international labour, educational and human rights regimes that set international standards defining the minimum age of exit from education and entry to the labour force and standards of working conditions, unemployment provision, vocational schemes, public works and equality of treatment applicable to young members of the workforce. These initiatives gave concrete meaning to the otherwise abstract concepts of 'the right to work' and 'the right to education', and to intersections between them. We also note the formative influence of the ILO on the construction of legal-administrative categories of the youth workforce. These defined the active youth labour force and the conditions under which work was prohibited or permitted, including which elements of whole populations of young people were to be classed as *in*active. In doing so, the ILO defined who could count as unemployed – including though the gargantuan task of collecting the kinds of long-run, standardised, authoritative statistical records across many dimensions and variables of youth (un)employment for almost every country worldwide (see Chapters 5 and 6).

Second, the agentic structure of the field is characterised by close and enduring relations among the actors. IGOs are important deliberative forums for consciousness-raising and organising, functioning as more than technical-bureaucratic sites of policy-making. The ILO, as the lead IGO, was a critical actor in all these aspects. During the LoN era, its officials were members of international epistemic communities spanning labour and education in particular, while working closely with labour ministries, employers and workers' organisations through its tripartite structure. They dialogued with international education, health and welfare communities comprised of government ministries, non-governmental organisations (NGOs) and international non-governmental organisations (INGOs) channelled through the LoN Committees on Child Welfare, Intellectual Cooperation, and Health Organisation, and, later on, the Committee on Unemployment Among Young People. These outward-facing relations continued in the post-war period. The ILO and UNESCO formed a powerful alliance that successfully prosecuted setting (and then raising) the minimum age of entry to employment and promoting comprehensive vocational education, training and guidance systems. The Bretton Woods institutions are not irrelevant, even if they were a largely latent force in the active shaping of the global policy field of YU for most of the period examined in this chapter. Their significance becomes much more palpable after the 1970s – as we discuss in the next chapter.

Third, the myriad initiatives in this emergent field followed readily identifiable logics. One meaning of 'logics' is that of a global policy dynamic, in which the participation of diverse constituencies representing or giving voice to young people in global forums generated claims, practices, and norms that in turn propelled further initiatives. Such initiatives were propelled by an ever-widening understanding of (mainly) the ILO's mandate, but they were invariably stymied by the institutional limitations thrown up by a bifurcated system of global governance separating the social (consequences) from the economic (causes). A further meaning of 'logics' is in the sense of dominant policy approaches to YU. These, we found, reflected two impulses: protecting young people, be it from premature employment, overemployment, unemployment or labour exploitation, and ensuring young people were sufficiently available for work on reasonable financial terms. They invariably produced responses that clung tightly to supply-side labour economics. Indeed, the causes of and solutions to YU have struggled to be seen through any lenses other than supply-side ones, despite the dominance of the Keynesian paradigm within and outwith the ILO for much of the period this chapter has examined. Thus, global policy initiatives have been overwhelmingly oriented towards delaying the entry of new cohorts coming into the labour market each year, diverting them away from (un)employment towards prolonged periods of education and/or steering them to further periods of (vocational) training. Such proposals to use RoSLA to 'warehouse' young people in education amidst 'difficult' labour market circumstances have been evident since the 1930s, and have regularly surfaced and re-surfaced internationally and at the ILO since then, as the ostensibly 'easy' palliative in recurrent conditions of falling demand for young people's labour – especially in equally recurrent transnational and global economic and financial crises (identified in Chapters 5 and 6). Indeed, the seeds of what were, by the ILO's own assessment, merely palliative measures were sown in its earliest years and have not been uprooted since.

Socially liberal global policy logics clung all the while to nationally bounded conceptions of economic and social structure. Although YU was quickly recognised as a global social issue (in the sense that it was common in different ways and at different times to all member countries) it was not understood as an outcome of forces rooted in modes of socio-economic organisation transcending nation states. Indeed, policy discourses gravitated mainly around measures to be taken by national actors in domestic spheres of governance through processes of national policy-making in response to the circumstances of countries' national economies. This is not to deny that more globalist conceptions emerged from time to time, but they failed to generate the traction needed to take them forward. The best example of this is found in an expert group report that set out how a global policy of global full employment could be realised through global economic planning within a strong global economic governance framework (UN Department of Economic Affairs, 1949). The conspicuous failure to institute such institutions was all the more apparent given that economic organisation transcended countries and linked economies and young workforces into inescapably international relations of interconnectedness and interdependency that are the focus of Chapters 3 and 4.

The global oversight of YU developed through the succession of initiatives discussed in this chapter hardly challenged those intent on 'using' youth labour, in the most instrumental sense of that term, 'flexibly'. The global legal and normative framework may have restricted some usages of youth labour, but it legitimised others, and evidenced an overwhelming preoccupation with 'managing' its availability. International standard-setting activities – fused with an overwhelming orientation towards supply-side palliation that legitimised the international spread of such measures – were the interventions of first (and often final) resort. The development of such oversight did not seem to bring labour justice any closer to swathes of young people out of work; rather, it incrementally normalised an institutionalised tolerance of high and repeatedly rising levels of YU at the same time as it embedded a permissiveness towards economic development 'on the cheap'.

What of the wider significance of these multiple initiatives? At one level, the results were fairly meagre, and could hardly be said to have mobilised a global policy response proportionate to the scale of YU worldwide. Nevertheless, they contributed considerably to establishing international institutional machinery, processes and patterns for cooperation on matters of YU. Thus, it was during the LoN era that the human rights and full employment discourses were aired, discourses that became foundational to the UN-era international legal and normative order and to the ILO's embrace of 'the right to work' and 'full employment' concepts that became dominant features of this global policy field. Still, ILO forays into demand-side measures to prevent YU (circa 1935, 1950, 1976) were exceptional, and ultimately not sustained. When they surfaced, they remained at the discursive level – in the form of research reports and in UNGA Resolutions that urged action, mainly by governments. However powerful the theoretical case in favour of demand-side measures for full employment may have been, the ILO simply did not have the requisite mandate or resources to realise such ambitions in practice. In some respects at least, Chapter 8 charts fresh endeavours to address deficiencies in the demand for young people's labour. In doing so, it recounts an evolving history of the entry of other key IGO actors into this policy field alongside the ILO, and changing circumstances that threw into sharper relief the disturbing consequences of large-scale and endemic YU, from the 1980s onwards. These developments reflect and pick up on the significant changes in the global scale and distribution of YU that Chapters 5 and 6 described and endeavoured to interpret.

APPENDIX 7.1   LEGAL AND NORMATIVE AGREEMENTS
                AND KEY INITIATIVES OF PRINCIPAL
                INTERNATIONAL GOVERNMENTAL
                ORGANISATIONS PERTAINING TO YOUTH
                UNEMPLOYMENT, 1919–1979

*Table 7A.1   Legal and normative international agreements and key global initiatives on
               youth unemployment, 1919–1979*

Year	IGO	Agreement or initiative
1919	ILO	Unemployment Convention (C002) [addressed unemployment in general]
1919	ILO	Night Work of Young Persons (Industry) Convention (C006, 1919)
1919–21	ILO	Minimum working age Conventions: Industry (1919); Sea (1920); Agriculture (1921); Trimmers and Stokers (1921)
1921	ILO	Vocational Education (Agriculture) Recommendation (R015)
1924	League of Nations	Geneva Declaration of the Rights of the Child, Article 4
1925	League of Nations	International Committee on Intellectual Cooperation
1928	ILO	International Economic Conference on unemployment statistics
1931	League of Nations	Permanent Education Committee Resolution in favour of fixing 14 as the minimum school-leaving age
1932	ILO	Minimum working age Convention: non-industrial sectors (1932)
1934	ILO	Unemployment Provision Convention (C044) [unemployment in general]
1934	International Bureau of Education (IBE)/ ILO	International Conference on Public Education on 'compulsory education and the raising of the school-leaving age'; IBE Recommendation No. 2 concerning Access to Secondary Schools (R2)
1934	League of Nations	Child Welfare Committee considers effects of unemployment on child welfare; recommends compulsory school attendance for primary education, supplementary vocational courses, the institution of workers' allotments and suburban colonies or voluntary civil service in labour camps
1935	ILO	Unemployment (Young Persons) Recommendation, 1935 (R045) [withdrawn 2002]
1935	ILO	Forty-Hour Week Convention (C047)
1936	ILO	Reduction of Hours of Work (Public Works) Convention (C051)
1937	ILO	Minimum Age (Family Undertakings) Recommendation (R052)
1939	ILO	Vocational Training Recommendation (R057) [replaced by R117 in 1962]
1948	UNGA	Universal Declaration of Human Rights (A/RES/217(III) A)
1949	UNGA	Full Employment Resolution (A/RES/308(IV))
1949	ILO	Vocational Guidance Recommendation R087
1951	ILO/UNESCO	ILO report on child labour and compulsory education presented under the joint auspices of UNESCO and IBE to the 14th International Conference on Public Education. The report was published by UNESCO as *Child Labor in Relation to Compulsory Education*
1959	UNGA	Declaration of the Rights of the Child (A/RES/1386(XIV))

Year	IGO	Agreement or initiative
1959	ILO	Minimum Age (Fishermen) Convention (C112)
1962	ILO	Social Policy (Basic Aims and Standards) Convention (C117)
1962	ILO	Vocational Training Recommendation (R117)
1963	UNESCO	Recommendation concerning technical and vocational education (R56)
1965	ILO	Minimum Age (Underground Work) Convention (C123)
1966	UNGA	International Covenant on Economic, Social and Cultural Rights (ICESCR) [multilateral treaty adopted in December 1966, effective from January 1976]
1969	UNGA	Declaration on Social Progress and Development (A/RES/2542(XXIV))
1970	ILO	Special Youth Schemes Recommendation (R136)
1971	UNGA	Youth, its problems and needs, and its participation in social development (A/RES/2770(XXVI))
1973	ILO	Minimum Age Convention (C138)
1973	UNESCO	Recommendation No. 68 concerning the Relationship between Education, Training and Employment, with particular reference to secondary education, its aims, structure and content
1973	UNGA	Concerted action at national and international levels to meet the needs and aspirations of youth and to promote their participation in national and international development (A/RES/3140(XXVIII))
1975	ILO	Human Resources Development Convention (C142)
1976	ILO	Tripartite World Conference on Employment, Income Distribution, Social Progress and the International Division of Labour
1977	UN	Declaration on Multinational Enterprises and Social Policy
1977	UN	UN Taskforce on Youth
1977	UNGA	Channels of communication with youth and youth organizations (A/RES/32/135)

Source: The authors, derived from relevant IGO websites (accessed January 2020).

APPENDIX 7.2   SUMMARY OF PROVISIONS OF THE UNEMPLOYMENT (YOUNG PERSONS) RECOMMENDATION

Table 7A.2   Summary of provisions of the unemployment (young persons) reccommendation

Area	Provision
Education	Minimum age for leaving school and being admitted to employment 'not less than fifteen years, as soon as circumstances permit'. Those with the necessary aptitudes should be encouraged to attend secondary or technical schools beyond the minimum school-leaving age. Young people over the school-leaving age and under 18 years old who are unable to find suitable employment should be required to continue full-time attendance at school until suitable employment is available for them. Maintenance allowances should be paid to parents during this additional educational period. Curricula for young people in prolonged education should be designed primarily to promote their general education, but should also provide vocational education. Such attendance should at least be *made compulsory for unemployed juveniles*. Refusal to attend a required course may result in temporary disqualification, entirely or partly, from unemployment benefit and allowances.
Vocational Guidance, placing services	Young persons unable to secure employment after secondary, technical or higher studies be given opportunities to obtain practical experience in industrial, commercial and other undertakings and in public administration, with every precaution taken to prevent them from displacing regular workers. Vocational guidance should be provided to inform young people about 'overcrowded occupations' and 'to assist them to counteract prejudices which constitute barriers to their occupational readjustment'. National systems of public employment exchanges should include special youth placing services. Placing services for young persons aged 18 years or more should support their occupational readjustment, including relocation to districts in which occupations are expanding. Governments should facilitate international exchanges of student employees.
Employment Centres and Public Works	Special Employment Centres for young unemployed people aged between 18 and 24 should be set up 'to provide work under other than normal conditions of employment'. Strictly based on voluntary attendance only for the physically fit. Organisation of the centres should enable self-governance, particularly as regards discipline, and be professionally staffed by personnel with a 'thorough knowledge of social questions generally and of the problems of youth in particular'. Measures should be taken to 'develop team spirit among the persons attending the centres' and to encourage them to 'form cooperative working groups for employment on land settlement schemes, public works, handicrafts, etc.'. The centres' work programmes should avoid competition with workers in normal employment but should collaborate closely with public employment exchanges which play a key role in placing young attendees in normal employment. Attendees should be treated as employees, remunerated for their work and admitted to social insurance schemes. Special Public Works should be provided for Unemployed Young Persons who have terminated secondary, technical or higher studies. Such works should be adapted as far as possible to the training of such persons.

Source: ILO, 1935d (emphasis added).

8. The neo-liberalisation of global youth unemployment policy, 1980–2021

8.1 INTRODUCTION

This chapter continues to trace the historical construction of youth unemployment (YU) as a global field of social policy. Like Chapter 7, its principal focus lies with the socio-political processes of social problem and social policy response formation as they play out in multilateral spheres of cross-border governance. The chapter proceeds in much the same way as Chapter 7, tracing the institutional, programmatic, ideological and agentic features of the YU policy field, and organising the discussion chronologically over four decades from the early 1980s to 2020. This periodisation broadly corresponds with the break from 'embedded liberalism' (Chapter 7) and the ascendancy of neo-liberalism beginning in the 1970s. Our periodisation is sensitive to the 'varieties of liberalisms' argument (Gallagher, 2011), and we test the idea that the present period may be entering a new phase of liberalism as far as global YU policy is concerned, one that is associated with the fall-out from the global financial crisis (GFC) of 2007–08 and the reconfiguration of already-multipolar geo-political and -economic landscapes.

Within this frame, we continue to work between the macro-ideational features of the policy field and the 'sticky' inter-institutional terrain whereupon the contested and historically constituted global social politics of policy plays out. Our focus on key episodes in global policy development is not intended to conflate international organisation (IO) 'policy time' with 'political economy time', or to suggest that the episodes have any intrinsic meaning outside the context in which they occur. It does, however, enable a necessary degree of granularity that helps uncover the evolving structural and relational features of the global policy field. The discussion deliberately endeavours to foreground how (and, whenever possible, where) political contestation occurs, the relations of alliance and opposition among transnational policy actors, and the concrete meaning of the 'right to work' for young people in defined contexts, both organisational and political-economic. Our intention is to help illuminate how developments in global YU policy relate to structural political economy and not just the tactical manoeuvres of actors. We are also conscious of the need to strike a balance between providing a sufficiently detailed elucidation of the diverse textures of the field to satisfy social policy historians, while also drawing out the broader structures beyond any given intervention or event in order to meet sociological and political-economic perspectives. A detailed timeline of multilateral agreements and initiatives on YU for the period covered by this chapter is set out in Appendix 8.1.

The chapter is structured as follows. Section 8.2 covers global YU policy from the early 1980s to the turn of the century. Tracing the first two decades of the 'new' UN-wide youth initiative that rolled out against the backdrop of skyrocketing levels of YU, we discuss UN and ILO activity which saw, for the first time since the 1930s, a renewed focus on YU in the 1980s that adhered to palliative, supply-side, 'active' labour market measures, before declining to low levels of activity during the 1990s, and then culminating in the inclusion of YU-specific commitments in the Millennium Development Goals (MDGs) (2000). Section 8.3 focuses on the first decade of the new century up to the global financial crisis (GFC) during which the development paradigm of the MDG period saw the entry of new policy actors (notably the World Bank (WB)) and generated two global YU partnership structures led by the ILO and WB. The section discusses the origins and characteristics of these structures that were increasingly, over the years, to define the predominant means of 'delivering' global YU policy. Section 8.4 turns attention to the decade following the GFC, and discusses further shifts in global YU policy as seen in the continuity of supply-side emphases, the corporatisation of global partnerships addressing YU, the emergence of multi-sectoral approaches to YU and a focus on young people 'not in education, employment and training' (NEETs) as an increasingly important element of global YU policy – just as the Sustainable Development Goals (SDGs) were being negotiated and rolled out. Section 8.5 draws overall conclusions, looking across Chapters 7 and 8 and tying them together, to consider wider themes and imperatives structuring the century's-worth of global YU policy.

8.2   THE RETURN OF YOUTH UNEMPLOYMENT (1980–1999): THE RIGHT TO WORK AND THE 'NEW' DEVELOPMENT AGENDA

The 1980s opened a new chapter in global YU policy. Institutionally, YU was now a designated priority area in the UN's Taskforce on Youth and the UN's youth programme (Chapter 7, p. 176). This prioritisation marked a major shift in the UN's response to YU, not because it represented a new level of attention to YU as a global policy issue, but because mainstreaming YU into the heart of UN work meant that global YU policy would be shaped by a wider range of organisations than was previously the case. Even if the International Labour Organization (ILO) was at this time still the dominant international governmental organisation (IGO) in this policy field, the institutional and political dynamics shaping its development were to be markedly different.

An early indication of the 'new' politics of global policy in this area was provided in a UN General Assembly (UNGA) Resolution announcing the UN's third international development decade (1981–1990), which foregrounded employment objectives and efforts to build UN youth policy based on improved 'channels of communication' between the UN, young people and youth organisations (UNGA, 1980). This global push on overlapping employment and youth objectives combined to heighten focus on YU – as signalled by the first-ever UNGA Resolution to highlight the problem of YU:

> … unemployment of youth is a hindrance to the full participation of young people in the socio-economic life of their country, limits their ability to participate in the development process and is, furthermore, a source of increased social ills. (UNGA, 1981, A/RES/36/29, preamble)

The Resolution fell short of referencing full employment, and highlighted instead the importance of supply-side measures in realising the 'rights of youth with special regard for the right to work' (UNGA, 1981). Demand-led measures were notably absent – not only in that Resolution but also in the subsequent ones on youth that were passed almost annually in the lead up to the UN's International Youth Year (1985). Nevertheless, it was significant that the UN was now urging that YU be given the 'highest priority' (UNGA, 1985, A/RES/40/16), even if the most concrete reflection of this amounted to no more than a conference in Vienna in 1987 to develop a long-term programme on youth.

The material realities for hundreds of millions of young people around the world to which this Resolution was a response was captured by a UN Secretary-General report four years later on 'the social situation of youth' (UNSG, 1985) which highlighted how 'problems of YU and underemployment have worsened implacably' (p. 11).[1] Indeed, they had worsened. Table 8.1 (below) shows that in two-thirds (14 of 22) high-income countries (HICs) (with few exceptions, the only countries with continuous records during this period), YU rates increased substantially between 1980 and 1986. In 12 of the 22 countries they were above 10 per cent in most years and in six countries they exceeded 20 per cent in most years.[2]

As to the causes of these escalating rates, the UNSG report noted the effects of economic recession and made some oblique references to the adverse effects of neo-liberal social and economic policies (UNSG, 1985: 11, 14). In terms of policy responses, the main thrust of its recommendations revolved around the extension of education and training, but – notably – it also urged attention to demand-side measures, for example in the form of youth job impacts from 'new demands, fields or types of occupation' in specific fields such as new technologies, agro-industry and environmental protection. This was hardly an unequivocal embrace of demand-led approaches to YU, but it did at least move further towards emphasising governments' role in stimulating the creation of new youth jobs in the open economy through sector-specific economic development strategies. This intervention by the UNSG was all the more notable given that the prevailing discourse was about 'rolling back' the state to 'liberate' private agents of development.

It is worth pausing to reflect on points of similarity between the rise of YU as an explicit matter of global social policy at this time compared with the mid-1930s (Chapter 7). Not only did both periods see a rise of YU to very high levels, but they were met with an intensification of standard-setting activities by the ILO. Indeed, just as 50 years previously, the ILO responded to it through another Recommendation – the Employment Policy (Supplementary Provisions) Recommendation (ILO, 1984). This was the first ILO instrument to deal directly with YU since the 1935 Recommendation. It did not announce any change in the ILO's approach to YU, however: it stuck to its previously-noted preference for palliative measures (Chapter 7). As far as young people 'frequently having difficulties in finding lasting employment' were con-

---

[1]   Note also this alternate, coyly-euphemistic phrasing used by that report: 'Far too many young people's lives are characterized by an immense volatility of occupation, and by the fact that *the process whereby they try to become workers is often not consummated at all*' (UNSG, 1985: 15, emphasis added).
[2]   Note that 'ILO does not have global data for unemployment prior to 1991', and that 'to our knowledge such data does not exist elsewhere' (authors' email correspondence with the ILOStat team, 24 June 2020). This limited the number of HICs that could be included in Table 8.1, and more generally places significant limitations on historical analysis of trajectories of YU at country, world-regional and country income group levels.

Table 8.1   Youth unemployment rates, aged 20–24 years, high-income countries, 1980–1990

	Australia	Austria	Belgium	Canada	Germany	Denmark	Spain	Finland	France	Greece	Hong Kong	Ireland	Italy	Japan	Korea	Luxembourg	Norway	Singapore	Sweden	Taiwan	United Kingdom	United States
1980	8.8	–	–	10.6	–	–	23.8	5.9	–	–	5.1	–	20.8	3.3	10.3	–	–	4.3	–	3.1	–	11.5
1981	8.1	–	–	10.6	–	–	29.2	6.7	–	15.1	3.4	–	–	3.6	9.0	–	–	–	–	3.5	–	12.3
1982	10.3	6.2	–	16.2	–	–	33.1	7.6	–	19.7	4.6	16.8	24.1	4	8.9	–	–	3.6	6.1	5.4	–	14.9
1983	14.5	7.4	21.7	17.7	9.9	17.7	36.5	7.8	15.8	22.2	5.4	18.0	24.7	4.1	8.3	5.0	17.2	4.8	6.8	6.5	16.5	14.5
1984	12.8	5.8	23.5	16.0	9.5	15.8	41.4	7.1	20.3	23.0	5.2	20.4	27.4	4.4	8.2	2.8	–	4.1	6.5	6.2	16.9	11.5
1985	11.4	4.9	21.3	14.4	9.3	12.1	44.0	7.9	21.6	23.1	4.4	21.4	28.1	4.1	9.6	4.2	14.9	7.0	6.3	7.0	16.7	11.1
1986	11.2	4.3	19.9	13.6	8.2	9.0	44.1	7.7	21.0	22.9	4.3	21.8	29.5	4.6	8.7	3.4	–	9.6	5.3	6.7	17.0	10.7
1987	11.1	4.8	20.2	12.3	7.7	9.5	40.2	6.8	21.1	24.5	3.0	20.9	30.4	4.5	7.2	3.3	12.5	7.6	4.6	5.3	14.6	9.7
1988	10.3	4.9	17.3	10.6	7.0	10.1	38.5	5.4	20.7	24.7	2.6	18.3	30.7	4.2	6.7	3.0	12.1	5.6	–	4.7	12.4	8.7
1989	8.3	4.3	14.5	9.7	5.6	13.5	32.8	6.8	18.9	24.6	2.2	15.4	29.5	3.8	6.4	–	10.9	4.0	2.9	4.3	10.0	8.6
1990	10.1	4.0	13.4	11.2	4.7	13.5	29.9	5.4	18.8	22.5	2.5	21.1	26.6	3.7	6.2	2.4	9.4	–	3.4	4.8	9.49	8.8

Key:

	Most years < 10%
	Most years > 10%
	Most years > 20%

Notes: Figures shown are percentages. Table 8.1 includes YU data for all 22 countries for which at least six years of data had been recorded with the ILO in the period 1980–90. All are high-income countries. In all but eight of these countries, YU rates increased substantially over several years between 1980 and 1986. In 12 countries YU rates were above 10% for all or most of the years for which data is available; in six countries they exceeded 20% in most years. Four Asian countries and four European countries maintained YU rates below 10% throughout. Rates began to decline in most countries by 1988.
Source: the authors, based on ILOStat data, https://www.ilo.org/shinyapps/bulkexplorer (accessed 2 July 2020).

cerned, it emphasised education and training schemes of various kinds[3] as vital components of national policy responses, and highlighted that '[o]ther special measures should be taken for young people' (para. 17) – such as through local community projects with a 'social character'.[4]

Of course, the world economic context of this Recommendation and of youth (un)employment was markedly different compared with the mid-1930s. Not only was international economic interdependence now so much more extensive and intensive (Chapter 4), but the ILO was no longer the sole IGO in this policy field. UNESCO was already an ally in ILO's work on YU, but had approached YU from an educational perspective rather than a labour one, and furthermore it was a minor actor in doing so (Chapter 7). UNESCO stepped up its apparent interest in youth employment issues,[5] claiming they were a long-standing feature of its youth policy[6] and announced its intention to stake its rightful place at the table of global YU policy. This amounted to an informal consultation process on YU research that led to the underwhelming conclusion that UNESCO-commissioned research would prioritise coping mechanisms for youth unemployed, while not totally neglecting its causes (UNESCO, 1984).[7] Disappointing as this was, the stake it tried to claim as an influential actor in global YU policy may have been the only realistic one available in the face of resurgent monetarism and rampant neo-liberalisation.

By the mid-1980s, 'youth issues', notably the right to education and to work, were becoming increasingly prominent in the UN. The International Youth Year (1985) was a significant

---

[3]   These 'might include, inter alia – (a) general education accessible to all and vocational guidance and training programmes to assist these persons to find work ...; (b) the creation of a training system linked with both the educational system and the world of work; (c) counselling and employment services to assist individuals to enter the labour market ...; (d) programmes which create gainful employment in specific regions, areas or sectors; (e) programmes of adjustment to structural change; (f) measures of continuing training and retraining; (g) measures of vocational rehabilitation; (h) assistance for voluntary mobility; and (i) programmes for the promotion of self-employment and workers' co-operatives' (ILO, 1984, para 16).

[4]   Recommendation R169 was also clear that such programmes should not be a mandatory requirement. It set out principles for these special programmes: alternating training and work to assist young people in finding their first job; training adapted to technical and economic development; measures should ease the transition from school to work and promote integration into 'normal' employment on completion of training; highest priority should be given to protecting the safety and health of young workers. It also advised that '[t]hese measures should be carefully monitored ...'.

[5]   By UNESCO's own account, its involvement in youth employment included a film 'Being young and working' (1973–74), a Symposium of Young Workers (1976), a series of publications on unemployment and education (1980), five regional meetings on youth employment, and an international research programme (1983) on attitudes of young workers (UNESCO, 1984: 3).

[6]   *Youth: Ways of Life, Work and Employment, Research Trends* (UNESCO and Kazancigil, 1985), stated that '[a]t present, [UNESCO youth programmes] basically involve stimulating research, promoting the exchange of information, in cooperation with non-governmental youth organizations, and helping to draw up youth policies and programmes in Member States. ... we might mention two activities which UNESCO supports: the Issue Group on Technological Change, Youth and Employment of the International Social Science Council, ... and the research programme on youth, work and employment in Europe of the European Co-ordination Centre for Research and Documentation in Social Sciences (Vienna Centre). UNESCO also organised a World Congress of Youth (Barcelona, 8–15 July 1985), which covered such topics as: youth, education and work; youth and cultural development; youth and international co-operation' (UNESCO and Kazancigil, 1985: 426).

[7]   A UNESCO follow-up report to this consultation (UNESCO, 1985) highlighted a range of joint (research) activities of UNESCO and ILO, as well as OECD, on YU (UNESCO, 1985: 3).

factor in helping spur the development of global youth policy as an institutionalised field of UN activity in which employment and unemployment were one part. The ILO and UNESCO remained the principal specialised agencies leading on YU, though YU was increasingly being taken up elsewhere in the UN. A further UNSG (1987) report by the Secretary-General (UNSG, 1987) on YU recommended that international measures should 'include increasing job opportunities, developing co-operatives and providing vocational training' and claimed that '[p]articular attention has been paid to finding work for school dropouts and reabsorbing the unemployed into the job market' (UNSG, 1987: 9). More importantly, perhaps, a new UN Youth Fund was set up to support youth projects and UN capacity to facilitate interregional and/or global activities associated with the International Youth Year.[8] Otherwise, a growing emphasis on 'channels of communication'[9] between the UN and national and international NGOs 'contributed substantially to the assessment of the global situation of youth in the 1980s', helping highlight public awareness on youth issues (UNSG, 1987: 21). Overall, the Year galvanised the 'mainstreaming' of youth policy into UN business and cemented the central axis of the UN's approach to YU, that is, through the lens of young people's right to education and to work.[10] Worthy as such initiatives were, they were not remotely equal to addressing the geographical breadth, depth and scale of the escalating social crisis signalled by the rising YU rates (Table 8.1).

Regarding the international normative framework on youth and (un)employment, there was some progress on including young people in disability, night work and occupational safety provisions, but the most significant aspect was an ILO Convention on Employment Promotion and Protection against Unemployment (1988, C168) and an accompanying Recommendation (R176, 1988) that contained explicit reference to YU and the 'special circumstances' of 'new applicants for employment' (for example, young people). This intervention identified age as a basis of prohibited discrimination (Article 6) and, for the first time, designated young people as a priority group for strategies to extend social security coverage.[11] Controversially, the Convention endorsed reallocating public resources away from income-guarantee schemes in favour of vocational guidance and training schemes. Although the ILO had long promoted vocational guidance, training and rehabilitation as major anti-unemployment measures

---

[8]   The UN Youth Fund's budget amounted to a very modest US$280,000, which financially supported 36 projects across the arts, education (literacy), forestry, agriculture and welfare between 1984 and 1987. Country-based research was the largest single item (UNSG, 1987: 14).

[9]   The Vienna Non-governmental Organisation Committee on Youth, founded in 1982, comprises a group of international non-governmental organisations (INGOs) that are either wholly youth organisations, organisations with youth chapters or organisations interested in youth, including trade unions. Unemployment featured at a Round Table on Youth Unemployment (September 1987, Vienna) that subsequently led to the establishment of an (Austrian) 'Institute of Hope 87' to promote youth employment.

[10]   UNGA urged ECOSOC and all other UN bodies to give *regular* consideration to youth's right to education and work (UNGA, 1986, 1987). It reiterated YU as a development issue as well as the importance of education and access to vocational guidance and training.

[11]   Article 26 of C168 covers 'persons seeking work who have never been, or have ceased to be, recognised as unemployed or have never been, or have ceased to be, covered by schemes for the protection of the unemployed'. It stipulates that for each country at least three of ten categories of persons seeking work shall receive social benefits in accordance with prescribed terms and conditions: young persons who have completed their vocational training; young persons who have completed their studies; and young persons who have completed their compulsory military service.

(Chapter 7), C168 emphasised that these measures should be part of 'policies leading to stable, sustained, non-inflationary economic growth and a flexible response to change' (preamble, Convention). *Rarely have such few words signalled such a significant shift in the global politics of global YU policy*. They formally incorporated into the ILO's discursive and labour standards frameworks a neo-liberal, deregulatory labour market discourse on 'labour flexibility' and a decisive shift in favour of 'active labour market policies' (ALMPs) at the expense of 'passive' income security ones. Such a radical reversal of the ILO's longstanding historical priorities was further exacerbated by the Convention being devoid of reference to ILO minimum income standards for employment assistance and economic support (benefits) to unemployed people. Nor did it help that the Convention stipulated that '[i]n cases of full unemployment, benefits shall … avoid creating disincentives either to work or to employment creation' (Article 14). The conclusion of C168 was significant in a further respect: it was the most recent ILO instrument on young people and work, and no additional labour standards instruments pertaining to YU have since been agreed throughout the whole of the three-plus intervening decades.

The 1980s was a lost decade in terms of social and economic policies other than those that take their cue from monetarism and neo-liberalism. The rupture from the post-war Keynesian/liberal consensus was manifested in country-level policy landscapes, and in the rise of YU. At the global policy-making level, the authority of the UN system (and the ILO specifically) to deal with matters of YU (amongst other issues) was being challenged and whatever prospects had existed for gaining further ground in this field by building on the ILO's World Employment Programme (WEP) substantially receded. Indeed, the political context of global policy-making was transformed. Global policy took greater inspiration from Washington than from the Philadelphia Declaration of 1944. The IMF and World Bank structural adjustment programmes were addressed to domestic debt crises and poverty in ways that emphasised residual models of public provision to meet 'basic needs' instead of comprehensive programmes of redistribution to meet universal needs, and posited the informal economy as a springboard for latent entrepreneurship rather than as a source of poverty. 'Free' markets, export-oriented production and industrialisation, privatisation of industry and services, deregulation of wage and price controls, reduced public expenditure, cuts in progressive taxation and a depreciation in organisations representing workers were central tenets of the new global politics of global economic governance as it manifested at country level (Yeates, 2001).

Even if this project was unevenly realised in practice, it fundamentally reframed the political economy of global policy-making, and instituted profound regulatory shifts that took hold and gained pace during the 1990s. One aspect of this was that general policy space to extend regulatory initiatives shrunk while those that promised 'light touch' regulatory modes and methods expanded. Globally, non-binding agreements premised on voluntary self-regulation came to prevail on all matters except those relating to the global 'free' trade agenda. In this realm, legally-binding trade agreements assigned corporate enterprises unprecedented rights (Dunkley, 1997). The WEP had retained a place for the ILO at the table in this radically transformed political space, but it was drawn in as a participant overseeing these global shifts (Chapter 7, Section 7.5). If the ILO's aim was to achieve 'orderly oversight' of global economic restructuring, it failed. The new political priorities that transformed labour systems rendered the 1980s and much of the 1990s lost decades as measured against holistic development outcomes. The ILO, like other specialised agencies of the UN, including UNESCO, was ill-prepared to counter these forces that were recalibrating the political economy of global policy-making. They scrambled to adjust to the new politics of global governance on which supporters of neo-liberal globalism – notably WB, IMF and, later, the World Trade Organization (WTO) – imposed an increasingly large and dominant footprint (Yeates, 2001; Yeates and Pillinger, 2019).

The imprint of this new political-institutional terrain on global YU policy took different forms. One is the low level of global YU policy activity. Despite more than half of high-income countries having YU rates amongst 20–24-year-olds peaking at between 15 per cent and 44 per cent (Table 8.1; see also Chapter 5, Section 5.2.1 and Tables 5.1–5.3 for rates above 15 per cent worldwide), it was a mark of the debilitation of the ILO that it initiated unusually few Conventions, Recommendations, projects or programmes dedicated to YU between 1980 and (especially) the late 1990s (Appendix 8.1). Published reports and studies focused on child labour rather than youth and employment. This neo-liberal imprint was also manifested through the preference for UN-wide actions, declarative statements, action programmes and projects.

The first half of the decade saw several such initiatives, which give an apparent sense of a purposeful UN response to YU. In 1990, a new global youth programme was proposed to give 'priority ... to the enjoyment by youth of human rights, including the right to education and to work ...' (UNGA, 1990). The Centre for Social Development and Humanitarian Affairs of the Secretariat (later renamed the United Nations Department for Economic and Social Affairs (UNDESA)) became the designated UN focal point for monitoring the inclusion of youth matters into UN work on a range of issues, including employment. The *World Programme of Action for Youth to the Year 2000 and Beyond* (UNGA, 1995), the last 'big' youth-specific UN initiative of the century prior to the Millennium Development Goals (MDGs), re-stated the goal of full employment and emphasised partnerships among the public and private sector and among IGOs to achieve this. Tackling YU and underemployment also featured as a commitment by the 118 signatory states to the UN's Copenhagen Declaration on Social Development and Programme of Action (UN, 1995).

In some ways, such initiatives provided a platform for challenging neo-liberal globalisation. For example, the *World Programme of Action* reaffirmed the adverse impacts of high levels of YU, including long-term YU, on the realisation of international development goals, especially on the primary development objective – poverty eradication (UNGA, 1991). A 1998 meeting of the UN World Youth Forum highlighted the extent of social injustice and exclusion faced by young people, including growing YU, which it attributed mainly to 'the enormous inequities in income, wealth and power' brought about by unfair trade and investment agreements and relations (UNESCO, 1998a). In the same year, an international declaration of national ministers for youth (Lisbon Declaration on Youth Policies and Programmes) reaffirmed different priorities for national youth policies, including 'the ultimate societal goal of full employment' (Article 53) (UNESCO, 1998b).

This fightback was far from coordinated, however. Notably, the ILO failed to press home the demands contained within these declarations, not least because it had become a significantly diminished witness to its own marginalisation as a one-time hegemonic force in the spheres of global governance and global policy in relation to YU (and other fields). Making a significant rejoinder to its marginalisation in the face of the overwhelming combined forces of the 'iron triangle' of neo-liberalism (the World Bank (WB), International Monetary Fund

(IMF) and World Trade Organization (WTO) (O'Brien et al., 2000)), the ILO's *Declaration on Fundamental Principles and Rights at Work* (ILO, 1998) asserted that equitable social progress and the maintenance of existing labour standards could not be achieved by means of economic growth alone. It asserted a set of 'core' rights universally applicable to all workers worldwide,[12] but was widely criticised as retreating from its constitutional mandate to strengthen labour rights and standards (O'Brien, 2014). The ILO's favouring of voluntary codes of practice and recommendations instead of statutory instruments to realise labour rights and standards added to the sense of a partially compromised, less effective, less assertive actor not capable of supporting labour on the global stage (Deacon, 2013, 2015). The perception of a new global labour 'pact' was also buttressed by WB and IMF 'regularising' their relationships with trade unions through consultative processes with civil society organisations while simultaneously failing to embed core labour standards in development project contracts they issued (O'Brien, 2014). These developments were cognisant of the need for labour standards in some international contexts, while also allowing the expansion of unregulated labour in others.

The century closed with a vacuous UNGA resolution repeating the call for 'a focused global dialogue on youth-related issues' (UNGA, 1999) and an address by UN Secretary-General Kofi Annan to the Davos World Economic Forum that proposed to the world's global business elite the Global Compact on Human Rights, Labour Standards and Environmental Practices (hereafter, Global Compact) (UN, 2000). All ten principles of the Global Compact were expressed as expectations on business, when it came into effect in 2000. Four labour principles required businesses to uphold 'core' labour standards as defined in ILO's *Declaration on Fundamental Principles and Rights at Work*: freedom of association and the effective recognition of the right to collective bargaining, the elimination of forced or compulsory labour, effective abolition of child labour, and the elimination of discrimination in respect of employment and occupation (ILO, 1998). Embodying universal values and shared principles, the Global Compact would, he promised, give a 'human face' to the global market and sustain the open global economy. In principle, at least, Annan's proposal represented a robust and potentially progressive attempt to redress imbalances and limit the worldwide powers of ill-regulated and rampant global capital in favour of the social realm, including in relation to labour rights and standards.

Although Kofi Annan presented the Global Compact as a platform to further extend labour standards, this was far from being borne out by events, and especially not in relation to YU – not least because none of the Compact's four labour principles had any direct relevance to YU. The general principles might have provided a platform for further progress in responding to YU in the subsequent years, but there has been no evidence of this. For example, the ILO's (2008) 'Guide for Business on Principles 3–6 of the Global Compact' made no mention of YU, and the golden opportunity to recognise that eliminating child labour would extend employment opportunities for young workers was overlooked. More generally, it is unclear whether the voluntarism of the Global Compact countermands the 'obligations' of the 1998 *Declaration on Fundamental Principles and Rights at Work* (ILO, 1998), but the normative dilution of the ILO Declaration's impact was, de facto, inevitable. Indeed, the Global Compact

---

[12]   These concerned the abolition of child labour and forced or compulsory labour, the elimination of employment discrimination, and the maintenance of rights to collective bargaining.

has since come under severe criticism for allowing business to profit from association with the UN while compromising the UN's power to hold business to account, and for making little if any demonstrable contribution to levelling-up employment aspects of business practices (Thérien and Pouliot, 2006; Farnsworth, 2014; Yeates and Pillinger, 2019).[13]

The Millennium Declaration and MDGs at least held out more significant hope of slowing, if not reversing, escalating rates of YU that were underpinned by decades-worth of neo-liberal global policy. Indeed, throughout the 1990s, YU rates were averaging 10–13 per cent (14–16 per cent in high-income countries) – averages which concealed a great many extremes of YU. By 1999, the global YU count had risen above the 70 million threshold for the first time since comprehensive global records began.[14] In recognition of this parlous dearth of employment for young people, the UN Millennium Declaration resolved to 'develop and implement strategies that give young people everywhere a real chance to find decent and productive work' (UN, 2000). The assertive ambition of MDG Target 1.b ('achieve full and productive employment and decent work for all, including women and young people') effectively placed the relevant UN bodies on notice to secure a substantial reversal of the alarming, persistent increases in YU rates throughout the 1980s–90s. The inclusion of targets on youth employment in the MDGs raised the profile of YU as a global development issue of priority importance in ways that had not previously been seen. The targets were not, however, operationalised; in a repeat of post-war global employment policy history (Chapter 7, Section 7.4, pp. 171–74), member states refrained from specifying actual ranges for full employment globally.

Although it may have been overly optimistic to expect that the MDGs would reverse more than two decades of neo-liberal economic restructuring, they did usher in a new global policy dynamic that was to prove highly significant in global YU policy in other ways. Notably, the MDGs' emphasis on global development partnerships promoted inter-agency working, not just within the UN but between the UN and other IGOs and INGOs, and, increasingly – as per the principles of the Global Compact – with the business sector. The ILO, UNESCO and UNDESA were to work as partners, as they had done for many decades, and from the beginning of the new millennium the World Bank was to join as a partner. In the event, as we discuss in the next sections, this emphasis on inter-IGO working and the attempt it represented to overcome fragmentation in global development governance played a significant role in drawing in corporate and third-sector partners. It was a shift that was to transform YU policy-making and interventions henceforth.

---

[13] Farnsworth (2014: 95), for example, argued that the Global Compact 'has won support from companies precisely because it is voluntary and it provides good opportunities for corporations to associate themselves, or their products, with the UN's positive "brand"'. Global Compact-badged initiatives are sometimes referred to as 'blue-washing' because of the entitlement of participating businesses to use the UN's blue logo (sometimes apparently masking corporate abuses).

[14] See Tables and ILO-sourced graphics throughout Chapter 5. ILOStat data show YU rates for just 15 countries for 1980, and two countries (Japan and the USA) for 1971 (see also Table 8.1, above). This places significant limits on historical analysis of trajectories of YU at country, world-regional and country income group levels.

8.3   INTERNATIONAL ORGANISATIONS' POLICY RESPONSES TO YOUTH UNEMPLOYMENT (2000–2008): THE GLOBAL DEVELOPMENT POLICY AGENDA

Since the UN was established, UNESCO and the ILO had constituted, defined and developed global YU policy. Until 2000, their combined powers had resided in their capacities to introduce quasi-legislative, regulatory or normative changes intended to reduce the risks of YU internationally, and to urge, enable or require other institutions and UN member states to act. The ILO had continued its work of establishing Conventions and Recommendations that had direct or indirect relevance to labour and (un)employment, albeit only until the late 1980s. It might therefore have been expected that the ILO and UNESCO would lead the pursuit of MDG Target 1.b. However, other forces evidently prevailed. From 2001 onwards, UNESCO became largely absent from this policy field,[15] and the WB joined it as a completely new entrant in global YU policy.[16] This was a radical reconfiguration of IOs in this field. It was also politically sensitive. Historically, the ILO and WB had been mutually distant and unconnected, pursuing very different agendas and goals that were typically actually or potentially conflicting. Since 1919, the ILO had epitomised the global face and voice of human labour, committed in its aims of securing decent working conditions, labour rights and fair pay across all nations. The WB's historical disregard for (and, often, its opposition to) many UN organisations' social, economic, labour and human rights priorities is well documented, especially in relation to its leading role alongside the IMF during the period of 'structural adjustment' programmes beginning in the 1980s.[17] While there are also countervailing analyses and interpretations of the WB's more recent priorities, notably during the GFC (see Barrientos et al., 2011; Alderman and Yemtsov, 2012), at the time of WB's and ILO's 'required' collaboration it was clear that they were not (and would be unlikely to become) cognate or even complementary analysts, thinkers and actors on the terrain of mass and endemic youth unemployment (EYU).

These major shifts not only altered the terrain and scope of ILO and WB activities, they facilitated a sea-change in IGO responses to escalating and endemic levels of YU. 'Towards global partnerships' (UNGA, 2001), set as an objective for IGOs the creation of partnerships with the private sector, NGOs and civil society bodies, and encouragement for the private sector to 'accept and implement the principle of good corporate citizenship', including through multi-stakeholder initiatives. The first realisation of partnerships in this reconfigured terrain was the newly-created Youth Employment Network (YEN). It was established in 2001 under the auspices of UNDESA (for the UN), with the ILO and WB as the key partners and dominant

---

[15]   Exceptions were occasional publications (see, for example, UNESCO, 2006) and participation in the First Global Forum on Youth Policies in 2014: see https://en.unesco.org/events/global-forum-youth-policies (accessed 22 June 2020).

[16]   Following the Second World War, the WB made a major contribution to borrowing and lending between national governments to establish full employment. Since then, identifiable work of *direct* involvement in addressing YU policy by the WB had been rare.

[17]   For detailed accounts of some of the tensions and conflicts between the WB and some IGOs, see, for example, Deacon et al. (1997); Deacon (2007); Rodgers et al. (2009); Helleiner (2014); and Maul (2019).

actors.[18] The ILO and WB agreed 'to prioritize youth employment on the development agenda and to exchange knowledge on effective policies and programmes to improve employment opportunities for youth'.[19] YEN was significant in part because it aimed to redefine YU as a social development issue, impelling the ILO and WB to attempt some accommodation of their disparate positions by pioneering complementary ways of reducing YU rates. YEN was based at the ILO's office in Geneva, serviced by ILO's permanent secretariat. It also worked out of ILO's regional offices in Senegal and Tanzania and in 20 lead countries across several world-regions. It was financed by three national governments (Denmark, Sweden, the UK), the International Olympic Committee, Accenture PLC, the WB and the United Nations Industrial Development Organization (UNIDO). The ILO continued to be the leading IGO throughout the YEN period, building on its earlier work setting international labour standards and employment rights, as well as maintaining its international networks and bases.

In common with some subsequent partnerships, evidence of the effectiveness and outcomes of YEN is extremely sparse and mostly inaccessible to secondary research. More than a decade after its inception, a nominally-independent evaluation described it as 'mainly a platform for data collection and information sharing that provides technical advice to find new solutions to the youth employment challenge' (World Bank Independent Evaluation Group, 2013: 32). The report comments that 'Although YEN has had some success in resource mobilization, the funding issue remains a major obstacle to the sustainability of YEN and its Secretariat' (p. 32). A separate independent assessment found major shortcomings in YEN's systematic impact evaluation of programmes (Eichhorst and Rinne, 2015: 46).

The YEN Secretariat – and so, in effect, YEN as a separate independent partnership – ceased to function in 2014. The WB was evidently the junior partner in YEN, and its intention to assert other priorities was already clear soon after YEN became operational.[20] The WB's annual *World Development Report* (*WDR*) for 2007 indicated its preferred direction of travel. Subtitled 'Development and the Next Generation' (World Bank, 2006), it focused on invest-ment in youth by 'expanding opportunities, enhancing capabilities, and providing second chances'. It also referenced MDG 8, 'partnerships for international development' (World Bank, 2006), thereby anticipating the WB's later Social Protection and Labour (SPL) strategy (World Bank, 2011). The 2007 *WDR* also anticipated WB's plans for a new breakaway part-nership for youth employment. By 2008 WB had instigated its Global Partnership for Youth Employment (GPYE), incorporating YEN as one partner alongside several third-sector bodies and an inter-agency UN body (ILO, 2012a, 2012b).[21] GPYE focused on three main activities: providing applied research and learning to better understand school-to-work transitions and increase the employability of youth; promoting policy dialogue; and supporting technical assistance for local governments and capacity-building for stakeholders from the public sector and civil society, to enhance their engagement (ILO, 2012a, 2012b). The ILO continued to run YEN, independently of the WB, but YEN's inclusion in GPYE had the effect of maintaining

---

[18]   UNDESA's role was principally a coordinating one, though it was judged to be minimal over the long run by an ILO evaluation report (International Labour Office Evaluation Unit, 2012).
[19]   See   https://www.ilo.org/global/about-the-ilo/newsroom/news/WCMS_143025/lang--en/index .htm (accessed 22 June 2020).
[20]   This view is cautiously acknowledged by the ILO's Evaluation Unit (International Labour Office Evaluation Unit, 2012: 4).
[21]   Fergusson (2021) discusses the politics of partnerships in this policy field in depth.

a nominal ILO presence in oversight of this new partnership. GPYE was short-lived, and little publicly-available evidence of its work and impact appears to have survived.[22] By 2014, GPYE had been devolved to the International Youth Foundation and apparently ceased to function shortly afterwards.[23]

At the heart of the ILO's and WB's differences seems to have been the WB's prioritisation of supply-side measures intended to make young people more employable in pursuit of economic development, in contrast to the ILO's orientation towards job creation and demand-side projects. Alongside these differences were the WB's traditionally unsympathetic and often hostile predispositions towards social security for the unemployed, compared to the ILO's recognition of its necessity.[24] In an early presentation on the plans for YEN, the ILO's Deputy Director drew attention to the importance of GDP growth and the management of aggregate demand to increase levels of employment. His remarks suggested that enhanced employability skills can *only* be used if new jobs are also created, giving the example of infrastructure projects requiring labour-intensive public works that can be implemented speedily (Miller, 2001: 7–8).[25]

Mostly out of step with this advice, a key element of YEN's early plans was its focus on 'The four Es': employability, entrepreneurship, employment creation, and equal opportunities – the first two being predominantly supply-side activities, the third demand-side oriented. This nevertheless reflected a degree of accommodation between the ILO and the WB in the early stages of YEN. The differences between supply-side and demand-side analyses of the causes of YU have long been evident in ILO and WB discourses. The ILO's pre-GFC policies – especially its Global Employment Agenda – emphasised labour market reform, job creation and institutional reform. But ILO policies also advocated active labour market programmes (ALMPs), targeted employment incentives, promotion of entrepreneurship and other supply-side measures, albeit alongside demand-side interventions (see, for example, ILO, 2008). In contrast, the WB's early approach to YU was firmly grounded in human capital theory, with predominantly supply-side oriented interpretations referencing premature exit from schooling, poor skills, qualifications and attitudes as well as skills mismatches as causes of high YU rates. The WB's 2007 *WDR* is replete with references to implied deficiencies in young people's basic skills, skills matches, skills accumulation, skills that are relevant to labour market needs and continuing skills development (World Bank, 2006: 96–107). Deficiency of demand for young workers' labour receives a single mention in 300 pages.[26]

---

[22]   The World Bank Research and Publications website identifies no GPYE outputs. Residual outline records of GPYE's activity are held by Solutions for Youth Employment (S4YE), GPYE's successor. No independent analysis of GPYE has been undertaken, but a single substantial 'how to' guide to monitoring and evaluation of youth livelihood interventions survives (Hempel and Fiala, 2012). See https://openknowledge.worldbank.org and https://www.s4ye.org/taxonomy/term/386 (both accessed 25 February 2020).

[23]   The International Youth Federation (IYF) produced two GPYE outputs. See https://www.iyfnet .org/initiatives/global-partnership-youth-employment-gpye (accessed 25 February 2020).

[24]   For interpretation of these tensions, see Fergusson and Yeates (2013, 2014). Here, we focus on the supply-side/demand-side issues. The welfare and social protection issues nevertheless continue to be of great importance (see Chapter 2, Section 2.4).

[25]   Miller's (2001) observations are consistent with Okun's Law (see Chapter 6, Section 6.2).

[26]   Other major differences are evident in the ILO's and WB's literature concerning the circumstances and provision of social protection and welfare arrangements for young people without work. Although

Counterfactually, soon after GPYE was initiated – in the same year as the onset of the GFC – it would have been reasonable to surmise that the post-MDG era of ILO–WB partnerships was already drawing to a close. Just as the ILO had clearly been the leading partner in YEN, so the WB emerged as the lead IGO for GPYE, so much so that the ILO was apparently only nominally active in GPYE. In effect, the partners appeared to have become disconnected, and to be operating independently of each other, with the WB running GPYE and the ILO running YEN. This trajectory of separation continued throughout the early years of the GFC, but the huge impact of the crisis on YU globally was to result in three major programmes intended to re-establish partnership between the key IGO actors, in the form of 'Solutions for Youth Employment', the 'Global Initiative on Decent Jobs for Youth' and 'Generation Unlimited' – all in pursuit of a much more robust agenda for *eliminating* YU worldwide set by the Sustainable Development Goals of 2015.

8.4 INTERNATIONAL ORGANISATIONS' POLICY RESPONSES TO YOUTH UNEMPLOYMENT (2009–2020): THE GLOBAL FINANCIAL CRISIS

8.4.1 International Organisations and Global Financial Crises

The global financial crisis of 2007/08 transformed the profile of YU in much of the world (see Chapter 5). Its economic consequences were profound in many countries. As Chapter 6 demonstrated, consistent with Okun's Law, mass YU at endemic scales is primarily associated with declining GDP. When economies shrink sharply, young people are, with great consistency across countries, the most immediate victims. While this relationship is strongest in high-income countries and less strong in middle-income countries, it is the most significant and reliable correlate and highly probable cause of YU worldwide. As the GFC 'set in', a stronger global response to the economic effects of the GFC and its implications across policy fields – especially those concerned with mass unemployment – was needed. How IGOs anticipated and responded to the consequent economic crises is essential to understanding the impact of the GFC on young people's opportunities.

Historical political-economic contexts provide important insights into IGOs' responses to financial and economic crises. In the aftermaths of two world wars, the urgent need to address massive financial deficits, restore national economies and facilitate international trade was conspicuously clear, as was the need for dedicated IGOs to secure social and economic recovery and propose policies capable of mitigating at least some of the risks of future catastrophic global conflict. It was twelve years after the end of the First World War before the Hague Conference established the Bank for International Settlements (BIS) to settle international reparations. At the end of the Second World War the Bretton Woods Conference established the IMF with the purpose of avoiding future financial crises. The IMF's 1945 Articles of

---

their positions were not typically material to their collaboration or the management of local projects, the symbolic significance of their major differences – and by implication their limited compatibility as partners – is apparent (see Fergusson and Yeates, 2013, 2014, 2017). For detailed analysis of the evolution of these and other IO partnerships, see Fergusson (2021). For source documents that illustrate typical differences, see ILO (2004a, 2004b, 2005); World Bank (2006); and ILO and IMF (2010).

Agreement established worldwide fixed currency exchange rates based on the US dollar and bound national governments to maintaining currency values. Movement of capital between currency areas was restricted, and no further regulatory arrangements were deemed necessary. Between 1945 and 1975, major international banking crises were exceptional rarities. The gold standard was abandoned in 1971 and currency values were allowed to float in accordance with rates determined by worldwide demand in financial markets.

Early responses to this transformative shift in the regulation of global financial transactions were slow and limited.[27] There was no effective anticipation of the GFC. Seven decades after it was established the BIS was the only IO to warn of an impending crisis. Its warnings passed unheeded, and in 2007 the sub-prime mortgage crisis in the US triggered multiple bank collapses which became global in 2008, with economic consequences that affected most countries at magnitudes not witnessed since the 1930s.[28] Schoenbaum (2012: 84) argues that the GFC 'exposed the weakness of IMF supervision of the global economy, the inadequacy of IMF resources, and the shortcomings of the IMF conditionality program for extending loans'. The IMF's own Independent Evaluation Office's report (IMF/IEO, 2011) was excoriating in its criticisms of the Fund. The only organisation with genuinely global economic oversight, the IMF, failed to identify the risks. The stability of international finance had depended entirely on the self-regulatory capacity of international financial markets, and by 2007 self-regulation had failed.

8.4.2　Early Responses to the GFC

The extraordinary harms the GFC inflicted on young people's prospects of employment worldwide prompted the WB to become an even more prominent actor in the YU policy field than it was after the MDGs, and to modify some of the tenets of its earlier policy stances. As national governments began to face the implications for youth (un)employment, the ILO presented its Global Jobs Pact (ILO, 2009), based on its Decent Work Agenda, and its International Labour Conference (ILC) called on donor countries and multilateral agencies to provide funding in response. Surprisingly, the Pact made no substantive reference to YU rates, which had risen in 2009 but had yet to peak, even though the UN General Assembly recognised 'the special vulnerability of young people in the current financial and economic crisis, in particular with regard to youth unemployment and precarious working conditions' (UNGA, 2009: 2). By 2010, for the first time, the WB advocated demand-side measures that would provide financial incentives to firms to hire workers, and wage subsidies to bring pay closer to market rates (World Bank, 2010: 2, 3, 5). This was a remarkable departure for an IGO committed to the competence and efficiency of 'free' market systems.[29]

---

[27]　See Schoenbaum (2012) on the work of the International Organization of Securities Commissions; the Basel Committee on Banking Supervision; and the International Association of Insurance Supervisors.

[28]　For an authoritative comprehensive analysis, see Tooze, 2018; also brief summaries of his analyses in Chapter 5 (Section 5.2.2, above).

[29]　The WB's own evaluation of youth employment programmes funded with the International Finance Corporation (IFC) emphasised the economic and social costs of YU soon afterwards (World Bank, 2012), while Lundberg et al. (2012: 21) stressed the damaging effects of crises and their longer-term costs to young people.

It was not until 2011 that the need for greater urgency became clear to the UN, and over the next four years a succession of initiatives was launched. A High-level Meeting of the General Assembly on Youth that year urged member states 'to address the global challenge of youth unemployment by … regional and national particularities' (UNGA, 2011a: 5; see also UNGA (2011b)). In 2012 the first Youth Forum taking place under the auspices of UN ECOSOC set as its overall theme high quality jobs as a route to youth empowerment (ECOSOC, 2012). The same year, the ILC issued a major 'call for action' to address what it now termed the 'youth employment crisis' and requested that the call emphasise demand-side policies of pro-employment growth, creation of decent jobs and the ambition for full employment (ILO, 2012a: 4).[30] This was followed up by a UNGA Resolution on youth recognising the multi-faceted nature of young people's labour market position and experiences and incor- porating commitments on YU, unacceptable employment experiences, and the influence of globalisation processes on those experiences (UNGA, 2013: 3). It is nonetheless notable that UNGA Resolutions on policies involving youth in most subsequent years to 2019 reliably reit- erated a commitment to the pursuit of skills as a precursor to job creation – thereby continuing to reinforce supply-side strategies in preference to demand-side ones.

From 2013, improved coordination across UN agencies was facilitated through a System-wide Action Plan on Youth (Youth-SWAP) to guide youth programmes across the UN within the framework of the 15 priority areas of the (now-ageing) *World Programme of Action for Youth to the Year 2000 and Beyond* (see Section 8.2 above). SWAP's thematic area of Employment and Entrepreneurship committed stakeholders to ensuring 'greater opportunities for youth to secure decent work and income over the life-cycle, contributing to a virtuous circle of poverty reduction, sustainable development and social inclusion', with a particular stress on gender-sensitive strategies (UN, 2013). A further UNGA resolution in support of World Youth Skills Day reiterated concerns about the 75 million unemployed youth, and reinforced a continuing preoccupation with supply-side measures (UNGA, 2014).

Throughout this period, an ever-growing emphasis on multi-stakeholder partnerships with civil society and businesses ushered in a growing corporatisation of global partnerships in this policy field as facilitated by the UN's Global Compact (see pp. 191–92, above). The ILO's long-standing emphasis on full employment and demand-led analyses of YU continued to advocate skills development, and technical and vocational education and training (TVET), and added entrepreneurship to its priorities. These trends intensified as the ideational, technical and financial capacities of the World Bank became fully engaged with the YU crisis, and reinforced these priorities amongst the policies of UN bodies.

Other countervailing trends amongst UN IGOs made specific connections between youth (un)employment and social development. Recognition that youth (un)employment is not only about decent productive work, but that it also encompasses poverty, hunger and illiteracy, and contributes to wider social development goals of social integration and solidarity, were key themes at the 2007 meeting of the UN Commission for Social Development. This implied an urgent need for recognising the plights of youth extending well beyond policies concerning YU, and, importantly, for the involvement of agencies beyond the ILO. The point that youth (un)employment is a matter of youth development and of social and economic development

---

[30] Others included knowledge development, technical assistance, partnership and advocacy (ILO, 2012a: 13–15).

more widely was amplified (UNGA, 2007), as was the idea that 'measures to address YU should extend beyond the realms of education, training, social integration and mobility to include reconciliation of family life and working life, equal opportunities, solidarity between the generations, health and lifelong learning' (para. 8e, p. 3). Awareness of these trends had endured in some UN agencies, but were far from ubiquitous. In any case, supply-side biases remained evident in the continued emphasis on skills development and the multiple needs of young people most at risk of joblessness, as did the absence of reference to demand-led measures. In this context, ILO's embrace of supply-side measures and especially of youth entrepreneurship hardly looked out of place.

8.4.3   Separate Development: ILO and WB

From 2009 onwards, the extreme effects of the GFC on YU rates worldwide were starkly evident. The spike in YU rates in high-income and lower middle-income countries (HICs and LMICs) was exceptional (see Figure 5.8, Chapter 5, p. 99). The relationship between declining national GDP and rising YU rates left little doubt that economic decline caused by the GFC was driving up YU rates sharply. As Chapter 6 demonstrated, in almost all HICs, the GDP–YU relationship was at high levels of statistical significance, and this pattern recurred in almost half of upper middle-income countries (UMICs) and a quarter of LMICs (see Appendix 6.2, Table 6A.2.1). By 2012, the average YU rate for HICs was recovering rapidly (although rates in some HICs remained acutely high: see Table 5.2). In contrast, the average rates for LMICs and UMICs continued to escalate – sometimes sharply – and endemic levels of YU continue unabated in many of these countries.[31]

In 2012, following the ILC's crisis call for action on global YU, the WB proposed a new multi-stakeholder partnership: Solutions for Youth Employment (S4YE). It was launched in 2014 with an extraordinary longer-term ambition to place 150 million more young people in employment. Like the earlier WB-led GPYE it drew heavily on third-sector partnerships as well as global corporates, financiers, banks and government representatives. S4YE's structures, governance, lead actors and finances have epitomised the corporatisation of YU programmes. As lead IGO, the WB was the main enabler of projects around the world under the leadership of delegated authorities of the central body, accountable to, but distinct from, the WB. How far each project resembles a corporate enterprise expected to break even financially or generate surplus remains opaque. It is also difficult to establish whether S4YE resembles an IO, an international charity, a third-sector corporate, a commercial trader, or an amalgam of these statuses. Similarly, it is unclear how S4YE's activities are made publicly accountable. By 2020 it was overseeing 44 Impact Portfolios across 38 countries.[32] Although discursively committed to building increased demand for young people's labour, S4YE's strategic framework is dominated by programmes intended to strengthen labour supply by means of upskilling and cognate projects (S4YE, 2015: 27). Notably, rights to social and labour protection are

---

[31]   Amongst UMICs, YU rates persisted at 40–50 per cent and above in Gabon, Namibia, South Africa, Bosnia and Herzegovina, Georgia, Montenegro, North Macedonia, and Algeria, for example. Amongst LMICs, in Egypt, Sudan and Tunisia, YU has been at or above 30 per cent almost continuously for three decades. See Table 5.2.

[32]   See   https://www.s4ye.org/sites/default/files/2020-01/FINAL.S4YE.FACTBOOK.2020_0.pdf (accessed 23 August 2020).

not referred to in presented information, while independent evaluations query the value of the supply-side measures adopted.[33]

In the same year that S4YE launched, the ILO began work on its Global Initiative on Decent Jobs for Youth (GIDJY) (latterly known as Decent Jobs for Youth (DJY)). Like S4YE it is a multi-stakeholder partnership, aiming to involve five million young people in at least 26 projects worldwide, including some job creation projects, with a strong emphasis on job quality, decent work conditions and gender equality, signalling prioritisation of demand-side programmes, as well as providing supply-side measures (ILO, 2015b). Notably, DJY's model and partners do not match the corporatised model of S4YE, being predominantly UN agencies, charities, international development agencies and not-for-profit entities, government representatives (including the Global South) and an international development bank. DJY's three global corporate business partners (MacDonald's, Microsoft, Nestlé) constitute a much smaller element of DJY than of S4YE. DJY began operations in 2017. Significantly, previous reciprocities of partnership observed in YEN and GPYE appear to have lapsed: the WB is not represented or involved in DJY, while the ILO appears to be no more than a nominal member of the Board of S4YE.

Whether these arrangements signal a change from attempted collaboration to apparent separate development between these two major IOs is not yet wholly clear. What is beyond doubt is that a subsequent UN intervention radically altered the terrain and the dynamics of power and influence in shaping global responses to an unabated crisis of YU. The 2015 Sustainable Development Goals (SDGs) established a much stronger ambition for addressing YU: 'By 2030, achieve full and productive employment and decent work for all women and men, including for young people and persons with disabilities, and equal pay for work of equal value' (Goal 8.5) and 'By 2020, substantially reduce the proportion of youth not in employment, education or training' (Goal 8.6). No standards for achieving these full employment targets were set (for example, ranges of unemployment rates to be achieved worldwide for young people), just as for the MDGs and, before then, for the UN's full employment programme (Chapter 7, Section 7.4, p. 172). Well before 2020, though, it was evident that the 'waymark' SDG 8.6 would not be met. The UN made clear that 'action to meet the Goals is not yet advancing at the speed or scale required. 2020 needs to usher in a decade of ambitious action to deliver the Goals by 2030' (UN, 2020). The prospects for meeting SDG 8.5 by 2030, too, were clearly in very serious doubt.

8.4.4   Direct Intervention on the Faltering Path to SDG 8

On the eve of the adoption of the SDGs, the UN highlighted a huge decline in global youth employment rates between 1991 and 2015, from 50 per cent to 40 per cent (UN, 2015). This recognition of substantial prospective shortfalls on the ambitions of SDGs 8.5 and 8.6 prompted a further set of initiatives. In September 2018 the 73rd UNGA moved to establish

---

[33]   In 2013, the WB's evaluation group found that WB projects spent half as much on job creation as on supply-side-oriented projects (World Bank Independent Evaluation Group, 2013), noting that supply-side measures are generally ineffective in high-unemployment environments, and that demand-side interventions are needed. S4YE's early analysis found that that 52 per cent of ILO and WB expenditure was on supply-side labour market measures, compared to 29 per cent spent on demand-side measures (S4YE, 2015).

its new youth strategy programme as part of the UN's Agenda 2030 programme (UN, 2018). A key element of the strategy was the creation of Generation Unlimited (GenU), led by UNICEF, and described as 'a global partnership that aims to ensure that every young person is in education, learning, training or employment by 2030' (UNICEF, 2018). GenU's focus is 'youth engagement, participation and advocacy; supporting young people's greater access to quality education and skills development; and economic empowerment through decent jobs'. It is described as a

> global multi-sector partnership to meet the urgent need for expanded education, training and employ-ment opportunities for young people, aged 10 to 24, on an unprecedented scale' intended to address the needs of 'the largest cohort ever – an unprecedented 1.8 billion – who require a new inclusive approach, given the extraordinary economic, social and cultural challenges they face. (Generation Unlimited, n.d.)

The UN's larger Youth Strategy, *Youth 2030: working with and for young people*, is said to act 'as an umbrella framework to guide the entire UN as it steps up its work with and for young people' (UN, 2018: 5). Its third priority is to 'support young people's greater access to decent work and productive employment' (UN, 2018: 11). This includes a commitment to engaging member states and partners to

> advocate for a balanced approach to stimulate demand for youth labour and prompt improvements in skills development systems, with the objective of easing the school-to-work transition and reducing the youth NEET [not in education, employment or training] rate, particularly among young women and disadvantaged youth'. (p. 11)

This is an encouraging statement, particularly because of its apparent reference to demand-side interventions, even if somewhat equivocally so. The strategy document and other online outputs place a very strong emphasis on attracting and 'leveraging' global and national invest-ment in GenU's activities, allowing successful initiatives to be up-scaled and to demonstrate financial returns.

GenU's Executive Committee comprises the World Bank's Vice President for Human Development, UNICEF's Special Representative for Young People, three CEOs of global corporates, a senior national civil servant, and the CEO of a third-sector organisation. The 53-member Global Board has a diverse membership.[34] It is noteworthy that the IMF is not a member; that the World Bank and UNICEF are the only IGO members of the Executive Committee; and that the ILO and UNESCO are members of the Global Board but not the Executive Committee. UNICEF's inclusion in a key role in GenU is significant inasmuch as historically it has had a surprisingly low profile in YU issues, given its responsibility for children and young people up to the age of 17 (one to two years above eligibility for formal employment in many countries) (Chapter 7). Its inclusion in a dominant position in partnership with WB also marks a prospective major shift in the priorities of GenU (see also below).

---

[34]   The Board comprises most Executive Committee members, representatives of six UN agencies and the European Commission, the ILO's Director-General, the Secretary-General of the OECD, and ten representatives of private-sector corporate bodies, six national governments (equally Global North and South), 15 third-sector organisations and ten IGOs.

By 2020 GenU was working in approximately 40 mainly low-income and lower middle-income countries. Two major advances in GenU's work were the partnerships brokered with the World Bank, which led to an allocation of $1 billion; and with the African Union, which aims to reach 10 million young people by 2021. GenU's websites convey a strong sense that the initial projects and endeavours are already supply-side dominated, with a very strong emphasis on skills development before leaving school, on educational improvement, and on vocational projects and employability. But there is no information on how the demand-side element of the commitment to a balanced approach is to be achieved. Rather, most of the narrative is dominated by references to skills development, training, entrepreneurship, investment in human capital and digital connectivity.

The World Bank's 'ground-breaking' GenU partnership with UNICEF is heralded as a new commitment to 'promote education, skills and training for young people in developing countries with the goal of boosting their employment prospects' (Generation Unlimited, 2019a). The $1 billion investment committed GenU to 'mobilizing countries to deliver more effective investments in people – especially young people ' (Generation Unlimited, 2019a). The four key foci are all essentially supply-side strategies. In different ways, the narratives are once again premised on deficit models of the supply of adequately skilled young entrants to labour markets. Only very occasionally do other demand-side discourses emerge: the CEO of Unilever recognises that 'the private sector has a big role to play in making jobs, education and skills training available to these young people', and the Director of GenU stresses the urgent need for job creation in Africa (Generation Unlimited, 2019b, 2020).

This casts an interesting light on UNICEF's emergence as a key player, especially since it has been almost entirely absent from debate among IGOs, including during the GFC, and its past policy discourse has displayed a surprising enthusiasm for supply-side measures.[35] One persuasive reading of the new alliance between the WB and UNICEF in GenU is that they share interpretations of the causes of YU and responses to it that contrast markedly with the interpretations of the ILO, UNESCO and ECOSOC. GenU's priorities recall well-worked historical debates in economics and education emanating from the Washington Consensus and global neo-liberalisation reflecting a fierce, long-standing and unresolved debate centred on human capital development and vocationalisation. On the political-economic right, a forceful case prioritised 'the needs of the economy' in the face of economic decline in leading advanced economies (for example, Carnoy and Levin, 1985). Long-standing critical assessments have however queried these premises and claims and the forms of social and economic reproduction that would ensue, particularly regarding entrenched inequalities of class, 'race' and gender (Apple, 1978, 1982, 1995, 2018; Dale, 1982, 1989). From the information available, GenU leans towards supply-side labour market strategies. These developments are resonant of the WB's and ILO's paths of 'separate development' described above.

Two important issues arise in relation to GenU. The first concerns the increasingly corporate nature of partnerships noted earlier in this global policy field. The incorporation of multi-stakeholder partnerships into the UN's 2030 Agenda for Sustainable Development has already drawn a wide range of social actors into shaping global policy. Particular concerns

---

[35] Fergusson and Yeates' (2014) analysis of IGOs' policy discourses identified UNICEF as the sole UN agency to align with the WB's supply-side oriented interpretations of YU between 2004 and 2012. See also Fergusson and Yeates (2013) for a fuller interpretation of WB's earlier premises and priorities.

accrue to the nature and effects of corporate private-sector involvement in global policy formation and implementation in relation to employment and labour rights, transparency and public
accountability. Multi-stakeholder partnerships should be positive developments in support of
innovative policy formation using knowledgeable local agencies, providers and employers.
But this cannot be assumed. Some partnerships have been underpinned by the post-2015
Partnership Platform for Philanthropy (UNDP et al., 2014), and some aspects of its work have
raised concerns about inadequate transparency, for example.[36] There are also questions that
the UN has sought to address concerning business practices in partnerships (UNSG, 2013),
referencing transparent legal and ethical standards and due diligence in respect of human
rights. Corporate-led approaches risk neglecting such expectations and straining partnerships.
In the long run, extending and enhancing the role of commercial interests in partnership with
public and third-sector organisations puts at risk implementation of normative standards to
ensure decent work and social protection at work for the youngest, most vulnerable entrants to
globalised labour markets.

The second issue concerns the speedy sequential emergence of three major new partnerships. One question concerns the need for a third global partnership in the same field as
S4YE and DJY. GenU was initiated within two years of the start dates of S4YE and DJY. Its
commitments replicate many aspects of S4YE's, which is very different from DJY's partnership with UN agencies. The co-existence of three programmes with ostensibly similar core
goals allows for important differences of objectives and/or strategies between partnerships.
But a plurality of priorities and methods may not ensure compatibility, productive outcomes
or an efficient use of resources. As we noted above, evaluations have queried some of the
approaches and effectiveness of past partnership programmes and projects. Finding solutions
to YU by means of projects and ground-level interventions depends on shared objectives
and common measures of success. Whether EYU is best tackled by prevailing on capital and
private enterprise, or by drawing on the public purse to generate demand for youthful labour
requires assessment against agreed criteria. In any case, GenU institutes a partnership revolving around NEETs – a policy sub-category of YU incorporated into the SDGs and commonly
used in some HICs. It remains to be seen whether GenU's approach can achieve a significant
development in responding to YU, equivalent to the ILO's powerful interventions a century
earlier (see Chapter 7).

8.5   CONCLUSIONS

It is inconceivable that these recently-reconfigured partnerships for addressing YU could
ever make more than a small impression on realising decent work for the 68 million
15–24-year-olds who were already known to be unemployed in 2019. Nevertheless, underlying these partnerships remain differences of approach and method that are important vestiges
of the deep historical political-economic rifts that have characterised the struggles defining
and distinguishing the globalised economies and societies of the twentieth century. Reflecting
these differences, each partnership would offer very different answers to some key questions

---

[36]   The SDG Platform is described as 'a vehicle for catalyzing multi-stakeholder partnerships to
advance the SDGs'. For critical commentary of the WB's Global Financing Facility (World Bank, 2015),
see the Bretton Woods Project (2017).

about how best to resolve EYU globally. Are supply-side programmes that reskill young people to match the needs of employers the most effective responses to YU – allowing that employers' needs are volatile and labour markets are unstable? Do demand-side measures that create publicly funded jobs achieve anything more than short-term one-off amelioration – merely smoothing out fluctuating YU rates until labour markets 'clear' and economic recovery 'solves the problem'? Are 'balanced approaches' and 'mixed economy' tactics preferable in that some interventions will inevitably result in beneficial job placements while others produce no useful outcome – because of constantly changing circumstances which enable employers to thrive financially on reserve armies of youthful labour?

There are few clearer illustrations of the tensions and struggles within and between the partnerships than their answers to these questions. They would almost certainly mirror the long-run ebb and flow of stances among the key IGO actors in the YU policy field over the last century. As this chapter and Chapter 7 have sought to show, these questions have been fought out through the politics of responding to mass and global EYU since the early twentieth century. Indeed, there are few turns in the evolution of this global social policy field that cannot be traced to the fractures and divisions that have emanated from struggles between these conflicting priorities and objectives. While this claim is not intended as an essentialist, reductionist re-assertion of a simplistic binary division between leading global actors, we highlight the constant push and pull between the clearly delineated forces that have been central to the formation of this global policy field. However named and labelled, the differences, struggles, and some-time partnerships amongst its IGOs have always pivoted on the rights and protections of young people in local and global labour markets, as against the rights and imperatives of industry and business to optimise productivity, efficiency and competitive success.

Our survey of the politics of global YU policy as played out in multilateral spheres of governance over the course of a century (1919–2020) has shown how integral these struggles and contestations have been to that history, and how they permeated almost every aspect of the construction of global YU policy as a coherent and distinctive global policy field, whether we 'read' this field through international norms and agreements, or through programmes of 'technical' assistance, research and advocacy that connected and embedded IGOs and other transnational actors, ideationally as well as institutionally. The ILO became the lead IGO in the agentic structure of YU policy-making and oversight, working in partnership with diverse international communities connected to YU, notably UNESCO in the post-war period. Working together, a global policy dynamic of identifiable logics with shared meanings had emerged by the mid-1930s. The policy approach was, then, formed relatively early on, certainly in terms of its normative underpinnings, and continued to be elaborated and refined during the post-war period, most intensively so up to the 1970s when the international commitment to full employment waned. By the late 1970s, expansive political-economic recalibration opened up a titanic struggle between the forces of social democracy and neo-liberalism across (but also beyond) the North Atlantic axis, a struggle that was successfully and effectively played out to the advantage of the WB and IMF, rather than to the ILO and UNESCO that had dominated in the post-war years. Most tangibly, this halted the expansive norms-building period and marked a shift towards projects formed within a UN-based global youth policy of which unemployment was one issue among many.

A significant milestone in this history is the post-2000 turn towards multi-stakeholder global partnerships as formalised structures through which relations of cooperation and competition are played out among national and transnational actors. Opaque in terms of structure, accountability, budget, modes of operation, projects and, most of all, effectiveness and impact, these partnerships have varied in terms of durability and composition, as well as the extent to which partnership was more satisfactory than separation. The partners in YEN and their conflicting published interpretations of political-economic causes of and solutions to mass and endemic YU proved at that time irreconcilable. The fate of this initial partnership was sealed by the GFC and the urgent need for an alternative – GPYE – which could never have been remotely equal to the task it faced in the aftermath. The SDGs' global development imperatives propelled new inter-IGO alliances but both the ILO and WB led new partnerships in which the other was either only nominally present (S4YE) or actually absent (DJY): partnership meant working with organisations other than each other.

The history of the WB's and ILO's collaborative endeavours to reduce and ameliorate YU from 2000 onwards has been one of creating, joining, withdrawing from and re-creating partnerships, with each other but primarily with other (mainly global) actors. Throughout the post-2000 period, supply-side palliation dominated, even as it was self-evidently unequal to burgeoning YU. So deeply has it been embedded, institutionally and ideationally, in global governance structures that we cannot but conclude that it is the dominant paradigm of global YU policy. From the perspective of the long course of history, this approach is the historically-dominant one. It has emerged within a fragmented global governance structure dating back to the LoN and continuing throughout the twentieth century and to the present day that separated global 'economic' (macro-economic, finance and trade) institutions from global 'social' ones. Keynesianism came closest to traversing the boundaries of this separation, but the boundaries remained 'hard-wired' in global institutional design. This was a global 'pact' of sorts, and one that relegated YU to the realm of palliative 'social policy' measures rather than a society-wide economic issue to be addressed principally through demand structures and the dynamics of a globalising economy. Although YU was belatedly recognised as a global social issue, from the outset it was never adequately understood as one whose dynamics inherently and substantially transcended nation states, including in the forceful face of continuous globalised economic restructuring.

Furthermore, a profound change has occurred in the operational structures of global YU policy that may signal deep-rooted transformations in the global political economy of YU – namely, that global corporate entities have become more prominent within the new global partnerships. Although business interests have long been involved in global YU policy through the ILO's tripartite structures, the post-2000 on-boarding of corporations in global YU partnerships is of a different order. Indeed, this has occurred continuously over two decades, and has permeated such structures to the extent that corporate involvement has become a routine feature of global YU policy. Now, it characterises and shapes most programmes. S4YE and DJY have already shown themselves to be major corporate enterprises, albeit enterprises that work in significantly different ways, often towards different ends. GenU may well establish a new pathway for up-scaling and consolidating this trend and exert a growing influence of business interests in global YU policy. It will be telling to observe at what juncture the efficiency of, and need to maintain, three separate youth employment partnerships working in parallel in the same policy field comes to be queried. Time, and shifts in the global balance of power will tell whether this signals a temporary or more permanent shift in global YU policy, whether it opens up a deeper pathway into liberalism (and what variant of liberalism), or whether some potentially transformative threats to global health on the cusp of the third decade of this millennium are of such moment in the face of unprecedented extremes of EYU as to force transformative thinking and radically-reconstructed IO partnerships – as the closing chapter contemplates.

Across the broad sweep of history that Chapters 7 and 8 have tried to capture, we conclude that the multilateralization of YU policy has tolerated the causes and harms of high levels of YU rather than demonstrating effectiveness in challenging them at source. At no point have standards for the attainment of the ostensibly core aim of realising full employment been set – not in the initial specification of the UN's full employment programme in the late 1940s, nor in the World Employment Programme of the 1970s, nor in the MDGs, nor, most recently in the SDGs. The specification of such standards for young people, such as global ranges for acceptable, sustainable global and national rates of YU, has proved, it seems, to be a step too far. Moreover, successive efforts to construct and develop the policy field have paralleled, overseen, and in some senses facilitated, the global re-organisation of youth labour (see Chapters 3–6). We return to these connections in Chapter 9. For now, whatever the future of these structures, two key issues that have become submerged in the evolution of IOs' responses to the challenges of mass and endemic YU will need to be addressed.

First is the critical issue of re-building and sustaining demand for young people's labour sufficient to make productive use of available supply. This has been allowed to fall in the hierarchy of priorities since the MDGs, alongside the decline and disappearance of calls for full employment as a policy priority. The majority of programmes instituted under the rubric of global YU policy are (albeit still to differing degrees) dominated by supply-side projects to improve employability and feed the changing needs of capital in globalised youth labour markets. It is difficult to find countervailing evidence of efforts to persuade national governments of policies that prioritise job creation towards stabilising the volatility of globalised labour forces – except perhaps in the most extreme emergencies of the kind we have alluded to (see also Chapter 9). Certainly, following the GFC, there remains clear evidence of the continuing domination of supply-side over demand-side measures.

The second issue is that *all* the key actors in this field of global policy and governance appear to have shrunk from the enormity of the task of tackling mass and EYU as an ostensibly *permanent* condition, and from doing so at scale. At one level, this is epitomised in emasculated UN initiatives. The Global Compact is one example of this. It was, as we saw, a missed opportunity to prioritise youth employment and hold businesses and governments to account for their failure to realise MDG commitments (and subsequently SDG ones) on youth employment. We also see this in how the ILO's core mission and its *raison d'être* has been radically redefined and substantially diluted. In large part, the ILO now functions as a consultancy service for countries and institutions striving to strengthen youth employment. Its most 'recent' major global initiative of 15 years' standing pre-dated the GFC: the ILO's 'brochure' (*sic*) for the 2005 Youth Employment Programme (YEP) described it as providing 'knowledge development and dissemination … advocacy and partnerships, [and] … technical assistance and capacity building' (ILO, n.d.: 6). Apart from the ILO's one – albeit major and substantially financed – remaining programme, 'Decent Jobs for Youth', it appears to be a facilitative rather than a leading IO.

The international community's reluctance to tackle mass and endemic YU is also evident, at another level, in apparent eschewal of direct or implied criticism of apparent shortcomings of the institutions of global governance in driving down YU rates. Such criticisms, when they happen, are typically exercised with great caution in public discourse; they surprise when they occur. One recent, bold exception, however, came from the lips of UN Secretary-General Antonio Guterres in April 2020 when he addressed the UN Security Council on the huge scale of insufficient jobs or other employment for young people,[37] which he described as 'frankly, failures … by those in power today'.[38] These genuinely 'frank' and welcome words are a stark reminder of the weaknesses of global governance, notably the institutional separation of economic governance (IMF, WB, WTO) from social governance (UN-based IGOs) that has plagued the development of global YU policy and severely limited IOs' capacities to address inexorably rising YU rates. As Chapter 9 discusses, the further global health adversities to which we have repeatedly alluded at several junctures may yet refresh public demand for strengthened capacities of these global institutions to achieve the social and economic justice on which international peace and security is founded – including by means of assuring the rights of all young people to productive employment in decent work, with equal pay for work of equal value, as agreed and encapsulated in SDG 8.5.

---

[37] The full speech can be sourced at https://www.un.org/sg/en/content/sg/statement/2020-04-27/secretary-generals-remarks-virtual-security-council-meeting-the-maintenance-of-international-peace-and-security-youth-peace-and-security-delivered (accessed 10 August 2020).

[38] Guterres' phrase echoes the ILO Director-General's comments in 2012 regarding worldwide youth activism in response to YU and the GFC (Somavia/ILO, 2012a, 2012b). See also Schmidt and Hassanien (2011), Tzannatos et al. (2011), and Singerman (2013) regarding YU and the Arab Spring of 2010–2012.

APPENDIX 8.1　　LEGAL AND NORMATIVE AGREEMENTS
AND KEY INITIATIVES OF PRINCIPAL
INTERNATIONAL GOVERNMENTAL
ORGANISATIONS PERTAINING TO YOUTH
UNEMPLOYMENT, 1980–2020

Table 8A.1　　*Legal and normative international agreements and key global initiatives on youth unemployment, 1980–2020*

Year	IGO	Agreement or initiative
1981	UNESCO	Recommendation No. 73 to the Ministries of Education concerning the interaction between education and productive work
1981	UNGA	Efforts and measures for securing the implementation and the enjoyment by youth of human rights, particularly the right to education and to work (A/RES/36/29)
1981	UNGA	Channels of communication between the United Nations and youth and youth organizations (A/RES/36/17)
1982	UNGA	Efforts and measures for securing the implementation and the enjoyment of youth of human rights, particularly the right to education and to work (A/RES/37/49)
1982	UN	Vienna Non-Governmental Organisation Committee on Youth
1984	ILO	Employment Policy (Supplementary Provisions) Recommendation (R169)
1984	UN	UN Youth Fund
1985	UN	International Youth Year: Participation, Development, Peace
1985	UNGA	Opportunities for youth (A/RES/40/16)
1986	UNGA	Efforts and measures for securing the implementation and the enjoyment by youth of human rights, particularly the right to education and to work (A/RES/41/98)
1987	UNGA	Efforts and Measures for Securing the Implementation by States and the Enjoyment by Youth of Human Rights in Conditions of Peace, Particularly the Right to Education and to Work (A/RES/42/52)
1988	UNGA	Question of youth (A/RES/43/94)
1988	ILO	Convention on Employment Promotion and Protection against Unemployment (C168), and Recommendation (R176)
1989	UNESCO	Convention on Technical and Vocational Education
1989	UN	Convention on the Rights of the Child (A/RES/44/25)
1991	UNGA	International cooperation for the eradication of poverty in developing countries (A/RES/46/141)
1995	UNGA	A World Programme of Action for Youth to the Year 2000 and Beyond (A/RES/50/81)
1995	UN	Copenhagen Declaration on Social Development, and Programme of Action of the World Summit for Social Development (A/Conf.166/9)
1998	UN World Youth Forum	Braga Youth Action Plan
1998	World Conference of Ministers Responsible for Youth	Lisbon Declaration on Youth Policies and Programmes
1999	UNGA	Policies and Programmes Involving Youth (A/RES/54/120)

Year	IGO	Agreement or initiative
2000	UN	Millennium Declaration (A/RES/55/2) and Millennium Development Goals, target 1.b: 'Achieve full and productive employment and decent work for all, including … young people'
2000	UN	Global Compact Initiative
2001	UNGA	Policies and programmes involving youth (A/RES/56/117)
2001	UN	World Youth Forum – Dakar Youth Empowerment Strategy
2001	ILO	Global Agenda for Employment
2001	ILO/WB/UNESCO	Youth Employment Network (YEN)
2001	UNSG	High-level Panel on Youth Employment
2002	UNGA	Promoting youth employment (A/RES/57/165)
2003	UN Commission for Social Development	Draft resolution Policies and Programmes on Youth (Review of UN plans and programmes for action for youth – draft resolution sent to ECOSOC for adoption – see https://undocs.org/E/CN.5/2003/9
2003	UNGA	Policies and programmes involving youth (A/RES/58/133)
2004	UNGA	Policies and programmes involving youth: tenth anniversary of the World Programme of Action for Youth to the Year 2000 and Beyond (A/RES/59/148)
2005	UNDESA	World Youth Report
2005	UNGA	Policies and programmes involving youth (A/RES/60/2)
2005	UNGA	2005 World Summit Outcome (A/RES/60/1)
2006	UNSG	Follow-up to the World Programme of Action for Youth to the Year 2000 and Beyond. Report of the Secretary-General (A/62/61)
2007	UN Secretary-General	Goals and targets for monitoring the progress of youth in the global economy (A/62/61–E/2007/7; A/62/61/Add.1–E/2007/7/Add.1)
2007	UN Commission for Social Development	'Promoting Full Employment and Decent Work for All' priority theme, and Resolution 45/2 'Youth'
2007	UNGA	Policies and programmes involving youth: youth in the global economy – promoting youth participation in social and economic development (A/RES/62/126)
2008	WB/ILO	Global Partnership for Youth Employment (GPYE)
2008	ILO	Declaration on Social Justice for a Fair Globalization
2009	UNGA	Policies and programmes involving youth (A/RES/64/130)
2009	ILO	Global Jobs Pact
2010	UN	International Year of Youth (2010–11)
2011	UN	High-level Meeting of the General Assembly on Youth: Dialogue and Mutual Understanding (outcome document A/RES/65/312)
2011	UNGA	Policies and programmes involving youth (A/RES/66/121)
2012	ECOSOC	First annual Youth Forum – 'Creating a Sustainable Future: Empowering Youth with Better Job Opportunities'
2012	ILO	The youth employment crisis: a call for action (ILC Resolution)
2013	UNGA	Policies and programmes involving youth (A/RES/68/130)
2013	UN	System-wide Action Plan on Youth (Youth-SWAP)
2014	UNGA	World Youth Skills Day (A/RES/69/145)
2014	UNDP/UNESCO/UN Youth Envoy	First Global Forum on Youth Policies

Year	IGO	Agreement or initiative
2015	UN	Transforming our World: the 2030 Agenda for Sustainable Development
2015	WB	Solutions for Youth Employment (S4YE)
2015	UNGA	Policies and programmes involving youth (A/RES/70/127)
2015	ILO	[Global Initiative on] Decent Jobs for Youth ([GI]DJY)
2017	UNGA	Policies and programmes involving youth (A/RES/72/146)
2018	UN	Youth 2030: The United Nations Youth Strategy
2018	WB/UNICEF/ILO	Generation Unlimited (GenU) partnership
2019	UNGA	Policies and programmes involving youth (A/RES/74/121)

Source: The authors, derived from relevant IGO websites (accessed January 2020).

9. Conclusion: towards a global compact for youth employment

9.1 INTRODUCTION

This book has inscribed 'the global' into youth unemployment (YU) and undertaken an expansive analytical and empirical survey of the nature and impacts of global YU. In this, we have not aimed to provide a once-and-for-all account or definitive assessment of global YU, but to elaborate some principal elements, dynamics and implications of looking at it through a *globalist* analytical lens, on an extensively international scale, and over the long course of history. As we set out in Chapter 1, the thesis of this book is that YU must inevitably be grasped as a matter of *global* structures and processes that condition the social organisation and social relations of youth labour within and between countries worldwide. Thus, YU must be explained primarily in terms of the huge influence of the world economy and trade, the globalising strategies of corporate enterprises and states, and the institutions of global govern-ance. This thesis, we recognise, challenges dominant explanations of YU as first and foremost a matter of national social, political and economic structures that necessitate unilateral national responses. It insists that YU is not wholly explicable within paradigms that point to the 'normal' fluctuations of business cycles or labour force deficiencies across various employa-bility attributes. And it asserts that YU must be appreciated as a matter of *social policy* – that is, as a matter of the socio-institutional arrangements, policies and measures that determine the distribution and redistribution of resources within and between countries, and that shape who is incorporated into or excluded from the active labour force and on what basis, and who can access social protection when necessary and on what terms (Chapter 2). Our thesis applies to YU in the poorest parts of the world no less than it does in the richest. It also applies to YU a century ago no less than to the present.

Such global 'optics' offer a novel and vital perspective on the causes of and responses to YU that has been sorely missing from, or at best very deeply submerged within, theoretical and policy-oriented research on YU and youth labour forces. First, they relate YU to a the-oretically-expansive and empirically-substantiated conception of global youth labour forces. In this regard, we emphasised universal features of the social organisation of youth labour that are culturally and institutionally embedded and persist over time and place. Second, they draw attention to endemic youth unemployment (EYU) – a persistent, prevalent form of YU that has become increasingly extensive and normalised worldwide since 2008 but has built on rising levels of EYU long pre-dating the global financial crisis (GFC). EYU signals, we suggest, the emergence of a new phase of global liberalism that is challenging liberal and authoritarian democracies alike. Third, our global 'optics' draw attention to the influence of institutions and organisations of global economic and social governance that in turn substantially influence who gets what sorts of jobs, on what terms and under what conditions. In this, we highlighted a global YU policy stretching back a century that set the normative and institutional foundations of responses to YU and youth labour forces worldwide, and how this policy bears, even today, the marks of deep schisms and contradictions in global governance.

The book's wide-ranging analytical and empirical gaze should not be interpreted as an attempt to assert a totalising position that obscures difference and denies agency. Indeed, it is precisely *because* we use an historically informed, internationally extensive global perspective on the social organisation, governance and regulation of YU that we have been able to 'surface' the multitudinous expressions and meanings of YU over time and place, and highlight how the contexts, processes, institutions and policies that produce, amplify, stabilise, de-stabilise, prevent, and mitigate YU are differentiated not uniform, and fluid not fixed. At the same time, our emphasis on multiplicity and heterogeneity should not be mistaken for an eschewal of structural patterning; there are strong and enduring common features, dominant trends and overarching themes in the global landscape of YU. We have aimed to present as rich a picture of these distinctions and similarities over as much of the last century as the limits of reliable evidence and space allow. In keeping with the spirit of academic endeavour, we hope that this, the first systematic globalist study of YU spanning such a wide terrain and extensive timeframe, provides a stimulus to further debate and research that builds on what we have started. Our aim has been to engage all those concerned with YU in a consideration of problems and responses in often unfamiliar contexts, and to draw out some key points for focused discussion, research and analysis.

This closing chapter brings together the critical commentaries, research findings and conclusions of Chapters 2–8 and considers their wider significance. It is structured around three further sections. Section 9.2 recaps on the different stages and focus of our discussion of global YU, drawing together principal insights regarding each of the three 'dialogic terrains' set out in Section 1.5 of Chapter 1 and the wider concerns of the book. Section 9.3 argues for a (re-) vitalisation of global youth unemployment policy, including by means of a Global Compact for Youth Employment. The YU and -related Sustainable Development Goals (SDGs), a *transformative* social policy paradigm (UNRISD, 2016), and ideas of global economic planning for full employment developed at the UN in the 1940s are among the principal reference points for this. Section 9.4 completes the book by considering the prospective effects of the 2020 global Coronavirus pandemic (GCP) (Covid-19) on endemic YU worldwide.

9.2   A CENTURY OF GLOBAL YOUTH UNEMPLOYMENT: THREE DIALOGIC TERRAINS

In this section we summarily review the conclusions from each of the chapters that have cumulatively elaborated the meaning of global YU in worldwide and historical contexts. The discussion is organised around the three 'dialogic terrains' we identified in Chapter 1: global economic restructuring and endemic youth unemployment (the particular foci of Chapters 3 and 4); global financial crises and endemic youth unemployment (Chapters 5 and 6); and global governance and EYU (Chapters 7 and 8). While these terrains broadly map onto the three pairs of chapters, we make clear relevant contributions of chapters from 'other' pairings. First, though, we return to Chapter 2, which elaborated a fundamental premise of our approach: *that developing a holistic understanding of global YU* (Chapter 1) necessitates analysing and interpreting YU *primarily as a social policy issue*, as a social phenomenon that spans multiple interlinked socio-institutional contexts, sectors and actors. In this way, we develop and refine political economy perspectives through which YU tends to be more often understood – often, that is, to the occlusion (sometimes purposive exclusion) of social policy, and the dynamics of social organisation and the social relations of welfare.

9.2.1 Youth Unemployment as a Social Policy Issue

From the outset, a fundamental premise of our approach has been that YU – whether endemic or otherwise – is to be understood as a matter of social policy, while taking full account of key contributions to its analysis from economics and political economy. Thus, YU cannot be adequately observed, interpreted or addressed independently of the social institutions, social organisation and social relations of welfare. The marginalisation of these elements for interpreting and addressing YU, we have endeavoured to demonstrate, has impeded holistic analyses of its causes, persistence, harms and, crucially, prospective solutions. Economic analyses are not sufficient means of explaining and addressing recurrent cycles of escalating YU within and across countries of almost every type.

Chapter 2 advanced these claims by discussing the scarring effects of YU, as seen through: deprivation of income; economic insecurity; damage to mental health and well-being; insufficient housing and its propensity to impede young people's social as well as economic independence; and the deepening privations of inadequate or absent social security, in terms of financial and welfare needs. Such scarring undermines the advancement of young people's personal development across all countries, mostly regardless of mean income, profile of distributional (in)equality, social structure or political character. Perhaps the most telling manifestation of long-standing failures to prevent recurrent and endemic YU through the 'soft' powers of governance and management is the mobilisation of 'hard' power in response to young people's resistance to unemployment. Such resistance takes the form of mass and coordinated protests like those in the wake of the GFC; or routine refusal of thinly disguised palliative modes of 'airbrushing' YU that agencies of state deploy, in order to funnel, corral or harass young people into participation in unremunerated simulacra of genuine employment – often under threat of withdrawal of such minor monetary 'training allowances' as may accrue to participants.

As we concluded, inherent in YU are fundamental tensions that are universal and applicable to all country 'types' and that must ultimately be reconciled. They concern universal entitlement to full and productive employment and decent work on the basis of equality, for women and men of all ages (UN SDG 8.5); the universal imperative to ensure the availability of copious supplies of new entrants to the labour market; and the universal operation of forces of supply of and demand for available supplies of human labour according to economic priorities and business needs. We estimate that the governments and democratic governing forums of the great majority of countries worldwide engage (or are prevailed upon to engage) in continuous struggles between these positions. We conclude that pro-social decent work priorities fall very far short of being globally dominant.

Throughout, we have aimed to show how and why EYU can only be fully understood as a phenomenon that transcends the priorities and actions of a multiplicity of individual countries, however closely aligned, dominant or preponderant. Its specific causes are to be found in the three-way interaction between the processes of global economic restructuring, global financial crises and global governance. We have also aimed to embed social policy within our analyses across all of Chapters 3–8. As we now turn to review those chapters within the framework of these three dialogic terrains, we urge cognisance of the need for matters of social policy to be central to all analyses, including and especially when political-economic and economic analyses are necessarily to the fore, empirically or theoretically.

9.2.2   Globalisation, Economic Restructuring and Endemic Youth Unemployment

Chapters 3 and 4 elaborated primary meanings of global YU: first, as an intrinsic feature of global youth labour forces and, second, as indelibly embroiled in processes of global economic restructuring. To this end, they set out our theoretical idea of the global youth labour force and our associated concepts of global reserve 'armies' of youth labour (GRAoYL) and the new international division of youth labour (NIDYL), and began to discern some principal features of global YU, notably its size and composition in relation to the global labour force, its role in labour force management, and its relationship to capitalist dynamism, past and present.

We presented the first-ever calculation of the size and composition of the global youth labour force (Chapter 3). The first of our datasets generated a snapshot picture for 2018 of 62 per cent of the world's youth population (approximately 757 million 15–24-year-olds), showing that just one in four of the global youth labour force is a waged worker and three in four of this labour force is unemployed. Using this maximal method of calculating unemployment, the overwhelming majority of young unemployed people are concealed in informal and subsistence economies or 'warehoused' in education or training (or prison). This global youth workforce is structurally differentiated: rich countries contain the greatest proportion of young wage workers whereas poor ones contain the greatest proportion of hidden unemployed. Lower middle-income countries (LMICs) have the greatest proportion of economically inactive young people, while low-income countries (LICs) have the greatest proportion of young people subsisting in the informal economy. There is remarkably little variation in the proportion of openly unemployed young people around the world; the highest is in upper middle-income countries (UMICs) (8.5 per cent), the lowest in LICs (4.9 per cent).

We argued that the global dynamics of YU only make sense in relation to the global labour force and world economy more widely. One aspect of this is that the global labour force is structurally differentiated by age – the idea that young people occupy a universally disadvantageous position within the labour force, and that the youngest are the most disadvantaged within that. Indeed, outside of slavery or certain forms of unwaged labour, young people constitute the quintessentially neo-liberal global workforce, combining as they do availability and exploitability. Young people are exceptionally susceptible to employer predation due to their lack of experience and labour organisation. Such workforce qualities render them more exploitable than older groups (25 years+); indeed, they are sought-after by corporate strategists seeking to manage wage inflation and enhance labour discipline. Youth labour reservoirs are ones from which employers can readily recruit in times of high product demand or into which they can expel employees in times of slump in demand. It is precisely the bi-directional fluidity of movement of young workers between employment and unemployment that makes them such a distinctively attractive labour force for employers. This is an enduring and universal principle transcending variants or periods of capitalism: our conclusions are as tenable today following four decades of neo-liberal global restructuring as they were in the mid-nineteenth century when Engels observed that young age was a predictor of adverse incorporation into waged labour, or in the mid-twentieth century prior to neo-liberal globalisation when young people predominated in offshored industrial workforces in peripheral countries.

We further elaborated the relationship between global YU and economic restructuring through detailed analysis of how youth labour is drawn into, expelled from or excluded from the formation of global circuits of capital in several 'frontier' industries (Chapter 4). We showed that even the most intensive centres of world market production are vulnerable to competition from alternative ones where youth labour supply and other key factors of production are more advantageous to capital accumulation. Sites where labour is youngest, most needy and least organised are especially attractive. By such means, youth labour is equally vulnerable to low-waged precarious predation in newly offshored global factories and to the desertion of unfavourable 'old' locations.

The interconnectedness of youth labour markets worldwide is accorded theoretical significance when seen through the lens of capital valorisation strategies that are a mainstay of the world economy. Capitalist dynamism depends on harnessing elements of the youth labour force – the global reserve army of youth labour (GRAoYL). In particular, we showed that high rates of YU function as markers of sites in which capital valorisation strategies can be productively realised. In other words, from the perspective of capital, the presence of a large reserve army of youth labour confers distinct advantages where the aim is to reduce overall labour costs more than is possible without relocation, provided all other requisite conditions for efficient production and distribution are met. Put another way, if capital valorisation leads firms to seek out areas of labour surplus, then high rates of open and hidden YU indicate high profit levels. It (almost) goes without saying that this is a no-win process for young people, their families and communities, even if such processes are often heralded by many apologists for and advocates of capital valorisation as creating 'new' youth jobs. In the locations from which production is withdrawn, new dynamics of unemployment are created, the effects of which are felt inter-generationally, often in the production of high rates of youth unemployment among those from the most disadvantaged backgrounds. In the locations at which re-siting is directed, relatively privileged groups of young people are drawn into waged labour in world-market industries, undertaking work on adverse terms and for which they are often vastly over-qualified. The arrival of such world market factories makes little to no appreciable dent in levels of YU in the chosen sites, but, instead, restructures local social institutions (labour markets, education and training systems) and reconfigures social inequalities *among* youth cohorts as well as between young and older cohorts.

We emphatically concluded that the condition of youth labour in general and youth unemployment specifically must be explained by reference to such dynamics at the level of the world economy. Jobless young people are a major and critical element of an evolving new international division of youth labour (NIDYL) and of a global youth labour force that is notable for its mobility, adaptability, exploitability and impermanence. Integral to this is a global youth labour ideology that is surprisingly enduring over time and place. Adding significant new evidence about how the production of new – or the reconfiguration of extant – social inequalities among young people, nationally and globally, have themselves been reconfigured (including through a continuing gendered and racialised segmentation of youth labour markets (Chapters 1 and 5)), we insistently underline that young age is a clearly identifiable social division of labour and a major axis of global labour exploitation. Marxian conceptualisations of the global labour force are especially valuable in understanding the distinctive condition and significance of YU contemporarily. To repeat: the distinctive characteristics of the NIDYL and the resultant global reserve army of youth labour (GRAoYL) are the volume, availability and bi-directional fluidity of movement of populations of young workers (in and out of employment), and the capacity to warehouse suitably educated and skilled youthful labour power until it is required (Chapter 4).

9.2.3   Global Financial Crises and Endemic Youth Unemployment

If, as we have argued, global economic restructuring during the nineteenth and twentieth centuries rendered YU an essentially global phenomenon that contributed to the endemic character of YU throughout much of the world, then successive financial and economic crises have compounded the increasingly endemic character of YU over time and across territories (Chapter 5). As one effect was layered upon the other, the impacts of GFCs in countries that were already 'losers' in transnational battles for retaining versus gaining jobs were inevitably deeper and/or more prolonged. Empirically, we have presented clear examples of escalations in YU rates spanning almost a century. For the financial crises of the 1920s and 1930s, the first-recorded impacts on youth and adult unemployment (Tables 3.1–3.3) reached rates of 20–40 per cent over several years in most of the high-income countries (HICs) for which data are available. A series of national banking and transnational financial crises throughout the 1980s were associated with spikes in YU rates within a similar range across much of Asia, Australasia, Europe and North America (with prolonged extremes in Belgium, France, Greece, Italy and Spain – all exceeding EYU thresholds) (Table 8.1). And, after the onset of the GFC in 2008, all country income groups (CIGs) except the low-income group saw a rapid escalation in YU over five years, most extremely amongst the 79 HICs – peaking at an 18 per cent mean. Lower mean rates have continued to rise continuously since 2008 amongst UMICs and LMICs (Figure 5.8).

We comprehensively analysed the extent to which changes in YU rates were associated with economic change measured by gross domestic product (GDP) year-on-year, maximally between 1980 and 2018, before and during the GFC period, for a total of 74 countries (Chapter 6). We found that 15–24-year-olds were very significantly more likely to be at risk of being unemployed than adults aged 25+, in many cases by substantial or very substantial margins. Overall, changes in GDP growth were associated with *larger changes* in unemployment *after* the onset of the GFC than before it. In HICs, the relationship between annual changes in GDP and in YU always found higher YU rates amongst 15–24-year-olds than amongst adults aged 25+. However, the 25+ age group consistently experienced a *proportionately* greater increase in unemployment if comparing the difference in their YU rates before and during the GFC period – that is to say, the differential between the pre-GFC and GFC periods was greater amongst the older than the younger age group. In UMICs, the association between YU and GDP was less strong than in HICs for both age groups, but considerably stronger for 15–24-year-olds than those aged 25+, and consistently stronger during the GFC period than before it. These findings leave no room for doubt that amongst the world's more affluent countries young people (and young women especially) are generally much more adversely affected by economic downturns than older people, and that, across both age ranges, the effect on unemployment was greater in the wake of the GFC than it was in the years immediately preceding it. We find little room for doubt that there is a causal relationship between GFC-induced economic decline and rising worldwide YU, above and beyond the conditioning effects of national factors.

These findings address (and in many cases resolve) some critically important questions we raised in Chapter 1. First, the GFC was unprecedented in its effects on the scale and persistence of YU. Second, while its negative impact on youth and adult employment rates garnered most international attention because of its acute impact in HICs, these effects were also clearly present amongst UMICs. Third, the ostensibly relatively rapid recovery from the GFC indicated in the global mean was initially almost entirely attributable to the lower YU rate in UMICs (between 2009 and 2014). However, this recovery period was immediately followed by a sharp reversal in the YU profiles of the three different groups. Amongst HICs there was a remarkable recovery between 2014 and 2019 when YU rates fell to their lowest level in almost three decades (Figure 5.8), while rates escalated dramatically in UMICs and LMICs during the same five-year period. It is highly likely that this complete reciprocal reversal in YU trends between HICs versus UMICs and LMICs is in part a stark manifestation of global economic restructuring in action. It is beyond the scope of this study to establish whether, for example, HICs 'repatriated' some of their offshored production, or whether they escalated offshoring at the expense of UMICs' endeavours to maintain or begin their own ventures in outsourcing. Probing the distributional gains and losses between countries in the different groups merits a major programme of further research into the global dynamics of youth labour during and after intense episodes of economic crisis and restructuring. Fourth, although the degree of volatility in YU rates in HICs since 1991 is inevitably most prominent, the underlying trends of steadily escalating YU over three decades amongst UMICs (a seven-percentage point escalation to 2019) and LMICs (a four-percentage point escalation) stand out.

Seen in the long view (Figure 5.8), it is LMICs that have experienced the most enduring, persistent and almost constantly escalating average rates of YU over three decades – closely followed by UMICs. Fifteen of the 25 countries that we identified as typifying the highest extremes of endemic YU worldwide are UMICs, most of which experienced YU rates of 40–60 per cent for between *three and 29 years* since 1991 (Table 5.2). If we follow the maximalist principle of calculating youth unemployment (Chapter 3), LICs, too, would, beyond serious doubt, have similar or worse average YU profiles. These are deeply troubling findings that should give major cause for concern.

9.2.4 Global Governance and Endemic Youth Unemployment

Chapters 7 and 8 scrutinised the 'place' of YU in cross-border spheres of governance and policy-making over the course of a century. Our extensive archival research covering multilateral initiatives on YU from 1919 to 2020 shone a vital spotlight on this hitherto untold history of YU and social policy and revealed the extent to which YU has been defined as a matter for global collective action, the nature of international governmental organisations' (IGOs) powers to address YU, and the approaches they take and the initiatives they institute (Chapter 1, Section 1.5.3). We emphatically showed that YU was one of the earliest social policy issues identified for routine inter-state policy dialogue and that it has been an ongoing matter for a wide range of institutions and actors in global governance ever since. Across a hundred years, IGOs have been key forums through which international awareness of the magnitude and consequences of YU as a *global* issue and as an appropriate matter for supra-national and extensively international action have been raised. They have been key institutional spaces for advocacy initiatives on matters of YU, have established normative frameworks and standards governing state and civil society policy responses to YU, and have instituted (and run) YU programmes and projects.

The global policy field is decidedly highly internationalised, multi-actored, multi-sectoral and, regrettably, fragmented. Although it was the sole IGO in the early twentieth century to have addressed YU, the ILO was nonetheless embedded within a range of youth-related international social policy fields, notably education, child welfare, and health, as well as in labour economics (Chapter 7). Advocates for young unemployed people were mostly international professional associations that worked in strategic alliance with the ILO, socialist youth labour groups that fought hard for stronger ILO action on YU, and many national and international youth associations. Civil society organisation was internationally extensive and civil society organisations' engagement with global YU policy-making was pronounced. The early 'face' of global YU policy took shape through ILO Conventions and Recommendations that sought to set labour standards for all adult and child members of the labour force; only one Recommendation was addressed specifically to YU, passed in the mid-1930s at a time of global economic and political crises. The ILO defined YU as first and foremost an issue of labour justice and institutionalised a policy approach founded more in palliative supply-side measures rather than preventative and demand-led ones. This approach remains the signature of the ILO and of global YU policy to the present day.

The ILO retained its dominant position as a global policy actor and its policy approach to YU during most of the post-Second World War period to date, prioritising League of Nations (LoN)-era 'unfinished business' on vocational training in a new global social policy context of full employment and expanded social protection goals. The incorporation of YU into a fledgling multi-sectoral UN Youth Policy in the late 1970s instituted a 'rupture' with post-Second World War peace and justice goals. It coincided with the ascendancy of new (neo-liberal) political priorities, the unleashing of further waves of global economic restructuring, and surges in YU that have been a feature of the world economy and which have since dominated global YU policy-making (cf. Chapters 3–6, and Chapter 8). This neo-liberal global social policy re-set was consolidated through the emphasis on global partnerships since the early 2000s and the UN's push towards greater involvement of multinational business and third-sector corporations in YU policy funding and delivery (Chapter 8). We found that the character and focus of the ILO's work in the field of YU was re-steered, away from strengthening international instruments to better protect young people's employment rights (the last such normative instrument dates back to the late 1980s). The new direction of travel oversaw – and in many ways facilitated – the great global jobs shift and the associated rise in global EYU (see Section 9.2.3, above); it endeavoured to resolve the ills of mass and endemic YU 'on location' by directly running or overseeing projects and programmes to create temporary work or develop young people's skills in readiness for calls for their labour, should they arrive. In effect, then, the ILO was gradually re-positioned away from being a strategic actor with a defined international quasi-legislative role that promulgated the case for renewed demand for young people's labour; and towards managing tactical oversight of localised palliative country-level projects that may benefit some individuals without creating enduring labour market effects or leveraging commitments to strengthen the enforcement of existing rights.

This incremental re-steering of the ILO also shifted much of its discourse and many of its practices away from demand-side approaches (and their emphasis on preventing unemployment through comprehensive macro-economic planning and management), and towards supply-side ones that emphasise the skills, education or personal deficits of young people and which, by implication, attribute responsibility for unemployment to its victims (Chapter 8).

Overall, our reading of the global politics of YU through the lens of the (re)making of global social policy on YU has emphasised diverse currents, tensions and struggles among myriad policy actors in a highly contested policy domain. Forces of protection, competition and exploitation reflect constant strains; relations of cooperation and opposition, alliance and contestation among the multiple policy actors are tightly interwoven; and the outcomes of struggles are determined by political contestation among actors with highly differential power bases and resources. As we have argued, global YU policy is the outcome of complex dynamics; it has institutionalised elements of protection, competition and exploitation in different combinations over time. This global policy history emphatically locates it as integral to the (re-)making of welfare and work landscapes, international struggles over young people's rights to work, and the current 'shape' of youth unemployment policy worldwide.

Across this long history of global policy and global governance, three key points stand out. First, the alliance between the international labour and educational communities, incarnated in the ILO and UNESCO, respectively, has been by far the most enduring and, in many ways successful partnership. This alliance, gravitating around aligning the minimum age of exit from education with a minimum age of entry to employment, proved to be the dominant axis. Together, the ILO and UNESCO have defined YU as a global social policy issue located at the interstices of the rights to work, to education and to social security. This policy paradigm was established by the early twentieth century and was successively institutionalised in global standard-setting initiatives thereafter; it continues to characterise present-day global policy. The proliferation of inter-IGO partnerships since then has not disrupted or succeeded in breaking from that approach, despite the diffusion and diversification of efforts that it has introduced.

Second, the prevailing global policy approach remains essentially a palliative one, in that although it sets standards for a wide range of measures on YU, it is ultimately directed at reducing the length of time young people are openly unemployed. Demand-led approaches to YU that pressed the case for job creation were present for just a short time in global policy history, circa 1950–79, when they challenged the dominant supply-side approach. Despite the nominal discursive attachment to full employment that characterised the post-Second World War period and continues to be evident presently, the relative retreat of the ILO from advocating demand-led approaches – in contrast to its historic commitments – means there is, in effect, no IGO prioritising state-led job creation towards substantially reducing global YU.

Third, however we periodise global YU policy history, we conclude that missing from that history was a vision of how to fashion and govern a world economy capable of providing employment to all young people who wanted it. This is attributable, we concluded, to the schism between global economic and social governance designed into the global institutional architecture from the outset, first in the LoN and then in the UN, and successively further embedded in and reified through each global YU policy strategy, programme, project or partnership formulated over the decades since. This schism is the principal cause of the institutional fragmentation and weakness of global governance that has long hindered the development of an effective global social policy capable of realising the ILO's long-held advocacy of decent, productive work for all young people worldwide.

9.3   THE GLOBAL COMPACT FOR YOUTH EMPLOYMENT

Our research has found irrefutable evidence that YU has fallen through the cracks of a broken system of global economic and social governance for much of the last century, most especially over the last 40–50 years; and that even the depredations of the GFC have failed to stimulate a set of global responses concomitant with the magnitude of burgeoning rates of YU that followed it, worldwide. As a result, we conclude, the international community has sleep-walked into a world of rising and *endemic* YU that is choking the futures of tens and potentially hundreds of millions of young people and postponing the development dividends that would otherwise emanate from their contributions to shared prosperity.

Within the century's-worth of global youth labour history that is the subject of this study, the last two decades stand out for the repeated attempts to reaffirm the world's commitments to international labour rights. Each of them, separately and in combination, offered an opportunity at critical conjunctures to recapture ILO's historic mission to create a world in which labour is not a commodity. Yet none of these have satisfactorily grappled with YU or strengthened the global institutional architectures needed to do so (see Section 9.2, above). All past endeavours for addressing global YU – of which by far the most concerted, purposive and effective was the work of the ILO between its inception and the 1970s – are no longer remotely adequate for today's challenges. Despite the constantly dwindling labour force participation rate amongst 15–24-year-olds over three decades, YU rates increase year-on-year. Yet even these data significantly underestimate the true scale of YU. As we have stressed throughout, open unemployment rates may be little more than the tip of a very sizeable iceberg: hidden beneath its waterline is a great depth of youth unemployment among informal, vulnerably employed and contributing family workers amongst populations aged under 25 years.

The UN's *Youth 2030* strategy is a welcome response but hardly conveys the significance and urgency of reducing YU as a global priority of the first order. Its Third Priority, 'Economic Empowerment through Decent Work – Support young people's greater access to decent work and productive employment' (UN, 2018: 11–12) understates the magnitude and significance of YU, while four of its commitments lack specificity, in different ways. The UN's first pledge, to 'renew and strengthen efforts towards decent work for young people', is as much notable for its lack of commitment to guaranteeing work for all (even allowing for unavoidable 'frictional' unemployment) as for its commendable intention. Its second pledge, to 'advocate for a balanced approach to stimulate the youth labour demand and prompt improvements in skills development systems', is also welcome, but there is very little evidence of a systematic – still less worldwide – advocacy strategy beyond the small cadre of dedicated actors working in programmes like Decent Jobs for Youth (DJY) and Generation Unlimited (GenU). It also demonstrates a persistent reluctance to acknowledge that supply-side approaches to resolving YU have made a diminutive impression on global YU and are nowhere close to resolving its scale. The third commitment, to 'guide and support Member States and other partners ... to develop and operationalise strategies that prioritise the improvement of both the quantity and quality of jobs', pinpoints some relevant mitigative policies, but its crucial yet unelaborated reference to 'economic and labour market policies' effectively side-steps how they are to be given force, and not left to voluntaristic enactments that depend on benign pro-social change. The final pledge, to 'engage Member States and other partners to ... enhance the capacity of the green economy to create more and better employment opportunities for young people in wage and self-employment', is laudable but, on recent records at least, likely to be marginal in its impacts on all but the most economically advanced countries. It also begs the questions: who are the 'other partners', what are the means of enhancement, and where are the incentives to action, *and* the disincentives to inaction?

Youth 2030 is a necessarily short document. But the need for brevity is all too revealing of these silences. It also lacks a sense of urgency, advocacy and structures of incentives and disincentives. Most of all, its silences actively signal the lack of governmental commitment and state power to propel and galvanise all stakeholders: a sense of strong normative pressure; strong financial and economic disincentives to maintaining high rates of YU; the funding of projects and programmes that is contingent on meeting international standards; robust monitoring and accountability processes of the (in)actions of states and business communities; the necessity of full transparent reporting; and ultimately, the need for internationally-imposed sanctions attached to international initiatives funded or overseen by IGOs.

It is now clearer than ever that, as welcome as *Youth 2030* is, making serious inroads into global YU requires concerted multilateral cooperation and robust global governance responses of a kind not contemplated since the late 1940s, if ever. The question now is, *what role can and should the institutions of global governance play in addressing global YU*? The discussion that follows is informed by the idea of a *transformative* approach to social policy, as proposed by UNRISD (2016). Although not developed specifically in relation to YU or to global governance, its generic principles hold true for our purposes. As related to YU, it directs attention to the need for strong global leadership to foster and support responses that, first, go beyond mitigation to substantively address upstream causes of YU rooted in the global economy; second, are grounded in normative values of global social justice and social sustainability, cognisant that the existing model of economic development will not be able to absorb the world's unemployed youth labour; third, are multi-sectoral and policy-driven; and, fourth, are premised on inclusive, democratic multi-stakeholder partnerships among state and non-state actors.

In this regard, the teleological case for what we term a Global Compact for Youth Employment (GCfYE) is irresistible. Its *raison d'être* is to reverse *endemic* YU, scaling it down to minimalist frictional levels that cannot be eliminated, even through public policy interventions. The rationale for a GCfYE is a function of this teleological purpose: it pre-supposes the benefits of the desired outcome, on grounds of the compelling evidence presented in Chapters 2–8 and the prospective harms to individual young people, societies, economies and, ultimately, to conflicted relationships between countries. There is no doubt that reversing EYU would realise the ideal of inclusive, equitable economic development, bringing enormous benefits for individual and collective welfare and for wider social development. While the challenges in addressing global YU are considerable, they are eminently achievable provided that the right level of investment is made and the shared international will is strong, in fast-changing circumstances. In support of these claims, we confine ourselves to briefly outlining the contours of such a Global Compact and indicate some priorities for action.

A first – and urgent – priority is to agree clear targets, and clear standards for their attainment, to give concrete meaning to SDG 8.5's pursuit of productive decent work for young people with equal pay for work of equal value. For this, we repurpose recommendations of the UN report *National and International Measures for Full Employment* (UN, 1949). Specifically, we propose a full employment target for young people. Such a target, we argue, should be measured in terms of youth unemployment rather than youth employment. An age range and specification for the maximum internationally acceptable period without employment would need to be agreed, but the YU target should be expressed in terms of the smallest percentage of youth unemployment consistent with frictional and temporary unemployment that can be reasonably maintained. By providing an operational standard for policy measures, such a target would be a vital step to eliminating endemic YU. Within limits, the target percentage of YU would vary according to country circumstances, though in general the target can *and must* be set at a much lower percentage YU rate than is currently tolerated and – as we have emphasised throughout – normalised. The target would also need to take account of unemployment which bears inequitably upon excluded and disadvantaged sections of the youth population.

A principal medium-term objective would be to facilitate substantial levelling-up of the viable employment possibilities for young people in country income groups in which YU has long been persistent and/or hidden. The purpose of the YU target becomes meaningful in this context: its aim is to benchmark change in the YU rate so that any change above the upper limit of the range agreed could be regarded as evidence of policy failure (and the obverse as evidence of policy success). A YU target therefore takes on real meaning when seen as part of a wider youth employment stabilisation policy. Such a policy should be oriented towards maintaining effective demand for youth labour at the level necessary to keep YU within target. Obligations upon states and upon all businesses producing and trading goods and services between states to generate such demand would be a central pillar of such a stabilisation policy. Commensurate progress between states 'in step' with one another would facilitate mutual confidence that the least assiduous were not gaining economic advantage while others put economic 'inclusionary-ness' before the maximisation of economic output.

There are many ways of increasing demand for youth labour. Fiscal policy is one useful element. Illustratively, judicious use of general taxation and/or supplementary levies should lead to incentives for young people's labour market participation, and incentives for companies to employ young people in productive employment. Reducing the ratio of vulnerable-to-securely contracted young workers with working conditions consistent with practices benchmarked against international labour standards would be an essential objective. Such employment should be realised on the basis of equality and consistent with international labour standards and human rights law. Companies and governments would be recognised for reaching (and additionally for exceeding) agreed proportionate quotas of young people in their labour forces on these terms. Strong, clear, enforceable disincentives would be essential responses to failing to meet targets, which should be regulatorily monitored using methods that require competent participation in the monitoring process, overseen by a designated IGO.

Participatory modes of social policy formation should underpin the GCfYE. Consensual international communities built from four pillars – governments, workers' organisations, employers and youth non-governmental organisations (NGOs) – participating on the basis of equality would be expected to elaborate the principles, goals, and means for realising the YU target, and to lead their institutionalisation through youth employment stabilisation policies. The Compact would bear upon all states once endorsed by a worldwide majority of states under the auspices of the UN, backed by clear plans for implementation that include powers to award (and so also to withhold or retract) funds. Failure to reach agreement within the UN at global level would not preclude world-regional communities of participants from each of these four pillars from moving ahead with regional youth employment compacts. Specialist advice from selected pools of youth employment and unemployment advisers, not limited to labour economists and including social policy analysts, would be made available to countries with YU rates persistently above YU targets.

A core principle of the Compact is that it would bridge the current deeply rooted dysfunctional fragmentation between global economic and global social governance. To this end, we invoke the idea of a UN Economic and Social *Council*. An empowered ECOSOC, working in tandem with an expert advisory Global Commission on Youth Unemployment answerable to ECOSOC, can be tasked to work through and oversee the detailed procedures involved in formulating an encompassing Global Youth Employment Programme, including the global (and sub-global) targets and national and international aspects of global youth employment stabilisation policies, and in monitoring and reporting on progress (or lack of progress) at regular intervals, drawing ECOSOC's and UN's attention to emerging problems.

Leading bodies from what are presently and separately thought of as 'economic' and 'social' realms of global governance would work together on a basis of parity of esteem and equality. The redistributive powers of the International Monetary Fund (IMF) and the World Bank (WB) would be redirected to contributing substantially to funding in countries in which the initial assumptions of the Compact were not sustainable. Empowered UN social agencies, notably the ILO and UNESCO, with newly assigned financial and legal 'teeth' and radical ambition to match them, would be expected to lead the elaboration of a strengthened global regulatory and policy framework that supports the realisation of the Compact in all parts of the world. This might include building in reserve powers to call upon selected governments and global corporate entities when necessary to provide additional support to enable countries that struggle to meet YU targets and accompanying standards. No presumptions should be entertained as to which countries would be the most urgent beneficiaries.

The integration of social and economic realms of global governance might also direct attention towards ensuring that young people's working conditions are within the effective jurisdiction of individual states and the realm of strengthened global policy enforcement mechanisms. It might also include capacity-building to support each of the four pillars to participate in the formulation and implementation of the Compact, globally, regionally and nationally. One priority here would be to support global non-state actors mobilising around youth unemployment *and* youth employment to 'visibilise' YU as a global, regional and national policy issue, and to empower them to participate in the Compact at the level of policy formulation as well as in monitoring and implementation.

Those who conceive these objectives and methods as economically and politically illiterate are invited to pause to consider the social and political costs and incompetence of hobbling the prospects of financial independence and self-sufficiency for one in every seven young people up to and well beyond the age of 25 years (to reference our most conservative threshold for EYU at country level), and for three in every four young people worldwide if we take account of mass unrecorded unemployment as our barometer. They are also invited to contemplate the economic and political as well as the personal and social costs of responding to the harms done to or by young people whose frustration overspills into despair, violence and hatred of perceived 'others' who can be semi-plausibly held to be responsible for their plights, by virtue of their class, their gender, their 'race', their religion, or their political or social beliefs.

We closed Chapter 8 with the words of the UN Secretary-General, to the effect that unemployment amongst young people is a failure on the part of all who hold relevant governmental powers; and with reminders of the profound anxieties caused by mass youth protest during the GFC period, epitomised in the frustrations and actions of young people during the Arab Spring and elsewhere. In such circumstances, prioritising the very narrow versions of economic literacy that are presently globally dominant in the face of such injustices, harms and threats to social and political stability internationally itself seems less than economically literate or politically competent.

The importance of having the vision to step outside the prevailing social policy paradigm was never better expressed than in the following crisp assertion from a long-since deceased English civil servant and economic liberal, whose leadership during and after the Second World War re-made UK social policy: 'A revolutionary moment in the world's history is a time for revolutions, not for patching' (UK Government (1942) *Social Insurance and Allied Services* (Cmd. 6404), Paragraph 7; known as the Beveridge Report, after its author, William Beveridge). The following, closing, section of this book establishes a view of the current context that may make Beveridge's epithet and our proposals for a GCfYE of even greater relevance than the already-compelling evidence would have suggested.

9.4   THE GLOBAL CORONAVIRUS PANDEMIC AND THE ECONOMIC CRISIS OF 2020

The tenth anniversary of the onset of the GFC in 2018 prompted multiple predictions that a new financial crisis followed by a global recession in 2020 looked likely.[1] An extensive Special Report in *The Economist* argued that, 'Much of the world is likely to have to fight the next downturn with its armoury severely depleted … The global finance system is more prone to havoc than previously appreciated and its recession-fighting tools no longer pack a punch' (13 October 2018: 7, 12).

These strong cautionary comments were easily forgotten in the glare of what followed. But they remain significant. The seriousness of the Global Coronavirus Pandemic (GCP) was recognised by most governments during the second quarter of 2020 (Q2-2020). Its destructive economic and social potential remains beyond estimation, although the interaction between the already impending recession and the effects of the GCP will probably never be convincingly disentangled. If we confine the warnings from 2018 to the employment prospects for young people alone, average YU counts and rates in UMICs and LMICs have been climbing in almost every year since the GFC, to the highest levels seen since reliable comprehensive data were available. LMICs' average YU rates have been rising above the 15 per cent marker in every year since 2015, with predictions that this trajectory would continue beyond 2019 (see Chapter 5, Figure 5.8). The YU count was then predicted to edge higher every year, to reach 32.3 million in 2021. The trajectory is similar in UMICs, at and just above 15 per cent,

---

[1]   Contemporaneous academic support for these claims was widely published (for example, *The Financial Times* (11 September 2018), *The Washington Post* (10 October 2018)). See also Thompson (2018) for key indicators of impending recession.

although the open YU count has been declining below 24 million (Chapter 5). In many CIGs and world-regions, recovery from the GFC remained slow or absent (Tables 5.1–5.4 and Table 5.5 (Column 9)). While it is fruitless to speculate about future trajectories, seen from Q1-2021 as well as from the data that follows in Section 9.4.1 (below), it is evident that these combined economic forces may well trigger the greatest, most geographically far-reaching and prolonged extremes of YU in recorded history.

9.4.1   Economic Consequences of Covid-19

As of July 2020, modelled data from leading IGOs was presenting parlous predictions of unprecedented economic decline, not only in HICs but also far beyond them.[2] In March 2020, when the spread of the Covid-19 virus beyond China was first recognised, the Secretary-General of the OECD was already predicting that affected countries would continue to experience the economic fall-out 'for years to come', and compared the OECD's plan to deal with the outbreak to the Marshall Plan after the Second World War.[3] In June, the WB predicted a 5.2 per cent contraction in global GDP, with the HICs' economies expected to shrink by seven percentage points on average.[4] It anticipated that most countries would experience recessions, resulting in the most extensive global recession since records began in 1870. East Asia and the Pacific was likely to be the least affected region with positive growth of 0.5 per cent, with Europe and Central Asia (−4.7 per cent) and Latin America (−7.2 per cent) experiencing extremes of negative growth. The humanitarian and economic toll of recession, the WB expected, was likely to fall especially heavily on countries with extensive informal sectors (*c.* 70 per cent of total employment and above) – typically LICs and LMICs. The WB's president anticipated that up to 60 million people would be pushed into extreme poverty (updating this to 100 million two months later), adding that we should anticipate 'people in the poor countries being not only unemployed, but unable to get any work even in the informal sector. And that's going to have consequences for a decade'.[5] The IMF described the pandemic as 'A Crisis Like No Other', predicting declining global growth of −4.9 per cent in 2020 and −5.4 per cent in 2021.[6]

By July 2020, the European Commission had forecast a 9 percentage point contraction in the Euro area economy during 2020 (the deepest recession in EU history).[7] The UK Office for Budget Responsibility (OBR) predicted for the UK 'the largest decline in annual GDP for 300 years, with output falling by more than 10 per cent in 2020' and an 'unprecedented peacetime

---

[2]   Most of the data in this section reflect records for the first 3–4 months of the pandemic.

[3]   See https://www.bbc.co.uk/news/business-52000219 (broadcast 23 March 2020) (accessed 18 July 2020).

[4]   WB data and commentary: https://www.worldbank.org/en/news/feature/2020/06/08/the-global-economic-outlook-during-the-covid-19-pandemic-a-changed-world (accessed 18 July 2020).

[5]   See https://www.bbc.co.uk/news/business-52939846 (broadcast 7 June 2020) (accessed 18 July 2020).

[6]   IMF (2020) World Economic Output Update, June 2020. In HICs, economic output projections were negative across the board, ranging from −6 per cent in Japan, −8 per cent in the USA, −10 per cent in the UK, up to −13 per cent in France, Italy and Spain (table 1). In UMICs they range from +1 per cent in China to −10 per cent in Mexico. See https://www.imf.org/en/Publications/WEO/Issues/2020/06/24/WEOUpdateJune2020 (accessed 18 July 2020).

[7]   See https://ec.europa.eu/commission/presscorner/detail/en/ip_20_1269 (accessed 18 July 2020).

rise in [government] borrowing this year to between 13 and 21 per cent of GDP, lifting debt above 100 per cent of GDP' (OBR, 2020: 3). In May, the Bank of England had projected a 30 per cent decline in the UK's economic output by mid-year, and this was later partially confirmed by a 22 per cent decline in Q2-2020 (ONS, 2020).[8] OBR modelling indicated that it would be 2024–25 before the budget deficit returned to the pre-pandemic forecast (2.2 per cent of GDP).[9] UK government debt reached £2 trillion in July 2020. By January 2021, at least three fast-spreading mutated versions of the virus said to have originated in the UK, South Africa and Brazil caused spikes in transmission rates, leading to indicative risks of significantly increased spread of the virus pending full implementation of national vaccination programmes, and of substantial negative economic impacts. Addressing his Executive Board, the Director-General of the WHO said 'I need to be blunt: the world is on the brink of a cata-strophic moral failure – and the price of this failure will be paid with lives and livelihoods in the world's poorest countries'.[10] He was referring to the speed and energy with which HICs were buying up large quantities of protective vaccines through bilateral deals with companies, thereby 'driving up prices and attempting to jump to the front of the queue'. This out-bidding would inevitably slow or exclude middle- and low-income countries' access to vaccines, thereby increasing the risks of international transmission of the virus (and its variants) and prolonging the pandemic and the widespread economic havoc it would cause.

9.4.2   Implications for Youth (Un)employment

Predictions of this kind rapidly translated into expectations for unemployment trajectories. In the UK, barely a month into the first national 'lockdown', almost half of 18–24-year-olds had been furloughed, lost their job or lost working hours (Cominetti et al., 2020). The Institute of Fiscal Studies confirmed that 30 per cent of all job losses were amongst those aged below 25 years.[11] By June 2020, 15–19 per cent of young people were claiming unemployment benefits in 50 UK parliamentary constituencies.[12] The Institute for Employment Studies predicted that the unemployment rate for that group 'could be on its way towards 25% in the coming months'.[13] YU rates look set to continue to rise for some time: Resolution Foundation model-ling found that

> [A] 6.1 percentage point hike in the unemployment rate at the point of leaving full-time education … entails a 13 per cent lower likelihood of a graduate being in employment three years after having left education. For those with mid-level … and lower-level … qualifications, these figures are 27 and 37 per cent, respectively. (Henehan, 2020: 4)

---

[8]   See https://www.ft.com/content/734e604b-93d9-43a6-a6ec-19e8b22dad3c (accessed 18 July 2020).

[9]   See OBR (2020) *Financial Sustainability Report* at https://cdn.obr.uk/FSR2020_Pressnotice.pdf (accessed 18 July 2020).

[10]   See   https://www.who.int/director-general/speeches/detail/who-director-general-s-opening -remarks-at-148th-session-of-the-executive-board. (accessed 18 January 2021).

[11]   See https://www.ifs.org.uk/publications/14791 (accessed 18 July 2020).

[12]   See https://www.bbc.co.uk/news/uk-53430775 (accessed 20 July 2020).

[13]   See https://www.employment-studies.co.uk/resource/labour-market-statistics-june-2020-ies-anal ysis (accessed 18 July 2020).

In April the African Union (AU, 2020: 21) predicted that '[n]early 20 million jobs, both in the formal and informal sectors, are threatened with destruction on the continent if the situation continues'. Early 'hard' data came via the ILO's monthly recording of national working hours, which provide a useful indication of prospective rising unemployment rates across all age groups in the months ahead. Declining hours records for April included Mexico (60 per cent decline), Colombia (*c.*50 per cent) and Philippines (*c.*60 per cent), comparing unfavourably to Canada (30 per cent) and the USA (20 per cent) (ILO, 2020b).[14] A month later, Blanchflower was reporting that YU rates in the USA had increased from 4 per cent to 20 per cent in just six weeks, followed by a further increase to 33 per cent, anticipating rates exceeding those of the Great Depression.[15] The UN predicted the loss of 400 million jobs worldwide by Q2-2020, plus losses of livelihoods for 1.6 *billion* workers in the informal economy.[16]

Our findings on the relationship between declining GDP and rising YU would have predicted these impacts of the GCP. They showed that, on average, YU rates increase when GDP shrinks in the countries of all of the three higher-income groups – especially so in high-income countries, least so in lower middle-income countries (Chapter 6, Section 6.3.2 and Table 6.1). But the ILO's 'early' data also indicate that in Q2-2020 it was in lower middle-income countries that lost working hours were between two and five percentage points greater than in the other income groups (ILO, 2020b, figure 3). This suggests that the pattern of effects on YU during and after the GCP may well be quite different, perhaps affecting lower-income countries much more adversely than previously. But in general, across country income groups, young people's employment prospects currently look unprecedently bleak.

9.4.3   The Renewal of Global Governance

The threat to public health of the GCP makes a compelling case for renewed institutional strengthening amongst leading IGOs in this and other policy fields if it proves to be cyclical, prolonged or recurrent. It supports our argument for a Global Compact for Youth Employment outlined in Section 9.3 above. With international support and restored authority, the GCfYE could generate capacity to resolve historical tensions that have so substantially undermined the efficacy of global YU policy. A Compact that is conceived and delivered in collaboration on the basis of participatory policy-making, equality and universalism could still meet SDGs 8.5 and 8.6 by 2030. It would herald an unrivalled ability to generate solutions to the enduring harms of mass and endemic YU caused by Covid-19 or some other (as yet unknown) future pandemic, and to the urgent need for a bulwark against recurrent YU crises.

The short-term costs of an effectively renewed and re-empowered ILO, working alongside a similarly ambitious UNESCO, in this global policy field would be substantial, but so also would the costs to the economic security of tens (potentially hundreds) of millions of young people, and consequently to the nation states that would otherwise have little choice but to provide short-term palliatives on an unprecedented scale if the GCP continues. If it does,

---

[14]   Also available at https://www.ilo.org/wcmsp5/groups/public/@dgreports/@dcomm/documents/briefingnote/wcms_749399.pdf (accessed 18 July 2020).
[15]   BBC World Service, 'Covid Generation', https://www.bbc.co.uk/programmes/w3ct0v0j (broadcast 31 May 2020) (accessed 18 July 2020).
[16]   See https://sdgs.un.org/goals/goal8 (accessed 13 August 2020).

history provides no guides: the points of comparison between the so-called 'Spanish Flu' pandemic of 1918–19 and the current GCP are very limited (Webel and Culler Freeman, 2020). Then, many economies were debilitated by youth labour shortages and consequent wage inflation – but not by youth labour surplus and probable wage deflation as at present (Colvin and McLaughlin, 2020). But if the potential for inference and deduction between the two pandemics is limited, what is certain is that our findings of continuous annual upward gradients of YU rates in LMICs and UMICs demonstrate a great many countries' lack of resilience to economic shocks, and an even greater vulnerability if pandemic conditions are not arrested and reversed.

The UN Secretary-General's response to the pandemic and the global tensions that accompany it in his 2020 Nelson Mandela Lecture identified a generational opportunity to 'build back a more equal and sustainable world ... based on a New Social Contract and a New Global Deal that create equal opportunities for all, and respect the rights and freedoms of all'.[17] The New Social Contract, he argued, 'must integrate employment, sustainable development and social protection, based on equal rights and opportunities for all'. In a 'trail' for his lecture, Antonio Guterres commented on the failure of the G20 group of nations to cooperate in the face of the GCP of 2020, contrasting it to the G20's constructive collaborative work at the start of the GFC in 2008, and urged global institutions to adjust to current problems.[18]

We suggest that our proposed Global Compact for Youth Employment would make a substantial contribution to Guterres' proposed New Social Contract that, as of January 2021, remains short on the specifics of its youth employment features beyond the role of entrepreneurship in addressing YU (UNGA, 2020). If the ILO can be restored to its visionary leadership on demand-side labour economics; if UNESCO can resume close historic partnership with the ILO in making progressive connections between education and young people's employment; if UNICEF can play a full role in supporting the ambitious renewal of global YU policy; if the WB can suspend its conviction that YU is principally a supply-side problem; and if the IMF can provide the financial underpinnings of a global youth employment stabilisation programme, these five singularly powerful IGOs can forge genuine collaborations that exploit their best distinctive knowledges, understandings, competences and financial powers. If their governing bodies can be convinced that resolving burgeoning YU is a global policy priority and that a Global Compact for Youth Employment along the lines we have outlined is the best way of realising that priority, the GCP would have provided the conditions for a transformative global social policy to break through – one that revitalises global governance in the interests of ending endemic and mass YU, permanently and worldwide, and that commits global leaders to leaving no young person behind, anywhere. In the closing words of Guterres' Nelson Mandela lecture:

> Now is the time for global leaders to decide: Will we succumb to chaos, division and inequality? Or will we right the wrongs of the past and move forward together, for the good of all? We are at breaking point. But we know which side of history we are on.

---

[17]   'Tackling the Inequality Pandemic: A New Social Contract for a New Era', New York, 18 July 2020, https://www.nelsonmandela.org/news/entry/annual-lecture-2020-secretary-general-guterress-full-speech (accessed 19 July 2020).
[18]   BBC Radio 4, https://www.bbc.co.uk/programmes/m000l1bs (broadcast 18 July 2020) (accessed 18 July 2020).

References

Abé Ndjié, A., Atangana Ondoa, H. and Ngoa Tabi, H. (2019), 'Governance and youth unemployment in Africa', *Labor History*, 60 (6), 869–82.

Acemoglu, D., Autor, D., Dorn, D., Hanson, G.H. and Price, B. (2016), 'Import competition and the great US employment sag of the 2000s', *Journal of Labor Economics*, 34 (1, pt 2), S141–98.

ACEVO [Association of Chief Executives of Voluntary Organisations] (2012), 'Youth-unemployment: the crisis we cannot afford', London: ACEVO, https://www.acevo.org.uk/wp-content/uploads/2019/07/Youth-Unemployment-the-crisis-we-cannot-afford.pdf (accessed 18 August 2020).

Ackum, S. (1991), 'Youth unemployment, labor market programs and subsequent earnings', *The Scandinavian Journal of Economics*, 93 (4), 531–43.

ActionAid Afghanistan (2009), *ActionAid Afghanistan Brochure*, http://www3.actionaid.org/afghanistan/1764.html (accessed 25 March 2019).

Alderman, H. and Yemtsov, R. (2012), 'Productive role of social protection, social protection and labor', Discussion Paper No. 1203, Washington, DC: World Bank.

Appadurai, A. (1990), 'Disjuncture and difference in the global cultural economy', *Theory, Culture & Society*, 7, 295–310.

Apple, M.W. (1978), 'Ideology, reproduction, and educational reform', *Comparative Education Review*, 22 (3), 367–87.

Apple, M.W. (1982), 'Reproduction and contradiction in education', in Apple, M.W (ed.), *Cultural and Economic Reproduction in Education: Essays on Class, Ideology and the State*, Abingdon: Routledge, pp. 1–31.

Apple, M.W. (1995), *Education and Power*, Abingdon: Routledge.

Apple, M.W. (2018), *Ideology and Curriculum* (4th edition), Abingdon: Routledge.

Aruoba, S.B., Diebold, F.X., Kose, M.A. and Terrones, M.E. (2010), 'Globalization, the business cycle, and macroeconomic monitoring', Working Paper No. 16264, Cambridge, MA: National Bureau of Economic Research.

AU [African Union] (2020), 'Impact of the coronavirus (Covid 19) on the African economy', April, https://au.int/sites/default/files/documents/38326-doc-covid-19_impact_on_african_economy.pdf (accessed 18 July 2020).

Autor, D. (2014), 'Skills, education, and the rise of earnings inequality among the "other 99 percent"', *Science*, 344 (6186), 843–51.

Autor, D. and Dorn, D. (2013), 'The growth of low-skill service jobs and the polarization of the U.S. labor market', *American Economic Review*, 103 (5), 1553–97.

Autor, D.H., Dorn, D. and Hanson, G.H. (2013), 'The China syndrome: local labor market effects of import competition in the United States', *American Economic Review*, 103 (6), 2121–68.

Autor, D.H., Dorn, D., Hanson, G.H. and Song, J. (2014), 'Trade adjustment: worker-level evidence', *Quarterly Journal of Economics*, 129 (4), 1799–860.

Baah-Boateng, W. (2016), 'The youth unemployment challenge in Africa: what are the drivers?', *The Economic and Labour Relations Review*, 27 (4), 413–31.

Baerreson, D.B. (1971), *The Border Industrialisation Programme of Mexico*, Lexington, KY: Lexington Books.

Banerji, A., Lin, H. and Saksonovs, S. (2015), 'Youth unemployment in advanced Europe: Okun's Law and beyond', IMF Working Papers WP/15/5, New York: International Monetary Fund.

Barrientos, A., Kanbur, R. and Matkovic, G. (2011), 'Statement of the Advisory Panel IEG Evaluation of World Bank support to social safety nets, 2000–2010', https://pdfs.semanticscholar.org/f3cf/7111a008aacd0f50c73f63200d3c960861f7.pdf (accessed 25 March 2020).

Bates, I., Clarke, J., Cohen, P., Finn, D., Moore, R. and Willis, P. (1984), *Schooling for the Dole? The New Vocationalism*, Basingstoke: Macmillan International Higher Education.

Bayoumi, T. and Bui, T.T. (2010), 'Deconstructing the international business cycle: why does a US sneeze give the rest of the world a cold?', IMF Working Paper 10/239, Washington, DC: IMF.

Beach, D. (2017), 'Process-tracing methods in social science', in *Oxford Research Encyclopedia of Politics*, DOI: 10.1093/acrefore/9780190228637.013.176 (accessed 2 February 2020).

Beaudry, P., Green, D.A. and Sand, B. (2013), 'The great reversal in the demand for skill and cogitive tasks', *Journal of Labor Economics*, 34 (S1), S199–S247.

Becker, B.E. and Hills, S.M. (1980), 'Teenage unemployment: some evidence of the long-run effects on wages', *Journal of Human Resources*, 15 (3), 354–72.

Beerepoot, N. and Vogelzang, E. (2015), 'Service outsourcing to smaller cities in the Philippines: the formation of an emerging local middle class', in Lambregts, B., Beerepoot, N. and Kloosterman, R.C. (eds), *Local Impact of Globalization in South and Southeast Asia: Offshore Business Processes in Services Industries*, Abingdon: Routledge, pp. 195–207.

Bell, D.N. and Blanchflower, D.G. (2010), 'Youth unemployment: déjà vu?', Discussion Paper No. 4705, Bonn: IZA.

Bell, D.N. and Blanchflower, D.G. (2011), 'Young people and the Great Recession', *Oxford Review of Economic Policy*, 27 (2), 241–67.

Bellamy-Foster, J., McChesney, R.W. and Jonna, R.J. (2011), 'The global reserve army of labor and the new imperialism', *Monthly Review*, 63 (6), n.p.n., https://monthlyreview.org/2011/11/01/the-global-reserve-army-of-labor-and-the-new-imperialism/ (accessed 18 August 2020).

Benanav, A. (2014), 'A global history of unemployment: surplus populations in the world economy, 1949–2010', PhD Thesis, UCLA, Los Angeles, CA: UCLA, https://escholarship.org/uc/item/7r14v2bq (accessed 27 January 2020).

Benanav, A. (2019), 'The origins of informality: the ILO at the limit of the concept of unemployment', *Journal of Global History*, 14 (1), 107–25.

Bergson, A., Ngnemzué, L. and Mayer, T. (2019), 'Youth unemployment, neoliberal reforms, and emigration in West Africa', in Mayer, T., Moorti, S. and McCallum, J.K. (eds), *The Crisis of Youth Unemployment*, Abingdon: Routledge, pp. 140–55.

Bessant, J., Farthing, R. and Watts, R. (2017), *The Precarious Generation: A Political Economy of Young People*, Abingdon: Taylor and Francis.

Betcherman, G. and Khan, T. (2015), *Youth Employment in Sub-Saharan Africa: Taking Stock of the Evidence and Knowledge Gaps*, Ottawa: International Development Research Centre.

Betcherman, G. and Khan, T. (2018), 'Jobs for Africa's expanding youth cohort: a stocktaking of employment prospects and policy interventions', *IZA Journal of Development and Migration*, 8 (13), 2–20.

Beveridge, W. (1909), *Unemployment: A Problem of Industry*, Harlow: Longmans, Green and Co. [re-published 1930].

Bheemaiah, K. and Smith, M. (2015), 'Inequality, technology and job polarization of the youth labor market in Europe', Paper to Society for the Advancement of Socio-economics 27th Annual Mini-Conference, 'Inequality in the 21st Century', London: LSE, 2–4 July 2015.

Bhorat, H., Cassim, A., Kanbur, R., Stanwix, B. and Yu, D. (2016), 'Minimum wages and youth: the case of South Africa', *Journal of African Economies*, 25 (Suppl. 1), i61–i102.

Biersteker, T.J. (1992), 'The "triumph" of neoclassical economics in the developing world: policy convergence and bases of governance in the international economic order', in Rosenau, J.N. and Czempiel, E.-O. (eds), *Governance without Government: Order and Change in World Politics*, Cambridge: Cambridge University Press, pp. 102–31.

Biersteker, T.J. (2013), 'State, sovereignty, and territory', in Carlsnaes, W., Risse, T. and Simmons, B.A. (eds), *Handbook of International Relations: State, Sovereignty, and Territory*, London: Sage, pp. 245–72.

Biggart, A. and Furlong, A. (1996), 'Educating "discouraged workers": cultural diversity in the upper secondary school', *British Journal of Sociology of Education*, 17 (3), 253–66.

Billari, F. (2004), 'Becoming an adult in Europe: a macro(/micro)-demographic perspective', *Demographic Research*, 3 (2), 15–44.

Blossfeld, H.-P., Buchholz, S., Bukodi, E. and Kurz, K. (eds) (2008), *Young Workers, Globalization and the Labor Market: Comparing Early Working Life in Eleven Countries*, Cheltenham, UK and Northampton, MA, USA: Edward Elgar Publishing.

Blossfeld, H.-P., Klizing, E., Mills, M. and Kurz, K. (eds) (2005), *Globalization, Uncertainty and Youth in Society*, London: Routledge.

Bölükbaş, M. (2018), 'Do inflation and economic growth substantially affect youth unemployment? Evidence from 20 emerging economies', *International Journal of Economic and Administrative Studies (UİİİD-IJEAS)*, 18, 55–66.

Bordo, M.D. and Murshid, A.P. (2000), 'Are financial crises becoming increasingly more contagious? What is the historical evidence on contagion?', Working Paper No. 7900, Cambridge, MA: National Bureau of Economic Research.

Bowles, S. and Gintis, H. (1976), *Schooling in Capitalist America: Educational Reform and Contradictions of Economic Life*, London: Routledge and Kegan Paul.

Brandt, M. and Hank, K. (2014), 'Scars that will not disappear: long-term associations between early and later life unemployment under different welfare regimes', *Journal of Social Policy*, 43 (4), 727–43.

Braverman, H. (1974), *Labor and Monopoly Capital: The Degradation of Work in the Twentieth Century*, New York: Monthly Review Press.

Bretton Woods Project (2017), 'Global financing facility falls short on family planning', London: Bretton Woods Project, https://www.brettonwoodsproject.org/2017/01/gff-falls-short-family-planning/ (accessed 11 July 2020).

Brown, P., Power, S., Tholen, G. and Allouch, A. (2014), 'Credentials, talent and cultural capital: a comparative study of educational elites in England and France', *British Journal of Sociology of Education*, 37 (2), 191–211.

Bruno, G.S., Choudhry Tanveer, M., Marelli, E. and Signorelli, M. (2017), 'The short-and long-run impacts of financial crises on youth unemployment in OECD countries', *Applied Economics*, 49 (34), 3372–94.

Bruno, G.S., Marelli, E. and Signorelli, M. (2014), 'The rise of NEET and youth unemployment in EU regions after the crisis', *Comparative Economic Studies*, 56 (4), 592–615.

Buck, T. (2014), *International Child Law*, London: Routledge.

Bukodi, E., Ebralidze, E., Schmelzer, P. and Blossfeld, H.-P. (2008), 'Struggling to become an insider: does increasing flexibility at labor market entry affect early careers? A theoretical framework', in Blossfeld, H.-P., Buchholz, S., Bukodi, E. and Kurz, K. (eds), *Young Workers, Globalization and the Labor Market*, Cheltenham, UK and Northampton, MA, USA: Edward Elgar Publishing, pp. 3–28.

Bynner, J., Chisholm, L. and Furlong, A. (eds) (1997), *Youth, Citizenship and Social Change in a European Context*, London: Routledge.

Cairns, D., de Almeida Alves, N., Alexandre, A. and Correia, A. (2016), *Youth Unemployment and Job Precariousness: Political Participation in a Neo-liberal Era*, London: Springer.

Cameron, C., Lush, A. and Meara, G. (1943), *Disinherited Youth*, Edinburgh: Carnegie Trust.

Cantin, E. and Taylor, M. (2008), 'Making the "workshop of the world": China and the international division of labour', in Taylor, M. (ed.), *Global Economy Contested: Power and Conflict across the International Division of Labour*, Abingdon: Routledge, pp. 51–75.

Caporale, G.M. and Gil-Alana, L. (2014), 'Youth unemployment in Europe: persistence and macroeconomic determinants', *Comparative Economic Studies*, 56 (4), 581–91.

Carnoy, M. and Levin, H. (1985), *Schooling and Work in the Democratic State*, Redwood City, CA: Stanford University Press.

Carr, H. and Hunter, C. (2008), 'Managing vulnerability: homelessness law and the interplay of the social, the political and the technical', *Journal of Social Welfare and Family Law*, 30 (4), 293–307.

Casson, M. (1979), *Youth Unemployment*, London: Palgrave Macmillan.

Cedefop (2010), *Skill Mismatch in Europe*, Brussels: European Centre for the Development of Vocational Training.

Cedefop (2014), *EU Skills Panorama*, Brussels: European Commission.

Chamberlain, G. (2011), 'Okun's Law revisited', *Economic and Labour Market Review*, 5 (2), 104–32.

Chauvel, L. (2010), 'The long-term destabilization of youth, scarring effects, and the future of the welfare regime in post-trente glorieuses France', *French Politics, Culture and Society*, 28 (3), 74–96.

Cho, Y., Margolis, D., Newhouse, D. and Robalino, D. (2012), *Labor Markets in Low and Middle-Income Countries: Trends and Implications for Social Protection and Labor Policies*, Social Protection and Labor Discussion Paper No. 1207, Washington, DC: World Bank.

Choudhry, M.T., Marelli, E. and Signorelli, M. (2012), 'Youth unemployment rate and impact of financial crises', *International Journal of Manpower*, 33 (1), 76–95.

Clarke, J., Cochrane, A. and McLaughlin, J. (eds) (1994), *Managing Social Policy*, London: Sage.

Clarke, J., Gewirtz, S. and McLaughlin, J. (eds) (2000), *New Managerialism, New Welfare?*, London: Sage.

Clarke, T., Baker, P., Watts, C.J., Henderson, H., Evans, T. and Sherr, L. (2001), 'Self-harm in younger people: audit of prevalence and provision', *Psychology, Health and Medicine*, 6 (4), 349–59.

Cockx, B. and Picchio, M. (2013), 'Scarring effects of remaining unemployed for long-term unemployed school-leavers', *Journal of the Royal Statistical Society: Series A (Statistics in Society)*, 176 (4), 951–80.

Coffield, F., Borrill, C. and Marshall, S. (1983), 'How young people try to survive being unemployed', *New Society*, 64 (1072), 332–4.

Coffield, F., Borrill, C. and Marshall, S. (1986), *Growing Up at the Margins: Young Adults in the North East*, Milton Keynes: Open University Press.

Cohen, R.B., Felton, F., Nkosi, M. and van Liere, J. (eds) (1979), *The Multinational Corporation: A Radical Approach: Papers by Stephen Herbert Hymer*, Cambridge: Cambridge University Press.

Coles, B. (1995), *Youth and Social Policy*, London: UCL Press.

Collier, D. (2011), 'Understanding process tracing', *Political Science and Politics*, 44 (4), 823–30.

Colvin, C. and McLaughlin, E. (2020), 'Coronavirus and Spanish flu: economic lessons to learn from the last truly global pandemic', *The Conversation*, 11 March, https://theconversation.com/coronavirus-and-spanish-flu-economic-lessons-to-learn-from-the-last-truly-global-pandemic-133176 (accessed 18 July 2020).

Cominetti, N., Gardiner, L. and Slaughter, H. (2020), 'The full monty: facing up to the challenge of the coronavirus labour market crisis', Resolution Foundation, June, https://www.resolutionfoundation.org/app/uploads/2020/06/The-Full-Monty.pdf (accessed 18 August 2020).

Commission on Global Governance (1995), *Our Global Neighbourhood: The Report of the Commission on Global Governance*, New York: Oxford University Press.

Cowling, K. and Sugden, R. (1987), *Transnational Monopoly Capitalism*, Brighton: Wheatsheaf.

Craig, G. (1988), *Young People at the Crossroads*, London: Family Policy Studies Centre.

Crouch, C. (2015), 'Labour market governance and the creation of outsiders', *British Journal of Industrial Relations*, 53 (1), 27–48.

Cuervo, H. and Wyn, J. (2016), 'An unspoken crisis: the "scarring effects" of the complex nexus between education and work on two generations of young Australians', *International Journal of Lifelong Education*, 35 (2), 122–35.

Dale, R. (1982), 'Education and the capitalist state: contributions and contradictions', in Apple, M.W. (ed.), *Cultural and Economic Reproduction in Education: Essays on Class, Ideology and the State*, Abingdon: Routledge, pp. 127–61.

Dale, R. (1989), *The State and Education Policy*, Milton Keynes: Open University Press.

Danielsson, J., Valenzuela, M. and Zer, I. (2018), 'Learning from history: volatility and financial crises', *The Review of Financial Studies*, 31 (7), 2774–805.

D'Cruz, P. and Noronha, E. (2010), 'Employee dilemmas in the Indian ITES-BPO sector', in Messenger, J.C. and Ghosheh, N. (eds), *Offshoring and Working Conditions in Remote Work*, International Labour Organization; Basingstoke: Palgrave Macmillan, pp. 60–100.

de Lange, M., Gesthuizen, M. and Wolbers, M.H.J. (2014), 'Youth labour market integration across Europe', *European Societies*, 16 (2), 194–212.

Deacon, B. (2007), *Global Social Policy and Governance*, London: Sage.

Deacon, B. (2013), *Global Social Policy in the Making: The Foundations of the Social Protection Floor*, Bristol: Policy Press.

Deacon, B. (2015), 'The International Labour Organization and global social governance – the 100 year search for social justice within capitalism', in Kaasch, A. and Martens, K. (eds), *Actors and Agency in Global Social Governance*, Oxford: Oxford University Press, pp. 45–63.

Deacon, B., Hulse, M. and Stubbs, P. (1997), *Global Social Policy: International Organisations and the Future of Welfare*, London: Sage.

Dean, H. (2006), 'Underclass or undermined? Young people and social citizenship', in MacDonald, R. (ed.), *Youth, the 'Underclass' and Social Exclusion*, Abingdon, Routledge, pp. 67–81.

Dicken, P. (2003), *Global Shift: Reshaping the Global Economic Map in the 21st Century* (4th edition), London: Sage.

Dicken, P. (2009), 'The world is "not" flat: the intense geographical unevenness of globalization', in *The Multiple Faces of Globalization*, Madrid: BBVA, https://www.bbvaopenmind.com/en/articles/the-world-is-not-flat-the-intense-geographical-unevenness-of-globalization/ (accessed 15 December 2019).

Dicken, P. (2011), *Global Shift: Mapping the Changing Contours of the World Economy* (5th edition), New York: The Guilford Press.

Dixon, J. (1995), *Social Security in Global Perspective*, Westport, CT: Praeger.

Dixon, R., Lim, G.C. and van Ours, J.C. (2017), 'Revisiting the Okun relationship', *Applied Economics*, 49 (28), 2749–65.

D'Mello, M. and Sahay, S. (2008), 'Betwixt and between? Exploring mobilities in a global workplace in India', in Upadhya, C. and Vasavi, A.R. (eds), *In an Outpost of the Global Economy: Work and Workers in India's Information Technology Industry*, London: Routledge, pp. 76–100.

Domínguez, E., Icaza, R., Quintero, C., López, S. and Stenman, A. (2010), 'Women workers in the Maquiladoras and the debate on global labour standards', *Feminist Economics*, 16 (4), 185–209.

Dorling, D. (2013), 'Generation jobless', *New Statesman* (16 August), pp. 16–22.

Ductor, L. and Leiva-Leon, D. (2016), 'Dynamics of global business cycle interdependence', *Journal of International Economics*, 102 (September), 110–27.

Dunkley, G. (1997), *The Free Trade Adventure: The WTO, the Uruguay Round and Globalism: A Critique*, London: Zed Books.

Dunning, J.H. (1993), *Multinational Enterprises and the Global Economy*, Harlow: Addison-Wesley.

Dunsch, S. (2016), 'Okun's Law and youth unemployment in Germany and Poland', *International Journal of Management and Economics*, 49 (1), 34–57.

Dunsch, S. (2017), 'Age- and gender-specific unemployment and Okun's Law in CEE countries', *Eastern European Economics*, 55 (4), 377–93.

Ebaidalla, E.M. (2016), 'Determinants of youth unemployment in OIC member states: a dynamic panel data analysis', *Journal of Economic Cooperation and Development*, 37 (2), 81–102.

ECOSOC (2012), *Creating a Sustainable Future: Empowering Youth with Better Job Opportunities*, New York: United Nations.

Eichengreen, B. and Hatton, T.J. (1988), 'Interwar unemployment in international perspective: an overview', in Eichengreen, B. and Hatton, T.J. (eds), *Interwar Unemployment in International Perspective*, Dordrecht: Springer, pp. 1–59.

Eichhorst, W. and Rinne, U. (2015), 'An assessment of the youth employment inventory and implications for Germany's development policy', No. 67, Bonn: Institute for the Study of Labor (IZA).

Ellwood, D.T. (1982), 'Teenage unemployment: permanent scars or temporary blemishes?', in Freeman, R.B. and Wise, D.A. (eds), *The Youth Labor Market Problem: Its Nature, Causes, and Consequences*, Chicago, IL: University of Chicago Press, pp. 349–90.

Elson, D. and Pearson, R. (1981), '"Nimble fingers make cheap workers": an analysis of women's employment in third world export manufacturing', *Feminist Review*, 7 (1), 87–107.

Emmenegger, P., Häusermann, S., Palier, B. and Seeleib-Kaiser, M. (2012). 'How we grow unequal', in Emmenegger, P., Häusermann, S., Palier, B. and Seeleib-Kaiser, M. (eds), *The Age of Dualization: The Changing Face of Inequality in Deindustrializing Societies*, Oxford: Oxford University Press, pp. 3–26.

Engels, F. (2009), *The Condition of the Working Class in England*, London: Penguin.

Enloe, C. (1983), 'Women textile workers in the militarization of Southeast Asia', in Nash, J. and Fernández-Kelly, M.P. (eds), *Women, Men, and the International Division of Labor*, Albany: University of New York Press, pp. 407–25.

Eraydin, A. and Erendil, E. (1999), 'The role of female labour in industrial restructuring: new production processes and labour market relations in the Istanbul clothing industry', *Gender, Place and Culture: A Journal of Feminist Geography*, 6 (3), 259–72.

Errighi, L., Khatiwada, S. and Bodwell, C. (2016), 'Business process outsourcing in the Philippines: challenges for decent work', ILO Asia-Pacific Working Paper Series, Bangkok: International Labour Organization, https://www.ilo.org/asia/publications/WCMS_538193/lang--en/index.htm (accessed 19 August 2020).

Farnsworth, K. (2014), 'Business and global social policy', in Yeates, N. (ed.), *Understanding Global Social Policy* (2nd edition), Bristol: Policy Press.

Fergusson, R. (2002), 'Rethinking youth transitions: policy transfer and new exclusions in New Labour's New Deal', *Policy Studies*, 23 (3), 173–90.

Fergusson, R. (2004), 'Discourses of exclusion: reconceptualising participation amongst young people', *Journal of Social Policy*, 33 (2), 289–320.

Fergusson, R. (2014), 'Warehouse, marketise, shelter, juridify: on the political economy and governance of extending school participation in England', in Farnsworth, K., Irving, Z. and Fenger, M. (eds), *Social Policy Review 26: Analysis and Debate in Social Policy*, Bristol: Policy Press, pp. 47–64.

Fergusson, R. (2016a), 'Global actors and policies on youth unemployment', paper presented at the International Sociological Association, 'Economy and Society' Research Committee, ISA Forum, Vienna, Austria, 14 July.

Fergusson, R. (2016b), *Young People, Welfare and Crime: Governing Non-participation*, Bristol: Policy Press.

Fergusson, R. (2017), 'Shifting policy responses amongst transnational actors to endemic youth unemployment', paper presented at 'Doing Comparative Social Policy Analysis in Changing Global Context' Conference, Hong Kong: Lingnan University, 8 December.

Fergusson, R. (2021), 'International organisations' involvement in youth unemployment as a global policy field, and the global financial crisis', in Martens, K., Niemann, D. and Kaasch, A. (eds), *International Organisations in Global Social Governance*, Basingstoke: Palgrave Macmillan.

Fergusson, R. and Yeates, N. (2012), 'The globalisation of youth unemployment policy', paper presented at the Policy and Politics Conference '40 years of Policy and Politics: Critical Reflections and Strategies for the Future', Bristol University, 18–19 September.

Fergusson, R. and Yeates, N. (2013), 'Business, as usual: the policy priorities of the World Bank's discourses on youth unemployment, and the global financial crisis', *Journal of International and Comparative Social Policy*, 29 (1), 64–78.

Fergusson, R. and Yeates, N. (2014), 'International governmental organisations and global youth unemployment: the normative and ideational foundations of policy discourses', *Policy and Politics*, 42 (3), 439–58 [first published online in 2013].

Fergusson, R. and Yeates, N. (2017), 'Partners or adversaries? Global policy responses to crises of youth unemployment', paper presented to Social Policy Association conference, 'Social Inequalities: Research, Theory and Policy', 9–11 July, University of Durham.

Fergusson, R., Pye, D., Esland, G., McLaughlin, E. and Muncie, J. (2000), 'Normalized dislocation and new subjectivities in post-16 markets for education and work', *Critical Social Policy*, 20 (3), 283–305.

Fiddy, R. (ed.) (1983), *In Place of Work: Policy and Provision for the Young Unemployed*, Abingdon: Taylor and Francis.

Filmer, D. and Fox, L. (2014), *Youth Employment in Sub-Saharan Africa*, Washington, DC: World Bank.

Finn, D. (1987), *Training Without Jobs: New Deals and Broken Promises*, Macmillan International Higher Education, London: Palgrave Macmillan.

Finn, D. (2003), 'The "employment-first" welfare state: lessons from the New Deal for young people', *Social Policy and Administration*, 37 (7), 709–24.

Foray, D. and Lundvall, B. (1996), 'The knowledge-based economy: from the economics of knowledge to the learning economy', in Foray, D. and Lundvall, B. (eds), *Employment and Growth in the Knowledge-Based Economy*, Paris: OECD, pp. 11–32.

Ford, J., Rugg, J. and Burrows, R. (2002), 'Conceptualising the contemporary role of housing in the transition to adult life in England', *Urban Studies*, 39 (13), 2455–67.

Fox, L. and Thomas, A. (2016), 'Africa's got work to do: a diagnostic of youth employment challenges in sub-Saharan Africa', *Journal of African Economies*, 25 (Supplement 1), i16–i36.

Fox, L., Senbet, L.W. and Simbanegavi, W. (2016), 'Youth employment in sub-Saharan Africa: challenges, constraints and opportunities', *Journal of African Economies*, 25, Supplement 1, i3–i15.

France, A. (2016), *Understanding Youth in the Global Economic Crisis*, Bristol: Policy Press.

Freedman, D.H. (1977), *The Idle Threat: Unemployed Youth*, Geneva: ILO.

Freeman, C. (2000), *High Tech and High Heels in the Global Economy: Women, Work and Pink-Collar Identities*, Durham, NC: Duke University Press.

Fröbel, F., Heinrichs, J. and Kreye, O. (1980), *The New International Division of Labour: Structural Unemployment in Industrial Countries and Industrialisation in Developing Countries*, Cambridge: Cambridge University Press.

Fuller, C. and Narasimhan, H. (2008), 'Empowerment and constraint: women, work and the family in Chennai's software industry', in Upadhya, C. and Vasavi, A. (eds), *In an Outpost of the Global Economy: Work and Workers in India's Information Technology Industry*, London: Routledge, pp. 190–210.

Furlong, A. (2013), *Youth Studies: An Introduction*, Abingdon: Routledge.

Furlong, A. and Cartmel, F. (2006), *Young People and Social Change*, Maidenhead: McGraw-Hill Education.

Galenson, W. and Zellner, A. (1957), 'International comparison of unemployment rates', in Long, C.D. (ed.), *The Measurement and Behavior of Unemployment*, Cambridge, MA: National Bureau of Economic Research, pp. 439–584.

Gallagher, K. (2011), 'Regaining control? Capital controls and the global financial crisis', Working Paper Series No. 250, February, Political Economy Research Institute, Amherst: University of Massachusetts.

Gallie, D. and Paugam, S. (eds) (2000), *Welfare Regimes and the Experience of Unemployment in Europe*, Oxford: Oxford University Press.

Gallis, H. (1977), 'Youth unemployment: a statistical analysis', World Employment Programme Research Working Paper, Youth Unemployment in Industrialised Market Economies series, Geneva: ILO.

Garland, D. (2001), *The Culture of Control: Crime and Social Order in Contemporary Society*, Oxford: Oxford University Press.

Generation Unlimited (2019a), 'World Bank and UNICEF partner to promote education, skills and training for young people', https://www.generationunlimited.org/news-and-stories/world-bank-unicef-education-skills-training-young-people (accessed 5 July 2020).

Generation Unlimited (2019b), 'UNICEF prepares the largest generation in history with support from SAP', https://www.generationunlimited.org/news-and-stories/unicef-prepares-largest-generation-history-with-SAP-support (accessed 5 July 2020).

Generation Unlimited (2020), 'Message to business from UNICEF Executive Director Henrietta Fore and Unilever CEO Alan Jope', https://www.generationunlimited.org/news-and-stories/message-to-business-from-unicef-executive-director-henrietta-fore-and-unilever-ceo-alan-jope (accessed 5 July 2020).

Generation Unlimited (n.d.), 'Our work: how Generation Unlimited is helping young people reach their full potential', https://www.generationunlimited.org/our-work (accessed 5 July 2020).

Gereffi, G. and Korzeniewicz, M. (eds) (1994), *Commodity Chains and Global Capitalism*, Westport, CT: Praeger.

Godfrey, M. (2003), 'Youth employment policy in developing and transition countries – prevention as well as cure', Social Protection Unit, Human Development Network, Washington, DC: World Bank.

Goldman-Mellor, S., Caspi, A., Arseneault, L., Ajala, N., Ambler, A., Danese, A., Fisher, H., Hucker, A., Odgers, C., Williams, T. and Wong, C. (2016), 'Committed to work but vulnerable: self-perceptions and mental health in NEET 18-year-olds from a contemporary British cohort', *Journal of Child Psychology and Psychiatry*, 57 (2), 196–203.

Goldsmith, A.H., Veum, J.R. and Darity Jr, W. (1997), 'Unemployment, joblessness, psychological well-being and self-esteem: theory and evidence', *The Journal of Socio-Economics*, 26 (2), 133–58.

Gollan, J. (1937), *Youth in British Industry*, London: Gollancz.

Göransson, K. (2013), 'Reassessing the intergenerational contract', *Journal of Intergenerational Relationships*, 11 (1), 62–75.

Goyal, A. (2006), 'Global sourcing: east–west divide or synthesis?', in Kehal, H. and Singh, V. (eds), *Outsourcing and Offshoring in the 21st Century: A Socio-Economic Perspective*, London: Idea Group Publishing, pp. 54–74.

Gregg, P. (2001), 'The impact of youth unemployment on adult unemployment in the NCDS', *The Economic Journal*, 111 (475), F626–F653.

Gregg, P. and Tominey, E. (2005), 'The wage scar from male youth unemployment', *Labour Economics*, 12 (4), 487–509.

Grossman, R. (1979), 'Women's place in the integrated circuit', *Southeast Asia Chronicle*, 66 (joint issue with Pacific Research, 9 (5/6)), 2–17.

Guerrero, T.J. (2017), *Youth in Transition: Housing, Employment, Social Policies and Families in France and Spain*, Abingdon: Routledge.

Hagan, J. and McCarthy, B. (1998), *Mean Streets: Youth Crime and Homelessness*, Cambridge: Cambridge University Press.

Hamaguchi, N., Henstridge, M., Hino, H. and Mwabu, G. (2013), 'Empowering young Africans to live their dreams', Report to the fifth Tokyo international conference on African development, 2 June, Tokyo: Japan International Cooperation Agency.

Hammer, B., Istenič, T. and Vargha, L. (2018), 'The broken generational contract in Europe: generous transfers to the elderly population, low investments in children', *Intergenerational Justice Review*, 4 (1), 21–31.

Hanna, N.K. (2010), *Enabling Enterprise Transformation: Business and Grassroots Innovation for the Knowledge Economy*, New York: Springer.

Hardy, J., Shelley, S., Calveley, M., Kubisa, J. and Zahn, R. (2016), 'Scaling the mobility of health workers in an enlarged Europe: an open political-economy perspective', *European Urban and Regional Studies* 23 (4), 798–815.

Harris, N.S. (1989), *Social Security for Young People*, Aldershot: Gower.

Haurin, R.J., Haurin, D.R., Hendershott, P.H. and Bourassa, S.C. (1997), 'Home or alone: the costs of independent living for youth', *Social Science Research*, 26 (2), 135–52.

Heinz, W.R. (1987), 'The transition from school to work in crisis: coping with threatening unemployment', *Journal of Adolescent Research*, 2 (2), 127–41.

Helleiner, E. (2014), *Forgotten Foundations of Bretton Woods: International Development and the Making of the Postwar Order*, Ithaca, NY: Cornell University Press.

Hempel, K. and Fiala, N. (2012), 'Measuring success of youth livelihood interventions: a practical guide to monitoring and evaluation', Washington, DC: World Bank.

Henehan, H. (2020), 'Class of 2020: education leavers in the current crisis', Resolution Foundation, May, https://www.resolutionfoundation.org/publications/class-of-2020/ (accessed 18 July 2020).

Hermon, E. (1987), 'Peace education between the world wars: an historical overview of the origins of the organized transnational peace education movement', *Peace Research*, 19 (2), 2–6, 75–8.

Hirst, P. and Thompson, G. (1996), *Globalization in Question: The International Economy and the Possibilities of Governance*, Cambridge: Polity Press.

Hobbs, B.K. (2013), 'Okun's Law', in Cate, T. (ed.), *An Encyclopaedia of Keynesian Economics* (2nd edition), Cheltenham, UK and Northampton, MA, USA: Edward Elgar Publishing.

Hobsbawm, E. (2014), *Worlds of Labour: Further Studies in the History of Labour*, London: Orion.

Honohan, P. and Laeven, L. (eds) (2005), *Systemic Financial Crises: Containment and Resolution*, Cambridge: Cambridge University Press.

Hutengs, O. and Stadtmann, G. (2013), 'Age effects in Okun's law within the Eurozone', *Applied Economics Letters*, 20 (9), 821–5.

Hutengs, O. and Stadtmann, G. (2014), 'Age- and gender-specific unemployment in Scandinavian countries: an analysis based on Okun's law', *Comparative Economic Studies*, 56 (4), 567–80.

Hvinden, B., O'Reilly, J., Schoyen, M.A. and Hyggen, C. (2019a), *Negotiating Early Job Insecurity: Well-being, Scarring and Resilience of European Youth*, Cheltenham, UK and Northampton, MA, USA: Edward Elgar Publishing.

Hvinden, B., Hyggen, C., Schoyen, M.A. and Sirovátka, T. (eds) (2019b), *Youth Unemployment and Jobs Insecurity in Europe: Problems, Risk Factories and Policies*, Cheltenham, UK and Northampton, MA, USA: Edward Elgar Publishing.

Hymer, S.H. (1972), 'The multinational corporation and the law of uneven development', in Baghwati, J. (ed.), *Economics and World Order*, London: Macmillan, pp. 113–40.

Hymer, S.H. (1976), *The International Operations of National Firms: A Study of Direct Foreign Investment*, Cambridge, MA: MIT Press.

IBE/UNESCO [International Bureau of Education/United Nations Educational, Scientific and Cultural Organization] (1934), *Recommendation No. 2 concerning Admission to Secondary Schools (R2)*, Paris: IBE/UNESCO, http://www.ibe.unesco.org/sites/default/files/R01.pdf (accessed 19 August 2020).

IBE/UNESCO [International Bureau of Education/United Nations Educational, Scientific and Cultural Organization] (1951), *Recommendation No. 32 concerning Compulsory Education and its Prolongation (R32)*, Paris: IBE/UNESCO, http://www.ibe.unesco.org/en/international-conference -education/archive-ice-sessions-and-recommendations (accessed 19 August 2020).

IBE/UNESCO [International Bureau of Education/United Nations Educational, Scientific and Cultural Organization] (1981), *Recommendation No. 73 to the Ministries of Education concerning the Interaction between Education and Productive Work*, Paris: IBE/UNESCO, http://www.ibe.unesco .org/sites/default/files/REC_73_E.PDF (accessed 19 August 2020).

Ihensekhien, O.A. and Aisien, I.N. (2019), 'Growth–youth unemployment nexus in upper-middle-income countries in sub-Saharan Africa', *Turkish Economic Review*, 6 (1), 62–76.

Ihensekhien, O.A. and Asekome, M.O. (2017), 'Youth unemployment and economic growth: lesson from low-income countries in sub-Saharan Africa', *European Journal of Economics, Law and Politics (ELP)*, 4 (1), 1–15.

ILO [International Labour Organization] (1919a), *Constitution*, Geneva: ILO, https://www.ilo.org/ dyn/normlex/en/f?p=1000:62:0::NO:62:P62_LIST_ENTRIE_ID:2453907:NO (accessed 19 August 2020).

ILO [International Labour Organization] (1919b), *Unemployment Convention* (C002), Geneva: ILO.

ILO [International Labour Organization] (1919c), *Night Work of Young Persons (Industry) Convention* (C006), Geneva: ILO.

ILO [International Labour Organization] (1919d), *Minimum Age (Industry) Convention* (C005), Geneva: ILO.

ILO [International Labour Organization] (1919e), *Night Work (Women) Convention* (C004), Geneva: ILO.

ILO [International Labour Organization] (1919f), *First Annual Meeting*, Washington, DC: League of Nations, 29 October–29 November, https://www.ilo.org/public/libdoc/ilo/P/09616/09616(1919-1) .pdf (accessed 19 August 2020).

ILO [International Labour Organization] (1921a), *Minimum Age (Agriculture) Convention* (C010), Geneva: ILO.

ILO [International Labour Organization] (1921b), *Vocational Education (Agriculture) Recommendation* (R015), Geneva: ILO.

ILO [International Labour Organization] (1929), *Unemployment: Some International Aspects, 1920–1928*, report presented to the 12th session of the International Labour Conference, Geneva: ILO, May–June.

ILO [International Labour Organization] (1931), *Unemployment and Public Works, Studies and Reports*, Series C, No. 15, Geneva: ILO.

ILO [International Labour Organization] (1932), *Minimum Age (Non-Industrial Employment) Convention* (C033), Geneva: ILO.

ILO [International Labour Organization] (1933), *Annual Report of the Director* (17th session, Geneva, Switzerland), International Labour Office, Director-General, Geneva: ILO.

ILO [International Labour Organization] (1934a), *Annual Report of the Director* (18th session, Geneva, Switzerland), International Labour Office, Director-General, Geneva: ILO.

ILO [International Labour Organization] (1934b), *Unemployment Provision Convention* (C044), Geneva: ILO.

ILO [International Labour Organization] (1935a), *Annual Report of Director* (19th session, Geneva, Switzerland), International Labour Office, Director-General, Geneva: ILO.

ILO [International Labour Organization] (1935b), *Unemployment Among Young Persons*, International Labour Conference, 19th Session, Geneva: ILO.

ILO [International Labour Organization] (1935c), *International Labour Conference*, 19th Session, Geneva, 1935, Record of Proceedings, Geneva: International Labour Office, https://www.ilo.org/public/libdoc/ilo/P/09616/09616%281935-19%29.pdf (accessed 19 August 2020).

ILO [International Labour Organization] (1935d), *Unemployment (Young Persons) Recommendation* (R045), Geneva: ILO.

ILO [International Labour Organization] (1936), *Annual Report of the Director, International Labour Conference* (20th session, Geneva, Switzerland), International Labour Office, Director-General, Geneva: ILO.

ILO [International Labour Organization] (1937), *Vocational Training Recommendation* (R057), Geneva: ILO.

ILO [International Labour Organization] (1944a), *Constitution of the ILO and Declaration concerning the aims and purposes of the International Labour Organizations* (Declaration of Philadelphia), Geneva: ILO.

ILO [International Labour Organization] (1944b), *Report of the Director, International Labour Conference* (26th session, Geneva, Switzerland), International Labour Office, Director-General, Geneva: ILO.

ILO [International Labour Organization] (1950), *Report of the Director General, International Labour Conference* (33rd session, Geneva, Switzerland), International Labour Office, Geneva: ILO.

ILO [International Labour Organization] (1951), 'Child labour in relation to compulsory education', *International Labour Review*, 64 (1), 462–72.

ILO [International Labour Organization] (1976), *Declaration of Principles and Programme of Action*, adopted by the Tripartite World Conference on Employment, Income Distribution, Social Progress and the International Division of Labour, Geneva, Geneva: ILO, 4–17 June.

ILO [International Labour Organization] (1978), 'Youth unemployment in industrialised market economy countries; proceedings of an informal consultants' meeting', Geneva, World Employment Programme Research Working Paper, Youth Unemployment in Industrialised Market Economies series, ILO-EMP 47-1/WP.4, Geneva: ILO, 2–4 November 1977.

ILO [International Labour Organization] (1984), *Employment Policy (Supplementary Provisions) Recommendation* (R169), Geneva: ILO.

ILO [International Labour Organization] (1998), *ILO Declaration on Fundamental Principles and Rights at Work*, Geneva: ILO.

ILO [International Labour Organization] (2003), *Employment and Social Policy in Respect of Export Processing Zones* (EPZs), International Labour Office, GB.286/ESP/3, 286th Session Governing Body, Geneva, March, https://www.ilo.org/public/english/standards/relm/gb/docs/gb286/pdf/esp-3.pdf (accessed 12 December 2020).

ILO [International Labour Organization] (2004a), *Starting Right: Decent Work for Young People*, Background Paper to the Tripartite Meeting on Youth Employment: The Way Forward, TMYEWF/2004/, Geneva: ILO.

ILO [International Labour Organization] (2004b), *Conclusions of the Tripartite Meeting on Youth Employment: The Way Forward*, TMYEWF/2004/7, Geneva: ILO.

ILO [International Labour Organization] (2005), *Youth: Pathways to Decent Work: Report VI – Promoting Youth Employment, Tackling the Challenge*, Geneva: ILO.

ILO [International Labour Organization] (2008), *The Labour Principles of the United Nations Global Compact: A Guide for Business*, Geneva, International Labour Office, https://d306pr3pise04h.cloudfront.net/docs/issues_doc%2Flabour%2Fthe_labour_principles_a_guide_for_business.pdf (accessed 16 August 2020).

ILO [International Labour Organization] (2009), *Recovering from the Crisis: A Global Jobs Pact*, Geneva: ILO.

ILO [International Labour Organization] (2012a), *The Youth Employment Crisis: Time for Action*, Geneva: ILO.

ILO [International Labour Organization] (2012b), International Labour Conference 101st session, Committee on Youth Employment (C.E.J./D. 186), Geneva: ILO, https://www.ilo.org/wcmsp5/groups/public/---ed_norm/---relconf/documents/meetingdocument/wcms_182840.pdf (accessed 14 August 2019).

ILO [International Labour Organization] (2015a), *World Employment and Social Outlook 2015: The Changing Nature of Jobs*, Geneva: ILO.

ILO [International Labour Organization] (2015b), *Global Initiative on Decent Jobs for Youth: The Strategy Document*, Geneva: ILO.

ILO [International Labour Organization] (2016), *World Employment and Social Outlook 2016: Transforming Jobs to End Poverty*, Geneva: ILO.

ILO [International Labour Organization] (2017a), *Global Employment Trends for Youth 2017: Paths to a Better Working Future*, Geneva: ILO.

ILO [International Labour Organization] (2017b), *World Social Protection Report 2017–19: Universal Social Protection to Achieve the Sustainable Development Goals*, Geneva: ILO.

ILO [International Labour Organization] (2017c), *Multinational Enterprises and Social Policy*, Geneva: ILO.

ILO [International Labour Organization] (2020a), *Global Employment Trends for Youth 2020: Technology and the Future of Jobs*, Geneva: ILO.

ILO [International Labour Organization] (2020b), *ILO Monitor: COVID-19 and the World of Work* (5th edition), Geneva: ILO.

ILO [International Labour Organization] (n.d.), *Unemployment Rate*, Geneva: ILO, https://www.ilo.org/ilostat-files/Documents/description_UR_EN.pdf (accessed 2 February 2020).

ILO [International Labour Organization] (n.d.) *The ILO's Programme on Youth Employment*, https://www.ilo.org/wcmsp5/groups/public/---ed_emp/documents/publication/wcms_547338.pdf (accessed 16 August 2020).

ILO/IILS [International Labour Organization/International Institute of Labour Studies] (2011), *World of Work Report: Making Markets Work for Jobs*, Geneva: IILS.

ILO/IMF [International Labour Organization/International Monetary Fund] (2010), 'The challenges of growth, employment and social cohesion: discussion document', joint ILO–IMF conference in cooperation with the office of the Prime Minister of Norway, Oslo, Norway, 13 September.

IMF/IEO [International Monetary Fund/Independent Evaluation Office] (2011), *IEO Annual Report, 2011*, Washington, DC: IMF, https://www.imf.org/en/Publications/Independent-Evaluation-Office-Reports/Issues/2016/12/31/IEO-Annual-Report-2011-2490 (accessed 11 July 2020).

International Labour Office Evaluation Unit (2012), *Annual Evaluation Report 2011–12*, Geneva: ILO, https://www.ilo.org/wcmsp5/groups/public/---ed_mas/---eval/documents/publication/wcms_226358.pdf (accessed 19 August 2020).

Jakobi, A.P. (2009), 'Global education policy in the making: international organisations and lifelong learning', *Globalisation, Societies and Education*, 7 (4), 473–87.

Jenkins, M. (n.d.), 'Economic and social effects of export processing zones in Costa Rica', Working Paper No. 97, Geneva: ILO.

Jerven, M. (2013), *Poor Numbers: How We Are Misled by African Development Statistics and What To Do About It*, New York: Cornell University Press.

Jewkes, J. and Winterbottom, A. (1933), *Juvenile Unemployment*, London: Allen and Unwin.

Joshi, S. (2004), 'Tertiary sector-driven growth in India: impact on employment and poverty', *Economic and Political Weekly*, 39 (37), 4175–8.

Kaasch, A. and Martens, K. (eds) (2015), *Actors and Agency in Global Social Governance*, Oxford: Oxford University Press.

Kinsella, R. and Kinsella, M. (2011), 'The rise and rise of long term and youth unemployment in Ireland: the scarring of a generation', *Studies: An Irish Quarterly Review*, 100 (397), 83–102.

Kirk, N. (2003), *Comrades and Cousins: Globalisation, Workers and Labour Movements in Britain, the USA and Australia from the 1880s to 1914*, London: Merlin Press.

Kirk, N., MacRaild, D.M. and Nolan, M. (2009), 'Introduction: transnational ideas, activities and organisations in labour history, c.1860s to 1920', *Labour History Review*, 74 (3), 221–32.

Knowles, J., Pernia, E. and Racelis, M. (1999), *Social Consequences of the Financial Crisis in Asia*, Manila: Asia Development Bank.

Kose, M.A., Otrok, C. and Prasad, E. (2012), 'Global business cycles: convergence or decoupling?', *International Economic Review*, 53 (2), 511–38.

Kuchibhotla, M., Orazem, P.F. and Ravi, S. (2019), 'The scarring effects of youth joblessness in Sri Lanka', *Review of Development Economics*, 24 (1), 269–87.

Kurz, K., Buchhold, S., Schmelzer, P. and Blossfeld, H.-P. (2008), 'Young people's employment chances in flexible labour markets: a comparison of changes in eleven modern societies', in Blossfeld, H.-P., Buchholz, S., Bukodi, E. and Kurz, K. (eds), *Young Workers, Globalization and the Labor Market*, Cheltenham, UK and Northampton, MA, USA: Edward Elgar Publishing, pp. 337–54.

Lambregts, B., Beerepoot, N. and Kloosterman, R.C. (2016), 'The Local Impact of Services Offshoring in South and Southeast Asia: Introduction and Overview', in Lambregts, B., Beerepoot, N. and Kloosterman, R.C. (eds), *Local Impact of Globalization in South and Southeast Asia: Offshore business processes in services industries*, Abingdon: Routledge, pp. 1–14.

League of Nations (1924), *Geneva Declaration of the Rights of the Child*, adopted 26 September, Geneva: League of Nations, http://www.un-documents.net/gdrc1924.htm (accessed 19 August 2020).

Lee, K., Buse, K. and Fustukian, S. (eds) (2002), *Health Policy in a Globalising World*, Cambridge: Cambridge University Press.

Lee, S., Dwyer, J., Paul, E., Clarke, D., Treleaven, S. and Roseby, R. (2019), 'Differences by age and sex in adolescent suicide', *Australian and New Zealand Journal of Public Health*, 43 (3), 248–53.

Lenin, V.I. (1967), *V.I. Lenin on Youth*, Moscow: Progress Publishers.

Leschke, J. and Finn, M. (2019), 'Labor market flexibility and income security: changes for European youth during the Great Recession', in O'Reilly, J., Leschke, R.O., Seelib-Kaiser, M. and Villa, P. (eds), *Youth Labor in Transition*, New York: Oxford University Press, pp. 132–62.

Levy-Vroelant, C. (2010), 'Housing vulnerable groups: the development of a new public action sector', *International Journal of Housing Policy*, 10 (4), 443–56.

Li, H., Li, L., Wu, B. and Xiong, Y. (2012), 'The end of cheap Chinese labor', *Journal of Economic Perspectives*, 26 (4), 57–74.

Lim, L. and Fong, P.E. (1981), 'Technology choice and employment creation: A case study of three multinational enterprises in Singapore', Multinational Enterprises Programme Working Papers No. 16, Geneva: ILO. http://www.ilo.org/public/libdoc/ilo/1981/81B09_540_engl.pdf (accessed 28 January 2021).

Lin, J.Y. and Yu, M. (2015), 'Industrial upgrading and poverty reduction in China', in Naudé, W., Szirmai, A. and Haraguchi, N. (eds), *Structural Change and Industrial Development in the BRICS*, Oxford: Oxford University Press, pp. 93–118.

Livesey, F. (2018), 'Unpacking the possibilities of deglobalisation', *Cambridge Journal of Regions, Economy and Society*, 11 (1), 177–87.

London, B. and Ross, R. (1995), 'Political sociology of foreign direct investment: global capitalism and global mobility, 1965–1980', *International Journal of Comparative Sociology*, 36 (3–4), 198–218.

Lorentzen, T., Angelin, A., Dahl, E., Kauppinen, T., Moisio, P. and Salonen, T. (2014), 'Unemployment and economic security for young adults in Finland, Norway and Sweden: from unemployment protection to poverty relief', *International Journal of Social Welfare*, 23 (1), 41–51.

Lundberg, M., Weurmli, A. and World Bank (2012), *Children and Youth in Crisis: Protecting and Promoting Human Development in Times of Economic Shocks*, Washington, DC: World Bank.

Luxemburg, R. (1951), *The Accumulation of Capital*, London: Routledge.

Lydall, H. (1977), 'Unemployment in developing countries', World Employment Programme Research, Income Distribution and Employment Programme series, Working Paper, ILO-WEP 2-23/WP 50, Geneva: ILO.

Lynch, L.M. (1989), 'The youth labor market in the eighties: determinants of re-employment probabilities for young men and women', *The Review of Economics and Statistics*, 71 (1), 37–45.

MacDonald, R. (1994), 'Fiddly jobs, undeclared working and the something for nothing society', *Work, Employment and Society*, 8 (4), 507–30.

MacDonald, R. and Marsh, J. (2001), 'Disconnected youth?', *Journal of Youth Studies*, 4 (4), 373–91.

MacDonald, R. and Marsh, J. (2005), *Disconnected Youth? Growing Up in Britain's Poor Neighbourhoods*, Basingstoke: Palgrave Macmillan.

Madsen, P.K. (2015), 'Youth unemployment and the skills mismatch in Denmark', Directorate General for Internal Policies, Aalborg, Denmark: Aalborg University.

Mai, V.M. (2014), *The Capacity of Welfare Regimes to Absorb Macro-Economic Shocks: National Differences in the Development of Unemployment, Poverty and the Distribution of Income in the Aftermath of the Financial Crisis 2008*, Hamburg: Anchor Academic Publishing.

Majumder, S. and Sharma, R.P. (2014), 'Indian ITES industry going rural: the road ahead', *Journal of Business and Economic Policy*, 1 (2), 79–84.

Marasigan, M.L.C. (2016), 'How work in the BPO sector affects employability', in Lambregts, B., Beerepot, N. and Kloosterman, R.C. (eds), *The Local Impact of Services Offshoring in South and Southeast Asia: Offshore Business Processes in Services Industries*, Abingdon: Routledge, pp. 138–52.

Marconi, G., Beblavý, M. and Maselli, I. (2016), 'Age effects in Okun's law with different indicators of unemployment', *Applied Economics Letters*, 23 (8), 580–83.

Mars, B., Heron, J., Crane, C., Hawton, K., Lewis, G., Macleod, J., Tilling, K. and Gunnell, D. (2014), 'Clinical and social outcomes of adolescent self-harm: population-based birth cohort study', *British Medical Journal*, 349, g5954.

Martens, K., Niemann, D. and Kaasch, A. (eds) (2020), *International Organisations in Global Social Governance*, Basingstoke: Palgrave Macmillan.

Marx, K. (1887), 'Capital: A Critique of Political Economy', *Volume I Book One: The Process of Production of Capital*, https://www.marxists.org/archive/marx/works/download/pdf/Capital-Volume-I.pdf (accessed 6 February 2020).

Maul, D. (2019), *The International Labour Organization: 100 years of Global Social Policy*, Berlin: De Gruyter/ILO.

Mayer, T., Moorti, S. and McCallum, J.K. (eds) (2019), *The Crisis of Global Youth Unemployment*, London: Routledge.

Mazower, M. (2012), *Governing the World: The History of an Idea*, London: Penguin.

Melvyn, P. (1977), 'Youth unemployment: roots and remedies', World Employment Programme Research Working Paper, Youth Unemployment in Industrialised Market Economies series, ILO-EMP 47-1/WP.3, Geneva: ILO.

Miller, S.K. (2001), *Creating Decent Work for Young People: Policy Recommendations of the UN Secretary-General's Youth Employment Network*, Geneva: ILO.

Mills, C.W. (1959), *The Sociological Imagination*, New York: Oxford University Press.

Mittelman, J. (1995), 'Rethinking the international division of labour in the context of globalisation', *Third World Quarterly*, 16 (2), 273–95.

Mizen, P. (2003), 'The best days of your life? Youth, policy and Blair's New Labour', *Critical Social Policy*, 23 (4), 453–76.

Mizen, P. (2004), *The Changing State of Youth*, Basingstoke: Palgrave Macmillan.

Mojsoska-Blazevski, N., Petreski, M. and Bojadziev, M.I. (2017), 'Youth survival in the labour market: employment scarring in three transition economies', *The Economic and Labour Relations Review*, 28 (2), 312–31.

Morrell, S., Taylor, R., Quine, S., Kerr, C. and Western, J. (1994), 'A cohort study of unemployment as a cause of psychological disturbance in Australian youth', *Social Science and Medicine*, 38 (11), 1553–64.

Muncie, J. (2015), *Youth and Crime* (4th edition), London: Sage.

Munck, R. (2002), *Globalisation and Labour: The New 'Great Transformation'*, London: Zed Books.

Munck, R. and Waterman, P. (1999), *Labour Worldwide in the Era of Globalization*, Basingstoke: Macmillan.

Murray, A. (2017), 'The effect of import competition on employment in Canada: evidence from the "China Shock"', Centre for the Study of Living Standards Research Report 2017-03, July, Ottawa, ON: CSLS, http://www.csls.ca/reports/csls2017-03.pdf (accessed 15 August 2020).

Musson, A.E. (1959), 'The great depression in Britain, 1873–1896: a reappraisal', *The Journal of Economic History*, 19 (2), 199–228.

Nilsen, Ø.A. and Reiso, K.H. (2014), 'Scarring effects of early-career unemployment', *Nordic Economic Policy Review*, 1, 13–46.

O'Brien, R. (2014), 'Global labour policy', in Yeates, N. (ed.), *Understanding Global Social Policy* (2nd edition), Bristol: Policy Press, pp. 131–58.

O'Brien, R., Goetz, A.M., Scholte, J. and Williams, M. (2000), *Contesting Global Governance: Multilateral Economic Institutions and Global Social Movements*, Cambridge: Cambridge University Press.

OECD [Organisation for Economic Cooperation and Development] (2014), *Society at a Glance 2014: OECD Social Indicators: The Crisis and Its Aftermath*, Paris: OECD.

Ofreneo, R.E. (2016), 'Exclusion in Asia's evolving global production and service outsourcing', in Lambregts, B., Beerepoot, N. and Kloosterman, R.C. (eds), *The Local Impact of Services Offshoring in South and Southeast Asia: Offshore Business Processes in Services Industries*, Abingdon: Routledge, pp. 123–37.

O'Higgins, N. (2012), 'This time it's different? Youth labour markets during "the Great Recession"', *Comparative Economic Studies*, 54 (2), 395–412.

Okun, A.M. (1962), 'Potential GNP: its measurement and significance', *Proceedings of the Business and Economics Statistics Section*, Washington, DC: American Statistical Association.

O'Leary, E. and Negra, D. (2019), 'Irish youth unemployment and emigration, 2009–2014', in Mayer, T., Moorti, S. and McCallum, J.K. (eds), *The Crisis of Youth Unemployment*, London: Routledge, pp. 123–39.

Omori, Y. (1997), 'Stigma effects of nonemployment', *Economic Inquiry*, 35 (2), 394–416.

Ong, A. (1987), *Spirits of Resistance and Capitalist Discipline: Factory Women in Malaysia*, New York: State University of New York Press.

ONS [Office for National Statistics] (2020), *GDP First Quarterly Estimate, UK: April–June 2020*, London: ONS.

Orenstein, M.A. (2008), *Privatizing Pensions: The Transnational Campaign for Social Security Reform*, Princeton, NJ: Princeton University Press.

Osborne, D. and Gaebler, T. (1992), *Reinventing Government: How the Entrepreneurial Spirit is Transforming the Public Sector*, Oxford: Berg/Addison-Wesley.

Oshri, I., Kotlarsky, J. and Willcocks, L. (2011), *The Handbook of Global Outsourcing and Offshoring*, Basingstoke: Palgrave Macmillan.

Palier, B. and Thelen, K. (2010), 'Institutionalizing dualism: complementarities and change in France and Germany', *Politics and Society*, 38 (1), 119–48.

Papadopoulos, T. and Roumpakis, A. (2012), 'The Greek welfare state in the age of austerity: anti-social policy and the politico-economic crisis', in Kilkey, M., Ramia, G. and Farnsworth, K. (eds), *Social Policy Review 24: Analysis and Debate in Social Policy*, Bristol: Policy Press, pp. 205–30.

Peck, J. (2001), *Workfare States*, New York: Guilford Publications.

Pedersen, S. (2015), *The Guardians: The League of Nations and the Crisis of Empire*, Oxford: Oxford University Press.

Petreski, M., Mojsoska-Blazevski, N. and Bergolo, M. (2017), 'Labor-market scars when youth unemployment is extremely high: evidence from Macedonia', *Eastern European Economics*, 55 (2), 168–96.

Petzina, D. (1986), 'The extent and causes of unemployment in the Weimar Republic', in Stachura, D. (ed.), *Unemployment and the Great Depression in Weimar Germany*, London: Palgrave Macmillan, pp. 29–48.

Pierson, C. (1991), *Beyond the Welfare State? The New Political Economy of Welfare*, Cambridge: Polity Press.

Pollitt, C. (1990), *Managerialism and the Public Services: The Anglo-American Experience*, Oxford: Blackwell.

Power, E., Clarke, M., Kelleher, I., Coughlan, H., Lynch, F., Connor, D., Fitzpatrick, C., Harley, M. and Cannon, M. (2015), 'The association between economic inactivity and mental health among young people: a longitudinal study of young adults who are not in employment, education or training', *Irish Journal of Psychological Medicine*, 32 (1), 155–60.

Pratap, S. (2014), *Emerging Trends in Factory Asia: International Capital Mobility, Global Value Chains, and the Labour Movement*, Hong Kong: Asia Monitor Resource Centre, https://amrc.org .hk/sites/default/files/Emerging%20Trends%20in%20Factory%20Asia.pdf (accessed 15 December 2019).

Prince, H., Halasa-Rappel, Y. and Khan, A. (2018), 'Economic growth, youth unemployment, and political and social instability: a study of policies and outcomes in post-Arab Spring Egypt, Morocco, Jordan, and Tunisia', Working Paper 2018-12, Geneva: United Nations Research Institute for Social Development.

Ramos-Díaz, J. and Varela, A. (2012), 'From opportunity to austerity: crisis and social policy in Spain', in Kilkey, M., Ramia, G. and Farnsworth, K. (eds), *Social Policy Review 24: Analysis and Debate in Social Policy*, Bristol: Policy Press, pp. 231–56.

Reinalda, B. (2009), *Routledge History of International Organizations: From 1815 to the Present Day*, London: Routledge.

Reinhart, C.M. and Rogoff, K.S. (2008a), 'This time is different: a panoramic view of eight centuries of financial crises', Working Paper No. 13882, Cambridge, MA: National Bureau of Economic Research.

Reinhart, C.M. and Rogoff, K.S. (2008b), 'Is the 2007 US sub-prime financial crisis so different? An international historical comparison', *American Economic Review*, 98 (2), 339–44.

Reinhart, C.M. and Rogoff, K.S. (2009), 'The aftermath of financial crises', *American Economic Review*, 99 (2), 466–72.

Remesh, B.P. (2008), 'Work organisation, control and "empowerment": managing the contradictions of call centre work', in Upadhya, C. and Vasavi, A.R. (eds), *In an Outpost of the Global Economy: Work and Workers in India's Information Technology Industry*, London: Routledge, pp. 235–62.

Roberts, K. (1984), *School-leavers and Their Prospects: Youth in the Labour Market in the 1980s*, Milton Keynes: Open University Press.

Rodgers, G., Lee, E., Swepston, L. and Van Daele, J. (2009), *The International Labour Organization and the Quest for Social Justice, 1919–2009*, Michigan: International Labour Office.

Rose, N. (1989), *Governing the Soul: The Shaping of the Private Self*, London: Routledge.

Rose, N. (1999), *Powers of Freedom: Reframing Political Thought*, Cambridge: Cambridge University Press.

Rosen, D.M. (2005), *Armies of the Young: Child Soldiers in War and Terrorism*, London: Rutgers University Press.

Rosenberg, H. (1943), 'Political consequences of the Great Depression of 1873–1896 in Central Europe', *Economic History Review*, a13 (1–2), 58–73.

Ruggie, J. (1982), 'International regimes, transactions, and change: embedded liberalism in the post-war economic order', *International Organization*, 36 (2), 195–231.

S4YE [Solutions for Youth Employment] (2015), *Towards Solutions for Youth Employment: A 2015 Baseline Report*, Washington, DC: S4YE.

Sabolo, Y. (1975), 'Employment and unemployment, 1960–90', *International Labour Review*, 112 (6), 401–17.

Safa, H.I. (2013), 'Women and industrialisation in the Caribbean', in Stitcher, S. and Parpart, J. (eds), *Women, Employment and the Family in the International Division of Labour*, Basingstoke: Palgrave Macmillan, pp. 72–97.

Salaff, J.W. (2013), 'Women, the family and the state: Hong Kong, Taiwan, Singapore – newly industri-alised countries in Asia', in Stitcher, S. and Parpart, J. (eds), *Women, Employment and the Family in the International Division of Labour*, Basingstoke: Palgrave Macmillan, pp. 98–136.

Scarpetta, S., Sonnet, A. and Manfredi, T. (2010), 'Rising youth unemployment during the crisis: how to prevent negative long-term consequences on a generation?', OECD Social, Employment and Migration Working Papers, Issue 106, Paris: OECD.

Schmelzer, P. (2011), 'Unemployment in early career in the UK: a trap or a stepping stone?', *Acta Sociologica*, 54 (3), 251–65.

Schmidt, D. and Hassanien, D. (2011), 'In need of a future: causes and consequences of high youth unemployment – the case of North Africa', in Humanity in Action Denmark (ed.), *Youth for Democracy – Learning from Nonviolent Struggles around the World*, Copenhagen: Humanity in Action Denmark, https://www.humanityinaction.org/wp-content/uploads/2019/06/YouthF orDemocracyAnthology.pdf (accessed 11 August 2020).

Schneider, G. (1977), 'Youth unemployment: social aspects and attitudes', World Employment Programme Research Working Paper, Youth Unemployment in Industrialised Market Economies series, ILO-EMP 47-1/WP.1, Geneva: ILO.

Schoenbaum, T.J. (2012), *The Age of Austerity*, Cheltenham, UK and Northampton, MA, USA: Edward Elgar Publishing.

Silver, B. (2003), *Forces of Labor: Workers' Movements and Globalization since 1870*, Cambridge: Cambridge University Press.

Simmons, R., Thompson, R. and Russell, L. (2014), *Education, Work and Social Change: Young People and Marginalization in Post-industrial Britain*, Basingstoke: Palgrave Macmillan.

Singerman, D. (2013), 'Youth, gender, and dignity in the Egyptian uprising', *Journal of Middle East Women's Studies*, 9 (3), 1–27.

Sloam, J. (2014), 'New voice, less equal: the civic and political engagement of young people in the United States and Europe', *Comparative Political Studies*, 47 (5), 663–88.

Somavia, J./ILO (2012a), 'Director-General's opening address to the 101st International Labour Conference', 30 May, Geneva: ILO, https://www.ilo.org/global/about-the-ilo/newsroom/statements -and-speeches/WCMS_181894/lang--en/index.htm (accessed 19 August 2020).

Somavia, J./ILO (2012b), 'Director-General's address to the plenary of the 101st International Labour Conference', 6 June, Geneva: ILO, https://www.ilo.org/global/about-the-ilo/media-centre/statements -and-speeches/WCMS_182362/lang--en/index.htm (accessed 19 August 2020).

Song, J. (2012), 'Economic distress, labor market reforms, and dualism in Japan and Korea', *Governance*, 25 (3), 415–38.

Stachura, P.D. (1986), 'The social and welfare implications of youth unemployment in Weimar Germany, 1929–1933', in Stachura, P.D. (ed.), *Unemployment and the Great Depression in Weimar Germany*, London: Palgrave Macmillan, pp. 121–47.

Standing, G. (1999), *Global Labour Flexibility: Seeking Distributive Justice*, Basingstoke: Palgrave Macmillan.

Standing, G. (2011), *The Precariat: The New Dangerous Class*, London: Bloomsbury.

Stitcher, S. (2013), 'Women, employment and the family: current debates', in Stitcher, S. and Parpart, J. (eds), *Women, Employment and the Family in the International Division of Labour*, Basingstoke: Palgrave Macmillan, pp. 11–71.

Strandh, M., Nilsson, K., Nordlund, M. and Hammarström, A. (2015), 'Do open youth unemployment and youth programs leave the same mental health scars? Evidence from a Swedish 27-year cohort study', *BMC Public Health*, 15 (1), 1151–60.

Sukarieh, M. and Tannock, S. (2015), *Youth Rising? The Politics of Youth in the Global Economy*, New York and London: Routledge.

Tawney, R.H. (1909), 'Economics of boy labour', *Economic Journal*, 19 (76), 517–37.

Taylor, M. (ed.) (2011), *Renewing International Labour Studies*, London: Routledge.

Thelen, K. and Kume, I. (1999), 'The effects of globalization on labor revisited: lessons from Germany and Japan', *Politics and Society*, 27 (4), 477–505.

Thérien, J.-P. and Pouliot, V. (2006), 'The global compact: shifting the politics of international development?', *Global Governance*, 12 (1), 55–75.

Thompson, H. (2018), 'We are not in Kansas anymore: economic and political shocks', in Hay, C. and Hunt, T. (eds), *The Coming Crisis: Building a Sustainable Political Economy*, London: Palgrave Macmillan, pp. 11–16.

Tiano, S. (1990), 'Maquiladora women: a new category of workers?', in Ward, K. (ed.), *Women Workers and Global Restructuring*, Ithaca, NY: Cornell University Press, pp. 193–223.

Tooze, A. (2018), *Crashed: How a Decade of Financial Crises Changed the World*, London: Allen Lane.

Toro, P.A., Lesperance, T.M. and Braciszewski, J.M. (2011), 'The heterogeneity of homeless youth in America: examining typologies', Washington, DC: Homelessness Research Institute, pp. 1–13.

Torres, E. (2014), 'Philippines: a Magna Carta for call centre workers', *Equal Times*, 28 February, https://www.equaltimes.org/philippines-a-magna-carta-for-call?lang=en#.XXEhM0xFyM- (accessed 5 September 2019).

Tschang, T. (2011), *The Philippines' IT-enabled Services Industry*, Singapore: Lee Kong Chian School of Business, Singapore Management University, http://siteresources.worldbank.org/INTPHILIPPINES/Resources/Tschang-word.pdf (accessed 5 September 2019).

Turnham, D. (1973), 'Empirical evidence of open unemployment in developing countries', in Jolly, R. (ed.), *Third World Employment, Problems and Strategy*, London: Penguin, pp. 42–54.

Tyler, D.I. (2013), *Revolting Subjects: Social Abjection and Resistance in Neoliberal Britain*, London: Zed Books.

Tzannatos, Z., Haq, T. and Schmidt, D. (2011), 'The labour market in the Arab states: recent trends, policy responses and future challenges', in International Labour Office (ed.), *The Global Crisis: Causes, Responses and Challenges*, Geneva: ILO, pp. 51–65.

UK Government (1942), *Social Insurance and Allied Services* (Cmd. 6404), https://www.nationalarchives.gov.uk/wp-content/uploads/2014/03/prem-4-891.jpg (accessed 19 August 2020).

UN [United Nations] (1945), *Charter of the United Nations*, signed 26 June 1945, effective 24 October 1945, New York: UN, https://www.un.org/en/charter-united-nations/index.html (accessed 19 August 2020).

UN [United Nations] (1948), *Universal Declaration of Human Rights* (A/RES/217(III) A), New York: UN.

UN [United Nations] (1949), *National and International Measures for Full Employment*, Report by a Group of Experts appointed by the Secretary-General, E/1584, New York: UN.

UN [United Nations] (1959), *Declaration of the Rights of the Child*, New York: UN.

UN [United Nations] (1966), *International Covenant on Economic, Social and Cultural Rights (ICESCR)*, New York: UN.

UN [United Nations] (1969), *Declaration on Social Progress and Development*, New York: UN.

UN [United Nations] (1971a), *1970 Report on the World Social Situation*, New York: UN.

UN [United Nations] (1971b), *World Economic Survey, 1969–1970: The Developing Countries in the 1960s, the Problem of Appraising Progress*, New York: UN.

UN [United Nations] (1972), *World Economic Survey 1971: Current Economic Developments*, E/5144 ST/ECA/159, New York: UN.

UN [United Nations] (1995), *Copenhagen Declaration on Social Development and Programme of Action*, A/CONF.166/9, New York: UN.

UN [United Nations] (2000), *Millennium Declaration*, A/RES/55/2, New York: UN.

UN [United Nations] (2013), *System-wide Action Plan on Youth* (Youth-SWAP), New York: UN, https://www.unsystem.org/content/un-system-wide-action-plan-youth (accessed 2 July 2020).

UN [United Nations] (2015), *End Poverty: Millennium Development Goals and Beyond 2015*, New York: UN, https://www.un.org/millenniumgoals/poverty.shtml (accessed 2 July 2020).

UN [United Nations] (2018), *Youth 2030: Working with and for Young People: UN Youth Strategy*, New York: UN, https://www.un.org/youthenvoy/youth-un/ (accessed 19 August 2020).

UN [United Nations] (2020), *Sustainable Development Goals: Decade of Action*, New York: UN, https://www.un.org/sustainabledevelopment/decade-of-action/ (accessed 2 July 2020).

UN Department of Economic Affairs (1949), 'National and international measures for full employment, Report by a group of experts appointed by the Secretary-General', Working Paper E/1584, New York: UN.

UNDESA [UN Department of Economic and Social Affairs] (2007), *Young People's Transitions into Adulthood: Progress and Change*, New York: United Nations.

UNDP [United Nations Development Programme], Rockefeller Philanthropy Advisors and Leading Foundations (2014), 'Post-2015 Partnership Platform for Philanthropy', New York: UNDP, https://www.undp.org/content/undp/en/home/presscenter/pressreleases/2014/11/20/undp-foundation-center-and-rpa-partner-with-leading-foundations-to-engage-philanthropic-sector-in-post-2015-global-development-process-.html (accessed 22 August 2020).

UNESCO [United Nations Educational, Scientific and Cultural Organization] (1951), *Recommendation No. 32 concerning Compulsory Education and its Prolongation*, Paris: IBE/UNESCO, http://www.ibe.unesco.org/sites/default/files/R32.pdf (accessed 19 August 2020).

UNESCO [United Nations Educational, Scientific and Cultural Organization] (1963), *Recommendation No. 56 to the Ministries of Education concerning the Organisation of Educational and Vocational*

Guidance, Paris: IBE/UNESCO, http://www.ibe.unesco.org/sites/default/files/R56.pdf (accessed 19 August 2020).

UNESCO [United Nations Educational, Scientific and Cultural Organization] (1973), *Revision of the Recommendation Concerning Technical and Vocational Education*, ED/MD/28, Paris: UNESCO, 14 September, https://unesdoc.unesco.org/ark:/48223/pf0000005523?posInSet=1andqueryId=3c84cb81-1247-4fbf-af61-d522bafc2bf2 (accessed 19 August 2020).

UNESCO [United Nations Educational, Scientific and Cultural Organization] (1979), *International Conference on Education: Recommendations, 1934–77*, Paris: UNESCO.

UNESCO [United Nations Educational, Scientific and Cultural Organization] (1984), *Informal Consultation to Advise on the Research on the Nature, the Causes and the Consequences of Youth Unemployment*, UNESCO Paris, 25–27 April 1984. Final Report, SHS-84/WS/42, Paris: UNESCO.

UNESCO [United Nations Educational, Scientific and Cultural Organization] (1985), 'Social Sciences, and the Nature, Causes and Consequences of Youth Unemployment in Europe', Meeting of Experts on Youth Unemployment, 18–20 September 1985. SHS/85/Conf.615/6, Paris: UNESCO.

UNESCO [United Nations Educational, Scientific and Cultural Organization] (1998a), *Braga Youth Action Plan*. Third World Youth Forum of the UN System, Braga, Portugal, 1–7 August 1998. Paris: UNESCO, http://portal.unesco.org/en/ev.php-URL_ID=22125andURL_DO=DO_TOPICandURL_SECTION=201.html (accessed 19 August 2020).

UNESCO [United Nations Educational, Scientific and Cultural Organization] (1998b), *Lisbon Declaration on Youth Policies and Programmes*, Lisbon, Portugal, 12 August 1998, https://www.youthpolicy.org/library/wp-content/uploads/library/1998_Lisbon_Declaration_Eng.pdf#:~:text=Lisbon%20Declaration%20on%20Youth%20Policies%20and%20Programmes%20Lisbon%2C,in%20its%20resolution%201997%2F55%20have%20welcomed%20the%20 (accessed 19 August 2020).

UNESCO [and Uganda Youth Development Link (UYDEL)] (2006), *Non-Formal Education and Livelihood Skills for Marginalised Street and Slum Youth in Uganda*, Kampala: UYDEL/UNESCO.

UNESCO and Kazancigil, A. (1985), 'Youth: ways of life, work and employment, research trends', *International Social Science Journal*, 38 (106), 425–6.

UNGA [United Nations General Assembly] (1971), 'Youth, its problems and needs, and its participation in social development', A/RES/2770 (XXVI), New York: UN.

UNGA [United Nations General Assembly] (1974a), *Declaration on the Establishment of a New International Economic Order*, A/RES/3201 (S-VI), New York: UN.

UNGA [United Nations General Assembly] (1974b), *Programme of Action on the Establishment of a New International Economic Order*, A/RES/3202 (S-VI), New York: UN.

UNGA [United Nations General Assembly] (1980), *Third United Nations Development Decade*, A/RES/35/56, New York: UN.

UNGA [United Nations General Assembly] (1981), *Youth Rights to Education and to Work*, A/RES/36/29, New York: UN.

UNGA [United Nations General Assembly] (1985), *Opportunities for Youth*, A/RES/40/16, New York: UN.

UNGA [United Nations General Assembly] (1986), *Youth Rights to Education and to Work*, A/RES/41/98, New York: UN.

UNGA [United Nations General Assembly] (1987), *Opportunities for Youth*, A/RES/42/53, New York: UN.

UNGA [United Nations General Assembly] (1990), *Policies and Programmes Involving Youth*, A/RES/45/103, New York: UN.

UNGA [United Nations General Assembly] (1991), *International Cooperation for the Eradication of Poverty in Developing Countries*, A/RES/46/141, New York: UN.

UNGA [United Nations General Assembly] (1995), *World Programme of Action for Youth*, A/RES/50/81, New York: UN.

UNGA [United Nations General Assembly] (1999), *Policies and Programmes Involving Youth*, A/RES/54/120, New York: UN.

UNGA [United Nations General Assembly] (2001), *Towards Global Partnership for Youth*, A/RES/56/76, New York: UN.

UNGA [United Nations General Assembly] (2007), *Promoting Youth Participation in Social and Economic Development*, A/RES/62/126, New York: UN.

UNGA [United Nations General Assembly] (2009), *Policies and Programmes Involving Youth*, A/RES/64/130, New York: UN.

UNGA [United Nations General Assembly] (2011a), *High-level Meeting of the General Assembly on Youth: Dialogue and Mutual Understanding*, A/RES/65/312, New York: UN.

UNGA [United Nations General Assembly] (2011b), *Policies and Programmes Involving Youth*, A/RES/66/121, New York: UN.

UNGA [United Nations General Assembly] (2013), *Policies and Programmes Involving Youth*, A/RES/68/130, New York: UN.

UNGA [United Nations General Assembly] (2014), *World Youth Skills Day*, A/RES/69/145, New York: UN.

UNGA [United Nations General Assembly] (2020), *Entrepreneurship for Sustainable Development*, A/RES/75/211, 21st December 2020. New York: United Nations.

UNICEF [United Nations International Children's Emergency Fund] (2018), *UNICEF and Young People: A Generation Full of Potential and the Power to Change the World*, New York: UNICEF, https://www.unicef.org/young-people (accessed 2 July 2020).

UNRISD [United Nations Research Institute for Social Development] (2016), *Policy Innovations for Transformative Change*, UNRISD 2016 Flagship Report, https://www.unrisd.org/flagship2016 (accessed 18 August 2020).

UNSG [United Nations Secretary-General] (1985), *Situation of Youth in the 1980s*, A/40/64, E/1985/5 January 1985, New York: UN.

UNSG [United Nations Secretary-General] (1987), *Policies and Programmes involving Young People: Participation, Development, Peace*, A/42/595, October 1987, New York: UN.

UNSG [United Nations Secretary-General] (2013), *Report of the Secretary-General on Enhanced Cooperation between the United Nations and all Relevant Partners, in Particular the Private Sector*, A/68/326, New York: UN.

Upadhya, C. and Vasavi, A.R. (2006), *Work, Culture and Sociality in the Indian IT Industry: A Sociological Study*, Final Report submitted to IDPAD. Bangalore: National Institute of Advanced Studies.

Upadhya, C. and Vasavi, A.R. (2008), 'Outposts of the global information economy: work and workers in India's outsourcing industry', in Upadhya, C. and Vasavi, A.R. (eds), *An Outpost of the Global Economy: Work and Workers in India's Information Technology Industry*, London: Routledge, pp. 9–49.

van Bergeijk, P.A.G. (2017), 'One is not enough! An economic history perspective on world trade collapses and deglobalization', International Institute of Social Studies, Working Paper No. 628, Rotterdam: IISS.

Van Berkel, R. (2010), 'The provision of income protection and activation services for the unemployed in "active" welfare states: an international comparison', *Journal of Social Policy*, 39 (1), 17–34.

Van den Bree, M.B., Shelton, K., Bonner, A., Moss, S., Thomas, H. and Taylor, P.J. (2009), 'A longitudinal population-based study of factors in adolescence predicting homelessness in young adulthood', *Journal of Adolescent Health*, 45 (6), 571–8.

Van der Linden, M. (2003), *Transnational Labour History*, Aldershot: Ashgate.

Van der Linden, M. (ed.) (2008), *Workers of the World: Essays toward a Global Labor History*, Leiden: Brill.

Van der Ploeg, J. and Scholte, E. (1997), *Homeless Youth*, London: Sage.

Van Ginneken, W. (1999), *Social Security for the Excluded Majority: Case Studies of Developing Countries*, Geneva: ILO.

Vasavi, A.R. (2008), 'Serviced from India: the making of India's global youth workforce', in Upadhya, C. and Vasavi, A.R. (eds), *An Outpost of the Global Economy: Work and Workers in India's Information Technology Industry*, London: Routledge, pp. 211–34.

Verick, S. (2009), 'Who is hit hardest during a financial crisis? The vulnerability of young men and women to unemployment in an economic downturn', Discussion Paper No. 4359, Bonn: IZA.

Verick, S. (2011), 'The impact of the global financial crisis on labour markets in OECD countries: why youth and other vulnerable groups have been hit hard', in Islam, R. and Verick, S. (eds), *From the Great Recession to Labour Market Recovery*, London: Palgrave Macmillan, pp. 119–45.

Versailles, Treaty of (1919), signed 28 June, entered into force 10 January 1920, Versailles, France.

Vodopivec, M. (2006), 'Choosing a system of unemployment income support: guidelines for developing and transition countries', *The World Bank Research Observer*, 21 (1), 49–89.

Vogel, P. (2015), *Generation Jobless? Turning the Youth Unemployment Crisis into Opportunity*, Basingstoke: Palgrave Macmillan.

Wacquant, L. (2009), *Punishing the Poor: The Neoliberal Government of Social Insecurity*, Durham, NC and London: Duke University Press.

Wallace, C. (1987), *For Richer, for Poorer: Growing Up In and Out of Work*, London: Tavistock.

Wallerstein, I.M. (1974), *The Modern World-System*, New York: Academic Press.

Wallerstein, I.M. (2004), *World-Systems Analysis: An Introduction*, Durham, NC: Duke University Press.

Walters, W. (2000), *Unemployment and Government: Genealogies of the Social*, Cambridge: Cambridge University Press.

Ward, K. (1984), *Women in the World-System*, New York: Praeger Publishers.

Watanabe, H.R. (2018), 'Labour market dualism and diversification in Japan', *British Journal of Industrial Relations*, 56 (3), 579–602.

Watson, K. (1983), *Youth, Education and Employment: International Perspectives*, London: Croom Helm.

Webel, M. and Culler Freeman, M. (2020), 'Compare the flu pandemic of 1918 and COVID-19 with caution – the past is not a prediction', *The Conversation*, 4 June, https://theconversation.com/compare-the-flu-pandemic-of-1918-and-covid-19-with-caution-the-past-is-not-a-prediction-138895 (accessed 19 August 2020).

Webster, C., Simpson, D., MacDonald, R., Abbas, A., Simpson, M., Shildrick, T. and Cieslik, M. (2004), *Poor Transitions: Social Exclusion and Young Adults*, Bristol: Policy Press.

Weiss, T.G. and Wilkinson, R. (2014), 'International organisation and global governance: what matters and why', in Weiss, T.G. and Wilkinson, R. (eds), *International Organisation and Global Governance*, London: Routledge, pp. 3–22.

Whitbeck, L.B., Hoyt, D.R. and Yoder, K.A. (1999), 'A risk-amplification model of victimization and depressive symptoms among runaway and homeless adolescents', *American Journal of Community Psychology*, 27 (2), 273–96.

Woodin, T., McCulloch, G. and Cowar, S. (2013), *Secondary Education and the Raising of the School Leaving Age: Coming of Age?*, Basingstoke: Palgrave Macmillan.

World Bank (2006), *World Development Report 2007: Development and the Next Generation*, Washington, DC: World Bank.

World Bank (2010), 'Active labor market programs for youth: a framework to guide youth employment interventions', World Bank Employment Policy Primer No. 16, Washington, DC: World Bank.

World Bank (2011), *Social Protection and Labor Strategy 2012–2022: Resilience, Equity and Opportunity*, Washington, DC: World Bank.

World Bank (2012), *World Development Report 2013: Jobs*, Washington, DC: World Bank.

World Bank (2015), *Global Financing Facility in Support of Every Woman Every Child: Business Plan*, Washington, DC: World Bank, http://pubdocs.worldbank.org/en/598311437686176148/1515268-GFF-Business-Plan.pdf (accessed 25 June 2020).

World Bank (2016), *World Development Report: Digital Dividends*, Washington, DC: World Bank.

World Bank Independent Evaluation Group (2013), 'Youth employment programs: an evaluation of World Bank and international finance corporation support', Washington, DC: World Bank.

Wright, L., Head, J. and Jivraj, S. (2019), 'What moderates the scarring effect of youth unemployment on later life mental health?', *Journal of Epidemiology and Community Health*, 73 (Supplement 1), A6.

Yeates, N. (1999), 'Social politics and policy in an era of globalisation', *Social Policy and Administration*, 33 (4), 372–93.

Yeates, N. (2001), *Globalisation and Social Policy*, London: Sage.

Yeates, N. (2002), 'Globalization and social policy: from global neoliberal hegemony to global political pluralism', *Global Social Policy*, 2 (1), 69–91.

Yeates, N. (2007), 'The global and supra-national dimensions of the welfare mix', in Powell, M. (ed.), *Understanding the Mixed Economy of Welfare*, Bristol: Policy Press, pp. 199–219.

Yeates, N. (ed.) (2014), *Understanding Global Social Policy*, 2nd edition, Bristol: Policy Press.

Yeates, N. (2018), 'Global approaches to social policy: a survey of analytical methods', United Nations Research Institute for Social Development Thematic Paper, New Directions in Social Policy Series, WP 2018-2. Geneva: UNRISD.

Yeates, N. and Holden, C. (eds) (forthcoming), *Understanding Global Social Policy* (3rd edition), Bristol: Policy Press.

Yeates, N. and Pillinger, J. (2019), *International Health Worker Migration and Recruitment: Global Governance, Politics and Policy*, London: Routledge.

Zanin, L. (2014), 'On Okun's law in OECD countries: an analysis by age cohorts', *Economics Letters*, 125 (2), 243–8.

Zuccotti, C.V. and O'Reilly, J. (2019), 'Do scarring effects vary by ethnicity and gender?', in O'Reilly, J., Leschke, R.O., Seelib-Kaiser, M. and Villa, P. (eds), *Youth Labor in Transition*, New York: Oxford University Press, pp. 560–96.

Index

Please note:
Terms in footnotes and appendices are included in the index, referenced by page number.
At country income group, continent and world-region levels, readers should also look up the names of individual countries listed.

inequality / inequalities 1, 14, 15, 17, 36, 68,
    175, 202, 215
    economic inequality and social protests 33,
        34,
    family support and unemployed young
        people 7
    and GenU 202
    global dynamics of 15
    and the global youth workforce 60, 72, 74,
        75, 77, 99, 212–13
    and ITES/BPO sector employment 64, 67,
        74
    see also age; disabilities; gender; social class
informal economy workers 1, 3, 5–6, 7, 19, 49,
    57, 65–8, 74–5, 77, 78, 88–9, 102, 214,
    220, 225, 227
    as excluded workers 48–9
    and global economic governance 186
    and the global reserve army of youth labour
        (GRAoYL) 90
    ILO data on 48, 99
    and social protection 31–2
    and unemployment rates and totals 87–8
information and communications technology
        (ICT) 38–9
    and the global services economy 63–4
    global youth workforce 64–5, 74–5
information technology-enabled services (ITES)
    call centres 64
    global youth workforce 64–5, 67, 68, 69–70,
        74, 75
INGOs *see* international non-governmental
    organisations
intergenerational contract failures 26
International Association of Insurance
    Supervisors 197
International Bank for Reconstruction and
    Development (IBRD) 170, 172, 173
    see also World Bank
International Bureau of Education (IBE) 164,
    173
    International Conference on Public
        Education (1934) 180
    Recommendation on Access to Secondary
        Schools (R2) 180
    see also UNESCO
International Conference on Public Education
    (ICPE) 164, 173, 180
International Covenant on Economic, Social and
    Cultural Rights (ICESCR) (1966) 181
international division of labour *see* new
    international division of youth labour
    (NIDYL)
International Finance Corporation (IFC) 197

international governmental organisations (IGOs)
    20, 33, 157
    and the Global Compact for Youth
        Employment (GCfYE) proposal
        220–4, 227
    and the global financial crisis 196–203
    global youth unemployment policy 156–82,
        183–210
    legal and normative agreements and key
        initiatives, overview 180–1, 208–10
    literature on youth unemployment 10–12
    partnerships 190–6, 198–207, 218, 219, 221
    and social unrest 34
    see also International Labour Organization
        (ILO); International Monetary Fund
        (IMF); global governance; League of
        Nations (LoN); United Nations (UN);
        World Bank (WB); World Health
        Organization (WHO); World Trade
        Organization (WTO)
International Labour Conference (ILC) 20, 161,
    163, 165, 166, 168, 169, 197, 198, 199,
    209
International Labour Organization (ILO) 17–20,
    34, 47–50, 63–4, 88–97, 103–4, 157–9,
    160–9, 174–182, 183–200, 201, 202, 203,
    204–07, 208–10, 218–20, 220, 223, 227–8
    and Bellamy-Foster et. al's categories of
        labour force participation 103–4
    Constitution 157–9
    Convention on Employment Promotion and
        Protection Against Unemployment
        (1988) 188–9, 208
    on the Coronavirus pandemic (GCP) 227–8
    country designations 50
    Decent Jobs for Youth (DJY) programme
        200, 203, 205, 210, 220
    Decent Work Agenda 197
    *Declaration on Fundamental Principles and
        Rights at Work* 191
    *Declaration on Multinational Enterprises
        and Social Policy* 176, 181
    *Declaration on Social Justice for a Fair
        Globalization* 209
    definition of 'in' and 'not in' the labour force
        88
        see also Bellamy-Foster, J.; global
            reserve army of youth labour
            (GRAoYL)
    definition of youth 48
    Economic and Financial Section 159
    Employment Policy (Supplementary
        Provisions) Recommendation (1984)
        185–7, 208